Welcome to
McGraw-Hill's
NURSING SCHOOL ENTRANCE EXAMS

*C*ongratulations! You've chosen the Nursing School Entrance Exam guide from America's leading educational publisher. You probably know us from many of the textbooks you used in school. Now we're ready to help you take the next step—and get into the nursing program of your choice.

This book gives you everything you need to succeed in any of the four major nursing school entrance exams. You'll get in-depth instruction and review of every topic tested, tips and strategies for every question type, and plenty of practice exams to boost your test-taking confidence.

In addition, in the following pages you'll find:

▶ **How to Get the Most from This Book:** Step-by-step instructions to help you make the best use of the test-prep materials in this guide.

▶ **How to Use the Practice Tests:** Tips and strategies to guide your test-taking practice and to help you understand entrance exam scoring.

▶ **Your Entrance Exam Training Schedule:** How to make the best use of your time from now until test day.

▶ **25 Top Strategies for Test Day:** Use this list to check your knowledge, or as a last-minute refresher before the exam.

▶ **How to Choose a Nursing Program:** Tips from the experts on what to look for in a professional program.

▶ **Incredibly Useful Resources:** Websites and test prep you can use today to prepare for an outstanding test score and a great start to your health care career.

ABOUT McGRAW-HILL EDUCATION

This book has been created by a unit of McGraw-Hill Education, a division of The McGraw-Hill Companies. McGraw-Hill Education is a leading global provider of instructional, assessment, and reference materials in both print and digital form. McGraw-Hill Education has offices in 33 countries and publishes in more than 65 languages. With a broad range of products and services—from traditional textbooks to the latest in online and multimedia learning—we engage, stimulate, and empower students and professionals of all ages, helping them meet the increasing challenges of the 21st century knowledge economy.

Learn more. McGraw Hill Do more.

How to Get the Most from This Book

This book contains general information about four nursing school entrance exams and chapters on each of the test topics. It also contains a Diagnostic Test and practice tests with explanatory answers.

Count backward from your test day to determine how much time you have to prepare. If you have at least 3 weeks but preferably 12 to 18 weeks before test day, you should work through the entire book. You can follow the four-step program shown below. If you have less than 3 weeks, take the Diagnostic Test. Then use your score there to focus on the chapters that cover the content that caused you the most trouble. Do as many practice questions as you can in the areas where you are weakest.

1 Start with the Diagnostic Test

The Diagnostic Test in Chapter 5 of this book is divided into the topics you will face on whichever nursing school entrance exam you take. Take the test as the first step in your test-preparation program. It will help you to pinpoint areas of strength and weakness in your knowledge base and your skill set. After you have scored the Diagnostic Test, you should review the parts of Chapters 6 to 9 that cover any content areas you found difficult.

2 Learn Test-Taking Strategies

Chapter 4 describes important test-taking strategies that can help you earn extra points. You will learn about strategic thinking, using your energy wisely, and when to guess if you don't know the answer to a question.

3 Prepare for Each Test Section

Chapters 6 to 9 cover the main sections of any nursing school entrance exam: Verbal Ability, Reading Comprehension, Mathematical Ability, and Science. Each chapter offers concept reviews and specific strategies for answering the given question type, along with plenty of practice exercises with answers. Pay special attention to the Science Review. Whereas the Verbal, Reading, and Mathematics sections of nursing school entrance exams are often fairly basic, you may need to brush up on your chemistry, physics, and human anatomy skills.

4 Take the Practice Tests

Chapter 10 of this book contains two practice tests in each of the main topics: Verbal Skills, Reading Comprehension, Mathematics, and Science. They are followed by explanatory answers that give you further information about any items you may have missed. Use these tests to check your progress, to gain experience with typical nursing school entrance exam formats, and to learn to pace yourself to get your highest possible score.

How to Use the Practice Tests

Take the Diagnostic Test Under Realistic Testing Conditions

Time yourself to get a sense of how long things take you to complete. Use the time limits shown on the test. Take the test in a library or in a quiet room that simulates the quiet atmosphere of a testing site.

After Your Review, Tackle the Practice Tests

When you have finished your review of the instructional material in Chapters 6 to 9, start tackling the practice tests in Chapter 10. Each test is one section from a typical nursing school entrance exam. The tests contain a variety of question types and subjects that parallel the kinds of questions you will see on the nursing school entrance exam that you take. If you work through all of the material provided, you shouldn't have any surprises on test day.

Review the Explanations as Necessary

There is a brief explanation for each of the practice questions in this book. You will probably not need to read all of these explanations. Sometimes you can tell right away why you got a wrong answer. Perhaps you added when you should have subtracted, or you mixed up two events in a passage. We call such errors "concentration errors." Everyone makes them from time to time, and you should not worry when they occur. Training properly with the aid of this book will help you to avoid concentration errors. Try to distinguish between that kind of error and any actual gaps in your knowledge base. If you have time, read the explanations for any questions that were challenging for you. Notice where you guessed correctly or answered correctly but for the wrong reason.

Keep Your Score Results in Perspective

Standardized-test scores are sensitive to factors such as fatigue and stress. Your stress should ease as you become comfortable with the test formats. Use the information you gain from reading the explanatory answers to help you improve.

A Note on Scoring the Practice Tests

Nursing school entrance exams are unusual in that no two nursing schools require the same scores. Be sure to check with the school or schools of your choice to find out their requirements. The tests in this book, because they do not correlate identically to any one test, merely give you a clue to your proficiency. Instead of obsessing over your percentage of correct answers on Test 1, see whether your score improves when you take Test 2. If you have reviewed explanatory answers and perhaps returned to the instructional material in Chapters 6 to 9 after taking Test 1, your Test 2 scores should show some level of improvement. Reviewing those answers and doing some more studying of concepts you missed should prepare you for the best score of all on the actual test date.

Nursing School Entrance Exam Training Schedule

Around eight weeks before your exam

- Find a quiet place, such as a library, and take the Diagnostic Test (Chapter 5) under actual test conditions. Evaluate your results and pinpoint your areas of strength and weakness. Register for your exam, either online or at your community college or nursing school.

The first four to six weeks of training

- Review the material in Chapters 6 to 9 of this book. Use your textbooks or library or online resources to supplement the material here with any information that you feel you should review.

Two or three weeks before your exam

- Start with Verbal Skills Test 1 in Chapter 10. Take all of the Test 1 tests. Time yourself to get a sense of how long you need. Use the results to fine-tune your training. Review the explanatory answers and any relevant chapters in this book.

One or two weeks before your exam

- Start with Verbal Skills Test 2 in Chapter 10. Take all of the Test 2 tests. Time yourself again. Review the explanatory answers and compare your scores to the scores for Test 1. Do you see an improvement? Are there any concepts you still need to review? Start planning a fun event for after your exam!

Two to five days before your exam

- Make sure you know how to get to the testing center and where to park. Figure out what you are going to wear on test day. Gather your materials (admission ticket or user ID and password, photo ID, pencils, calculator if you are allowed to bring one). Adjust your sleep schedule, if necessary, so that you are able to wake up early if the test starts early in the morning. Confirm your plans for fun after the exam!

The day before your exam

- Stop cramming. Rest and relax. Get some physical activity so that you are better able to sleep and because the endorphins that you release in your brain will help with stress management. Make sure that you take care of your transportation issues and wake-up plan.

Test day!

- Get up early. Eat breakfast. Read something to warm up your brain. Bring your materials. Be on time. Avoid any fellow test-takers who sap your energy and stress you out. Remember that you have done everything you can do to prepare for this test. Breathe deeply and evenly. When the test is over, try not to think about it until you get your score report.

25 Top Strategies for Test Day

When it's almost test day and you've read this book and taken the practice tests, review these two pages. Here you'll find 25 essential strategies that can definitely help you to earn more points on your nursing school entrance exam. Use this review to check your test readiness and make sure you're prepared to get your best score.

General Test-Taking Strategies

Relax

1 **Don't panic!** If you are having a hard time answering the questions, use your best guess. If you cannot guess, move on.

2 **Breathe.** Take a few moments to breathe deeply and relax if you get stressed during the test. You will feel better.

Be Aware of Time

3 **Pace yourself.** Budget enough time for each question so that you won't have to rush at the end of the section.

4 **Stay focused.** Ignore the things going on around you that you cannot control.

Guess Carefully

5 **Answer everything.** There is no direct scoring penalty for wrong answers, so it pays to answer every question, even if you have to guess.

6 **Use what you know.** When you don't know the answer and need to guess, try to make an educated guess by eliminating answer choices that you know are wrong. The more you can eliminate, the better your chance of getting the answer right.

Strategies for Computer-Based Tests

The Computer System

7 **Be aware of scroll bars.** Some images and text are too big to fit on your screen and require you to scroll down to view them.

8 **Estimate.** If you have access to an online calculator, estimate your answers first. Sometimes online calculators can be "sticky." Test the calculator before you begin answering questions.

Answering Questions

9 **Know the format and rules.** Some computer-based tests allow you to return to questions and change answers. Others do not. Before you begin testing, be sure that you know whether you can move back and forth within a section of the test.

Verbal Test Strategies

10 Listen to your brain. Read "aloud" in your head. If it sounds right to you, it probably is.

11 Try the answer choices. Read each choice back into the sentence. Then choose the one that is correct.

12 Check all the answers. Some questions, such as those with two or more blanks in a sentence, have multiple answers. All answers in the answer choice must be correct. There is no partial credit.

13 Use context clues. Often the words surrounding an unknown word can help you to determine its meaning.

14 Use word roots and families. Even if you have never seen the word before, you may recognize part of it, or it may look similar to a word you do know.

Reading Test Strategies

15 Read the question stems first. It may help you to focus your reading if you know what will be asked.

16 Locate the correct part of the text. If a question refers to paragraph 3, be sure you're not looking at paragraph 4.

17 Skim and scan. Don't reread slowly and carefully to find a single word or fact. Use your skimming and scanning skills to locate what you need quickly and efficiently.

Math Test Strategies

18 Draw pictures. If you are allowed to use scratch paper, sketch things out to visualize the problem.

19 Think before computing. Ask: Will the answer be around 10, 100, or 1,000? Don't just grab your calculator. Think about what's reasonable.

20 Answer what's being asked. Ignore irrelevant information. Complete all the steps in the problem—don't quit early.

21 Know your conversions. Study a chart of metric-to-standard conversions, and memorize conversions within the metric and standard systems.

Science Test Strategies

22 Memorize some key science. Examples of topics that will appear on most nursing school entrance exams include: the periodic table of elements, basic anatomical directions, organs and functions, Newton's laws, basic physics formulas, and the stages of cellular reproduction.

23 Watch your calculations. Physics problems involve a lot of math. Don't miss a difficult question for a simple reason. Check your computations.

24 Watch for EXCEPTions. Some questions may ask you to find an exception to a rule or an exemption from a group. Make sure that your answer fits the question.

25 Don't pronounce. Science vocabulary can be intimidating. Don't waste time trying to pronounce difficult vocabulary in your head. If you recognize the word, great. If you don't, try to figure it out from context; compare it to words you know; or if all else fails, simply ignore it.

McGraw-Hill's

NURSING SCHOOL
ENTRANCE EXAMS

McGraw-Hill's

NURSING SCHOOL
ENTRANCE EXAMS

National League for Nursing Pre-Admission
Examination (NLN PAX-RN) • Test of Essential
Academic Skills (TEAS) • Psychological Services
Bureau (PSB) Nursing School Aptitude
Examination (RN) • Evolve Reach (HESI)
Admission Assessment (A2)

THOMAS A. EVANGELIST
TAMRA B. ORR
JUDY UNREIN
KATHY A. ZAHLER

New York I Chicago I San Francisco I Lisbon I London I Madrid I Mexico City I
Milan I New Delhi I San Juan I Seoul I Singapore I Sydney I Toronto

Copyright © 2013, 2009 by The McGraw-Hill Companies, Inc. All rights reserved. Printed in the United States of America. Except as permitted under the United States Copyright Act of 1976, no part of this publication may be reproduced or distributed in any form of by any means, or stored in a database of retrieval system, without the prior written permission of the publisher.

1 2 3 4 5 6 7 8 9 10 QDB/QDB 2 0 1 9 8 7 6 5 4 3 (0-07-181049-8)
1 2 3 4 5 6 7 8 9 10 QDB/QDB 2 0 1 9 8 7 6 5 4 3 (0-07-181145-1)

ISBN   978-0-07-181049-4 (book alone)
MHID   0-07-181049-8

ISBN   978-0-07-181145-3 (book for set)
MHID   0-07-181145-1

ISBN   978-0-07-181146-0 (set)
MHID   0-07-181146-X

e-ISBN 978-0-07-181048-7
e-MHID 0-07-181048-X

Cataloging-in-Publishing Data is on file with the Library of Congress

The NLN PAX-RN is produced by the National League for Nursing. TEAS is a trademark of the Assessment Technologies Institute™ LLC. The PSB Nursing School Aptitude Examination (RN) is produced by the Psychological Services Bureau. The "Evolve Reach (HESI) Admission Assessment (A2) is produced by Evolve Learning Systems, a division of Elsevier Publishing. Evolve® is a registered trademark of Elsevier Inc. in the United States and other jurisdictions. These organizations were not involved in the production of, and do not endorse, this product.

McGraw-Hill books are available at special quantity discounts to use as premiums and sales or for use in corporate training programs. To contact a representative, please e-mail us at bulksales@mcgraw-hill.com.

This book is printed on acid-free paper.

Contents

How to Use This Book

Welcome to *McGraw-Hill's Nursing School Entrance Exams*. You have made the decision to become a nurse, and you are looking forward to all the advantages and rewards of a nursing career, but now you need to succeed on your nursing school entrance test. We are here to help you.

This book has been created by a dedicated team of teachers and test-prep experts. Together they have helped thousands of students score high on all kinds of exams. They have pooled their knowledge to make this the most effective test-prep program available for nursing school entrance exams.

McGraw-Hill's Nursing School Entrance Exams contains a wealth of features to help you do your best. Follow these steps to get the most out of your study time:

- **Read Chapter 1** to learn important basic information for people entering the nursing field. Written by a leading nursing professional, this chapter will tell you what kinds of nursing education programs are available to you, how the admissions process works, and how you can apply for financial aid. This chapter also includes important advice on how to decide if nursing is the right career field for you.
- **Read Chapter 2** to find out about the major admissions test used by nursing schools nationwide. You will learn how the tests are structured, what subjects they cover, what kinds of questions they ask, and how they are scored. Find out which of these tests is required by the school to which you are applying, and then focus your preparation accordingly.
- **Read Chapter 3** to learn how to set up your study plan. A handy chart is provided to show you which subjects are covered on which tests. This will help you decide which of the following chapters in this book are the ones you need to focus on.
- **Read Chapter 4** to learn some important test-taking strategies that can help you improve your score.
- **Take a Diagnostic Test in Chapter 5.** This test covers the same subjects as the real nursing school entrance exams and includes many questions in similar formats. Use the results to help you pinpoint your strengths and weaknesses and to identify which subjects you need to study most carefully.
- **Read Chapters 6 through 9 to find comprehensive reviews** of the subjects tested on nursing school entrance exams. Focus on the subjects that are on the exam you will be taking. Concentrate particularly on the subjects that gave you the most difficulty on the Diagnostic Test in Chapter 5.
- **Find practice tests in Chapter 10** for all the subject areas that are on nursing school entrance exams. Take the ones on the subjects that will be

on your real exam. For some exams, you will want to try all of the practice tests. For each one, set aside enough time to take the whole test at one sitting, screen out distractions, and concentrate in doing your best. If you approach these tests as you would the real exam, they should give you a good idea of how well you are prepared. After you take the tests, read through the explanations for each question, paying particular attention to those you answered incorrectly or had to guess on. If necessary, go back and reread the corresponding sections in the subject reviews in Chapters 6 through 9.

Different people have different ways or preparing for tests. You need to find a preparation method that suits your schedule and your learning style. We have tried to make this book flexible enough for you to use in a way that works best for you. However, for this as for any other test, there is no substitute for serious intensive review and study. The more time and effort you devote to preparing, the better your chances of achieving your goal.

McGraw-Hill's

NURSING SCHOOL
ENTRANCE EXAMS

CHAPTER 1

Getting Into Nursing School
Mary Ann Cantrell, PhD, RN

Nursing is the protection, promotion, and optimization of health and abilities; prevention of illness and injury; alleviation of suffering through the diagnosis and treatment of human response; and advocacy in the care of individuals, families, communities, and populations.
—The American Nurses Association (ANA)

Read this chapter to learn

- How to decide whether a nursing career is right for you
- What the advantages and rewards of a nursing career are
- What types of nursing education programs are available
- How to decide which program is right for you
- How to apply to nursing schools
- How to obtain financial aid

WHAT IS A NURSE?

A nurse is a person who combines science and technology with people skills such as communication, problem solving, teaching, and compassion to meet the health care needs of individuals, families, and communities. Nurses are the backbone of the U.S. health care system. In addition for caring for the sick, nurses work to:

- Promote health
- Prevent disease

- Help patients and their families cope with illnesses, emergencies, and long-term disease
- Save lives
- Build healthier communities

A career in nursing is very demanding, not just physically but also intellectually, emotionally, and spiritually. But it can also be extremely rewarding. The common saying "what you put into something is what you get out of it" definitely holds true for nursing.

To become a registered nurse (RN), you must:

- Graduate from a state-approved school of nursing
- Pass a state licensing examination called the National Council Licensure Examination for Registered Nurses (NCLEX-RN)

Registered Nurse versus Licensed Practical Nurse

Students who are considering a nursing career may not know the differences between a registered nurse (RN) and a licensed practical nurse (LPN), sometimes referred to as a licensed vocation nurse (LVN). To become an LPN, a person must:

- Graduate from a year-long program that is usually provided at a vocational or technical school
- Take and successfully pass an examination called the NCLEX-PN (a different examination from the NCLEX-RN required for an RN license)

An LPN functions under the direction of an RN and consequently has less autonomy and a more narrow scope in his or her practice or role in providing care. The salary of an LPN is also considerably lower than the average salary of an RN. According to the Bureau of Labor Statistics, in 2010 there were over 752,000 LPNs and LVNs in the United States, with a faster-than-average job growth rate of close to 22 percent. The median pay for LPNs that year was about $40,380 or $19.42 per hour. Comparable figures for RNs were 2.7 million employed, with a job growth rate of 26 percent and median pay of $64,690 or $31.10 an hour.

IS A NURSING CAREER RIGHT FOR YOU?

How can you tell if a nursing career is right for you? To answer that question, you will need to think carefully about your own personal and professional goals. Also, and just as important, you will need to find out exactly what a nursing career entails. You can begin this process by searching nursing career options on the Internet or reading career materials in a bookstore or in a guidance counselor's office. These activities are a good starting point, but you will probably want to learn still more about what nurses actually do.

One way to do this is to volunteer at a local hospital. Volunteering gives you a first-hand view of the hospitalization experience and the role of the nurse. Most nurses, whether they work in a hospital, an outpatient clinic, or a nurse-run clinic, are willing to talk to others interested in becoming a nurse. If you get the opportunity, ask a nurse about his or her typical day, what challenges he or she faces, and what advice he or she would give to someone who is starting a career in nursing.

Volunteering in a hospital also helps you understand the environment in which nurses practice. Approximately 55 percent of all practicing nurses work in an acute care hospital setting. Being aware of a typical hospital culture can help you decide if being a nurse is right for you.

Besides finding out what nursing actually entails, you will also want to make a thorough assessment of your personal strengths, weaknesses, unique qualities, and educational interests. As part of this process, think about how you are likely to respond to the nursing situations that you see during your volunteer work. Could you handle these situations if you were the nurse on duty? Do you have the strengths and abilities that you admire in the nurses at work around you? And ultimately, do you find nursing work personally rewarding and fulfilling? If so, then you can be confident that nursing is a good career choice for you.

ADVANTAGES AND REWARDS OF A NURSING CAREER

For nursing, it may be true that what you put into it is what you get out of it, but there are also many important rewards for nurses. One obvious reward is the financial compensation that nurses receive, and another is the job security that nurses have as a result of the ongoing demand for RNs. But beyond that, there are emotional and spiritual rewards, such as the reward of watching a person regain his or her previous state of health after a serious injury or illness, or the reward of watching a teenager quit a high-risk behavior such as drinking after a behavioral-education program conducted by a nurse in the community. These and many similar situations are among the intangible rewards that nurses can expect to receive in their careers.

Effective nurses are professionals who have a strong theoretical background in the sciences and nursing theory, as well as the ability to apply these concepts in clinical practice. They also have strong communication skills that help them achieve meaningful conversations and interactions with patients, families, and other health care professionals. These skills create positive patient care outcomes and are a source of real satisfaction for nursing professionals. Yet great nurses also base their practice on the following premise: *it is the little things that count*. Some nursing professionals identify this as part of the care ethic of nursing, whereas others would define it as the art of nursing practice. Whichever it is, focusing on the little things seems to provide the most satisfaction and recognition among patients, families, and other health care professionals. In turn, the recognition that comes as a result of these small, insignificant acts is often a nurse's greatest source of satisfaction and sense of reward in his or her career.

What are these "little things" that count so much? One example is the nurse who while starting an intravenous infusion of chemotherapy (which requires a significant amount of knowledge, skill, and concentration) can at the same time look the patient in the eyes, stop what he or she is doing for a moment, and (as if there is nothing else on her mind) ask, "How are you? How is your family? What do you need?" The well-known nursing leader Virginia Henderson believes that the nurse should ". . . get inside the skin of each of (her) patients in order to know what (he) needs." These simple questions are perhaps one way to make tangible what Henderson is talking about. In return, for the nurse who can make someone understand that he or she really cares and wants to meet the patient's needs, there is the concrete reward of the patient responding, "I am so glad you are my nurse, I feel safe with you!"

These small acts are really so important to patients, yet they can be often overlooked in the hectic day-to-day practice of nursing. And it is not just in the hospital where the pace is hectic; it is also in clinics, in patients' homes, and in long-term care facilities. In all of these settings, nurses are challenged to create opportunities for offering these "little things" that mean so much to patients. When nurses are able to give of themselves in the care and support of patients, they may find that they will be rewarded tenfold in patients' spoken and unspoken gratitude and appreciation.

Learning About Nursing Careers: Online Resources

Before you make your nursing career decisions, you will also want to learn all you can about the nature of nursing. A good way to begin is to visit the Web sites of the following professional organizations, which are considered the leadership organizations for the nursing profession. Each site offers detailed information about nursing and about nursing career options.

- The National League for Nursing (NLN): www.nln.org
- American Nurses Association (ANA): www.nursingworld.org
- American Association of Colleges of Nursing (AACN): www.aacn.nche.edu

TYPES OF NURSING EDUCATION PROGRAMS

There are essentially three types of nursing education programs that prepare students to become RNs. They are as follows:

- A three-year diploma program
- A two- to three-year associate's degree program
- A four-year university program

Many consider a four-year university program to be the entry degree for the profession. Although all of these programs prepare you to be a registered nurse, they differ in the scope and depth of nursing theory courses offered and also in whether they include courses that do not directly focus on the practice of nursing. For example, diploma nursing programs do not normally offer a course on nursing research.

All three types of programs teach theory content on the fundamentals of nursing, medical-surgical nursing, psychiatric nursing, obstetrical and gynecological nursing, pediatric nursing, and public and community health nursing. All three also involve classroom learning, practicing nursing skills in a lab environment, and learning how to care for patients in real-life health care settings. Classroom learning focuses on learning the theory and concepts that support the science of nursing. Clinical nursing courses, which are also part of all three program types, provide opportunities to apply theory knowledge either in a lab or clinical setting.

In certain areas of the country, where many nursing education programs are offered, a diploma program, an associate's degree program, and a four-year university program may use the same health care institution for the clinical teaching of their students. It is common to have nursing students from all three program types at one health care institution on the same day.

Whichever type of program people graduate from, they must still take and successfully pass the NCLEX-RN exam to practice as a RN.

Now let us look at each of the three types in more detail.

Three-Year Diploma in Nursing Program

A diploma in nursing is awarded from a hospital. When nurses began to be formally educated in the United States, this was the initial program offered. Although once a common educational route for RNs, the number of diploma programs has decreased as nursing education has shifted from hospitals to academic institutions. The trend in the past 20 years has been either to disband diploma nursing programs outright or combine them with associate degree programs offered at community colleges. Today, only a small percentage of all basic RN education programs are diploma programs.

Two- to Three-Year Associate's Degree in Nursing (ADN) Program

A program granting an Associate's Degree in Nursing (ADN) prepares you for a defined technical scope of practice. The clinical and classroom components of ADN programs prepare you for nursing roles that require nursing theory and technical proficiency. Although you may assume that all associate's degrees are earned in two years, in fact, the ADN typically takes three, partly due to the large number of prerequisite courses. According to the

Health Resources and Services administration, in 2008, just over 36 percent of RNs achieved their degree via an associate's program.

In most health care settings, RNs with associate's degrees can provide care with the same degree of scope and breadth as those who have bachelor's degrees. However, nurses with associate's degrees often return to school to earn Bachelor of Science in Nursing (BSN) degrees.

In her book *The Ultimate Guide to Getting into Nursing School*, Genevieve Chandler offers three common reasons why RNs with associate's degrees return to school for the BSN degree:

- An employing institution, usually a hospital, is urging the RN to obtain the BSN.
- The RN seeks to learn more in-depth knowledge to provide more effective patient care.
- The RN wants to advance his or her career, and a BSN degree is needed to earn an advanced degree in nursing.

Four-Year University Program in Nursing (BSN) Program

The four-year, university-based Bachelor of Science in Nursing (BSN) degree provides the nursing theory, sciences, humanities, and behavioral science preparation necessary for the full scope of professional nursing responsibilities, as well as the knowledge base necessary for advanced education in specialized clinical practice, research, or primary health care. There are a variety of paths to the BSN. Some students begin with a traditional, four-year BSN plan. Others transition from RN to BSN or from ADN to BSN. Still others complete their BSN via online courses or academic-service partnerships that allow them to earn credits while holding down a nursing job.

The AACN offers the following description of a typical four-year program:

- During the first two years, most programs concentrate on psychology, human growth and development, biology, microbiology, organic chemistry, nutrition, and anatomy and physiology.
- During the last two years, many programs begin the focused nursing curriculum, including adult acute and chronic disease, maternal/child health, pediatrics, psychiatric/mental health nursing, and community health nursing. Also covered are nursing theory, bioethics, management, research and statistics, health assessment, pharmacology, pathophysiology, and electives in complex nursing processes.
- The final two years is also the time when students apply nursing theory in clinical practice in hospitals, nursing homes, and community settings.

A BSN is required for admission to graduate nursing programs that include nurse practitioner, clinical nurse specialist, and other leadership positions in health care. A number of recent studies indicate a strong correlation between higher, specialized degrees and positive patient outcomes.

Second Degree Program

Second degree programs in nursing enable individuals who have earned a college degree in another discipline, such as accounting, to earn a BSN degree. Those who enter these programs can be young adults who have recently graduated college or older adults who earned their college degree 10 to 15 years previously. The college credits that these students have already earned are counted toward the BSN degree. These programs are often referred to as "fast-track" programs, because most students can complete them in 12 to 14 months. Before a student formally enters a second degree program, he or she often has to earn credits in prerequisite courses, such as pathophysiology and pharmacology. Second degree programs are very intense because they must be completed within a short time frame. Most programs admit students in May and graduate them by the end of August the following year without significant breaks between semesters.

WHICH PROGRAM IS RIGHT FOR YOU?

When choosing among nursing programs, you will want to consider a variety of factors, including location, cost, time, and career goals.

Location

Depending on where you live in the United States, you may have several of the three types of programs located nearby, or you may only have a limited selection of programs and/or types programs to choose from. Many students entering college to earn a BSN degree are willing to move to another city or state to enroll in the school of their choice. Students seeking an associate's degree, a diploma program, or a second degree program are usually less willing to relocate.

Cost

The cost of nursing programs varies widely based on the type of program and whether the sponsoring institution is public or private. In 2010–2011, according to the National Center for Education Statistics, the cost of a nursing education at a public four-year college was more than $20,000 per year, including tuition, fees, books, room and board, transportation, and miscellaneous expenses. The cost at a private undergraduate college or university was estimated at close to $40,000 per year. Diploma in nursing programs and associate degree programs are traditionally lower in cost than university-based BSN programs. When you are choosing a nursing program, you will need to think carefully about what you can afford. Chandler offers the following questions for consideration in *The Ultimate Guide to Getting Into Nursing School*:

- Does the nursing program offer tuition reimbursement programs where you sign an agreement to work at a health care facility for a specified period of time after graduation for free tuition?
- Is working during school feasible?
- Are there work-study programs?
- Can you earn money or tuition credit as a teaching assistant?
- Can you earn money as a research assistant?
- Can you consider working as a Certified Nursing Assistant or an Emergency Medical Technician?
- Can you consider working as a Student Nursing Assistant, Nurse Extern, or Nurse Technician during the school year?
- What financial aid is available at this particular institution?

Time

Earning a BSN degree takes four years of study, and even an associate's degree may take three years. Depending on your life circumstances, how much time you can allow for your nursing studies will be an important factor in your choice of program. Most people who enroll in a nursing program, whatever the type, find that the time commitment required for classroom and clinical courses severely limits the time available for other activities, including working and fulfilling family responsibilities.

Career Goals

The AACN suggests that you ask yourself the following questions when considering whether a particular nursing program meets your career goals:

- How involved is the faculty in developing students for today's health care industry?
- How strong is the school's affiliation with clinics and hospitals?
- Is there any assurance that a student will gain an up-to-date educational experience for the current job market?
- Are a variety of care settings available?
- How much time in clinics will be needed for graduation?
- What are the program's resources in terms of computer and science laboratories?
- Does the school work with hospitals and community-based centers to provide health care?
- How available is the faculty to oversee a student's curriculum?
- What kind of student support is available in terms of study groups and technological aids?
- What kind of counseling from faculty members and administrators is available to help students develop well-rounded, effective progress through the program?

THE ADMISSIONS PROCESS AND HOW TO APPLY

Identifying Nursing Programs of Interest to You

Once you have decided whether to pursue a four-year degree, an associate's degree, or a diploma in nursing, the next step is to identify particular programs to which you would like to apply. When you have a list, you will need to find out each program's admission requirements and obtain application forms. Information and forms are usually available on each program's Website or by calling or writing to the school to request these materials. Most schools of nursing also include a "mission statement": a short explanation of what specific kind of education the school seeks to provide. A careful examination of a program's mission statement gives you a clear idea of the program's values and its philosophy of nursing education that will, in turn, have a strong influence on its curriculum and student learning experiences.

Programs vary in their entrance requirements, but a high school diploma or equivalent is necessary. Most colleges consider an applicant's SAT or ACT scores along with high school grade point average (GPA).

Because the application process is time-consuming and requires a significant amount of energy, it makes sense to limit the number of programs to which you apply. However, be sure to apply to more than one program so that you are not staking everything on a single application. Also, you may want to rank the programs that you have applied to in order of preference in case you are ultimately accepted by more than one.

Submitting Your Application

Most applications for admission into nursing programs ask you to include the following materials:

- An official copy of your high school transcript that includes your course work and final GPA and, if applying as a second degree student, an official copy of your college transcript that includes your course work and GPA
- A list and description of your extracurricular activities
- A list and description of your community service
- A list and description of your leadership activities
- Letters of recommendation
- An essay describing your interests in a nursing career

Completing an application requires a significant amount of time. You may be able to fill out and submit the application online; this is increasingly common. If you plan to submit a "hard copy" (paper) application, it is important to type your responses to the various questions. A typed application is easier to read, is less likely to be misinterpreted, and looks more professional.

If your application is hard to read or looks sloppy, the admissions committee may reject it even if you have good credentials. Take the time to read the directions, to assemble the requested information, and to insert that information in the correct spaces on the application form. Once you have submitted your application, you should receive confirmation from the admissions officer that it has been received. Most programs let you know when a decision regarding your application will be made and when you will receive notification.

The Essay and the Interview

As part of the application process, you will probably be asked to write an essay about why you are pursuing a career in nursing. You may also be asked to participate in a face-to-face interview with an admissions officer or someone designated by the admissions office. In both the essay and the interview, you need to be able to state clearly why you are interested in a nursing career. If you cannot clearly articulate your career plans and goals, that will quickly become evident to the admissions officer. Nursing school admissions are competitive, and having clear goals and a realistic understanding of nursing as a career may be the factor that causes the admissions officer to choose you over another equally qualified candidate.

Follow-Up Actions

After any interview, it is very important to send a thank-you note. This can be in the form of an e-mail or a handwritten note sent through the U.S. postal service. In the note, be sure to thank the interviewer for sharing time with you. You might also share your general impressions about the information you gained from the interview and mention your continued interest in the program. If for some reason you have decided that you are no longer interested in a particular program, it is courteous to notify the admissions officer of your decision to withdraw your application.

Once you start hearing from nursing programs to which you have applied, you may find that you have been accepted by more than one. If that is the case, you will need to consider several factors when making your final choice. Cost and geographic location are, of course, always major factors, but you should also carefully examine each school's mission and values and choose one that aligns with your personal goals.

FINANCIAL AID FOR NURSING STUDENTS

Financial aid is money made available by the government and other sources to help students pay for the costs of their education. Due to the high demand for registered nurses and the short supply of these professionals currently in the workforce, many funding opportunities have been created to offset the costs of a nursing education. The federal government and many state governments have created funding mechanisms to assist students in payment for their nursing degree. The Health Resources and Services Administration nursing programs of the federal government address the nation's RN shortage by providing scholarships, loans, and loan repayments to nursing students, RNs, and nursing faculty. These federal programs also provide grants to RN training programs to increase the number of nurses, improve nurses' skills, and keep nurses in the nursing field. The Nursing Reinvestment Act is one federal program that provides scholarships to qualified undergraduate students. Information about this scholarship can be found at bhpr.hrsa.gov/loanscholarships/scholarships/Nursing/.

The Web site of AACN has a comprehensive list of scholarships, loans, and grants available to undergraduate nursing students. Go to www.aacn.nche.edu/students/financial-aid#general to learn more.

Financial aid can be in the form of loans, grants, work-payback programs, work-study programs, and scholarships. Scholarships and grants are considered gifts and do not have to be repaid. Loans are borrowed money that must be repaid with interest, usually after graduation. Student employment provides jobs during the academic year for which students are paid. Sources of financial aid for nursing students include:

- The federal government
- State and local governments
- Private sources such as corporations

Eligibility for financial aid is based either on need or merit. Most need-based financial aid comes from the federal government and is given to individuals or families who cannot afford the entire cost of a nursing education. Eligibility for need-based financial aid is determined by the Federal Need Analysis Methodology. A free on-line application called the Free Application for Student Aid (FAFSA) can be obtained online at www.fafsa.ed.gov. The processing and outcome of this application determines a student's Expected Family Contribution (EFC), which is the amount of money a family is expected to contribute toward educational expenses. The federal government offers several grants and loans. The table at the end of this chapter briefly summarizes some of the federal aid programs available to undergraduate students.

Financial aid from state governments is provided primarily in the form of scholarships and grants awarded to students attending college in their home states. Financial aid from private sources such as corporations and foundations is usually based on merit or on the fulfillment of certain specific qualifications rather than on need.

Applying for financial aid can be a daunting task. A large amount of detailed information is required to complete the necessary forms. The first step in this process is to complete the FAFSA application to determine your calculated EFC. Students are highly encouraged to complete the FAFSA soon after January 1 to be eligible for federal and state financial aid programs for the upcoming academic year. Although the latest version of the form becomes available each year in late fall, a completed FAFSA form will not be accepted for processing until January 1 of the next year. Two to four weeks after submitting your FAFSA, you will receive a Student Aid Report that shows the information you reported and your calculated EFC. At the same time, the financial aid office at each school that accepts you examines your need as well as your expected ability to pay for some part of your education. The financial aid office then tells you how much financial aid you can expect to receive if you attend that school. This notification usually comes sometime in the spring prior to the fall semester. You are also assigned a financial aid officer who assists you in this process. This individual is your "point" person whom you may contact to answer your questions. An offer is usually composed of need-based loans and grants.

Federal Aid Programs for Undergraduates*	
Name	**Description**
Pell Grant www.2012pellgrant.com/	Available to undergraduate students with extreme financial need who meet certain eligibility requirements. The maximum amount of the grant per year is $5,400 and does not have to be repaid.
Federal Supplemental Educational Opportunity Grant (SEOG) www.fseog.com/	This grant is available for full-time students with financial need. The maximum amount of the grant per year is $4,000 and does not have to be repaid.
Federal Nursing Student Loan www.hrsa .gov/loanscholarships/ loans/nursing.html	This is a 5% interest loan provided to students with financial need. The maximum amount of this loan per year is $3,300, with an increase to $5,200 for nursing students in their last two years of study. Loan repayment must begin approximately nine months after graduation.
Stafford/Direct Loans www.staffordloan.com	This loan varies based on a student's progress in a program: $3,500 subsidized/$2,000 unsubsidized (freshman); $4,500 subsidized/$2,000 unsubsidized (sophomore); $5,500 subsidized/$2,000 unsubsidized (junior/senior). Amounts are higher for students who are independent (unsupported by parents).
Parent PLUS Loans www.parentplusloan.com	This is loan program for parents of students who are considered their dependents. The loan amount can be up to the full cost of the education. Parents can make payments immediately or defer them until the student graduates.

*Information based on 2012 figures.

All About the Exams

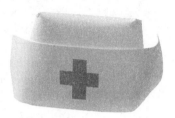

Read this chapter to learn

- Which different tests are used for nursing school admissions
- What kinds of questions are on each test
- How the tests are scored

You have decided that a nursing career is right for you, and you are getting ready to apply to nursing school. Soon it will be up to you to succeed on the entrance exam. Nursing schools across America use many different exams to assess student applicants. Four of the most widely used exams are the following:

- National League for Nursing Pre-Admission Examination (NLN PAX-RN)
- Test of Essential Academic Skills (TEAS)
- Psychological Services Bureau (PSB) Nursing School Aptitude Examination (RN)
- Evolve Reach (HESI) Admission Assessment Exam

Which test you take depends on which exam is required by the school or schools to which you are applying. When you start the application process, be sure to find out which test each school requires, so that you can focus your preparation accordingly. Note that in most cases, the school to which you are applying will tell you when and where to take the admission exam.

This chapter will present important information about these different exams. You will find out what kinds of questions are on each exam, what topics are covered, and how the different exams are scored. Now let us look in depth at each of these exams.

NATIONAL LEAGUE FOR NURSING PRE-ADMISSION EXAMINATION (NLN PAX-RN)

Format of the Test

The NLN PAX-RN is administered by the National League for Nursing, a leading professional organization for nurse faculty and others involved in nursing education. It is designed to measure your abilities in the academic areas that are central to nursing education. The NLN exam is available in two forms: a traditional paper-and-pencil test and a computer-based version. All of the questions on the NLN PAX-RN exam are multiple-choice items, each with four answer choices. The format of the test is shown in Table 2.1.

Table 2.1. NLN PAX-RN Format

Section	Number of Questions	Time Allowed	Content
Verbal Ability	80	1 hour	Word knowledge, reading comprehension
Mathematics	54	1 hour	Arithmetic, basic algebra, geometry, graphs, conversions, and data interpretation
Science	80	1 hour	High-school level biology, chemistry, physics, and earth science
Total	214	3 hours	

How the Test Is Scored

For each section of the NLN PAX-RN exam, you receive a "raw score" based on how many items you answered correctly. Some questions on the exam are included for experimental reasons and are therefore not scored. As a result, the highest possible scores for each section are as follows: Verbal Ability, 60; Mathematics, 40; and Science, 60. You will also receive a "composite score" that is a weighted combination of your scores on the separate test sections. Composite scores may range from 0 to 200. In addition, you receive percentile scores for each test section and for the test as a whole. These scores are developed using a statistical process. They show what portion of a so-called "norms group" of similar test-takers earned raw scores that are lower than yours. For example, if you earned a raw score of 52 on the Verbal Ability section with a corresponding percentile score of 85, that means that

85 percent of the test-takers in the norms group earned raw scores that were lower than yours. The NLN says that for each section, percentiles ranging from about 40 to 60 indicate average performance on the exam.

Note that there is no official passing score on this exam. The schools that require applicants to take the NLN PAX-RN establish their own criteria about what scores are considered acceptable for admission.

Types of Questions

On the NLN PAX-RN exam, the Verbal Ability questions are of two types. First, there are vocabulary questions that test your understanding of specific words. These questions may look like this:

> The candidates engaged in an *acrimonious* debate. ***Acrimonious*** means
>
> (A) polite.
> (B) public.
> (C) meaningless.
> (D) combative.
>
> Answer: D. *Acrimonious* means "combative."

The second type of Verbal Ability question is reading comprehension. In this type of question, you are given a reading passage of 400 to 500 words. The passage is usually on a topic in science or medicine. Following the passage are six questions about its content. Each question has four answer choices. You must pick the best answer choice based on your understanding of the passage. Here is an example:

> The "food pyramid" is a visual representation of how the different food groups can be combined to form a healthy diet. Although it has been a vital part of dietary guidelines for years, the pyramid is constantly undergoing analysis and revision as additional studying is done in nutritional fields. Recently, the pyramid has undergone another change regarding the unique dietary needs of seniors.
>
> According to an article published in the January 2008 issue of the *Journal of Nutrition,* modifications in the pyramid for older adults include an emphasis on fiber and calcium, as well as on vitamins D and B_{12}. By incorporating these changes, the pyramid now indicates that the nutrients found in a person's routine daily consumption typically are not enough for seniors. Seniors need supplementation.
>
> As people age, they tend to move less and thus need fewer calories to maintain their weight. Because seniors tend to eat a more limited amount, dietitians urge them to choose wisely. They are urged to eat nutrient-rich meals featuring such food as fruits, vegetables, low-fat dairy products, and high-fiber whole grains. Some experts recommend that older people purchase packaged versions of perishables because such foods

last longer than the fresh kind. For example, dried and frozen fruit have a much longer shelf life, as do frozen or canned vegetables. Having a supply of these in the cupboard means fewer trips to the grocery store and less risk of running out of nutritional snacks.

The newly designed pyramid also focuses on the importance for older people of ingesting adequate amounts of fluids on a daily basis. This helps ensure proper digestion and prevent any possibility of dehydration.

Finally, the revised pyramid includes information on incorporating exercise and other physical activities into the lives of older adults. Suggestions include swimming, walking, or simple yard work. Because recent reports have stated that obesity levels for people older than 70 years of age are climbing, performing some type of regular exercise is more essential than ever.

1. The best title for this selection is

    (A) America's Seniors Need Exercise.
    (B) A New Food Pyramid for Seniors.
    (C) Finding Supplementation for Aging.
    (D) Dietary Changes in Older Americans.

2. The purpose of updating the food pyramid as described in the passage is to

    (A) change how seniors eat.
    (B) increase food supplement sales.
    (C) encourage people to eat more fruit.
    (D) convince older people to start swimming.

3. The passage says that seniors should support their digestion by

    (A) taking vitamin D.
    (B) eating fewer calories.
    (C) drinking adequate fluids.
    (D) incorporating some exercise into their regular routine.

4. Dried and frozen fruit is often recommended by dietitians because it is

    (A) delicious.
    (B) easier to store.
    (C) more nutritional than fresh fruit.
    (D) known to have a much longer shelf life.

5. The reason that the author of the passage suggests exercise such as swimming, walking, and yard work is because those activities are

    (A) ways to interact with other people.
    (B) things that can be done alone.
    (C) low impact in nature and relatively safe.
    (D) useless for burning up calories.

6. The author's purpose in writing this passage was primarily to

    (A) alert people to the different dietary needs of seniors.
    (B) encourage students to study the pyramid's requirements.
    (C) inform nurses about what supplements are most essential.
    (D) educate physicians on the differences between dried and fresh fruit.

    Answers: 1. B; 2. A; 3. C; 4. D; 5. C; 6. A

The questions in the Mathematics section of the test are also multiple-choice items with four answer choices. Here is an example:

    The number 1,200 is what percent of 1,500?

    (A) 20%
    (B) 40%
    (C) 60%
    (D) 80%

    Answer: D. The number 1,200 is 80 percent, or 80%, of 1,500.

The questions in the Science portion of the exam are likewise multiple-choice items. Here is an example:

    Which of the following transports oxygen in human blood?

    (A) phagocytes and white blood cells
    (B) hemoglobin in red blood cells
    (C) platelets
    (D) lymph from lymph nodes

    Answer: B. Hemoglobin in the red blood cells transports oxygen in human blood.

Note that some of the questions in the Science portion of the exam include tables, charts, or illustrations. Sometimes two or more questions are based on the same chart or illustration.

TEST OF ESSENTIAL ACADEMIC SKILLS (TEAS)

Format of the Test

The TEAS is administered by the Assessment Technologies Institute, a private testing company based in Leawood, Kansas. It is designed to measure entry-level verbal and math skills that have been deemed appropriate for nursing school applicants by a panel of nursing program curriculum experts. The TEAS is offered in both traditional paper-and-pencil and computer-administered formats. All of the questions on the TEAS are multiple-choice items, each with four answer choices. Table 2.2 shows the format of the test.

Table 2.2. TEAS Format

Section	Number of Questions	Time Allowed	Content
Reading	48	58 minutes	Reading comprehension
Mathematics	34	51 minutes	Arithmetic, basic algebra, graphs, and diagrams
Science	54	66 minutes	High school level biology, chemistry, human physiology, physics, and general science
English and language usage	34	34 minutes	Grammar, spelling, punctuation, sentence structure, and vocabulary words in context
Total	170	209 minutes	

How the Test Is Scored

After you take the TEAS, you receive a score in each of the four general test areas. In addition, you receive 16 subscores covering specific content categories within the main test areas.

Note that there are no official passing scores on this exam. The schools that require the applicants to take the TEAS establish their own criteria about what scores are considered acceptable for admission.

Types of Questions

In the reading questions on the TEAS, you may be given a reading passage, or you may be given some kind of graphic—a chart, a map, a diagram, or a graph. You are then given two or three questions based on the information in the passage or graphic. The questions may ask you to do any one of the following:

- Identify the main idea of the passage
- Locate important details
- Draw a conclusion based on the passage or graphic
- Apply a conclusion to a new situation
- Identify the author's tone or attitude
- Tell the meaning of a word based on its context

You must pick the choice that best answers the question. Here is an example using the following chart:

Weather Report		
City	Today's High Temperature (°F)	Today's Low Temperature (°F)
Atlanta	96	83
Baltimore	95	82
Boston	84	71
Chicago	83	70
Cleveland	82	73
Dallas	93	83
Denver	78	64
Detroit	84	92
Kansas City	90	79
Las Vegas	96	83
Los Angeles	88	72
Miami	92	87
Minneapolis	83	64
New York	84	73
Philadelphia	86	75
Phoenix	98	89
Seattle	79	63
Washington, DC	88	79

According to the chart, which of the following cities is experiencing the greatest fluctuation in temperature today?

(A) Cleveland
(B) New York
(C) Denver
(D) Minneapolis

Answer: D. Minneapolis is experiencing a temperature fluctuation of 19°F, which is more than any of the other three cities listed as answer choices.

In another kind of reading comprehension question, you are given a set of step-by-step directions. Typically, the directions tell how to draw a particular geometric figure. You are instructed to follow the directions exactly. When you have completed all of the steps, you are then asked which of four given diagrams most resembles your drawing. If you have followed the directions correctly, you will choose the correct answer.

Mathematics questions on the TEAS cover the topics of numbers, operations, ratio and proportion, fractions and percents, basic algebra, measurements, and interpreting data from graphs and diagrams. Many of the questions are word problems based on everyday situations. Here is an example:

A customer bought two grilled cheese sandwiches, one order of potato salad, and two iced teas. How much did the customer's purchases cost?

MENU	
Green salad	$2.25
Grilled cheese sandwich	$3.25
Veggie burger	$3.19
Potato salad	$1.79
Iced tea	$1.49
Ice cream	$2.75

(A) $6.20
(B) $7.94
(C) $8.45
(D) $11.27

Answer: D. $3.25 + $3.25 + $1.79 + $1.49 + $1.49 = $11.27

Science questions on the TEAS cover life science (living systems, evolution, and similar topics), human physiology, chemistry (atomic structure, compounds and solutions, and similar topics), and physics (force, motion, and similar topics). In some of the questions, you will be asked to interpret charts, diagrams, or similar graphics. Here are some examples of typical TEAS science questions:

1. The retina transmits nerve impulses to the brain via the

(A) optic nerve.
(B) cranial nerve.
(C) cardiac nerve.
(D) esophagus.

Answer: A. *Optic* refers to the eye, where the retina is located.

2. The arteries are part of the _____ system.

Which of the following correctly completes the sentence above?

(A) nervous
(B) endocrine

(C) lymphatic

(D) cardiovascular

Answer: D. The arteries carry blood away from the heart.

English and Language Usage questions on the TEAS cover punctuation, grammar, spelling, and sentence structure. Here are some typical sample questions:

1. That book is his masterpiece; I have always enjoyed _____ wry humor and sly irony.

   Which of the following words correctly completes the sentence above?

   (A) it's

   (B) its'

   (C) it is

   (D) its

   Answer: D. The possessive pronoun *its* is correct here.

2. Because of the apathy of her party's voters, our governor lost her campaign for reelection.

   What is the simple subject of the sentence above?

   (A) voters

   (B) governor

   (C) campaign

   (D) reelection

   Answer: B. *Governor* is the simple subject of the sentence.

3. Which of the following words is written correctly?

   (A) wellliked

   (B) counter-act

   (C) end-less

   (D) antibiotic

   Answer: D. *Antibiotic* is spelled without a hyphen.

4. As I walked through the dark forest, I shuttered in fear.

   What is the error in the sentence above?

   (A) walked

   (B) forest

   (C) shuttered

   (D) fear

   Answer: C. The sentence should read "As I walked through the dark forest, I *shuddered* in fear."

5. Susan bought a stamp to send a "get well" card to her sick friend at the post office.

Which phrase is misplaced in the sentence above?

(A) bought a stamp
(B) to send a "get well" card
(C) to her sick friend
(D) at the post office

Answer: D. The sentence as originally written is ambiguous: Is the sick friend at the post office? The sentence should be rewritten as follows: "Susan bought a stamp at the post office to send a 'get well' card to her sick friend."

PSYCHOLOGICAL SERVICES BUREAU (PSB) NURSING SCHOOL APTITUDE EXAMINATION (RN)

Format of the Test

The PSB examination (RN) is administered by the Psychological Services Bureau, a private testing firm specializing in entry-level examinations for various health professions. The Nursing School Aptitude Examination (RN) is designed to measure a person's capability to successfully complete the educational requirements for becoming an RN. The format of the test is shown in Table 2.3.

Table 2.3 PSB Nursing School Aptitude Examination (RN) Format		
Section	**Number of Questions**	**Content**
Academic aptitude	30 Vocabulary 30 Arithmetic 30 Nonverbal	Synonyms and analogies, eighth-grade level arithmetic, comprehension of form and spatial relationships
Spelling	50	Spelling
Reading comprehension	40	Ability to read and interpret passages, understand author's purpose, understand organization of ideas
Information in the natural sciences	90	Elementary level biology, chemistry, health, and safety
Vocational adjustment index	90	Questions relating to the applicant's feelings, attitudes, characteristics, and behavioral traits
Total	**360**	

How the Test Is Scored

After you take the PSB Nursing School Aptitude Examination (RN), you receive an Academic Aptitude Total Score based on the combined raw scores earned on the Vocabulary, Arithmetic, and Nonverbal subtests in the Academic Aptitude section. You also receive raw scores on each of the other four sections of the test. Each raw score represents the number of questions you answered correctly in that particular test section.

Each raw score is also translated by statistical methods into a percentile score. The percentile score shows how your results compare with the results achieved by others who took the same exam. For example, a percentile score of 65 on a particular test section shows that you scored higher than 65 percent of others who took the same test section.

Types of Questions

The questions in the Academic Aptitude section of the test are of three types: vocabulary, arithmetic, and nonverbal. The arithmetic questions test skills and concepts normally learned in school up through eighth grade. The nonverbal questions are of a type that may be unfamiliar to you. They show you pictures of objects, then they may ask you to spot the difference between one object and another. Or they may ask you to mentally "manipulate" an object; that is, turn it around or upside down, and then pick the answer choice that shows the object in the new position.

The questions in the Spelling section measure your ability to spell words correctly based on the rules of standard written English. The questions in the Reading Comprehension section measure your ability to understand and interpret what you read. You may be asked to identify the meaning of a specific statement, to locate a particular item of information, or to identify the author's purpose in writing. The questions in the Information in the Natural Sciences section cover basic biology, chemistry, health, and safety.

The questions in the Vocational Adjustment Index section are designed to determine whether you have any feelings, attitudes, opinions, or behavioral traits that might not be desirable in a professional nurse.

EVOLVE REACH (HESI) ADMISSION ASSESSMENT (A2)
Format of the Test

The A2 is divided into eight academic modules within three broad content areas: English language, mathematics, and science. In addition, the A2 may include a section on critical thinking, which may be graded or ungraded, plus one or two ungraded tests under the heading "Learner Profile." Most nursing programs require some of the modules and not others. It is important to know the requirements for the program you wish to enter.

Table 2.4 shows the number of items (which may vary year to year) and time suggested for each section. Because the test is given online, the times given are only suggestions that will allow you to complete the entire test within a reasonable time.

How the Test Is Scored

Your scores may be reported in three ways—as a percentage score for each module administered; as a subject-area composite score (for all science modules, for example); and as a composite score (the average score for all the modules you complete). Whether your score is acceptable depends on the program to which you are applying. Some nursing programs have specific cut-off points for each module. Others require a certain composite score.

Types of Questions

Reading items on the A2 test your comprehension of informational reading passages. You will be asked to read a short, multi-paragraph passage and answer a variety of questions about it. The passages used for A2 all have a science or health theme and may be typical of the type of reading you will do in your professional life.

Here is an example of an A2 Reading Comprehension question. On the test itself, most reading passages will be longer than this one.

> Counterfeit medicine may be contaminated, or it may contain the wrong or no active ingredient. Counterfeit medicine is illegal and may be dangerous. The quality, safety, and efficacy of counterfeit medicines are not known. Counterfeit medicine is often sold illegally over the Internet or by illegal operators posing as licensed pharmacies.
>
> What is the author's primary purpose in writing this passage?
>
> (A) To inform
> (B) To persuade
> (C) To entertain
> (D) To analyze
>
> Answer: A. The author defines *counterfeit medicine* and presents some facts about it, which indicates that the purpose is to inform.

The Vocabulary section of the test includes terms that appear regularly in health care contexts as well as in general and academic use. You may be asked to select a word or phrase that defines an underlined word in a sentence, as shown below, or to identify a synonym for a given word.

Table 2.4. Evolve Reach (HESI) A2 Format

Content Area and Module	Number of Items	Time Suggested	Content
English Language			
Reading Comprehension	47	60 minutes	Main idea, details, word meaning, author's purpose, fact and opinion, conclusions and inferences, summaries, tone
Vocabulary and General Knowledge	50	50 minutes	Synonyms, definitions
Grammar	50	50 minutes	Agreement, misplaced modifiers, pronoun case, serial commas, troublesome word pairs
Mathematics			
Basic Math Skills	50	50 minutes	Computation, fractions, percents, ratios and proportions, money, military time, Roman numerals, conversions
Science			
Biology	25	25 minutes	Scientific method, taxonomy, molecules, cells, photosynthesis, reproduction, genetics
Chemistry	25	25 minutes	States of matter, atomic structure, chemical equations, acids and bases, reactions, molarity
Anatomy and Physiology	25	25 minutes	Cells and tissues, systems, body planes and directions
Physics*	25	50 minutes	Speed and acceleration, momentum, Newton's laws, energy, waves, electricity
Learner Profile			
Critical Thinking	30	30 minutes	Common sense questions about real-life scenarios
Learning Style	14	15 minutes	Questions that tell about the applicant as a learner
Personality Profile	15	15 minutes	Questions that test levels of extroversion or introversion

*Currently being piloted.

Select the correct definition of the underlined word.

The patient received a potent dose of sleeping medication.

(A) Average
(B) Invasive
(C) Powerful
(D) Initial

Answer: C. *Potent* means "strong," so a potent dose is a strong, or powerful, dose.

The Grammar section requires you to identify sentences that are grammatically correct, words or phrases that are not used correctly, and words that best complete a sentence to make it grammatically correct.

Select the word or phrase that makes this sentence grammatically correct.

Could you please hand _____ the tongue depressors?

(A) myself
(B) me
(C) I
(D) ourselves

Answer: B. The pronoun required is an object pronoun (it receives the action of the verb), so only *me* completes the sentence correctly.

Mathematics on the A2 is much like math on any other entrance exam, except that a few items in the section may be short answer, meaning that you must compute the answer rather than choosing from four possible responses. Here is an example:

How many fluid ounces are in a pint? (Enter numeric value only.)

_____

Answer: 16. There are 8 ounces in a cup and 2 cups in a pint, so the answer is 16.

Biology, Chemistry, Anatomy and Physiology, and Physics are typical multiple-choice tests. Unlike some other exams, the A2 uses few diagrams, graphs, or other illustrations. The example here is from the chemistry module.

What is the expected pH of orange juice?

(A) Between 3.0 and 4.0
(B) Between 6.0 and 7.0
(C) Between 8.0 and 9.0
(D) Between 11.0 and 12.0

Answer: A. Orange juice is fairly acidic, meaning that it would fall toward the lower end of the pH scale.

The Critical Thinking, Learning Style, and Personality Profile segments of the A2 are required by certain programs that want to know more about your common sense in given nursing scenarios, your preferred learning style and what it means about how you should study, and your level of introversion or extroversion. The only one that may affect your entry into a program is the Critical Thinking test. Some nursing programs use it as a pre- and post-test to see how well students improve over the course of training. Others require a particular score for entry. Like all of the A2 modules, these are required by some nursing programs and not by others.

CHAPTER 3

Setting Up Your Study Plan

Read this chapter to learn

- How to create a study plan that meets your needs

- How to use your time wisely

CREATE A PLAN THAT IS RIGHT FOR YOU

The first step in setting up your study plan is to find out which of the various nursing school entrance exams you are going to take. As you learned in Chapter 2, there are significant differences in what the various tests cover and in the kinds of questions that are on each one. Not all of the tests cover the same subjects. For example, some include a science section, and some do not. Some test grammar and punctuation, and some do not. You need to know which particular topics you need to study so that you can focus your preparation and not waste time on subjects that you will not need to know.

To help you, we have created the chart on the following page. It summarizes the different topics tested on each of the four major nursing entrance exams. Find out which exam is required by the nursing schools to which you are applying. Then use the chart to figure out which subjects you need to focus on, based on which test(s) you plan to take. Once you know which subjects you need to study, you can make plans to devote your study time to the chapters in this book that cover those subjects.

Topics Tested on Nursing School Entrance Exams

Test Topic	NLN	TEAS	PSB	A2*
English				
Grammar		√		√
Sentence structure		√		√
Spelling		√	√	√
Punctuation		√	√	√
Vocabulary	√	√	√	√
Reading Comprehension				
Reading comprehension	√	√	√	√
Mathematics				
Whole numbers	√	√	√	√
Decimals	√	√	√	√
Fractions	√	√	√	√
Percentages	√	√	√	√
Metric conversions	√	√		√
Algebra	√	√		√
Graphs	√	√		√
Applied mathematics	√	√	√	√
Geometry	√	√		
Ratio/Proportion		√		√
Spatial relations			√	
Military time				√
Science				
Biology	√	√	√	√
Chemistry	√	√	√	√
Physics	√	√	√	√
Earth Science	√	√		
Anatomy/Physiology		√	√	√

*On the Evolve Reach (HESI) A2 exam, *not* all topics will be required by all nursing programs. Check with your program to see which parts of the test you will be required to take.

Now you can use this book to review the topics that you need to study for your test.

- English topics are covered in Chapter 6.
- Reading comprehension is covered in Chapter 7.
- Mathematics topics are covered in Chapter 8.
- Science topics are covered in Chapter 9.

USE TIME WISELY

What kind of preparation program should you follow for your nursing school entrance exam? The answer depends on two things:

- How much time you have
- What kind of a student you are

So first, decide how much time you have. Do you have a month? Two weeks? Three days? The answer determines how much time you can devote to each step in the preparation process.

Next, think about your study habits. No one knows your learning style better than you do. Do you feel confident only when you are thoroughly prepared? Do you feel that you get stale if you prepare too far in advance? Do you feel well prepared already and are just looking to sharpen your focus? The answers to these questions also help you create your best study plan.

Make a study schedule. Be sure to set aside enough time at the end of your schedule to take the practice tests at the end of this book. Study with a friend if that works best for you. Often when preparing for a test, it helps to have someone who can quiz you about the test topics and whom you can quiz in return. If you do not have much time before the test, you may want to shorten your review time and focus instead entirely on the practice tests.

CHAPTER 4

Strategies to Raise Your Score

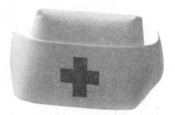

Read this chapter to learn

- How you can gain points with some simple test-taking strategies

- What to do on test day to help you do your best

This chapter presents some general test-taking strategies that apply to all or most of the tests required for nursing school admission. These strategies can help you gain valuable points when you take your test. At the end of the chapter you will also find some useful tips that can help you on test day.

GENERAL TEST-TAKING STRATEGIES

Take Advantage of the Multiple-Choice Format

With the exception of a few math questions on the Evolve Reach (HESI) A2 exam, all of the questions on the nursing school entrance exams are in multiple-choice format, which you have undoubtedly seen many times before. That means that for every question, the correct answer is right in front of you. All you have to do is pick it out from among three incorrect choices, called *distracters*. Consequently, you can use the process of elimination to rule out incorrect answer choices. The more answers you rule out, the easier it is to make the right choice.

Answer Every Question

On these exams, there is no penalty for choosing a wrong answer. Therefore, if you do not know the answer to a question, you have nothing to lose by guessing. So make sure that you answer every question. If you are taking one of the paper-and-pencil exams and find that you are running out of time, make sure to enter an answer for the questions that you have not tackled. With luck, you may be able to pick up a few extra points, even if your guesses are totally random.

Answer All of the Easy Problems First, Then Tackle the Hard Ones

Keep in mind that these tests all have specific time limits. There is not much time to spend trying to figure out the answers to harder problems, so skip them and come back to them later. There are three reasons why you should do this:

1. Every question counts the same in the scoring of the exam. That means that you are better off spending time answering the easier questions, where you are sure to pick up points.
2. Later on in the test you might come to a question or a set of answer choices that jogs your memory and helps you go back and answer the question you skipped.
3. By answering the easier questions, you will build your confidence and get into a helpful test-taking rhythm. Then when you go back to a question you skipped, you may find that it is not as hard as you first thought.

Note that some computerized tests, notably the Evolve Reach (HESI) A2, do not permit movement back and forth. On those tests, you will not be able to return to questions you have skipped. Your strategy will need to change. Make sure you are familiar with the format and rules for the test you are about to take.

Make Educated Guesses

What differentiates great test takers from merely good ones is the ability to guess in a way that maximizes the chance of guessing correctly. The way to do this is to use the process of elimination. Before you guess, try to eliminate one or more of the answer choices. That way, you can make an educated guess, and you have a better chance of picking the correct answer. Odds of one out of two or one out of three are better than one out of four!

Go with Your Gut

In those cases where you are not 100 percent sure of the answer you are choosing, it is often best to go with your gut feeling and stick with your first answer. If you decide to change that answer and pick another one, you may well pick the wrong answer because you have over-thought the problem. More often than not, if you know something about the subject, your first answer is likely to be the correct one.

Be Wary of Answer Choices That Look Familiar But Are Not Correct

Sometimes in the set of answer choices there will be one or more wrong answers that include familiar expressions or phrases. You might be tempted to pick one of these choices if you are working quickly or not paying complete attention. That is why it is important to think through each question thoroughly and carefully to make sure that you pick the correct answer choice.

TIPS FOR TEST DAY

Stay Calm

Once test day comes, you are as prepared as you are ever going to be, so there is no point in panicking. Use your energy to make sure that you are extra careful in answering questions and marking your answer choices.

Watch the Time

Make sure that you are on track to answer all of the questions within the time allowed. With so many questions to answer in a short time period, you are not going to have a lot of time to spare. Check yourself at 10- or 15-minute intervals using your watch or timer. Do not spend too much time on any one question. If you find yourself stuck for more than a minute or two on a question, then you should move on.

Do Not Panic if Time Runs Out

If you pace yourself and keep track of your progress, you should not run out of time. If you do, however, do not panic. Because there is no guessing penalty and you have nothing to lose by doing so, enter answers to all the remaining questions. If you are able to make educated guesses, you will probably be able to improve your score. However, even random guesses may help you pick up a few points. Guessing well is a skill that comes with practice, so incorporate it into your preparation program.

Use Extra Time to Check Your Work

If you have time left over at the end of a paper-and-pencil test, go back and check your work. Make sure that you have marked your answer sheet correctly. Check any calculations you may have made to make sure that they are correct. Resist the urge to second-guess too many of your answers, however, because this may lead you to change an already correct answer to a wrong one.

CHAPTER 5

Diagnostic Test

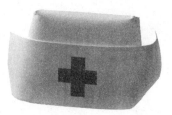

In this chapter you'll find

- A diagnostic test covering all subjects tested on nursing school entrance exams
- Sample questions like the ones on the real exams
- Answer explanations for every question

The diagnostic test in this chapter presents questions in all the subject areas tested on the most widely used nursing school entrance exams. The questions are in the multiple-choice format that you will encounter on the actual exam. They have also been designed to match the actual exams in degree of difficulty. Answer explanations for every question are provided at the end of the test.

This test gives you a very good idea of what you will face on test day. It is called a diagnostic test because it helps you "diagnose" how well prepared you are right now for the real exam and what subjects you need to review and study.

This test includes an answer sheet that you may want to remove from the book. Use this sheet to mark your answers. When you are finished with the test, carefully read the answer explanations, especially for any questions that you answered incorrectly. Pinpoint your weak areas by determining the topics in which you made the most errors. This knowledge helps you focus your study as you work your way through the subject review chapters in this book.

This test helps you gauge your test readiness if you treat it as an actual examination. Here are some hints on how to take the test under conditions similar to those of the actual exam.

- Find a time when you will not be interrupted.
- Complete the test in one session, following the suggested time limits.
- If you run out of time on any section, take note of where you ended when time ran out. This will help you determine if you need to speed up your pacing.

Diagnostic Test: Answer Sheet

SECTION 1. VERBAL SKILLS

1 (A) (B) (C) (D)   11 (A) (B) (C) (D)   21 (A) (B) (C) (D)
2 (A) (B) (C) (D)   12 (A) (B) (C) (D)   22 (A) (B) (C) (D)
3 (A) (B) (C) (D)   13 (A) (B) (C) (D)   23 (A) (B) (C) (D)
4 (A) (B) (C) (D)   14 (A) (B) (C) (D)   24 (A) (B) (C) (D)
5 (A) (B) (C) (D)   15 (A) (B) (C) (D)   25 (A) (B) (C) (D)
6 (A) (B) (C) (D)   16 (A) (B) (C) (D)   26 (A) (B) (C) (D)
7 (A) (B) (C) (D)   17 (A) (B) (C) (D)   27 (A) (B) (C) (D)
8 (A) (B) (C) (D)   18 (A) (B) (C) (D)   28 (A) (B) (C) (D)
9 (A) (B) (C) (D)   19 (A) (B) (C) (D)   29 (A) (B) (C) (D)
10 (A) (B) (C) (D)   20 (A) (B) (C) (D)   30 (A) (B) (C) (D)

SECTION 2. READING COMPREHENSION

1 (A) (B) (C) (D)   11 (A) (B) (C) (D)
2 (A) (B) (C) (D)   12 (A) (B) (C) (D)
3 (A) (B) (C) (D)   13 (A) (B) (C) (D)
4 (A) (B) (C) (D)   14 (A) (B) (C) (D)
5 (A) (B) (C) (D)   15 (A) (B) (C) (D)
6 (A) (B) (C) (D)
7 (A) (B) (C) (D)
8 (A) (B) (C) (D)
9 (A) (B) (C) (D)
10 (A) (B) (C) (D)

SECTION 3. MATHEMATICS

1 (A) (B) (C) (D)   11 (A) (B) (C) (D)   21 (A) (B) (C) (D)
2 (A) (B) (C) (D)   12 (A) (B) (C) (D)   22 (A) (B) (C) (D)
3 (A) (B) (C) (D)   13 (A) (B) (C) (D)   23 (A) (B) (C) (D)
4 (A) (B) (C) (D)   14 (A) (B) (C) (D)   24 (A) (B) (C) (D)
5 (A) (B) (C) (D)   15 (A) (B) (C) (D)   25 (A) (B) (C) (D)
6 (A) (B) (C) (D)   16 (A) (B) (C) (D)
7 (A) (B) (C) (D)   17 (A) (B) (C) (D)
8 (A) (B) (C) (D)   18 (A) (B) (C) (D)
9 (A) (B) (C) (D)   19 (A) (B) (C) (D)
10 (A) (B) (C) (D)   20 (A) (B) (C) (D)

SECTION 4. SCIENCE

1 (A) (B) (C) (D)   11 (A) (B) (C) (D)   21 (A) (B) (C) (D)
2 (A) (B) (C) (D)   12 (A) (B) (C) (D)   22 (A) (B) (C) (D)
3 (A) (B) (C) (D)   13 (A) (B) (C) (D)   23 (A) (B) (C) (D)
4 (A) (B) (C) (D)   14 (A) (B) (C) (D)   24 (A) (B) (C) (D)
5 (A) (B) (C) (D)   15 (A) (B) (C) (D)   25 (A) (B) (C) (D)
6 (A) (B) (C) (D)   16 (A) (B) (C) (D)   26 (A) (B) (C) (D)
7 (A) (B) (C) (D)   17 (A) (B) (C) (D)   27 (A) (B) (C) (D)
8 (A) (B) (C) (D)   18 (A) (B) (C) (D)   28 (A) (B) (C) (D)
9 (A) (B) (C) (D)   19 (A) (B) (C) (D)   29 (A) (B) (C) (D)
10 (A) (B) (C) (D)   20 (A) (B) (C) (D)   30 (A) (B) (C) (D)

SECTION 1. VERBAL SKILLS

30 Questions

Time Limit: 25 minutes

1. Which noun in the sentence below is the subject?

> The intensive care unit staff required all visitors to don plastic gloves and paper gowns before going in to see any of the patients.

(A) staff
(B) visitors
(C) gloves
(D) patients

2. Read the following sentence. Which word is the subject?

> Grab the charts and follow me because Dr. Tull and I are already behind schedule.

(A) charts
(B) you
(C) Dr. Tull
(D) I

3. Read the sentence below. Which pronoun can be used to replace "the patient"?

> Although the patient was nearly incoherent from the pain of his wounds, the patient was still able to answer all of the doctor's questions.

(A) she
(B) they
(C) I
(D) he

4. Read the sentence below. There is an error with the verb. Which answer corrects that error?

> While you are in with the physician, I is going to fill out all of the necessary papers.

(A) I are going to fill out
(B) I am going to fill out
(C) I is filling out
(D) I am filled out

GO ON TO THE NEXT PAGE

5. Which word in the following sentence is an adverb?

In the operating room the music played loudly, but the sedated patient was unaware of it.

(A) operating
(B) played
(C) loudly
(D) sedated

6. Which word in the following sentence is an adjective?

The huge bottle of lotion was tantalizingly out of reach on the table at the end of the bed.

(A) huge
(B) tantalizingly
(C) table
(D) bed

7. What type of word is needed to repair the error in the sentence below?

The blood pressure cuff, specifically designed to fit the upper arms of heavier patients.

(A) a subject
(B) a verb
(C) an adjective
(D) an adverb

8. What type of word is needed to repair the error in the sentence below?

Unable to control his temper, shoving the crash cart to the floor and knocking over both intravenous (IV) poles.

(A) a subject
(B) a verb
(C) an adverb
(D) an adjective

GO ON TO THE NEXT PAGE

9. All of the following corrections to the run-on sentence below are correct EXCEPT

> The photographer took a picture of the entire staff he managed to get everyone in one shot.

(A) The photographer took a picture of the entire staff, he managed to get everyone in one shot.
(B) The photographer took a picture of the entire staff; he managed to get everyone in one shot.
(C) The photographer took a picture of the entire staff, and he managed to get everyone in one shot.
(D) The photographer took a picture of the entire staff. He managed to get everyone in one shot.

10. Which of the following coordinating conjunctions fits best in the sentence below?

> Dr. Halbert will be out of town for the first two weeks of the month, _____ you will have to schedule her emergency patients with Dr. Carmen instead.

(A) nor
(B) yet
(C) so
(D) since

11. Which of the following subordinating conjunctions fits best in the sentence below?

> _____ our demands are met in full, we will all return to work tomorrow morning at 9:00 a.m.

(A) Even though
(B) Provided that
(C) Rather than
(D) So that

12. An independent clause is the same as a

(A) phrase.
(B) dependent clause.
(C) sentence.
(D) fragment.

13. Which of the following is an example of a dependent clause?

(A) The doctor's orders were carried out immediately.
(B) Who does not have her morning charts yet
(C) After all of their complaining and grievances
(D) Without a single thought of the consequences

GO ON TO THE NEXT PAGE

14. What type of clause is used in the sentence below?

> After seeing her photograph splashed across the front page of the newspaper, Dr. Carlton resigned.

(A) adverbial
(B) independent
(C) adjectival
(D) prepositional

15. Which of the following is the correct way to spell the word?

(A) calendar
(B) calander
(C) calender
(D) colendar

16. The word *discussed* is an example of which of the following?

(A) silent letter
(B) missing consonant
(C) homophone
(D) unstressed vowel

17. The word *climb* is an example of which of the following?

(A) missing consonant
(B) homophone
(C) unstressed vowel
(D) silent letter

18. What punctuation is needed in the sentence below to make it correct?

> "Nurse Connors" said Dr. Strauss, "just when did you plan to fill out this chart?"

(A) a comma
(B) a period
(C) an apostrophe
(D) a quotation mark

19. Where does a comma need to be added in the following sentence?

> Although I was already two hours past the end of my shift I stayed to help with the accident victims.

(A) after *hours*
(B) after *end*
(C) after *shift*
(D) after *help*

GO ON TO THE NEXT PAGE

20. What kind of punctuation is needed in this sentence?

The telephones would not quit ringing apparently there was an emergency of some kind in the neighborhood.

(A) a comma
(B) a colon
(C) a semicolon
(D) a question mark

21. Which word in the following sentence is missing an apostrophe?

You cannot fool me because I know my sisters lab coat when I see it, Cathy.

(A) cannot
(B) sisters
(C) coat
(D) Cathy

22. Which punctuation mark is missing from the following sentence?

My current shift a temporary assignment ends at noon, but I prefer to work in the afternoon or evening.

(A) an apostrophe
(B) a question mark
(C) a colon
(D) parentheses

23. What is one of the main purposes of an apostrophe?

(A) to indicate that a letter is missing
(B) to show that a word is plural
(C) to point out a time to pause
(D) to create a natural break

24. Although she apologized, the pain she had caused with her words was *irrevocable*. **Irrevocable** means

(A) permanent.
(B) repairable.
(C) compliant.
(D) accidental.

25. Someone who is filled with *lassitude* is

(A) energetic.
(B) determined.
(C) grieving.
(D) exhausted.

GO ON TO THE NEXT PAGE

26. If you ask a patient, "What was the last thing you *masticated*?" you are actually asking, "What was the last thing you _____?"

(A) did
(B) ate
(C) wore
(D) drank

27. The psychologist was positive that the patient was *sublimating* his feelings about the rape. **Sublimating** means

(A) supplementing.
(B) avoiding.
(C) repressing.
(D) admitting.

28. If a doctor informs you that the patient has a *vascular* problem, that means the patient has a condition involving the

(A) reproductive system.
(B) nervous system.
(C) circulatory system.
(D) digestive system.

29. A patient told you that the pain comes and goes in no recognized pattern. Which of the following words would you put into your notes to indicate this?

(A) acute
(B) sporadic
(C) chronic
(D) consistent

30. The new intern spoke with great *temerity*. **Temerity** means

(A) audacity.
(B) reticence.
(C) embarrassment.
(D) confidence.

STOP. IF YOU HAVE TIME LEFT OVER, CHECK YOUR WORK ON THIS SECTION ONLY.

SECTION 2. READING COMPREHENSION

15 questions

Time limit: 20 minutes

Questions 1–5 are based on the following passage.

It is hard to imagine that the virus that causes children to break out into itchy red dots and miss a few days of school is the same one that can send adults to the hospital begging for pain relief, but it is true. The varicella-zoster virus is responsible for both chickenpox in children and shingles in adults. Unlike many other viruses, this herpes virus can hibernate within the body for decades, only becoming noticeable when a person's immune system is severely compromised.

Shingles is often considered one of the most uncomfortable conditions because it causes burning and/or shooting pain, tingling and itching, and commonly rashes or blisters. Treatment ranges from a vaccine that prevents the virus from attacking in the first place to antiviral and pain medications for people who are already afflicted.

Every year, almost one million Americans seek help from the pain and discomfort of shingles, costing the United States $566 million in treatment. Unfortunately, a great many of these victims are also members of a very vulnerable population: the elderly. According to research, people 65 years of age or older are seven times more likely to develop shingles than younger people.

1. What is the main idea of this passage?

    (A) The varicella-zoster virus causes both chickenpox and shingles.
    (B) Shingles causes people a lot of pain and costs the medical system millions.
    (C) The elderly are the age group most at risk for contracting shingles.
    (D) A case of chickenpox can often cause children to miss several days of school.

2. Shingles causes all of the following symptoms EXCEPT

    (A) pain.
    (B) blisters.
    (C) fever.
    (D) itching.

3. Why is the vaccine the most effective type of treatment?

    (A) It is less expensive than the other available options.
    (B) It takes effect faster than antiviral and pain medications.
    (C) It is particularly effective with the elderly age group.
    (D) It prevents the condition from occurring in the first place.

GO ON TO THE NEXT PAGE

4. Shingles tend to appear in adults when

   (A) their immune system is compromised.
   (B) they are just past puberty.
   (C) the vaccine is administered.
   (D) they are younger than 65 years of age.

5. What makes this virus unusual?

   (A) It affects people of all ages.
   (B) It often attacks the elderly.
   (C) It causes some discomfort.
   (D) It can stay dormant for years.

Questions 6–10 are based on the following passage.

If statistics are to be believed, the surgeons on the popular television show *Nip/Tuck* seem to be inspiring many viewers to have cosmetic work. According to the American Society for Aesthetic Plastic Surgery, 11.7 million cosmetic procedures were performed in the United States in 2007 at an overall cost of approximately $13.2 billion. Since 1997, the number of regular surgical procedures has gone up by 114 percent, but the number of nonsurgical procedures has gone up an amazing 754 percent. The vast majority of cosmetic surgery patients are women, perhaps because in so many circumstances, women are more likely than men to be judged by their appearance.

By far, the most popular cosmetic surgical procedure is liposuction, followed by breast augmentation, eyelid surgery, abdominoplasty (often known as a "tummy tuck"), and breast reduction. Common nonsurgical cosmetic procedures include the extremely popular Botox injections, followed by laser hair removal, microdermabrasion, and laser skin resurfacing.

Although more than 90 percent of the patients who undergo cosmetic procedures are women, the number of men having some kind of work is slowly growing. To date, men's favorite procedure is injections to fill out wrinkles.

6. The best title for this passage is

   (A) Watching *Nip/Tuck* Is a Smart Thing to Do.
   (B) Cosmetic Procedures Are on the Rise.
   (C) Liposuction Remains a Popular Choice.
   (D) Men are Getting Rid of Wrinkles.

7. What can be inferred from the fact that women make up the majority of patients for cosmetic procedures?

   (A) Women have more money to spend than men.
   (B) Women feel more pressure to look attractive.
   (C) Women have done more research on the topic.
   (D) Women have more patience for recovery.

GO ON TO THE NEXT PAGE

8. Which of the following is one of the most popular types of cosmetic procedures for men?

    (A) liposuction
    (B) eyelid surgery
    (C) wrinkle injections
    (D) "tummy tucks"

9. Which of the following is the most popular type of nonsurgical cosmetic procedure for women?

    (A) Botox injections
    (B) Breast reduction
    (C) Microdermabrasion
    (D) Breast augmentation

10. What conclusion can be drawn from the fact that the number of men having cosmetic procedures is increasing?

    (A) Men are discovering the many cosmetic procedures that are available.
    (B) Men are finding out the psychological benefits of Botox injections.
    (C) Men are under more social pressure to maintain a handsome appearance.
    (D) Men are figuring out that liposuction can bring health benefits.

Questions 11–15 are based on the following passage.

Everyone knows that pepper is great for adding a little extra flavor to food, but a new study from Great Britain says that it may also have a medicinal purpose. Apparently, black pepper can help treat a disfiguring skin condition known as vitiligo.

Vitiligo is a disease that kills the skin's melanin, the element that gives skin its color and protects it from the sun's ultraviolet (UV) rays. It is the condition that the pop star Michael Jackson said was responsible for his skin color changes.

Researchers at King's College in London studied piperine, the compound in pepper that gives the spice its unique spicy flavor. Apparently piperine, along with its synthetic derivatives, helps stimulate pigmentation in people's skin, especially when phototherapy treatment is combined with UV radiation.

To date, treatment for vitiligo has consisted of steroids applied directly to the skin as well as phototherapy. However, a number of people do not respond effectively to hormones, and phototherapy always carries with it a risk of skin cancer. Piperine, on the other hand, when applied to the skin resulted in an even brown color within a mere six weeks.

GO ON TO THE NEXT PAGE

11. The best title for this selection is

    (A) Pepper Always Adds Flavor.
    (B) A Cure for Vitiligo.
    (C) Pepper Provides Pigmentation.
    (D) Pepper's Piperine.

12. What substance were the scientists studying?

    (A) piperine
    (B) melanin
    (C) pigmentation
    (D) phototherapy

13. Piperine gives pepper its

    (A) color.
    (B) flavor.
    (C) aroma.
    (D) shape.

14. What is one of the main functions of melanin?

    (A) to keep the skin supple
    (B) to release hormones
    (C) to provide taste
    (D) to provide protection from UV rays

15. Which treatment seems to have the highest risk?

    (A) piperine
    (B) phototherapy
    (C) steroids
    (D) hormones

STOP. IF YOU HAVE TIME LEFT OVER, CHECK YOUR WORK ON THIS SECTION ONLY.

SECTION 3. MATHEMATICS

25 questions

Time limit: 25 minutes

1. How is $\frac{8}{2}$ expressed as a percentage?

   (A) 4%
   (B) 40%
   (C) 400%
   (D) 4,000%

2. Doris is leaning a 10-ft ladder against a wall. If the ladder hits the wall at exactly 8 ft, how far away from the wall is the ladder placed on the floor?

   (A) 2 ft
   (B) 6 ft
   (C) 8 ft
   (D) 10 ft

3. What is the average (arithmetic mean) of 8, 3, 6, and 11?

   (A) 4
   (B) 6
   (C) 7
   (D) 9

4. If Melanie can complete 6 forms in 15 minutes, how long will it take her to complete 30 forms?

   (A) 12 minutes
   (B) 60 minutes
   (C) 75 minutes
   (D) 120 minutes

5. $3,892 + 364 =$

   (A) 4,126
   (B) 4,156
   (C) 4,256
   (D) 5,254

6. If Ryan is 2 years older than four times the age of his dog, Pixie, which expression represents that relationship?

   (A) $R = 4 + 2P$
   (B) $R = (2 + 4)P$
   (C) $R = \dfrac{2 + 4}{P}$
   (D) $R = 2 + 4P$

GO ON TO THE NEXT PAGE

7. If the longest distance across from edge to edge of a circle is 10 ft, what is the area of the circle?

(A) 5 ft
(B) 25π ft^2
(C) 50π ft^2
(D) 100π ft^2

8. What is the prime number between 34 and 39?

(A) 35
(B) 36
(C) 37
(D) 38

9. If $3 + 4x = 23$, what is the value of x?

(A) 2
(B) 3
(C) 4
(D) 5

10. $1\dfrac{2}{3} + \dfrac{4}{5} =$

(A) $\dfrac{7}{15}$

(B) $\dfrac{13}{15}$

(C) $\dfrac{37}{15}$

(D) $\dfrac{52}{15}$

Use the information below to answer questions 11 and 12.

	Cases Sold	Bottles Sold	Total Bottles
1997 Pinot Noir	5,437	15,229	80,473
1994 Pinot Gris	4,913	18,445	77,401
1991 Chardonnay	6,110	14,757	88,077
2001 Bordeaux	7,226	11,934	98,646

GO ON TO THE NEXT PAGE

11. Which wine sold the most cases but the fewest individual bottles?

(A) 1997 Pinot Noir
(B) 1994 Pinot Gris
(C) 1991 Chardonnay
(D) 2001 Bordeaux

12. Which wine had the largest percentage of sales in individual bottles?

(A) 1997 Pinot Noir
(B) 1994 Pinot Gris
(C) 1991 Chardonnay
(D) 2001 Bordeaux

13. $7,259 - 3,687 =$

(A) 3,572
(B) 3,672
(C) 4,572
(D) 5,472

14. If it is 90°F, approximately what temperature is it on the Celsius scale?

(A) 18°C
(B) 32°C
(C) 58°C
(D) 104°C

15. A certain rectangular room has an area of 196 ft². If the length and width of the room are the same, how wide is the room?

(A) 12 ft
(B) 13 ft
(C) 14 ft
(D) 16 ft

16. $3.98 \times 0.72 =$

(A) 3.26
(B) 2.8656
(C) 4.7
(D) 5.0293

17. The ratio of flour to sugar in a certain recipe is 3:2. If Don is making as much of the recipe as he can and he only has nine cups of flour, how much sugar will he use?

(A) 3
(B) 4.5
(C) 6
(D) 7.5

GO ON TO THE NEXT PAGE

18. What is the sum of the prime factors of 30?

(A) 2
(B) 5
(C) 10
(D) 15

19. The number 8 is what percent of 5?

(A) 62.5%
(B) 160%
(C) 162.5%
(D) 200%

20. $294 \times 35 =$

(A) 2,352
(B) 10,290
(C) 12,520
(D) 14,009

21.

is to as is to:

(A)   (C)

(B)   (D)

22. Which of the following expresses 65 percent as a decimal?

(A) 0.065
(B) 0.65
(C) 6.5
(D) 65

23. $(x^4)^5 =$

(A) $-x$
(B) x^9
(C) x^{12}
(D) x^{20}

GO ON TO THE NEXT PAGE

24. $385 \div 7 =$

    (A) 22

    (B) 35

    (C) 55

    (D) 62

25. If there are three foreign cars for every two domestic cars in a parking lot and their percentages are represented on a pie chart, what is the degree measure of the central angle that represents the foreign cars?

    (A) 60

    (B) 124

    (C) 144

    (D) 216

**STOP. IF YOU HAVE TIME LEFT OVER,
CHECK YOUR WORK ON THIS SECTION ONLY.**

SECTION 4. SCIENCE

30 questions

Time limit: 25 minutes

1. Which of the following statements is true?

   (A) DNA is made of amino acids.
   (B) RNA is double-stranded.
   (C) Cytosine replaces uracil in RNA.
   (D) Thymine pairs with adenine in DNA.

2. The genotype and phenotype for human life are determined by which of the following organic compounds?

   (A) water
   (B) carbohydrates
   (C) nucleic acids
   (D) amino acids

3. Which of the following transports oxygen in human blood?

   (A) phagocytes and white blood cells
   (B) hemoglobin in red blood cells
   (C) platelets
   (D) lymph from lymph nodes

4. Which of the following organelles controls the entry and exit of materials into and out of an animal cell?

   (A) cell membrane
   (B) cell wall
   (C) mitochondria
   (D) vacuole

5. Light is shined on a plant from a fixed position. As the plant grows, it tends to bend toward the light. This tendency is called

   (A) geotropism.
   (B) hydrotropism.
   (C) phototropism.
   (D) auxinism.

6. A change in the _____ leads to a mutation of an organism.

   (A) transfer RNA
   (B) amino acid in a protein synthesis
   (C) messenger RNA
   (D) nitrogen base sequence in DNA

GO ON TO THE NEXT PAGE

7. When a solute such as iodine is dissolved in _____, the solution is referred to as a tincture.

   (A) water
   (B) ether
   (C) alcohol
   (D) a base

8. A potassium ion (K^+) can be formed from a potassium atom (K) by

   (A) losing a neutron.
   (B) gaining a neutron.
   (C) gaining an electron.
   (D) losing an electron.

9. Among the following elements, which is a nonmetal?

   (A) mercury
   (B) magnesium
   (C) sulfur
   (D) potassium

10. Two organic compounds have the same formula but different molecular structures. These compounds are said to be

    (A) isofers.
    (B) isocompounds.
    (C) isotopes.
    (D) isomers.

11. A radioactive isotope has a half-life of 20 years. How many grams of a 6-gram sample will remain after 40 years?

    (A) 8 g
    (B) 1.5 g
    (C) 6 g
    (D) 3 g

12. The human embryo develops in the female's

    (A) menstrual cycle.
    (B) uterus.
    (C) vaginal canal.
    (D) cervix.

13. Which of the following develops so that nutrients can reach the human embryo?

    (A) ovary
    (B) sperm
    (C) amnion
    (D) placenta

GO ON TO THE NEXT PAGE

14. The small intestine has tiny structures designed for absorption. These structures are called

   (A) villi.
   (B) veins.
   (C) venoms.
   (D) root tips.

15. Within the human kidney, which of the following works to filter the blood?

   (A) nephron
   (B) urethra
   (C) neutron
   (D) epiglottis

16. When there are no cone cells in an animal's retina, that animal most likely cannot

   (A) determine various shades of colors.
   (B) see with that eye.
   (C) focus properly.
   (D) close its eyelid.

17. Of the following organisms, which is an invertebrate?

   (A) starfish
   (B) cat
   (C) human
   (D) mouse

18. Across which of the following does gas exchange take place?

   (A) skin
   (B) nasal cavity
   (C) capillaries
   (D) bronchioles

19. Which chamber of the heart receives blood from the lungs?

   (A) left atrium
   (B) right atrium
   (C) left ventricle
   (D) right ventricle

20. The space where a nervous impulse passes from one neuron to another is called the

   (A) gap.
   (B) neurotransmitter.
   (C) synapse.
   (D) sodium pump.

GO ON TO THE NEXT PAGE

21. Quantities having both magnitude and direction are

(A) scalar quantities.
(B) vector quantities.
(C) directional quantities.
(D) matrices.

22. The arrow in the following diagram represents the wave's

(A) period.
(B) frequency.
(C) amplitude.
(D) wavelength.

23. The diagram below illustrates which type of circuit?

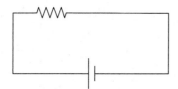

(A) series
(B) parallel
(C) complex
(D) open

24. In a sound wave with a constant velocity, the frequency is inversely proportional to the

(A) amplitude.
(B) reflection.
(C) wavelength.
(D) resonance.

25. Force multiplied by distance equals

(A) joules.
(B) work.
(C) power.
(D) potential energy.

26. An object is moving at a constant speed of 12 m/s. The object's acceleration is

(A) 0 m/s^2.
(B) 6 m/s^2.
(C) 12 m/s^2.
(D) 1 m/s^2.

GO ON TO THE NEXT PAGE

27. Newton's second law is shown by which of the following equations?

   (A) $PV = nRT$
   (B) $F = ma$
   (C) $p = mv$
   (D) $a = v/t$

28. The bending of light that takes place as light passes from air to quartz is called

   (A) deflection.
   (B) diffraction.
   (C) refraction.
   (D) absorption.

29. If the rate of change in velocity of an airplane has a negative value, the airplane has

   (A) stopped.
   (B) slowed down.
   (C) crashed an hour ago.
   (D) maintained a constant speed.

30. A runner sprints at a constant speed of 4 meters per second. How far will the runner travel in 20 seconds?

   (A) 5 meters
   (B) 800 meters
   (C) 120 meters
   (D) 80 meters

**STOP. IF YOU HAVE TIME LEFT OVER,
CHECK YOUR WORK ON THIS SECTION ONLY.**

Answer Key

Section 1. Verbal Skills

1. A	11. B	21. B
2. B	12. C	22. D
3. D	13. B	23. A
4. B	14. A	24. A
5. C	15. A	25. D
6. A	16. C	26. B
7. B	17. D	27. C
8. A	18. A	28. C
9. A	19. C	29. B
10. C	20. C	30. A

Section 2. Reading Comprehension

1. B	11. C
2. C	12. A
3. D	13. B
4. A	14. D
5. D	15. B
6. B	
7. B	
8. C	
9. A	
10. C	

Section 3. Mathematics

1. C	11. D	21. B
2. B	12. B	22. B
3. C	13. A	23. D
4. C	14. B	24. C
5. C	15. C	25. D
6. D	16. B	
7. B	17. C	
8. C	18. C	
9. D	19. B	
10. C	20. B	

Section 4. Science

1. D	11. B	21. B
2. C	12. B	22. C
3. B	13. D	23. A
4. A	14. A	24. C
5. C	15. A	25. B
6. D	16. A	26. A
7. C	17. A	27. B
8. D	18. C	28. C
9. C	19. A	29. B
10. D	20. C	30. D

EXPLANATIONS

Section 1. Verbal Skills

1. The correct choice is A.
The entire sentence is about the staff. *Intensive*, *care*, and *unit* are all adjectives telling about the staff. Choices B, C, and D are all nouns but are not the subject of the sentence.

2. The correct choice is B.
This is an example of an implied subject. Although choices A and C are nouns and choice D is a pronoun, none of them is what the sentence is about.

3. The correct choice is D.
The first part of the sentence clues you in that the patient is male, which eliminates *she* (choice A). *They* (choice B) is wrong because *patient* is singular and not plural, and *I* (choice C) is wrong because the pronoun must be in the third person, not the first.

4. The correct choice is B.
In the sentence, the verb *is* should be *am* to agree with the subject *I*. Choice A is plural and thus does not agree with the subject, choice C does not correct the error, and choice D changes the tense of the verb.

5. The correct choice is C.
Operating (choice A) is an adjective modifying *room*. *Played* (choice B) is the sentence's verb. *Sedated* (choice D) is an adjective modifying *patient*. Only *loudly* (choice C) is an adverb modifying the verb *played*.

6. The correct choice is A.
Tantalizingly (choice B) is an adverb modifying the adjective phrase "out of reach," and *table* (choice C) and *bed* (choice D) are both nouns.

7. The correct choice is B.
This is a fragment or incomplete sentence because it has no verb. Choice A is wrong because the fragment already has a subject (*cuff*). Choices C and D are wrong because no sentence has to have an adverb or adjective in order to be complete.

8. The correct choice is A.
This is a fragment or incomplete sentence because it has no subject. Choice B is wrong because the fragment already has verbs (*shoving, knocking*). Choices C and D are wrong because no sentence has to have an adverb or adjective to be complete.

9. The correct choice is A.
Adding a comma only creates a comma splice and does not repair the sentence. Choices B, C, and D all show correct ways to repair the run-on (adding a semicolon, adding a conjunction and a comma, or turning the run-on into two sentences).

10. The correct choice is C.
None of the other conjunctions fits the meaning of the sentence.

11. The correct choice is B.
None of the other conjunctions fits the meaning of the sentence.

12. The correct choice is C.
By definition, an independent clause is a complete sentence with a noun and a verb. A phrase cannot stand alone and neither can a dependent clause. A fragment is missing either the subject or verb.

13. The correct choice is B.
Choice A is an independent clause. Choices C and D are prepositional phrases.

14. The correct choice is A.
The adverb clause "After seeing her photograph splashed across the front page of the newspaper" modifies the verb *resigned*; it tells *when* Dr. Carlton resigned.

15. The correct choice is A.
Only choice A is spelled correctly.

16. The correct choice is C.
Discussed is a homophone for *disgust*. The two words are pronounced alike but spelled differently.

17. The correct choice is D.
In the word *climb*, the final *b* is not pronounced. It is a silent letter.

18. The correct choice is A.
A comma is missing after the word *Connors*. The comma is needed to set off the first part of the quotation. Otherwise, the sentence has quotation marks and a period where needed. No word in the sentence requires an apostrophe.

19. The correct choice is C.
A comma is needed at the end of the introductory adverb clause, after the word *shift*. Putting a comma anywhere else would be incorrect.

20. The correct choice is C.
This sentence is a run-on, so it needs a semicolon, period, or conjunction with a comma to separate its two parts. Merely adding a comma (choice A) would create a comma splice. A colon (choice B) is not needed because that punctuation mark is used to introduce a list. A question mark (choice D) is wrong because the sentence is not a question.

21. The correct choice is B.
An apostrophe is used in contractions or to show possession. *Sisters* is a possessive and should be written *sister's*. *Cannot* (choice A) is not a contraction, and *coat* (choice C) and *Cathy* (choice D) are neither contractions nor possessives.

22. The correct choice is D.
The sentence contains a side note of unnecessary information, so it needs parentheses before and after "a temporary assignment." An apostrophe (choice A) is not needed because there are no contractions or possessives.

A question mark (choice B) is not needed because the sentence is not a question. A colon (choice C) is not needed because there is no list to introduce.

23. The correct choice is A.
The apostrophe has two functions: to show possession and to indicate a missing letter in a contraction (choice A). The other three choices are not functions of this punctuation mark.

24. The correct choice is A.
Only *permanent* (choice A) has nearly the same meaning as *irrevocable*.

25. The correct choice is D.
A person who is filled with *lassitude* is extremely weary, or *exhausted* (choice D).

26. The correct choice is B.
Masticated means chewed; of the choices, only *ate* (choice B) has nearly the same meaning.

27. The correct choice is C.
Only *repressing* (choice C) has nearly the same meaning as *sublimating*.

28. The correct choice is C.
Vascular refers to blood vessels, which are part of the circulatory system (choice C).

29. The correct choice is B.
Sporadic (choice B) means "occurring in no recognizable pattern."

30. The correct choice is A.
Only *audacity* (choice B) has nearly the same meaning as *temerity*.

Section 2. Reading Comprehension

PASSAGE 1

1. The correct choice is B.
Choices A, C, and D are all details that support the main idea.

2. The correct choice is C.
All the other choices, except fever, are mentioned in the passage.

3. The correct choice is D.
There is nothing in the passage to support choices A, B, or C.

4. The correct choice is A.
A compromised immune system (choice A) is mentioned in the passage as a condition that may give shingles an opportunity to appear. The passage does not mention anything about a high risk at puberty (choice B) or indicate that there is a higher risk when a vaccine is given (choice C). It does say that the risk of contracting shingles goes up after 65 years of age but not before (choice D).

5. The correct choice is D.
According to the passage, the ability of the herpes virus to stay dormant in the body for long periods (choice D) makes it "unlike many other viruses."

PASSAGE 2

6. The correct choice is B.
Choice A is not relevant. Choice C is too specific because many different kinds of surgery are discussed. Choice D is also just a supporting detail rather than a main idea.

7. The correct choice is B.
According to the passage, "in so many circumstances, women are more likely than men to be judged by their appearance." From that statement, you may infer that women make up the majority of patients for cosmetic procedures because they feel more pressure to look attractive (choice B). All of the surgeries and procedures discussed in the passage are purely for improving overall appearance, so it is obvious that attractiveness is of paramount importance.

8. The correct choice is C.
The other types of surgery and procedures are mentioned as popular with women.

9. The correct choice is A.
Choices B and D are both surgical procedures. Choice C is not listed as the most popular procedure.

10. The correct choice is C.
Choice C is the most logical conclusion that can be drawn from information in the passage. There is nothing in the passage to support choices A, B, or D.

PASSAGE 3

11. The correct choice is C.
The main point of the passage is that pepper can help vitiligo victims get more pigmentation. Choice A is irrelevant. Choice B is too sweeping a claim; piperine is not a cure, just an improved treatment. Choice D is too vague.

12. The correct choice is A.
The scientists are studying piperine, not the skin's melanin or pigmentation abilities. Choice D is just a type of treatment.

13. The correct choice is B.
The passage states that the piperine is what gives the pepper its unique flavor (choice B). Piperine does not add to pepper's color, smell, or shape.

14. The correct choice is D.
Protection from UV rays is a main function described in the passage.

15. The correct choice is B.
There are no risks listed for piperine. Although steroids do have risks, these risks are not listed. Hormones are the same thing as steroids. Phototherapy has the risk of skin cancer.

Section 3. Mathematics

1. The correct choice is C.

The fraction $\frac{8}{2}$ reduces to 4. To convert to a percent, just move the decimal two places to the right, which gives 400%.

2. The correct choice is B.

The wall and the floor form the base and height of a right triangle, so the ladder is the hypotenuse. Using the Pythagorean theorem, $a^2 + b^2 = c^2$, plug in the numbers you know and get $8^2 + b^2 = 10^2$. Therefore $b^2 = 36$, and b, the distance on the floor from the wall to the ladder, is 6 feet.

3. The correct choice is C.

To find the average, add the numbers and then divide by the number of numerals listed; $(8 + 3 + 6 + 11) \div 4 = 28 \div 4 = 7$.

4. The correct choice is C.

Set up a proportion, or two equal fractions, to compare these two scenarios. For example, *6 forms* might go in the numerator on the left and *15 minutes* in the denominator. Then *30 forms* would then go in the numerator on the right, and x or another variable in the denominator. Cross-multiplying gives $6x = 450$, and dividing each side by 6 to solve for x gives 75.

5. The correct choice is C.

6. The correct choice is D.

You can translate this statement directly into algebra. The statement "Ryan is 2 years older than four times Pixie's age" becomes $R = 2 + 4P$, which is choice D.

7. The correct choice is B.

The longest distance across a circle, which in this case is 10 ft, is the same as its diameter; therefore, the radius is 5 ft. The formula for area of a circle is $A = \pi r^2$. Thus $A = \pi 5^2$, or 25π.

8. The correct choice is C.

Because prime numbers are divisible only by themselves and 1, the even numbers—36 and 38—are not prime. The number 35 is also divisible by 5 and 7, so it cannot be prime. The number 37 is the only answer choice that fits.

9. The correct choice is D.

When you solve for x, you get:

$3 - 3 + 4x = 23 - 3$

$4x = 20$

$\frac{4x}{4} = \frac{20}{4}$

$x = 5$

10. The correct choice is C.

First, you need to convert the mixed number, $1\frac{2}{3}$, to an improper fraction. Multiplying the integer by the denominator, you get 3, which you then add to the numerator to get $\frac{5}{3}$. Using the bowtie method to add $\frac{5}{3}$ and $\frac{4}{5}$ gives $\frac{25 + 12}{15}$, which equals $\frac{37}{15}$.

11. The correct choice is D.
Answering this question is mainly about making sure you are looking up the correct information in the table. The 2001 Bordeaux has the highest sales in cases, which is really all the information you need.

12. The correct choice is B.
To find what percentage of sales was in individual bottles, just consider the number of individual bottles divided by the number of bottles total. Because the math on this one is pretty time consuming, "ballpark" first to see if you can eliminate any answer choices. For the 1997 Pinot Noir, approximately 15,000 divided by approximately 80,000 is a little less than 20%. For the 1994 Pinot Gris, approximately 18,000 divided by approximately 77,000 is about 23%, or almost 25%. For the 1991 Chardonnay, approximately 15,000 divided by approximately 90,000 is about 20%. For the 2001 Bordeaux, approximately 12,000 divided by approximately 100,000 is about 12%. So the 1994 Pinot Gris has definitely the largest percentage of sales in individual bottles.

13. The correct choice is A.

14. The correct choice is B.
To convert from Fahrenheit to Celsius, subtract 32 and multiply by $\frac{5}{9}$. The calculation $(90 - 32) \times \frac{5}{9} = 58 \times \frac{5}{9}$ gives a little more than half of 58. Choice B is the only one that is close.

15. The correct choice is C.
If the length and width of the room are the same (and are integers, which they must be according to the answer choices), then a good knowledge of square roots helps solve the problem. The number 14 squared is 196, so 14 is the length and width of the room.

16. The correct choice is B.
Ignoring the decimals, $398 \times 72 = 28,656$. There are four spaces to the right of the decimal (collectively) in 3.98 and 0.72, so move the decimal four spaces to the left and get 2.8656.

17. The correct choice is C.
Constructing a proportion, or two equal fractions, is again a good way to go. The fraction on the left has 3 in the numerator and 2 in the denominator, and the fraction on the right has 9 in the numerator and x in the denominator. Cross-multiply and get $3x = 9 \times 2$, and solve to get $3x = 18$, or $x = 6$.

18. The correct choice is C.
The prime factors of 30 are 2, 3, and 5, and their sum is 10.

19. The correct choice is B.
A little translation is a big help on this problem: The question "8 is what percent of 5?" translates to "$8 = \frac{x}{100} \times 5$." To solve, $8 \times 100 = \frac{5x}{100} \times 100$, which comes out to $800 = 5x$, which becomes $\frac{800}{5} = \frac{5x}{5}$, or $160 = x$.

20. The correct choice is B.

21. The correct choice is B.
In the first pair, the shapes switch places: The circle becomes the inside shape and the square becomes the outside. Answer choice B is the only answer that repeats this same pattern; the downward-pointing triangle becomes the outside shape while the upward-pointing triangle becomes the inside shape.

22. The correct choice is B.
Converting a percent to a decimal just involves removing the percent sign and moving the decimal point two places to the left. Therefore, 65 percent becomes 0.65.

23. The correct choice is D.
When an exponent is raised to an exponent, multiply them to simplify. Use the expression $4 \times 5 = 20$. Therefore, the correct answer is x^{20}.

24. The correct choice is C.

25. The correct choice is D.
If there are three foreign cars to every two domestic, then foreign cars represent $\frac{3}{5}$ of the cars in the parking lot. This fraction is equal to 60 percent, and 60 percent of 360 (the number of degrees in a circle) is equal to 216.

Section 4. Science

1. The correct choice is D.
The pairings for DNA are guanine with cytosine and thymine with adenine. Uracil is found in RNA, where it pairs with adenine.

2. The correct choice is C.
Nucleic acids make up DNA, which codes for how humans develop.

3. The correct choice is B.
Red blood cells contain hemoglobin, which is responsible for transporting oxygen throughout the body.

4. The correct choice is A.
The cell membrane is said to be selectively permeable, controlling what enters and exits the cell.

5. The correct choice is C.
Because plants need light to survive, they tend to bend toward light sources. This tendency is termed phototropism.

6. The correct choice is D.
Changes in the base sequences in DNA can lead to the coding of different proteins. These mutations can eventually lead to cancer.

7. The correct choice is C.
Tinctures are solutions in which the solute is dissolved into alcohol.

8. The correct choice is D.
The gain or loss of electrons is what causes ions to form. Positive ions form because atoms have lost a negatively charged electron.

9. The correct choice is C.
Sulfur is located on the upper right side of the periodic table. It is soft, lacks luster, and does not conduct heat or electricity, making it a nonmetal.

10. The correct choice is D.
Isomers are organic compounds with the same molecular formulas but different structures. Examples are CH_3CH_2OH (an alcohol) and CH_3OCH_3 (an ether). Do not confuse isomers with isotopes, which have the same number of protons and are the same element. What makes isotopes different is the number of neutrons present, which makes the mass number vary as well.

11. The correct choice is B.
See the following diagram:
6 grams → (20 years) → 3 grams → (20 years, 40 years total) → 1.5 grams
After 20 years, the 6 grams you started out with will be 3 grams. After another 20 years (40 years total), one-half of 3 grams (1.5 grams) will remain.

12. The correct choice is B.
Zygotes settle in the uterus and develop into embryos.

13. The correct choice is D.
The placenta develops to "connect" the mother to the fetus so that the fetus can obtain oxygen and nutrients.

14. The correct choice is A.
Villi, like root tips, are designed to increase the surface area in which absorption occurs.

15. The correct choice is A.
The nephron's job is to filter the blood that enters the kidney. The ureter, also part of the excretory system, allows urine to exit the body.

16. The correct choice is A.
The cones in the eye are responsible for distinguishing between colors. People who are colorblind have defects with the cones and usually cannot see shades of greens and reds.

17. The correct choice is A.
Vertebrates have a spinal column, or backbone. A starfish is an invertebrate because it lacks this structure.

18. The correct choice is C.
Capillaries are one cell thick so that gas exchange can take place easily.

19. The correct choice is A.
The atria of the heart receive blood from other parts of the body. The left atrium receives oxygenated blood from the pulmonary veins, whereas the right atrium receives deoxygenated blood from the body.

20. The correct choice is C.
A synapse is the space between neurons. Neurotransmitters travel across this area so that one neuron can communicate with another.

21. The correct choice is B.
Vector quantities have both a magnitude and direction. Scalar quantities have only a magnitude.

22. The correct choice is C.
This arrow shows the distance from the normal of the wave to the maximum height above the normal. This represents the amplitude of the wave.

23. The correct choice is A.
This circuit is a series circuit because there is only one pathway that the current can take.

24. The correct choice is C.
According to the equation $v = f\lambda$, for velocity to remain constant, if the frequency increases, then the wavelength must decrease. If the frequency decreases, then the wavelength must increase. This is an inverse relationship.

25. The correct choice is B.
Work is equal to force times distance, $W = Fd$.

26. The correct choice is A.
If an object has a constant speed, it is not accelerating. Therefore, the acceleration is zero.

27. The correct choice is B.
Force is equal to mass times acceleration ($F = ma$). This is the equation for Newton's second law.

28. The correct choice is C.
Refraction is the bending of light that takes place as light travels from one medium into another. It occurs because of the change in speed of the light.

29. The correct choice is B.
A negative velocity indicates that an object is slowing down. If the airplane were at a constant speed, the rate of change would be zero.

30. The correct choice is D.
Distance is speed multiplied by time, $d = vt$. Multiplying 4 meters per second by 20 seconds gives 80 meters.

Verbal Ability

What does knowing the difference between a noun and a verb or if *i* comes before *e* in spelling have to do with nursing? That is a good question, but it is important to realize that being a nurse requires good written communication skills. Although a great deal of your time will be spent helping patients, talking to doctors, and performing essential medical processes, much of it will also be spent on filling out detailed reports, writing daily patient notes and recommendations, summarizing lab test results, and more. In other words, along with handling medications, needles, sponges, food trays, bedpans, and patients, you will also be handling words. The ability to use them well when you write is essential to both your understanding of what others write and their understanding of what you write.

There are five important verbal skills:

1. *Grammar,* which means knowing the parts of speech and how they are and are not meant to be used
2. *Sentence structure,* meaning how to make sure you avoid mistakes such as fragments and run-ons that can garble your writing
3. *Spelling,* which you need to master so that your words are not confusing or misleading
4. *Punctuation,* meaning everything from the simple commas, periods, end marks, and apostrophes to the more complex colons, quotation marks, and parentheses

5. *Vocabulary,* which you need so that you can understand the meaning of what people say and write and use appropriate terms in response

By becoming more skilled in English, you become a better reader and writer. By becoming a better reader and writer, you become better at overall communication. By becoming better at overall communication, you become a better nurse—and is not that the whole point?

Let us get started. Here is the process. We will briefly hit the high points about each one of the skills listed above and look at some examples. Next, for each skill, there will be a 10-question quiz. You will find answers for all the quizzes at the end of this chapter. Each answer will be explained so that if you do miss a question, you can figure out exactly why. Finally, you will have a chance to test your mastery of these skills by taking the verbal practice tests at the end of this book.

GRAMMAR

Merely hearing the word *grammar* is often enough to give some people the shudders. It is not one of the most popular topics, but it is an essential one. If you do not use proper grammar in speaking and/or writing, your communication may be confusing and may even cause others to conclude that you are not properly educated.

The odd thing about grammar is that when grammatical mistakes are made, most people recognize them on an intuitive level. For example, read the following sentence:

> The cardiac patient don't appear distressed yet has significantly elevated blood pressure readings.

You probably recognized that something was wrong. The sentence "sounded" wrong when you read it. When you read through it again, you probably were even able to point to the word *don't* and say, "Hey, this should be *doesn't,* right?"

You are correct. *Don't* should be *doesn't.* Good job. Chances are, however, that you did not say to yourself, "Hey, the subject of the sentence (*patient*) is singular, which requires the singular form of the verb *to do.* So *don't* should be changed to *doesn't* to agree with the subject." You simply recognized an error on an intuitive level.

This is good news because it will help you on your test. You will not have to state the rule that has been broken when there is a grammatical error. Instead, you will just have to recognize it and then know what has to be fixed. Everything you learn here will also help you to score higher on the reading comprehension test as well.

In preparation, let us do a quick overview of all that material you learned in high school English classes:

- Sentences
- Nouns

- Pronouns
- Verbs
- Adjectives
- Adverbs

Ready? Let us get started.

Sentences

A *sentence* is a group of words that contains a subject and at least one action word (verb). The *subject* is what or whom the sentence is about. For example, what is the subject of the following sentence?

> The cardiologist struggled to explain what had led him to select his chosen profession.

Who is struggling? The cardiologist. He is what the sentence is all about. Sometimes a sentence has more than one subject. Here's an example:

> Sharon and Kimberly offered to take the night shift for me this week.

What is the subject in this sentence? Sharon? Kimberly? Yes . . . and yes. The sentence has a double, or compound, subject.

In these first two examples, the subjects were right at the beginning of the sentence, but that is not always the case. Here is an example:

> Determined to score better on this test than on the last one, Sheila started studying weeks earlier.

Did you find the subject? It was halfway through the sentence. Who is the sentence about? Sheila! Right.

Finally, a sentence may also have what is called an *implied subject.* Here are some examples:

> Give me a sterile needle now!
> Call the doctor STAT!
> Close the patient's curtains.
> Call for a wheelchair, please.

None of these has a clear, stated subject, but to whom is the person talking? To **you!** *You* give me a needle. *You* call the doctor. *You* close the curtains. *You* is the implied subject here. It's sometimes referred to as *you-understood.*

The *predicate* of a sentence is the part that contains the action word (verb) that tells what the subject is or does. Let's return to our original example:

> The cardiologist *struggled to explain what had led him to select his chosen profession.*

All of the words in italics are the predicate of this sentence. The main action word is *struggled.* All of the other predicate words, *to explain what had led him to select his chosen profession*, tell about *struggled.*

Sentences can include smaller parts, called phrases and clauses (some of which can have their own subjects and predicates). We will look at those sentence parts in a later section of this chapter called Sentence Structure.

Nouns

Simply put, a *noun* is a word that names a person (Dr. Carter), a place (hospital), or a thing (medication). A noun can be the subject of a sentence. It can also perform other functions in the sentence.

Pronouns

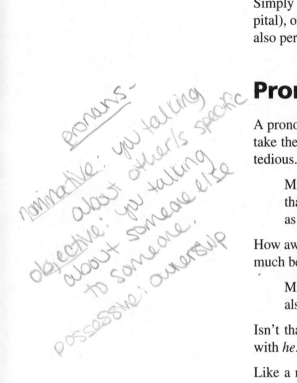

A pronoun is a type of word related to nouns. *Pronouns* are small words that take the place of nouns so that writing does not sound overly repetitive and tedious. For example:

> Mr. Clemens reported a high fever for six days and Mr. Clemens added that Mr. Clemens had also suffered various aches and pains for as long as Mr. Clemens could remember.

How awkward is that? The repetition of *Mr. Clemens* gets old very fast. How much better does it sound to say:

> Mr. Clemens reported a high fever for six days, and he added that he had also suffered various aches and pains for as long as he could remember.

Isn't that better? The three repetitions of *Mr. Clemens* have been replaced with *he*.

Like a noun, a pronoun can be the subject of a sentence (or the subject of a verb in a sentence part). A pronoun can also have other functions in the sentence. But unlike nouns, pronouns change form depending on their function. Pronouns have three forms called cases: *nominative, objective,* and *possessive.*

- A pronoun must be in the *nominative* case if it is the subject of a verb or if it follows a form of the verb *to be.*
- A pronoun must be in the *objective* case if it is "on the receiving end" of the action of a verb or if it follows a type of word called a *preposition.* (Common prepositions are *around, between, by, in, of, to,* and *with.*)
- A pronoun must be in the *possessive* case if it is used to indicate ownership. Some possessive pronouns can stand alone, such as *mine, yours, his, hers, ours, theirs,* and *whose.*

For example, look at how the possessive pronoun *hers* is used in this sentence:

> Mrs. Hastings says that the missing chart is hers.

Other possessive pronouns act as adjectives because they modify a noun. These include *my, your, his, her, its, our, their,* and *whose.*

Here is how this kind of possessive pronoun is used in sentences:

Susan, your coat is in the locker room.

My uniform needs to be washed and ironed before tomorrow.

The most commonly used pronouns, with their case forms, are the following:

Nominative	Objective	Possessive
I	me	my, mine
you	you	your, yours
he	him	his
she	her	her, hers
it	it	its
we	us	our, ours
they	them	their, theirs

The trick to learning how to use pronouns correctly is making sure you do not use an *indefinite* pronoun, or one in which you cannot tell what it refers to. Here's an example:

Mrs. Fredericks' appointment with Dr. Montana was at noon, but she was running an hour late.

Who is running late? Mrs. Fredericks? Dr. Montana? Who knows? You cannot tell from this example. How could it be improved? Here's one possibility:

Mrs. Fredericks' appointment with Dr. Montana was at noon, but the doctor was running an hour late.

Mystery solved. Now, how about this one?

When Sarah went to see Ms. Rodriguez, she was busy and asked if it could be postponed.

Confused? You should be. Who was busy? What was to be postponed? The pronoun *she* is indefinite because you do not know if the sentence means Sarah or Ms. Rodriguez. The pronoun *it* means nothing because there is nothing in the sentence to tell you what was to be postponed.

When Sarah went to see Ms. Rodriguez, Ms. Rodriguez was busy and asked if the meeting could be postponed.

Now this makes a lot more sense. Pronouns are helpful and make reading and understanding material easier if used properly. Just make sure that each one is clearly referring to only one person, place, or thing.

Verbs

Verbs are quite literally where the action is. A *verb* is a word that expresses action or says something about the condition of a subject. Verbs can be complicated creatures. There are linking verbs and helping verbs. Verbs come in tenses including past, present, and future—to name a few. Some are regular and some are irregular, and some are singular and some are plural. Again, if there is a mistake in any of these aspects, you most likely will know it on an intuitive level before you realize why it is wrong.

Let us cover some of the most important points about verbs.

1. **The verb must agree in number with its subject.** If the subject is singular (one only), the verb must be singular also. If the subject is plural (two or more), the verb must be plural also.

> The young nurse assist the patient onto the magnetic resonance imaging table.

> The physicians often confers on some of the most difficult cases.

As you read these sentences, are you aware of a problem? Do they "sound" wrong to you? That is because the verbs do not agree in number and subject. In the first example, *nurse* is singular, so the verb should be *assists*. Conversely, in the second example, *physicians* is plural, so the verb should be *confer*.

2. **The verb must be in the correct tense.** The sense of the sentence, often indicated by time words such as *now, then, tomorrow,* or *soon,* tells you which tense is correct. To write the correct tense, you need to write the correct verb ending and also sometimes add a helping verb such as *is, has,* or *will*. Here are some examples:

> The chiropractor adjusts a patient. (present)
> The chiropractor adjusted a patient. (past)
> The chiropractor will adjust a patient. (future)

> The meeting is starting. (present)
> The meeting has started. (past)
> The meeting will start. (future)

Look at the following statements and see if you can figure out what the error is in each one.

> A massage therapist works with a patient yesterday.
> The psychologist studied his session notes tomorrow.
> Dr. Connors will institute the new rules an hour ago.

Sound a little odd? They should. The verb tense does not match the other information in the sentence. Here is how they should read to be correct:

> A massage therapist worked with a patient yesterday.
> The psychologist will study his session notes tomorrow.
> Dr. Connors will institute the new rules in the next hour.

3. **Verbs can be regular and irregular in the way they form different tenses.** The regular ones are the simplest ones for sure. The ones used in the examples above are regular. To change their tense from present to past or future usually requires only the addition of *-s*, *-ing,* or *-ed.* The irregular ones are tricky because changing tense usually involves changing the basic spelling of the word.

The worst offender of all is the verb *to be*. It goes through amazing changes. Here is what this odd verb does:

Singular	Plural
Present Tense	
I am	we are
you are	you are
he, she, it is	they are
Past Tense	
I was	we were
you were	you were
he, she, it was	they were
Future Tense	
I will be	we will be
you will be	you will be
he, she, it will be	they will be

Here is a list of some of the other most common irregular verbs and how their spelling changes. Notice that the third column is yet another verb form called the *past participle*. This form is used with the helping verb *has* or *have*.

Present	Past	Past Participle
begin	began	begun
break	broke	broken
choose	chose	chosen
do	did	done
eat	ate	eaten
fly	flew	flown
go	went	gone
know	knew	known

Present	Past	Past Participle
lie	lay	lain
rise	rose	risen
see	saw	seen
shake	shook	shaken
speak	spoke	spoken
take	took	taken
write	wrote	written

Adjectives

Adjectives are words that describe or modify nouns. They give you more information about the subject and other nouns in the sentence. It is adjectives that add details and color to what you read and write. They provide specifics that you will need in reports that you handle. For example, you may read a report that says

> The patient stated that she had recently lost 20 pounds.

This gives you some basic information—but only the basics. You know little to nothing about the patient, so it is hard to begin to respond. How would your medical reaction change if each of the following adjectives were used?

> The *anorexic* patient stated that she had lost 20 pounds.
> The *elderly* patient stated that she had lost 20 pounds.
> The *cancer* patient stated that she had lost 20 pounds.
> The *obese* patient stated that she had lost 20 pounds.

The adjective is the key element in these sentences. The adjective is what gives you the detail that guides your response. These are simple examples that show you how important it is to include the extra words. When you add adjectives, keep them close to the noun they are describing or else you can cause confusion. Here are some examples of adjectives that stray a little distance from the nouns they modify.

> Their new uniforms were colorful and distinctive.
> The doctor's party was crowded and loud.

In the first sentence the adjectives *colorful* and *distinctive* modify the noun *uniforms*, even though the words are separated. In the second sentence, the adjectives *crowded* and *loud* modify the noun *party*.

When you are reading, pay close attention to adjectives. When you are writing, be sure to include them whenever they provide the clues that make a report or file more complete.

Adverbs

Adverbs also provide more details but adverbs modify verbs, adjectives, or other adverbs, not nouns. They tell you *when* or *how* something happened, or *how* something looks or sounds or feels. Using the same sentences as above, let us add some adverbs that give even more vital information.

> The obese patient stated that she had *recently* lost 20 pounds.
> The elderly patient stated that she had *unfortunately* lost 20 pounds.
> The cancer patient stated that she had *suddenly* lost 20 pounds.
> The anorexic patient stated that she had *obviously* lost 20 pounds.

Again, notice how these adverbs put an entirely different spin on the statement. Like adjectives, adverbs should be kept close to the word they are modifying. The vast majority of them, as is obvious in the above examples, end in *-ly*. One big and very common exception is the adverb *not*. Here is an example:

> The hospital staff was not pleased with the new payment rules.

In this sentence, the verb is *was pleased.* Modifying it with the adverb *not* changes the meaning of the verb to its direct opposite.

Let us look at a few more sentences before the quiz starts. Can you spot the two adverbs and two adjectives in the sentence below?

> Mrs. Cooper's recent accident regrettably left her with multiple abrasions, and she felt miserable.

Which words describe a noun? To answer this, find the nouns. The first noun is *Mrs. Cooper*. Nothing in the sentence describes her. The next noun is *accident*. It is described by *recent*, so that word is an adjective. The next noun is *abrasions*. Are there any details about it? Yes, the word *multiple* gives you more information about the abrasions. So *recent* and *multiple* are your two adjectives. How about adverbs? First, find the verbs. The first verb is *left*. The word *regrettably* tells how Mrs. Cooper was left, so it is an adverb. The second verb is *felt,* and it is described by the adverb *miserable*, which tells how Mrs. Cooper felt.

Okay, ready to see how much you absorbed from this first section? Take the quiz and see how you do.

GRAMMAR QUIZ

Circle the letter of your choice. Answers can be found on p. 101.

1. Read the sentence below. What is the subject?

> The new doctor was impatiently waiting for her night shift to be over so she could go home.

(A) doctor
(B) night
(C) shift
(D) home

2. Read the sentence below. What is the subject?

> The hospital maternity ward was busiest on the nights with a full moon.

(A) hospital
(B) ward
(C) nights
(D) moon

3. Read the sentence below. What is the subject?

> Plan to get to work at least 30 minutes earlier than usual during the holidays.

(A) work
(B) minutes
(C) you (understood)
(D) holidays

4. Read the sentence below. Which pronoun should be used to replace the second use of *the interns*?

> The interns met at the coffee house around the corner, and then the interns returned just in time for their shift to begin.

(A) he
(B) their
(C) me
(D) they

5. Read the sentence below. There is an error with the verb. Which answer corrects that error?

> The prescriptions for Mr. Hampton was picked up yesterday at the corner drugstore.

(A) was picking up yesterday
(B) were picks up yesterday
(C) was pick up yesterday
(D) were picked up yesterday

6. Read the sentence below. There is an error with the verb. Which answer corrects that error?

> Next month the support group meetings featured speakers from each department within the hospital.

(A) support group meetings featuring speakers
(B) support group meetings will feature speakers
(C) support group meetings have featured speakers
(D) support group meetings are featuring speakers

7. Which word in the following sentence is an adjective?

Holding a compress to the contusions on her face, the composed patient walked into the hospital.

(A) compress
(B) face
(C) composed
(D) hospital

8. Which two words in the following sentence are adjectives?

Because the nurse had never handled a psych patient before, he quickly called for additional help.

(A) nurse/patient
(B) psych/additional
(C) handled/called
(D) quickly/help

9. Which word in the following sentence is an adverb?

The record stated that the patient was not given his medication at the proper time.

(A) stated
(B) given
(C) not
(D) time

10. Which two words in the following sentence are adverbs?

The bullet had clearly entered his left shoulder and exited forcefully from his mid-back.

(A) bullet/left
(B) entered/exited
(C) shoulder/mid-back
(D) clearly/forcefully

SENTENCE STRUCTURE

Sentence structure means the parts used to build a sentence that make it complete and understandable. If parts are missing, just as when parts are missing from a building, the sentence is not as strong and does not hold up. Likewise, a sentence that tries to contain too much is unbalanced. To avoid these problems, you need to understand the difference between phrases and clauses and how to use them correctly. Likewise, you need to be familiar with the sentence structure concepts of *coordination* and *subordination*.

Let us look at each one of these concepts in turn so you know how to recognize a problem and avoid it in your writing.

Phrases

A *phrase* is a sentence part that lacks a subject and a verb. Here are some typical phrases:

> to the store
> in the street
> on the roof
> at the hospital
> with a stethoscope

The words *to, in, on, at*, and *with* are called prepositions, so phrases that use these words are called *prepositional phrases*. Prepositions were mentioned above in the section on pronouns. There are many more prepositions. Here are the top 30 that you will most likely use in nursing.

about	after	against
among	around	behind
below	beneath	between
beyond	despite	during
from	in	of
throughout	to	underneath
until	with	without

Another kind of phrase is the *participial phrase*. In the earlier section on verbs, you learned that a participle is a verb form. A participial phrase contains a participle but not a subject. When a participial phrase introduces and modifies a sentence, it is separated from the rest of the sentence by a comma. Here is an example:

> Pleased by the doctor's complimentary words, the nurse smiled.

Clauses

A *clause* is a sentence part that contains a subject and a verb. Clauses come in several forms: independent, dependent, adverb, adjective, and noun.

- An *independent clause* can stand on its own as a sentence. It has a subject and a verb and makes a complete thought.
- A *dependent clause,* on the other hand, is one that depends on other words to be added to it to make sense. It cannot stand alone because it does not form a complete thought. Here are some examples:

> Until the third shift comes on duty
> Because she missed punching in by 15 minutes
> Whenever the fire alarm went off in the hospital

Notice that after you read each one of these phrases, your mind said, "And . . . ?" That showed that you do not have all of the information you need to understand them. Each one of these clauses needs to be paired with more information to be complete.

A dependent clause that modifies a verb is called an *adverbial clause.* It can be placed at the beginning or at the end of the sentence.

> *Whenever the doctor operates*, he leaves virtually no scar.

The adverbial clause at the beginning modifies the verb *leaves.*

> Dr. Carmichael wanted to retire early *because a house on the ocean was waiting for him.*

The adverbial clause modifies the verb *wanted.*

A dependent clause that modifies a noun or pronoun is called an *adjectival clause.* Here are some examples:

> The only nurse on the shift *who is not from New York* is Angelina.
> It is obvious that the x-ray waiting room is a place *where you can catch up on your reading.*
> It never rains on the days *when I find a decent parking space.*

In the first sentence, "who is not from New York" modifies *nurse.* In the second, "where you can catch up on your reading" modifies *place.* In the third, "when I find a decent parking space" modifies *days.*

A clause that functions as a noun is called a *noun clause.* This kind of clause can be the subject of the sentence, or it can receive the action of the verb (that is, be an object). Here are two examples:

> *Where the patient's chart has gone* is anyone's guess.
> The nurses simply do not understand *why they have to put up with outdated supplies and equipment.*

In the first sentence, the noun clause functions as the subject. In the second sentence, the noun clause functions as the object of the verb *understand.*

Fragments

A sentence must have two things to be complete: a subject and a verb. If either one is missing, no matter how long the sentence is or how much additional information is added to it, it is still incomplete. For example, look at this sentence:

> The intensive care unit (ICU), busy from morning until night, especially after the massive 40-car pile-up on the highway in the evening.

It may look complete—it certainly is long enough—but it is not. There is no verb. Now look at this sentence:

> With detailed descriptions and multiple illustrations, far easier to understand than the nurse had expected.

In this sentence, the subject is missing. Did you think the subject was the nurse? Was he or she the one who had descriptions and illustrations? Was the nurse easier to understand? No, so he or she is not the subject of the sentence. Most likely the missing subject is something such as the *manual* or the *book.*

Clearly, a missing subject or verb can cause great confusion. Make sure that when you are writing you include a subject and verb in every sentence.

Run-On Sentences/Coordination and Subordination

A *run-on sentence* is one that contains two equal independent clauses, each with its own subject and verb, but there is no word such as *and* or *but* to link or separate the clauses, and the punctuation used between them is either missing or incorrect. Here are two examples:

> The hospital cafeteria has all new specials this week on Monday it is going to be Salisbury steak.
> The new cardiac equipment has finally arrived, the doctors plan to get it into place by the end of the month.

In each example, there are two independent clauses, each with its own subject and verb, but the word *and* that would link them is missing. In the first sentence, there is no punctuation between the two clauses. Without punctuation, the sentence is incorrect. In the second sentence, only a comma has been inserted between the two clauses. A run-on sentence in which the two independent clauses are separated only by a comma is called a *comma splice.* This, too, is incorrect.

Not all run-ons are long, mind you. Some are amazingly short but still incorrect.

> She intubated he observed.

So how do you correct a run-on? There are four ways:

1. Put a period between the two independent clauses to make two sentences.

   > The new cardiac equipment has finally arrived. The doctors plan to get it into place by the end of the month.

2. Put a semicolon between the two independent clauses. This is the correct punctuation.

   > The new cardiac equipment has finally arrived; the doctors plan to get it into place by the end of the month.

3. Add a word such as *and* or *but* to link the clauses in a *compound sentence,* and use a comma to separate the clauses.

   > The new cardiac equipment has finally arrived, and the doctors plan to get it into place by the end of the month.

Words used to link independent clauses in this way are called *coordinating conjunctions*. Here is a list of coordinating conjunctions: *and, but, for, nor, or, so,* and *yet.*

When adding a coordinating conjunction, make sure that it makes sense with the rest of the sentence. For example, *nor, or, for,* and *yet* would not make a lot of sense in the sample sentence above.

4. Use a *subordinating conjunction* to introduce one of the two clauses. This creates a *complex sentence.* In this kind of sentence, the clause without a subordinating conjunction becomes the *main clause.* Its subject and verb are considered the subject and verb of the whole sentence. The clause introduced with a subordinating conjunction becomes a dependent *subordinate clause.* The word *subordinate* means "of less importance." The information in the subordinate clause tells something about the information in the main clause. When this kind of clause introduces and modifies the sentence, it is separated from the rest of the sentence by a comma.

> Although the new cardiac equipment has finally arrived, the doctors plan to get it into place by the end of the month.

In this new sentence, *Although* is a subordinating conjunction. "Although the new cardiac equipment has finally arrived" is a subordinate clause. The main clause is "the doctors plan to get it into place by the end of the month." *Doctors* is the subject of the sentence as a whole. *Plan* is the verb of the sentence as a whole. The subordinate clause begins the sentence, so two clauses are separated by a comma.

The most common subordinating conjunctions are as follows:

after	although	as	as if
as long as	as much as	as soon as	as though
because	before	even if	even though
how	if	inasmuch as	in order that
now that	provided that	since	so that
than	that	though	unless
until	when	whenever	where
wherever	while		

Now let us take another quiz and see how well you remember this information.

SENTENCE STRUCTURE QUIZ

Circle the letter of your choice. Answers are on page 102.

1. What is needed to repair the error in the sentence below?

> The telemetry unit full of high-tech equipment and count-less computer systems.

(A) a verb
(B) a subject
(C) an adjective
(D) an adverb

2. What is needed to repair the error in the sentence below?

> Watched over the patients in the ICU, with an especially close eye on the electrocardiogram and blood pressure readings.

(A) a verb
(B) a subject
(C) a clause
(D) a phrase

3. All of the following corrections to the run-on sentence below are correct EXCEPT

> Maria ran through the checklist Sharon started on inventory.

(A) Maria ran through the checklist, and Sharon started on inventory.
(B) Maria ran through the checklist, Sharon started on inventory.
(C) Maria ran through the checklist. Sharon started on inventory.
(D) Maria ran through the checklist; Sharon started on inventory.

4. All of the following corrections to the run-on sentence below are correct EXCEPT

> Dr. Cooper scheduled surgery at noon he knew it would take all afternoon.

(A) Dr. Cooper scheduled surgery at noon because he knew it would take all afternoon.
(B) Dr. Cooper scheduled surgery at noon or he knew it would take all afternoon.
(C) Dr. Cooper scheduled surgery at noon. He knew it would take all afternoon.
(D) When Dr. Cooper scheduled surgery at noon, he knew it would take all afternoon.

5. Which of the following coordinating conjunctions fits best in the sentence below?

The pay raise will be implemented tomorrow, _____ our paychecks will not reflect it for two more weeks.

(A) nor
(B) so
(C) for
(D) but

6. Which of the following subordinating conjunctions fits best in the sentence below?

_____ the nursing department's holiday party starts in two hours, the caterer still has not shown up.

(A) Although
(B) Because
(C) Provided that
(D) In order that

7. An independent clause

(A) modifies an adjective.
(B) has no subject or verb.
(C) modifies an adverb.
(D) stands on its own.

8. A dependent clause

(A) has only a verb.
(B) has only a noun.
(C) cannot stand alone.
(D) starts with a preposition.

9. What type of clause is used in the following example?

The new doctor who is moving here from California will join our staff on January 1.

(A) independent
(B) adverbial
(C) prepositional
(D) adjectival

10. Which of the following is a prepositional phrase?

(A) she works
(B) she was exhausted
(C) to the lab
(D) when he operates

SPELLING

One of the easiest ways to make a mistake in writing is by spelling something wrong. Spelling errors are especially easy to make because the English language has some very odd rules. They do not make a lot of sense, but you cannot argue with them; you simply need to learn them. Here are some basic ones:

1. *i* **before** *e* **except after** *c.* Did you know there is a second line to this rule? It goes *or when sounded like* a *as in* neighbor *and* weigh. Here are some examples that illustrate this rule:

i before *e*	except after *c*	sounded like *a*	Words that don't follow the rule
achieve	ceiling	freight	either
believe	deceive	reign	neither
grief	deceit	sleigh	height
fierce	perceive	vein	leisure
piece	receipt	weight	seize

2. **Remember silent letters.** Some words contain letters that you do not hear when the word is pronounced. These letters are called *silent letters.* Here are some examples.

Silent Letters
ascertain
cupboard
diaphragm
ghastly
fascinate
gnarled
heir
listen
miscellaneous
pneumonia
psychology
subpoena
subtle
wrestle

3. **Spell homophones correctly.** *Homophones* are two or more words that sound alike but are spelled differently. Memorize the different spellings and make sure you use the correct one in your writing. If necessary, look up the different meanings of the words in a dictionary.

Homophones
accept/except
affect/effect
altar/alter
bare/bear
brake/break
complement/compliment
dear/deer
its/it's
lead/led
passed/past
principle/principal
stationary/stationery
their/they're/there
to/too/two
weather/whether
your/you're

Of course, one of the best ways to improve your spelling is the old-fashioned way; use a dictionary every single time you are not sure how to spell something. Although spelling errors are easy to make, they can truly make your writing look poor. Make learning how to spell properly a high priority, and your writing will benefit from it.

Now try the following spelling quiz.

SPELLING QUIZ

Circle the letter of your choice. Answers are on page 103.

1. Which of the following is spelled correctly?

(A) conciet
(B) cheif
(C) shriek
(D) nieghbor

2. Which of the following is the correct way to spell this word?

(A) temprature
(B) temperature
(C) temparature
(D) temperatire

3. The spelling of the word *principle* is an example of what?

(A) homophone
(B) silent letter
(C) exception to the "*i* before *e*" rule
(D) missing consonant

4. Which of the following words contains a silent letter?

(A) synonym
(B) beggar
(C) altar
(D) indict

5. Which of the following is the correct way to spell the word?

(A) porcelain
(B) porcelin
(C) porcelian
(D) porcilen

6. Certain words are known as "spelling demons." All four of these words are examples. Which one is spelled incorrectly?

(A) traveler
(B) embarrass
(C) geneology
(D) dysfunction

7. Which of the following words is spelled correctly?

(A) conceed
(B) healthful
(C) preceed
(D) beautifull

8. Which of the following words is spelled correctly?

(A) cieling
(B) disasterous
(C) miniuture
(D) pronunciation

9. Which of the following words is spelled correctly?

(A) seperate
(B) procede
(C) recognize
(D) complament

10. Which of the following words does not follow the usual "*i* before *e*" rule?

(A) fiend
(B) piece
(C) weird
(D) fierce

PUNCTUATION

Punctuation is very important because not including it or using the wrong kind can completely change the meaning of what you write. There are only a few types to learn, so let us get started.

The most common types of punctuation are:

.	**Period**
,	**Comma**
;	**Semicolon**
:	**Colon**
" "	**Quotation marks**
?	**Question mark**
!	**Exclamation point**
( )	**Parentheses**
'	**Apostrophe**

The *period* is the most frequently used form of punctuation. Its job is to tell the reader when to stop. It is used whenever a sentence is finished or complete. That is the only time it is used.

The *comma* is the second most frequently used form of punctuation. The comma's job is to tell the reader when to pause. There are several places that commas are needed:

• Between two main clauses linked by a coordinating conjunction such as *and, but,* or *or*

Dr. Smith is a general practitioner, but Dr. Rodriguez is a specialist.

- After an introductory prepositional phrase or series of phrases

    Against the doctor's orders, the head nurse allowed the children to come in and visit their mother for a few minutes.

- After an introductory participial phrase

    Surprised by the arrival of the equipment, Dr. Leonard quickly made room for it.

- After an introductory subordinate clause

    When the volunteers finally arrived, the nurses had a dozen jobs already lined up for them to do.

- After the greeting of an informal letter

    Dear Dr. Howard,

- At the close of any letter

    Yours truly,

- To set off words and expressions that interrupt the sentence

    Traveling nurses, I have heard, have one of the best possible jobs.

- To set off words of direct address

    Carmen, did you realize that you were scheduled to start an hour ago?

- With names and titles

    Mr. Henry Meade, Chief Administrator

- To set off words in apposition (that is, a group of words that describe or explain another word in the sentence)

    A native of Boston, the new head nurse had an amazing accent.

- To set off a clause containing information that is not essential to the meaning of the sentence

    The hospital's new chef, who formerly directed the biggest hospital cafeteria in New York, is starting next week.

- To separate items in a series

    The ambulance was stocked with bandages, antiseptic, oxygen, splints, a blood pressure monitor, and a stretcher.

- To set off a direct quotation

    "Mrs. Jenkins," she said, "you have to return for a check-up in three months."

- To separate the parts of an address

    Jefferson Community Hospital, 39745 S.W. McAdams St., Portland, OR

The *semicolon* is not used nearly as often, but it is still quite important. It is mainly used:

- To separate independent clauses that are not joined by a conjunction such as *and* or *but*

  Working the night shift is exhausting; working the morning one can be also.

- To separate independent clauses when one or both of them contains a comma

  After the intravenous needle was in, the nurse planned to add a unit of blood; but she had to go check the patient's blood type first.

- To separate independent clauses when the second clause begins with a conjunctive adverb such as *however, nevertheless, moreover, consequently,* or *for example*

  The new schedule format was a great idea; however, the morning shift, night shift, and part-timers did not like it.

The *colon,* a close relative to the semicolon, is also not a commonly used type of punctuation. It is primarily used:

- Before a list

  The supply closet was missing multiple items: two packages of gauze, six bottles of pain medication, three boxes of sterile needles, and four cotton swabs.

- Before a long quotation

  An anonymous person once said: "When you're a nurse you know that every day you will touch a life or a life will touch yours."

- After the salutation of a business letter

  Dear Staff Administrator:

Quotation marks are used when a person's exact words are quoted. The key to using quotation marks correctly is to put them before the first word of the quotation and after the last one, remembering to exclude all nonquote material. Also, remember that periods and commas always go inside the quotation marks.

  "Mr. Markham," said Dr. Troy, "your tests were negative."

The next two types of punctuation, the *question mark* and the *exclamation point,* are also quite self-explanatory. The question mark is used when a question is asked, and an exclamation point is used when a statement with great emotion is made.

  Hey, you! Get out of that room right now! Don't you know that visiting hours are over?

The last two punctuation marks are *parentheses* and *apostrophes.*

Parentheses are used to set off generally nonessential information. They give the reader additional information that is not necessary for understanding what is being written. Usually words are enclosed inside parentheses, but sometimes numbers and letters are inside parentheses, too.

> In your manual (see Chapter 8), you will find a description of that particular surgical procedure.

Apostrophes are used in three main ways:

- To show possession or ownership

   Elisha's reports are already filed and ready to go.

- To show the plural form of lowercase letters

   His algebra lesson was confusing because it seemed to be made up of nothing other than x's and y's.

- To show where a letter or number has been omitted, such as in contractions

   The head nurse couldn't remember the patient she had seen once in the 1970s.

Now it is time for another quiz. Remember that punctuation!

PUNCTUATION QUIZ

Circle the letter of your choice. Answers begin on page 103.

1. What punctuation is needed in this sentence to make it correct?

   She winced when she realized that the line started at the registration desk and went all the way out to the entrance doors

   (A) period
   (B) question mark
   (C) exclamation point
   (D) quotation mark

2. Where does a comma need to be added in the following sentence?

   For the very first time in my life I was placed in the ICU.

   (A) after *first*
   (B) after *life*
   (C) after *placed*
   (D) no comma needed

3. Where does a comma need to be added in the following sentence?

   When I finished Mrs. Carver's blood test I moved on to the next room.

   (A) after *finished*
   (B) after *Mrs. Carver's*
   (C) after *test*
   (D) no comma needed

4. Where does a comma need to be added in the following sentence?

She was completely intimidated by the appearance of the patient.

(A) after *completely*
(B) after *intimidated*
(C) after *appearance*
(D) no comma needed

5. What kind of punctuation is needed in this sentence?

The x-ray department had a major power outage patients are backed up for at least three hours.

(A) comma
(B) semicolon
(C) colon
(D) apostrophe

6. What kind of punctuation is needed in this sentence?

I repacked the first aid box with necessary supplies bandages, needles, tweezers, ice packs, antiseptic hand wash, scissors, splints, and gauze pads.

(A) question mark
(B) semicolon
(C) parentheses
(D) colon

7. Which punctuation mark is missing from the following sentence?

"Mrs. Becket, she called, "You can't leave until the doctor releases you!"

(A) comma
(B) quotation mark
(C) question mark
(D) apostrophe

8. Which punctuation mark is missing from the following?

"Look out The roof is about to cave in."

(A) quotation mark
(B) comma
(C) parentheses
(D) exclamation point

9. Which punctuation mark should be used when unnecessary information is inserted?

(A) semicolon
(B) apostrophe
(C) parentheses
(D) question mark

10. What punctuation mark do contractions require?

(A) apostrophe
(B) semicolon
(C) quotation marks
(D) parentheses

VOCABULARY

Your vocabulary is all the words that you use easily and comfortably in your spoken and written expression. The larger your vocabulary, the more clearly you can express yourself. A well-developed vocabulary can give you such a wide choice of words to use for describing patients, symptoms, processes, doctors, and everything else that you will be able to communicate whatever is necessary using the correct terms.

Nursing school entrance tests emphasize vocabulary heavily, so start preparing for it as soon as possible. This does not mean that you have to read a dictionary each night after work, but it does mean that you have to make learning new words a high priority. Some suggestions to help you do this include:

• Read, read, read. The more you read, the more words you will encounter. When you find a word you do not know, **look it up.** Also study the context clues, or the information around the word, that can give you clues to what the word means.
• Read more than the local paper and paperbacks from drugstore racks. Although those are good, they may not stretch your mind as much as reading publications such as the *Wall Street Journal,* the *New York Times, Discover Magazine,* and so on.
• Listen to local broadcasts of National Public Radio because it often introduces new ideas and vocabulary in its programs.
• Buy computer software vocabulary programs and use them.
• Have a thesaurus at hand. Looking up words that mean almost the same thing as a given word can teach you a lot about vocabulary.
• Get a computer or actual word a day e-mail/calendar.
• Play word games such as word searches and crossword puzzles. They definitely teach you new words. Also try Scrabble and Boggle for fun and learning.
• Watch the Public Broadcasting System (PBS) and other educational television stations.
• Take an online vocabulary course.

Although some vocabulary questions on nursing school entrance tests provide you with slight context clues, most of them simply expect you to know the word and what it means.

Here is the vocabulary quiz. How many words do you already know? If it is only a few of them, be sure to start studying now!

VOCABULARY QUIZ

Circle the letter of your choice. Answers begin on page 104.

1. A difference between two elements or issues is often referred to as a(n)

   (A) efficacy.
   (B) disparity.
   (C) impunity.
   (D) unction.

2. As she read the letter, the frown on her face was gradually *supplanted* by a smile. **Supplanted** means

   (A) replaced.
   (B) vindicated.
   (C) coerced.
   (D) supported.

3. The handsome new intern had an *entourage* behind him every step of the way. **Entourage** means

   (A) students.
   (B) followers.
   (C) colleagues.
   (D) nurses.

4. If history has taught us nothing else, it is that humans are consistently *fallible*. **Fallible** means

   (A) gullible.
   (B) amusing.
   (C) imperfect.
   (D) immortal.

5. On that rainy afternoon, lying on that comfortable couch, she was filled with a pervasive feeling of

   (A) ambition.
   (B) indolence.
   (C) gratitude.
   (D) frustration.

6. The sorrowful look on her face was a *harbinger* of bad news. ***Harbinger*** means

(A) bigot.
(B) servant.
(C) messenger.
(D) charlatan.

7. The woman spent 10 minutes *extolling* the virtues of her favorite plastic surgeon. ***Extolling*** means

(A) commending.
(B) fixating on.
(C) censoring.
(D) vouching for.

8. The crew worked for hours attempting to *extricate* the passengers trapped in the stalled elevator. ***Extricate*** means

(A) emanate.
(B) appease.
(C) free.
(D) fluctuate.

9. I was shocked when the family requested that I attend the funeral and give the

(A) tenet.
(B) eulogy.
(C) captions.
(D) litigation.

10. The plans had been in motion for months, and now at last they seemed to be coming to

(A) restoration.
(B) transition.
(C) zenith.
(D) fruition.

ANSWERS TO VERBAL ABILITY QUIZZES

GRAMMAR QUIZ

1. The correct choice is A.
If you ask yourself what the sentence is about, it is quickly clear that *doctor* is the subject. Although all four answer choices are nouns, the sentence is not about the *night,* a *shift,* or *home*. Instead, it is focused on what the doctor is doing.

2. The correct choice is B.
To correctly identify the subject, first eliminate the word *hospital*. In this sentence, it is an adjective describing the ward. The sentence is not about either the *night* or the *moon*. It is about the *ward* itself.

3. The correct choice is C.
This is an example of an implied subject, which is *you*. Although the other choices are nouns, none of them is the focus or subject of the sentence.

4. The correct choice is D.
Because there is more than one intern, the replacement pronoun needs to be plural. That rules out *he* and *me. Their* is a possessive pronoun, which also does not fit in the sentence. The only correct answer is *they*.

5. The correct choice is D.
Because the action of the sentence happened yesterday, the past tense of the verb is needed. Also, because *prescriptions* is plural, the verb must be plural. The only answer that provides both of these is choice D.

6. The correct choice is B.
The key here is that the meetings are happening next month, so the verb must be in the future tense. Only choice B adds the word *will*, so that the verb *feature* is in the future tense.

7. The correct choice is C.
An adjective is a word that modifies a noun. Choices A, B, and D are all nouns themselves, not words that modify nouns. The only choice that modifies a noun is choice C, *composed,* which describes the noun *patient*.

8. The correct choice is B.
The two words in choice A are both nouns, not adjectives. The words in choice C are both verbs. The words in choice D are an adverb and a noun. Only the two words in choice B modify nouns (*psych* modifies *patient* and *additional* modifies *help*).

9. The correct choice is C.
Remember that *not* (choice C) is one of the most common adverbs. In this sentence, it modifies the verb *was given*. Choice A is a verb, as is choice B. Choice D is a noun.

10. The correct choice is D.
You are looking for words that modify verbs, so find the verbs first. They are *entered* and *exited* (choice B). Look next to them and you will find the two

adverbs, *clearly* and *forcefully.* The words in choice A are a noun and an adjective. The words in choice C are both nouns.

SENTENCE STRUCTURE QUIZ

1. The correct choice is A.
This is a fragment because there is a subject (*unit*), but there is no verb, so choice A is correct.

2. The correct choice is B.
This is a fragment because there is no subject to go along with the verb (*watched*), so choice B is correct.

3. The correct choice is B.
There are several ways to correct a run-on sentence such as this one. One is adding a comma and the coordinating conjunction *and* as in choice A, another is dividing it into two complete sentences as in choice C, and still another is separating the two clauses with a semicolon as in choice D. Choice B, adding just a comma, creates a comma splice and does not fix the run-on sentence.

4. The correct choice is B.
There are several ways to correct this run-on sentence. One way (choice A) is to add the subordinating conjunction *because* to the second clause to make it a subordinate clause. Because the clause is at the end of the sentence, no punctuation is needed. A second way to correct the run-on sentence (choice C) is to divide it into two separate sentences. A third way (choice D) is to turn the first clause into an introductory subordinate clause by adding the subordinate conjunction *when.* Note that a comma is needed after this clause because it introduces and modifies the sentence.

5. The correct choice is D.
The way the statement is written, it implies contrast, and only *but* supports that relationship. None of the other choices makes sense.

6. The correct choice is A.
None of the choices here makes sense except choice A. Choice B implies a cause-and-effect relationship that does not exist.

7. The correct choice is D.
An independent clause is one that stands alone because it has a subject and verb and states a complete thought.

8. The correct choice is C.
A dependent clause has both a subject and a verb and does not start with a preposition, so only choice C is true.

9. The correct choice is D.
The clause "who is moving here from California" modifies the noun *doctor,* making this an adjectival clause. Choice A is incorrect because the clause is a dependent clause; choice B is incorrect because the clause does not modify a verb or an adjective, and choice C is incorrect because the clause does not start with a preposition.

10. The correct choice is C.

Among the choices, the only one that is a phrase is choice C, which begins with the preposition *to*. Each of the other choices contains a subject and a verb, so each one is a clause. Choices A and B can stand alone as independent clauses. Choice D cannot stand alone and is a dependent clause.

SPELLING QUIZ

1. The correct choice is C.
Choices A and B both have their *i*'s and *e*'s reversed. Choice D does, too.

2. The correct choice is B.
Only choice B has the letters in the correct order.

3. The correct choice is A.
Principle, meaning a rule or law, is one of a pair of homophones (words that sound alike but are spelled differently). Its partner is *principal*, meaning head person or chief.

4. The correct choice is D.
Choice D, *indict*, is pronounced "indite." The *c* is silent.

5. The correct choice is A.
All three other choices are spelled incorrectly.

6. The correct choice is C.
Choice C is spelled incorrectly. The correct spelling is *genealogy*.

7. The correct choice is B.
Choice A should be spelled *concede*. Choice C should be spelled *precede*. Choice D should be spelled *beautiful*.

8. The correct choice is D.
Choice A has the *e* and *i* reversed, choice B has an extra *e* between the *t* and the *r*, and choice C has a *u* instead of an *a*.

9. The correct choice is C.
Choice A should be spelled *separate*. Choice B should be spelled *proceed*. Choice D should be spelled *compliment* or *complement* (these two words are homophones).

10. The correct choice is C.
Choices A, B, and D do follow the rule.

PUNCTUATION QUIZ

1. The correct choice is A.
There is no end punctuation on this sentence. The sentence is not exclamatory, so it does not need an exclamation point. The sentence is not a question or a quote. A period is the correct choice.

2. The correct choice is B.
The sentence begins with a series of prepositional phrases: "for the very first time" and "in my life." A comma is needed after *life*.

3. The correct choice is C.
Commas are needed after introductory clauses. In this sentence, the introductory clause ends with the word *test*.

4. The correct choice is D.
No comma is needed because there is no introductory phrase or clause. The sentence is a single independent clause with two prepositional phrases ("by the appearance," "of the patient") at the end.

5. The correct choice is B.
This is an example of a run-on sentence. It consists of two independent clauses placed together with no punctuation between them. A semicolon is needed between *outage* and *patients*. A comma is not enough to repair the error; a coordinating conjunction such as *and* or *so* would be needed as well. A colon or an apostrophe is the wrong punctuation.

6. The correct choice is D.
This sentence includes a list, which should be set off by a colon following *supplies*.

7. The correct choice is B.
A second quotation mark is missing after the word *Becket*. The commas in the sentence are appropriate, and the apostrophe is where it should be. The sentence is not a question, so there is no need for a question mark. The end punctuation used is correct.

8. The correct choice is D.
"Look out" is an exclamatory statement that would be said with great emotion, so it requires an exclamation point at the end. The quotation marks are already there, there are no clauses needing commas, and there is no unnecessary information to enclose in parentheses.

9. The correct choice is C.
Only parentheses (choice C) are used to set off unnecessary information. The rest of the marks listed are used for distinctly different reasons.

10. The correct choice is A.
To indicate the missing letters in a contraction, an apostrophe is used. The other punctuation marks listed do not take care of this issue.

VOCABULARY QUIZ

1. The correct choice is B.
Disparity is the correct choice because it means "difference or dissimilarity." *Efficacy* means "the ability to produce the desired result." *Impunity* means "exemption from punishment." *Unction* means "real or pretended earnestness."

2. The correct choice is A.
Supplanted means "ousted, replaced, or overruled." *Vindicated* means "shown to be blameless" or "shown to be correct," *coerced* means "forced to do something," and *supported* means "encouraged or backed."

3. The correct choice is B.

An *entourage* is a group of people who follow someone of relative importance. *Students* is too specific because an entourage can be made up of different kinds of people, and *nurses* and *colleague*s are too specific as well.

4. The correct choice is C.

Fallible means "imperfect; liable to fail." *Gullible* means "liable to believe something too easily," *amusing* means funny and does not make sense with the context clue *consistently,* and *immortal* is definitely something that humans are not.

5. The correct choice is B.

There are a lot of context clues in this sentence. They add up to make *indolence* the best choice because it means "laziness or lethargy." *Ambition* is directly opposed to the sense of the context clues. *Gratitude* means "thankfulness," which does not make sense in the sentence. *Frustration* does not match the context clues either.

6. The correct choice is C.

A *harbinger* is an omen or foreteller of trouble to come, so *messenger* is the correct answer. A *bigot* is a person who is prejudiced against something or someone. A *servant* is someone who takes care of others, a meaning that makes no sense in the sentence. A *charlatan* is someone who is trying to scam another person, another meaning which does not fit the sentence.

7. The correct choice is A.

Extolling means "praising or complimenting," as in choice A, *commending.* *Fixating on* means "being obsessed with," whereas *censoring* means "leaving out potentially offensive material." *Vouching for* might make sense in the sentence, but it is not the correct definition of *extolling.*

8. The correct choice is C.

Extricate means "to remove from some difficulty," as is *free* in choice C. *Emanate* means "send out," whereas *appease* means "please or soothe." *Fluctuate* means "go from one state to another, back and forth."

9. The correct choice is B.

A *eulogy* is a speech at a funeral in praise of the deceased, so choice B is the correct answer. A *tenet* is a rule, whereas *captions* are the words that are provided to explain photographs. *Litigation* refers to the process of going to court.

10. The correct choice is D.

Fruition means "ripeness" or "completion," so it makes sense in the sentence. *Restoration* is the process of bringing something back to its original condition. *Transition* is the process of moving from one state or condition to another. A *zenith* is a peak or high point.

CHAPTER 7

Reading Comprehension

Read this chapter to learn

- What reading comprehension questions test
- How you can strengthen your reading comprehension skills
- How you can improve your reading speed

In contrast to a math or science test section, the reading comprehension section of a nursing school entrance exam does not test specific knowledge. Instead, it measures your ability to comprehend, analyze, and evaluate information from an unfamiliar written text. Its format will probably be familiar to you. You have probably taken many reading comprehension tests during your years in school.

Because a reading comprehension exam does not test specific knowledge, it is not possible to *study* for it. That said, however, there are some things you can do to *prepare* for it.

PREPARING FOR READING COMPREHENSION

By this stage in your educational career, you should have a pretty good sense of your reading skills. If you have achieved solid scores on reading comprehension tests in the past, the reading comprehension section of your nursing school entrance exam should be no problem at all. But if your comprehension skills are below par, if you freeze when faced with difficult reading passages, if you read very slowly, or if English is not your first language, you should take the time to work through this section of the book.

Read

The best way to learn to read better is to read more. If reading is not something that you do frequently, you are limiting yourself in a way that may show up on your test score. Reading broadly in subject areas that do not, at first glance, hold much appeal for you will train you to focus your attention on what you are reading. Pick up a journal in a field that is not familiar. Read an article. Summarize the key ideas. Consider the author's purpose. Decide whether the author's argument makes sense to you. Think about where the author might go next with his or her argument. Think about the author's tone.

All of this sounds like a chore, but it is the key to making yourself read actively. An active reader interacts with a text rather than bouncing off it. Success on reading comprehension tests requires active reading.

You can use any of the strategies below to focus your attention on your reading. You may use many of them already, quite automatically. Others may be just what you need to shift your reading comprehension into high gear.

Active Reading Strategies

- **Monitor your understanding.** When faced with a difficult text, it is all too easy to zone out and skip through challenging passages. Pay attention to how you are feeling about a text. Are you understanding the author's main points? Is there something that makes little or no sense? Are there words that you do not know? Figuring out what makes a passage hard for you is the first step toward correcting the problem. Once you figure it out, you can use one of the following strategies to improve your connection to the text.
- **Predict.** Your ability to make predictions is surprisingly important to your ability to read well. If a passage is well organized, you should be able to read the first few sentences and have a pretty good sense of where the author is going with the text. Practice this one starting with newspaper articles, where the main ideas are supposed to appear in the first paragraph. Move on to more difficult reading. See whether your expectation of a text holds up through the reading of the text. Making predictions about what you are about to read is an immediate way to engage with the text and to keep you engaged throughout your reading.
- **Ask questions.** Keep a running dialogue with yourself as you read. You do not have to stop reading; just pause to consider, "What does this mean? Why did the author use this word? Where is he or she going with this argument? Why is this important?" This will become second nature after a while. When you become acclimated to asking yourself questions as you read a test passage, you may discover that some of the questions you asked appear in different forms on the test itself.
- **Summarize.** You do this when you take notes in class or when you prepare an outline as you study for an exam. Try doing it as you read unfamiliar materials, but do it in your head. At the end of a particularly dense paragraph, try to reduce the author's verbiage to a single, cogent sentence that

states the main idea. At the end of a longer passage, see whether you can restate the theme or message in a phrase or two.

- **Connect.** Every piece of writing is a communication between the author and the reader. You connect to a text first by bringing your prior knowledge to that text and last by applying what you learn from the text to some area of your life. Even if you know nothing at all about architecture or archaeology, your lifetime of experience in the world carries a lot of weight as you read an article about those topics. Connecting to a text can lead to "Aha!" moments as you say to yourself, "I knew that!" or even "I never knew that!" If you are barreling through a text passively, you will not give yourself time to connect with it. You might as well tape the passage and play it under your pillow as you sleep.

Speed-Reading Strategies

You do not need to speed-read to perform well on the Reading Comprehension section, but you might benefit from some pointers that speed-readers use.

- **Avoid subvocalizing.** It is unlikely that you move your lips while you read, but you may find yourself "saying" the text in your head. This slows you down significantly, because you are slowing down to speech speed instead of revving up to reading speed. You do not need to "say" the words; the connection between your eyes and your brain is perfectly able to bypass that step.
- **Do not regress.** If you do not understand something, you may run your eyes back and forth and back and forth over it. Speed-readers know this as "regression," and it is a big drag on reading speed. It is better to read once all the way through and then reread a confusing section.
- **Bundle ideas.** Read phrases rather than words. Remember, you are being tested on overall meaning, which is not derived from single words but rather from phrases, sentences, and paragraphs. If you read word by word, your eye stops constantly, and that slows you down. Read bundles of meaning, and your eyes will flow over the page, improving both reading speed and comprehension.

TYPES OF READING COMPREHENSION QUESTIONS

When it comes to taking reading comprehension tests, knowing what to expect is half the battle. On nursing school entrance tests that include reading comprehension, you will usually be given a series of short or medium-length passages. Each passage is followed by several questions based on its content. The questions are in the multiple-choice format, usually with four answer choices.

The questions assess a variety of reading skills, from basic comprehension skills to higher-level analysis and evaluation skills. Here is a list of the skills that are usually tested in reading comprehension:

Find the Main Idea. This type of question asks you to identify the main idea of the passage as a whole. With this type of question, you need to be very careful to select the answer choice that reflects the main idea of the entire passage and not just a part of it. Don't pick choices that focus on supporting details or minor ideas in the passage. Here are some sample question stems for this kind of question:

- The main point of the passage is . . .
- The central thesis of the passage is . . .
- The best title for this selection is . . .

Locate a Detail. This type of question asks you to identify a detail that was mentioned somewhere in the passage. If you have read carefully, you should have a good idea of where the detail is located. Before finally selecting your answer choice, it is a good idea to look back at the passage and be sure that your memory of details is correct. Here are some sample question stems for this type of question:

- According to the passage . . .
- The passage suggests that . . .

Draw a Conclusion. This type of question asks you to think about ideas or facts given in the passage and to put them together to draw some kind of logical conclusion. In questions of this kind, it is very important to choose an answer that is directly supported by the facts in the passage. Incorrect answer choices will be statements that are not supported by anything in the passage. Here are some sample question stems for this type of question:

- The purpose of the process described in the passage is to . . .
- Why were the scientists studying . . .

Infer Information. This type of question asks you to look closely at ideas or facts stated in the passage and deduce something about them that the author has left unsaid. As with questions asking you to draw a conclusion, it is very important to choose an answer that is directly supported by some fact or idea in the passage. Incorrect answer choices will be statements that are not supported by anything in the passage. Here are some sample question stems for this type of question:

- Based on the passage, you can tell that . . .
- The passage implies that . . .
- The reason that the author suggests X is . . .
- When scientists began studying X, they already knew that . . .
- One group that will not be affected by X is . . .

Identify the Author's Purpose. This type of question asks you to tell why the author of the passage presents a certain fact or idea, or what that author is trying to do when he or she describes a given item or process. Here are some sample question stems for this type of question:

- The author's purpose in the third paragraph is . . .
- The author includes X to show . . .

Identify the meaning of a word in context. This kind of question asks you to identify the correct meaning a word used in the passage. Sometimes the word selected can have many different meanings, but only one will make sense within the context of the passage. Your task is to select that meaning. Here is how such questions are usually stated:

- What does the word *x* mean as used in this passage?

TEST-TAKING TIPS FOR READING COMPREHENSION

Because the format of reading comprehension tests is a familiar one, you may not need to preview the format itself. However, you may benefit from these tips on taking reading comprehension tests.

1. *Preview* the passage. Read the first paragraph. Skim the passage.
2. *Skim* the question stems (the part of each question that does not include the answer choices.) This will give you a quick idea of what to look for as you read.
3. *Read* the passage, using your active reading strategies.
4. *Answer* the questions. If a question stumps you, skip ahead and come back to it at the end of the question set.

QUIZZES AND ANSWERS

Each of the following passages is followed by questions based on its content. For each one, select the choice that best answers the question. Answers and explanations are given at the end of each question set.

Remember that on the actual test, you may be timed, so keep an eye on the clock and see how long it takes you to complete each one of these question sets. That will give you an idea of your average time, and you will know if you have to speed up before you take the actual test.

Passage 1

The "food pyramid" is a visual representation of how the different food groups can be combined to form a healthy diet. Although it has been a vital part of dietary guidelines for years, the pyramid is constantly undergoing analysis and revision as additional studying is done in nutritional fields. Recently, the pyramid has undergone another change regarding the unique dietary needs of seniors.

According to an article published in the January 2008 issue of the *Journal of Nutrition,* modifications in the pyramid for older adults include an emphasis on fiber and calcium, as well as on vitamins D and B_{12}. By incorporating these changes, the pyramid now indicates that the nutrients found in a person's routine daily consumption typically are not enough for seniors. Seniors need supplementation.

As people age, they tend to move less and thus need fewer calories to maintain their weight. Because seniors tend to eat a more limited amount, dietitians urge them to choose wisely. They are urged to eat nutrient-rich meals featuring such food as fruits, vegetables, low-fat dairy products, and high-fiber whole grains. Some experts recommend that older people purchase packaged versions of perishables because such foods last longer than the fresh kind. For example, dried and frozen fruit have a much longer shelf life, as do frozen or canned vegetables. Having a supply of these in the cupboard means fewer trips to the grocery store and less risk of running out of nutritional snacks.

The newly designed pyramid also focuses on the importance for older people of ingesting adequate amounts of fluids on a daily basis. This helps ensure proper digestion and prevent any possibility of dehydration.

Finally, the revised pyramid includes information on incorporating exercise and other physical activities into the lives of older adults. Suggestions include swimming, walking, or simple yard work. Because recent reports have stated that obesity levels for people older than 70 years of age are climbing, performing some type of regular exercise is more essential than ever.

1. The best title for this selection is

   (A) America's Seniors Need Exercise.
   (B) A New Food Pyramid for Seniors.
   (C) Finding Supplementation for Aging.
   (D) Dietary Changes in Older Americans.

2. The purpose of updating the food pyramid as described in the passage is to

   (A) change how seniors eat.
   (B) increase food supplement sales.
   (C) encourage people to eat more fruit.
   (D) convince older people to start swimming.

3. The passage says that seniors should support their digestion by

   (A) taking vitamin D.
   (B) eating fewer calories.
   (C) drinking adequate fluids.
   (D) incorporating some exercise into their regular routine.

4. Dried and frozen fruit is often recommended by dietitians because it is

   (A) delicious.
   (B) easier to store.
   (C) more nutritional than fresh fruit.
   (D) known to have a much longer shelf life.

5. The reason that the author of the passage suggests exercise such as swimming, walking, and yard work is because those activities are

(A) ways to interact with other people.
(B) things that can be done alone.
(C) low impact in nature and relatively safe.
(D) useless for burning up calories.

6. The author's purpose in writing this passage was primarily to

(A) alert people to the different dietary needs of seniors.
(B) encourage students to study the pyramid's requirements.
(C) inform nurses about what supplements are most essential.
(D) educate physicians on the differences between dried and fresh fruit.

ANSWERS AND EXPLANATIONS

1. The correct choice is B.
This is a question that asks you to *find the main idea of the passage*. The key is to ask yourself if each choice is too broad or too specific. You do not want to confuse details with the main idea. For example, choice A is too specific; the need for exercise was only one small detail at the end of the passage. Choice C is also too detailed; supplementation is only one detail from the passage. Choice D, however, is too broad; it does not focus on the pyramid's changes as the correct answer does.

2. The correct choice is A.
This is a question that asks you to *draw a conclusion* from the information you read. You are to think about the changes instituted in the food pyramid and determine their overall, general purpose. Those changes might have resulted in more sales of food supplements (choice B) and more fruit being consumed (choice C), but neither of those was the purpose of the changes. It is said that older people are being encouraged to swim (choice D), but that too was not the purpose of the changes to the food pyramid. The purpose was to get older people to change their eating habits.

3. The correct choice is C.
This is a *locate a detail* question to make sure you understood an important point made in the passage. Although all four answer choices are mentioned in the passage as something seniors should do, only one is actually associated with helping proper digestion.

4. The correct choice is D.
This question asks you to *locate a detail* based in the passage. Although choice A is correct (dried or frozen fruit is delicious), that is not the reason it is recommended. Choice B is not mentioned in the passage, and choice C is not a true statement.

5. The correct choice is C.
This question is asking you to *infer information* based on what is provided in the passage. None of these statements is directly stated, but by combining details from the passage, you can determine which is the correct answer. Choice A does not make sense because the activities listed are designed to

promote health; there is nothing to indicate that they are supposed to improve seniors' social lives. Choice B does not make sense because the point is not to find activities that seniors can do alone. Choice D is not correct because burning up calories is important for seniors. But the author is deliberately suggesting forms of exercise that would not be risky for older adults.

6. The correct choice is A.
This is an *identify the author's purpose* question. Choices B, C, and D are not correct because there is nothing to indicate that the passage was written specifically for students, nurses, or physicians. The purpose of the passage is to alert readers to the fact that according to modern research, seniors have special dietary needs.

Passage 2

Years of research have proven that Alzheimer's disease, along with other types of dementia, elevates the risk of dying early in the majority of patients. In a recent study performed by the Institute of Public Health at the University of Cambridge, scientists set out to determine just exactly how long people were likely to survive following the onset of dementia.

Currently, approximately 24 million people throughout the world suffer from the memory loss and orientation confusion that comes with Alzheimer's disease and other forms of dementia. That number appears to double every 20 years, and experts predict that by the year 2040, there will be 81 million people living with some level of the condition. The more the researchers and doctors can learn about what causes the problem, as well as how to treat it, the better prepared they will be to handle these millions of future patients.

To determine how people's life spans are affected by this medical condition, the scientists studied 13,000 seniors for a period of 14 years. During that time, 438 people developed dementia, the vast majority of whom died. The factors of age, disability, and gender were analyzed to see how they affected longevity as well.

Conclusions from the study showed that women tended to live slightly longer than men, averaging 4.6 years from the onset of dementia, as opposed to 4.1 years for men. The patients who were already weak or frail at the onset of the dementia died first, regardless of age. Marital status, living environment, and degree of mental decline, although relevant factors, were not shown to be influential.

Researchers from the University of Cambridge hope that this new information will help patients, clinicians, care providers, service providers, policy makers, and others who deal with dementia. The more they know, the better they will be able to respond to this heart-breaking condition.

1. The best title for this selection is

    (A) Alzheimer's Disease on the Rise.
    (B) Women's Life Spans Are Longer.
    (C) Average Time of Survival with Dementia.
    (D) The Effect of Marital Status on Longevity.

2. What fact did researchers already know before beginning this new study?

    (A) Women with Alzheimer's disease tend to live slightly longer than their male counterparts.
    (B) A patient's overall condition before dementia onset was a key factor in survival.
    (C) People diagnosed with some kind of dementia usually have a higher risk of dying early.
    (D) The living environment had a small influence on the overall life span of a patient with dementia.

3. The author mentions the number of patients with Alzheimer's disease to

    (A) point out the rarity of the disease.
    (B) emphasize the average age at which onset occurs.
    (C) clarify why the disease strikes one sex more than another.
    (D) explain why knowing more about the condition is so essential.

4. Why did the researchers undertake this new study on dementia?

    (A) to better understand the effects of the disease
    (B) to educate families on how to cope with the condition
    (C) to show physicians and other professionals a new kind of treatment
    (D) to prove that degree of mental decline is not the most important factor

5. According to the passage, the factor that affects dementia survival rate the most is

    (A) marital status.
    (B) health at onset.
    (C) living environment.
    (D) degree of mental decline.

6. Ironically, the one group of people mentioned in the passage who will be unable to make use of the conclusions of the study are

    (A) physicians.
    (B) nurses.
    (C) patients.
    (D) policy makers.

ANSWERS AND EXPLANATIONS

1. The correct choice is C.

This is a *main idea* question. By picking out the best title, you are pinpointing the focus of the passage. Choice A is not correct because the rise of Alzheimer's disease is a supporting detail rather than the main idea. Choice B highlights a relatively minor detail in the passage, and choice D does as well. The focus of the entire passage is best stated in choice C.

2. The correct choice is C.

This question asks you to *infer information*. If you look at how the passage was written, the only fact that the researchers knew before embarking on this experiment was that dementia patients had shorter life spans, which is stated in choice C. Choices A, B, and D were factors that researchers learned through their study.

3. The correct choice is D.

This question asks you to *identify the author's purpose* from details given in the passage. Choice A does not make sense with the information provided about the prevalence of the disease. The number of cases has no connection to the average age at onset as in choice B, and nothing in the passage discusses how the genders are affected differently (choice C). The reason that the author mentions the large number of patients with Alzheimer's disease is to support his or her claim that knowing about the condition is increasingly essential.

4. The correct choice is A.

This question asks you to *draw a conclusion*. The last paragraph is your best clue as to the right answer. Choice B is not true because there are no coping tips in this passage, choice C is wrong because there is nothing about treatment methods, and choice D is based on a fact discovered in the study but is not the reason why the research was done.

5. The correct choice is B.

This is a pure *locate a detail* question to make sure you comprehend what you read. All four answer choices are factors mentioned in the passage, but only choice B is pinpointed as an influential one. The rest are considered either not influential or not as relevant.

6. The correct choice is C.

This is another question that asks you to *infer information* based on what is in the passage. Physicians, nurses, and policy makers can all make use of the information provided by this study, but the patients themselves cannot do so and in fact would not even be aware of it.

Passage 3

In recent years, there have been frightening headlines about harmful ingredients such as mercury and lead in ordinary cosmetics. However, these are hardly the first examples of people paying a heavy price to conform to cultural ideals of beauty. That is a tradition that has been around for centuries.

Ancient Egyptians decorated their eyes with malachite (a green ore of copper), galena (a lead sulfide), and kohl (a paste made from soot, fat, and metals such as lead). This may have made them look more beautiful, but it also led to health problems such as insomnia and mental confusion.

The ancient Greeks went even further. They applied lead to their entire faces, supposedly to clear their complexions of any blemishes and improve the coloration of the skin. Health problems that resulted ranged from infertility to insanity. The lead ointment whitened their faces—a sure sign of beauty—so they then added some red lead to the cheeks for that rosy glow. As if that toxic mess was not enough, they also used hair dyes that contained lead. Some historians suspect that lead poisoning was part of what later led to the fall of the Roman Empire.

Lead played a huge role in cosmetics for centuries, but it was not until the mid-nineteenth century that the American Medical Association (AMA) published a paper about the connection between lead in cosmetics and health concerns. Despite the availability of this information, sellers still offered powders and potions that contained harmful chemicals and other materials. These products had innocuous names such as Snow White Enamel, Milk of Roses, and Berry's Freckle Ointment.

The Pure Food and Drug Act (1906) and the creation of the Food and Drug Administration (FDA) helped put an end to some of the most dangerous cosmetics, although products such as a lotion containing rat poison and a mascara that caused blindness still made it onto the market. In 1938 cosmetics came under the control of the FDA, and in 1977 a law was passed requiring cosmetic manufacturers to list all ingredients on their products.

Although these steps have helped ensure product safety, problems still exist. As recently as 2007, lipsticks for sale were found to contain lead, and mascara was found to contain mercury. An additional concern is phthalates, industrial chemicals that can cause birth defects and infertility. They are found in personal care products such as shampoos, lotions, perfume, and deodorants.

An old saying states that beauty has a price. Sometimes it just may be much higher than consumers realize.

1. Which of these topics is the main focus of the passage?

  (A) Frightening news stories from the past
  (B) Ancient Egyptian and Greek cultures
  (C) The dangers of cosmetics throughout history
  (D) The control of makeup by the FDA

2. Why did the ancient Greeks put white lead ointment on their faces?

  (A) to make themselves look younger
  (B) to clear up their complexions
  (C) to keep from getting seriously ill
  (D) to achieve an overall rosy glow

3. One might infer from this passage that

(A) beauty is more important than health.
(B) manufacturers of cosmetics will continue to ignore FDA rulings.
(C) the AMA regulates cosmetic ingredients.
(D) phthalates are not nearly as dangerous as ingredients used in the past.

4. Which of the following is identified in the passage as a health hazard resulting from lead?

(A) cancer
(B) paralysis
(C) infertility
(D) deafness

5. Which of the following types of cosmetics was not mentioned as containing toxic materials?

(A) lipstick
(B) deodorant
(C) mascara
(D) blush

6. What conclusion can be drawn from the fact that as recently as 2007, cosmetics were being pulled from store shelves?

(A) The FDA is no longer performing its job properly.
(B) The AMA believes that all cosmetics are completely safe now.
(C) Manufacturers are still using harmful ingredients in their products.
(D) Personal care products that contain phthalates are also being removed from stores.

ANSWERS AND EXPLANATIONS

1. The correct choice is C.
This is a *find the main idea* question. Although the passage starts out by referring to frightening headlines (choice A), that reference is merely an introduction and not the focus of the passage. Ancient Egyptian and Greek cultures (choice B) are mentioned as supporting details, but once again, they are not the main focus. Choice D is another supporting detail but not the main idea.

2. The correct choice is B.
This is a *locate a detail* question. Choice A is not correct because the idea of looking younger is never mentioned in the passage. Choice C is ironically wrong; the Greeks did not use lead ointment to stay healthy, and it actually made them sick. Choice D is not correct because a different kind of lead was used to provide the pink color.

3. The correct choice is A.

This is an *infer information* question. Choice B is not true because there is nothing in the passage to support this idea. Choice C is not true because the FDA regulates cosmetic ingredients, not the AMA. Choice D is not true because phthalates are just as dangerous as ingredients used in the past and even more prevalent.

4. The correct choice is C.

This is a *locate a detail* question. Choices A, B, and D are not mentioned in the passage. Only choice C is listed as one of the potential risks of lead.

5. The correct choice is D.

This is another *locate a detail* question. Choices A, B, and C were all mentioned as, at one time or another, containing toxic materials. Only choice D was not discussed.

6. The correct choice is C.

This question asks you to *draw a conclusion* from the information in the passage. Choice A is not correct because there is not enough information in the passage to support it. Choice B has no foundation in the passage and goes against the correct conclusion. Choice D is also wrong because these products are not being removed from the shelves.

Passage 4

Most people get a little grumpy when they do not get enough sleep, but when it comes to children, the problem may be more than just some extra irritation. Lack of sleep may also affect their weight, as well as their overall behavior.

A study conducted in New Zealand at the University of Auckland and published in the medical journal *Sleep* followed almost 600 children from infancy through seven years of age. Researchers observed the children's sleep patterns and found that generally they slept less on the weekends than during the week and even less during the summer months.

According to the findings, the children who tended to sleep the least were at greater risk for being overweight and/or experiencing behavioral problems. In fact, those who regularly slept less than nine hours a night were three times more likely than longer sleepers to be obese and to show signs of attention deficit disorder (ADD) and attention deficit hyperactivity disorder (ADHD). These results were based on questionnaires handed out to the children's parents and teachers.

How does sleep affect weight? The answer to that is still not clear, but experts suspect that chronic sleep deprivation somehow alters the hormones involved in appetite control and metabolism. This is a connection that still needs to be explored to be better understood.

How much sleep is enough for a child? Experts recommend that preschoolers get 11 to 13 hours of sleep each night, whereas school age children should get between 10 and 11 hours per night. Many children average only eight hours.

The study concluded that sleep duration is one risk factor that can be fairly easily altered to prevent future health problems for today's young people.

1. What would be the best title for this passage?

   (A) Preventing ADHD in Your Child
   (B) The Cure for Childhood Obesity
   (C) Hormones and Appetite Control
   (D) Children and the Need for Sleep

2. This passage suggests that children sleep the most during the

   (A) week.
   (B) weekend.
   (C) summer.
   (D) holidays.

3. This study was conducted primarily through

   (A) lab experiments.
   (B) questionnaires.
   (C) brief research.
   (D) years of interviews.

4. According to the passage, inadequate sleep can result in all of the following EXCEPT

   (A) hyperactivity.
   (B) obesity.
   (C) irritability.
   (D) anxiety.

5. What conclusion can you draw about the connection between sleep and young children?

   (A) Lack of sleep causes children to fail in school.
   (B) Inadequate rest raises the risk of behavioral and physical problems.
   (C) Sleeping less than 10 hours a night is guaranteed to result in obesity.
   (D) Eight hours of sleep each night meets the requirements of most children.

6. According to the passage, which of the following ideas needs further exploration?

   (A) How much sleep children actually need at each age
   (B) How children's sleep patterns change during the seasons
   (C) How sleep affects children's appetite and overall metabolism
   (D) How teachers and physicians determine a diagnosis of ADD or ADHD

ANSWERS AND EXPLANATIONS

1. The correct choice is D.

This is a *find the main idea* question. To pick out the best title, you have to grasp the focus of the entire article rather than just one or more supporting details. In this case, choice A is just one of the details in the passage. The passage does mention ADHD in children, but that is not the main idea. Obesity (choice B) is another detail mentioned in the passage, but nothing is said about a cure. Choice C implies that the whole article is about the link between hormones and appetite control, when in actuality, that is just one theory that is mentioned. The passage as a whole is about the importance of enough sleep for children.

2. The correct choice is A.

This is a *locate a detail* question. The passage states in the second paragraph that children sleep less in the summer and on weekends. Holidays are not mentioned. This means that the only correct answer is choice A.

3. The correct choice is B.

This is a *locate a detail* question. It requires you to identify details that you did and did not find in the passage. Choice A is wrong because no lab experiments are mentioned in the passage. Choice C is wrong because this study took place over seven years, so the word *brief* is incorrect. Choice D is also wrong because there is no mention of interviews.

4. The correct choice is D.

This is a *locate a detail* question. Looking back through the passage, you can see that choices A, B, and C are all mentioned in the passage as possible results of inadequate sleep. Only choice D is not found anywhere in the passage.

5. The correct choice is B.

This question asks you to *draw a conclusion* from the information presented in the passage. Based on the passage, choice A is not correct because it draws an unwarranted conclusion. Not enough sleep does not necessarily mean that a child will fail in school. Choice C is also incorrect because it is an unwarranted conclusion: obesity is a risk, not something guaranteed to occur. Choice D is also incorrect and goes against the evidence presented throughout the passage.

6. The correct choice is C.

This is an *infer information* question. You have to read the passage carefully to be sure of the correct answer to this question. Choice A is not up for further study; the numbers are made clear within the passage. Choice B is not considered an issue that needs to be further clarified. Choice D is beyond the scope of this passage.

Passage 5

Perhaps nothing mars the beauty and joy of a baby's arrival more than the presence of birth defects. Although the baby will certainly be just as welcomed and adored, these defects have the ability to have an impact these young new lives in unpleasant and even dangerous ways.

One of the best ways to prevent more than half of all possible birth defects to the brain and spine is extremely easy; women simply must make sure they are taking enough folic acid before they conceive and then continue to do so throughout the course of their pregnancy. Folic acid is primarily responsible for making new cells, and during early gestation, the cells of the neural tube, which eventually becomes the infant's spinal cord and brain, are particularly demanding. Having adequate amounts of folic acid at this point ensures proper cell division and specialization. If there is not enough folic acid in the mother's body at this point, neural tube defects (NTDs) can result in varying degrees. One example of NTD is spina bifida, a life-threatening situation; another is anencephaly, a fatal condition.

Experts recommend that women take 400 mcg of folic acid a day throughout their childbearing years. They can do this by taking daily multivitamin supplements that contain folic acid, by taking a single daily supplement of folic acid, or by adding fortified breakfast cereals to their daily menu. It is not adequate to wait until becoming pregnant to start supplementing with folic acid. The body must have a good supply before conception takes place. In addition, many women do not realize they are pregnant for several weeks, and by the time they do realize it and begin increasing their folic acid intake, the development phase for the embryo's brain and spinal cord has already passed.

In addition to causing NTDs, a lack of folic acid can also result in other health conditions such as cleft lip and cleft palate. It can also raise the risk of Parkinson's disease. On the other hand, adequate amounts of folic acid can lower the risks of cardiovascular disease and cancers of the colon, cervix, and breast, as well as Alzheimer's disease.

1. The major subject of this passage is

(A) dealing with spina bifida.
(B) finding natural sources of folic acid.
(C) recognizing the symptoms of Parkinson's disease.
(D) understanding the importance of folic acid during gestation.

2. According to the passage, when should a woman start making sure she has an adequate supply of folic acid?

(A) the minute she finds out that she is pregnant
(B) throughout childbearing age
(C) during the second and third trimester of pregnancy
(D) not before her obstetrician advises it

3. What conclusions can be drawn from the last sentence in the passage?

(A) Folic acid is not important after infancy.
(B) A good supply of folic acid prevents Alzheimer's disease.
(C) Folic acid plays an essential nutritional role throughout life.
(D) A lack of folic acid in adulthood can result in cleft palates and cleft lips.

4. All of the following are examples of conditions resulting from a lack of folic acid EXCEPT

    (A) cleft palate.
    (B) spina bifida.
    (C) anencephaly.
    (D) breast cancer.

5. What does the word *mars* mean as used in this passage?

    (A) emphasizes
    (B) tarnishes
    (C) exemplifies
    (D) characterizes

6. The passage suggests that women can take folic acid in all of the following ways EXCEPT

    (A) as a topical shot.
    (B) as a single supplement.
    (C) as part of a multivitamin supplement.
    (D) as part of fortified foods such as cereals.

ANSWERS AND EXPLANATIONS

1. The correct choice is D.
This is another *find the main idea* question. Choice A is not correct because there is no information in the passage about dealing with the condition, just basic information about the condition itself. Choice B is also incorrect because the sources of folic acid are not explored. Choice C is wrong because Parkinson's disease is only briefly mentioned and there is nothing about the symptoms.

2. The correct choice is B.
This is a *locate a detail* question. Choice A is incorrect: waiting until the woman knows she is pregnant is too late; vital development has already taken place. Choice C is also far too late for gestational development, and choice D is incorrect because a supplement may be needed well before a doctor suggests it.

3. The correct choice is C.
This question asks you to *draw a conclusion* based on the information in the passage. Choice A is not correct because the information in the last sentence indicates that folic acid influences health far into adulthood. Choice B is incorrect because it reaches an unwarranted conclusion; folic acid will lower the risks of Alzheimer's but not necessarily prevent it. Choice D is incorrect because cleft palates and lips result from a lack of folic acid during pregnancy, not afterwards.

4. The correct choice is D.
This is a *locate a detail* question. Answer choices A, B, and C are all incorrect because they were mentioned in the passage as possible conditions resulting from a lack of folic acid. The correct answer is choice D because the last paragraph indicates that folic acid helps prevent breast cancer, among other conditions.

5. The correct choice is B.

This kind of question asks you to *identify the meaning of a word in context*. To answer it, you have to reread the first sentence of the passage. That sentence makes it clear that the correct definition for the word as it used here is choice B. If you take the other choices and replace *mars* with any of them, the sentence does not make sense.

6. The correct choice is A.

This is a *locate a detail* question. To answer it, you have to refer to the passage's third paragraph, which states how women can increase their folic acid intake. Answer choices B, C, and D are all mentioned in the paragraph as ways in which women can take folic acid. Choice A, however, is never mentioned as an option so it is the correct answer.

Passage 6

What do pilots, astronauts, physicians, and risk managers have in common? In this case, they are all part of an organization based in Memphis, Tennessee, called Lifewings Partners. This unusual group focuses on finding ways to eliminate mistakes made accidentally in medical settings within the United States.

Lifewings Partners emphasizes the need for a watchdog in various medical settings. According to the National Institutes of Health, approximately 98,000 patients die each year in U.S. health care settings due to nothing more than medical error. Some other experts suspect that the number is much higher, reaching as high as 145,000. Examples include the man who had the wrong testicle removed in a Los Angeles hospital, a young boy who went in for a typical hernia surgery and ended up with brain damage from the anesthesia, and a hospital in Rhode Island that performed brain surgery on the wrong side of the brain—three times on three different patients in less than a year.

Since Lifewings Partners began seven years ago, more than 70 medical facilities have used their services. The company centers on ways to improve patient safety much in the same way that pilots work to keep their passengers safe while in the air. They do this through a five-step program that requires hospitals to change their medical and communication procedures, train their doctors and nurses, and establish checklists and measurements designed to track outcomes.

In addition to making internal changes in medical settings, Lifewings Partners also works to educate patients on safety before they even enter the hospital. The company suggests that all consumers do the following: go online to obtain public information on a hospital's safety, talk to their doctors to see what safety standards are in place already, and ask professionals about which facilities tend to have the best safety records. As Steve Harden, founder and CEO of the organization phrases it, "Just because a hospital has a great reputation for cutting-edge medicine doesn't necessarily mean the hospital is the safest place to go for routine procedures." After all, some mistakes are too big and too irrevocable to risk.

1. What is the main emphasis in this passage?

   (A) Medical mistakes are made in health centers every day.
   (B) Lifewings Partners is made up of an eclectic mix of people.
   (C) Lifewings Partners is working hard to prevent medical errors.
   (D) Consumers should talk to their doctors about hospital safety.

2. Which detail from the passage best supports the idea that some medical settings can be dangerous to patients?

   (A) A young boy went in to a hospital for a hernia operation and ended up with brain damage.
   (B) More than 70 medical facilities are currently using Lifewings Partners' services.
   (C) Lifewings Partners includes pilots, astronauts, doctors, and even risk managers.
   (D) Experts suspect that more medical mistakes are made than are actually reported to the National Institutes of Health.

3. Which of the following is a step that Lifewings Partners requires its client hospitals to implement?

   (A) Investigate the medical credentials of staff doctors and nurses.
   (B) Prescreen patients for medical conditions.
   (C) Enforce new rules regarding patients' health insurance.
   (D) Establish measurements designed to track patient outcomes.

4. Which of the following is a conclusion that can be drawn from the last paragraph of the passage?

   (A) Procedures that Lifewings Partners recommends are always effective.
   (B) Medical mistakes can happen at even the best hospitals.
   (C) Some hospitals know more about cutting-edge medicine than others.
   (D) Medical mistakes will one day be completely eradicated.

5. The word *watchdog* as used in the second paragraph of the passage can best be defined as

   (A) companion.
   (B) guard.
   (C) manager.
   (D) punisher.

6. On which group of people does Lifewings Partners focus education efforts?

   (A) students
   (B) CEOs
   (C) patients
   (D) pilots

ANSWERS AND EXPLANATIONS

1. The correct choice is C.

This is a *find the main idea question* and tests whether you can distinguish the primary idea from its supporting details. Choice A is too generic and is not the focus of the passage, choice B is a minor detail, and choice D is one step in a program for preventing medical errors. Choice C is the main idea in the passage.

2. The correct choice is A.

This is a *locate a detail* question. To answer it, you have to look at the different details from the passage and see which best supports the idea in the question. Choice B merely indicates that Lifewings Partners has many clients, whereas choice C just says who is involved in the organization. Choice D might be correct if rewritten to include the statistics, but in this case it is too vague.

3. The correct choice is D.

This is another *locate a detail* question. The passage says that Lifewings Partners requires its client hospitals "to change their medical and communication procedures, train their doctors and nurses, and establish checklists and measurements designed to track outcomes." Only choice D is included in that list.

4. The correct choice is B.

This is a *draw a conclusion* question. In the final paragraph of the passage, Lifewings Partners' CEO is quoted as follows: "Just because a hospital has a great reputation for cutting-edge medicine doesn't necessarily mean the hospital is the safest place to go for routine procedures." From this, you can conclude that medical mistakes can happen at even the finest hospitals. There is no support in the passage for any of the other choices.

5. The correct choice is B.

This is an *identify the meaning of a word in context* question. Context clues are very important here to understand the correct meaning. In this passage, the word *watchdog* is used to mean an organization that watches health care procedures and guards against medical errors.

6. The correct choice is C.

This is a *locate a detail* question. Choice A does not make sense because students are not part of the passage or the organization's target audience. Similarly, choice B is incorrect because CEOs are not the target audience. Choice D is incorrect, although the organization itself includes a pilot.

Passage 7

The health risks of coffee have long been debated, but a recent study has added another argument against too much coffee consumption. This study looked at the effect of drinking coffee on pregnant women. Conducted by physicians at Kaiser Permanente, the study explored the connection between caffeine and the risk of miscarriage.

The connection is one that has been explored before, but this study took a different approach. It took morning sickness into account, whereas other studies did not. The findings were significant: 200 milligrams of caffeine a day—about what is found in two cups of coffee—is enough to increase the risk of having a miscarriage. The source of the caffeine, whether coffee, tea, or soda, was irrelevant; the amount was the key.

This study followed more than 1,000 women who became pregnant within a two-year period. The amount of caffeine they drank was logged, as well as which women experienced a miscarriage. The results, as published in the January 2008 issue of the *American Journal of Obstetrics and Gynecology*, stated that the risk of miscarriage more than doubled in women who consumed 200 mg or more of caffeine per day.

Why does caffeine carry this risk? Researchers are not sure, but they theorize that the caffeine restricts blood flow to the placenta. This, in turn, can harm the developing fetus.

Does this mean the physicians will start advising women to quit drinking coffee while pregnant? Yes and no. Some doctors will certainly take this report to heart and encourage their patients to stay away from more than one cup of coffee a day, just as they recommend not drinking alcohol or smoking cigarettes. Others are not so convinced and doubt that this single study is enough to overturn the established guidelines of the American College of Obstetricians and Gynecologists. Instead, they believe that a lot more research needs to be done.

1. What is the main idea of this passage?

   (A) Coffee carries some obvious health risks for people.
   (B) Two cups of coffee a day may be enough to raise the risk of miscarriage.
   (C) There is a link between miscarriages and morning sickness.
   (D) Miscarriage rates are on the rise internationally.

2. Based on the study, which aspect of caffeine consumption seemed to be the key to the risk of miscarriage?

   (A) the source of the caffeine
   (B) the time the caffeine is ingested
   (C) the amount of caffeine ingested
   (D) the time between doses of caffeine

3. What do some researchers believe is the link between caffeine and miscarriages?

   (A) They think that caffeine inhibits placental blood flow.
   (B) They believe that caffeine makes the heart beat too rapidly.
   (C) They suspect that caffeine interferes with the immune system.
   (D) They theorize that caffeine prevents some nutrients from crossing the placenta.

4. The word *overturn* as used in the last paragraph of the passage can best be defined as

(A) justify.
(B) invalidate.
(C) support.
(D) review.

5. Based on this passage, what conclusion can best be drawn about the advice physicians will give their pregnant patients about coffee consumption?

(A) Almost all of them will advise women to stop drinking any caffeine until after the baby is born.
(B) The majority will ignore the study altogether and continue to advise caffeine in moderation as before.
(C) All of them will demand additional research to be done before they change what they tell their patients.
(D) Some will continue to make their normal recommendations about caffeine, while others will be more cautious than before.

6. Based on this passage, what conclusion can best be drawn about the potential effects of drinking coffee?

(A) It is completely safe for anyone.
(B) There are absolutely no concerns unless you are pregnant.
(C) It can be extremely dangerous for everyone.
(D) It may pose health risks for some people.

ANSWERS AND EXPLANATIONS

1. The correct choice is B.
Clearly, this is a *find the main idea* question. Choice A is too broad and goes beyond the scope of the passage, choice C is a side detail briefly mentioned, and choice D is not stated anywhere in the passage. Although the passage discusses miscarriages, it does not mention statistics.

2. The correct choice is C.
This question is a *locate a detail* question. If you read the passage carefully, you know that the answer is choice C. Where the caffeine came from and when it was ingested are irrelevant according to the passage.

3. The correct choice is A.
This is another *locate a detail* question. The answer is found in paragraph 4. Choice A is correct and is the only theory presented anywhere within the passage, making choices B, C, and D all incorrect.

4. The correct choice is B.
This is an *identify the meaning of a word in context* question. The findings of the study run counter to the established guidelines of the American College of Obstetricians and Gynecologists, so if accepted, the findings would invalidate those guidelines. None of the other choices fits the meaning in context.

5. The correct choice is D.

This is a *draw a conclusion* question. If you look at the last paragraph again, you see that the only correct answer is choice D. Some physicians will regard this study as conclusive and change their recommendations, whereas others will wait for more research.

6. The correct choice is D.

This is a *draw a conclusion* question. Choices A and C are sweeping conclusions that are not supported by the passage. There is also no reason to think that coffee is completely safe for anyone who is not pregnant, so choice B is incorrect. Choice D is the only conclusion that is supported by the passage.

Passage 8

In some schools around the country, physical education classes look a lot different than they did a generation or two ago. Kids are still in motion, stretching, running, lifting, and sweating. But instead of everyone doing the same activity at the same time as a team, they are exercising independently. They are being taught movements and activities that their teachers hope they will incorporate into their lives rather than just perform long enough to get a good grade.

By teaching kids the pleasure of exercise, gym teachers hope to instill important lessons about maintaining good health, staying fit, and keeping weight under control. By getting the chance to work at their own pace, rather than being forced to keep up with other classmates, students are often more willing to try new things and stick with them. They can also participate in low-impact sports like yoga, martial arts, and weightlifting. Instead of playing basketball or baseball, they can focus on more general skills like passing the ball.

A growing number of physical education (PE) teachers are also putting more of an emphasis on general nutrition and health. According to Craig Buschner, president of the National Association for Sport and Physical Education, "This field has to make changes." With the continual increase in the number of children who are obese, there is greater pressure to teach students about how to stay fit. To do this, gym teachers have to look at new ways to introduce exercise to their classes that will not intimidate or overwhelm them but instead intrigue and engage them.

One other difference found in some modern gym classes is the grading system. Instead of being graded on the ability to run laps in a set time or make a certain number of baskets, the students are graded simply on the effort they make in the class. Some even get extra credit if they are sweatiest student in the room!

1. What would be the best title for this passage?

    (A) Being a Team in PE
    (B) A New Kind of Grade
    (C) Learning Martial Arts
    (D) PE for School and Life

2. The term *instill* as used in the second paragraph of the passage can best be defined as

(A) encourage.
(B) indoctrinate.
(C) demand.
(D) create.

3. What can you conclude is the primary difference between traditional PE and how some PE classes are being taught today?

(A) For the first time, low-impact sports have been introduced.
(B) Today's students are stretching, running, and lifting.
(C) There is a greater emphasis on lifelong fitness.
(D) Gym teachers are grading more harshly.

4. What can be inferred about the "sweatiest student" referred to in the last sentence in the passage?

(A) This student is more overweight than anyone else.
(B) This student has worked hardest during class.
(C) This student does not need extra credit.
(D) This student is behind all of his/her classmates.

5. According to the passage, PE teachers are trying to teach students lessons about all of the following EXCEPT

(A) the importance of good nutrition for health.
(B) staying generally physically fit.
(C) ways to avoid contracting contagious diseases.
(D) keeping weight under control.

6. Why does the author quote Craig Buschner in the passage?

(A) to make an entirely new point about physical education
(B) to lend authority to ideas presented in the passage
(C) to demonstrate that not all PE teachers are in agreement
(D) to debunk the idea that childhood obesity is a growing problem

ANSWERS AND EXPLANATIONS

1. The correct choice is D.

This is a *find the main idea* question. Choice A is incorrect because this article is about how PE classes are focusing less on team activities and more on the individual. Choice B is not true because although grades are mentioned they are not the focus of the passage. Choice C is incorrect because it focuses on a very minor detail. Choice D is correct because the focus of the passage is on teaching PE in such a way that the lessons last a lifetime.

2. The correct choice is A.

This is an *identify the meaning of a word in context* question. If you look at the context clues in the sentence, the answer becomes clear. *Indoctrinate* (choice B) is much too harsh because it means "teach against one's will." *Demand* (choice C) and *create* (choice D) do not make sense in the sentence. Only choice A makes sense with the rest of the sentence.

3. The correct choice is C.

This is a *draw a conclusion* question. Choice A does not make sense because low-impact sports are not necessarily brand new. Choice B is wrong because students have been stretching, running, and lifting in PE class for years. Choice D is also false because there is nothing in the passage to indicate harsher grading, just different parameters. The correct answer is choice C because the emphasis in classes now is to teach physical exercise in a way that students will be encouraged to continue it for the rest of their lives.

4. The correct choice is B.

This is an *infer information* question. In this case, the clue to the answer comes in the sentence before the last one. It says that students are graded for the effort they put forth. This makes it clear that the sweatiest student who earns extra credit is one who has put forth a lot of effort in class. There is no support in the passage for any of the other choices.

5. The correct choice is C.

PE teachers incorporate a lot of new material into their classes, including choices A, B, and D. Only choice C is not mentioned, so it is the correct answer.

6. The correct choice is B.

This is an *identify the author's purpose* question. Craig Buschner is the president of the National Association for Sport and Physical Education, so his words lend authority to the idea that PE classes need to change to place greater emphasis on general physical fitness. There is no support in the passage for any of the other answer choices.

CHAPTER 8

Mathematical Ability

Read this chapter to learn

- How to solve problems in arithmetic
- How to solve problems in algebra and geometry
- How to interpret charts, tables, and graphs
- How to convert between U.S. and metric units of measure
- How to use mathematics to solve word problems

Y ou are probably not planning to become a nurse because you live for simplifying equations or calculating hypotenuses. However, there is math involved in the job, and that is why it is tested on nursing school entrance exams. If you are like many nursing school candidates, it has been a while since you were in math class. And if you are like most people, you have not necessarily used those skills a whole lot since leaving.

But do not worry. The math on nursing school entrance exams does not have to be scary. It is not as advanced as the math you studied in your high school classes, and we will make it as easy as possible to relearn the basics you need. If you have taken the math diagnostic test in Chapter 5 of this book, you can use your results to identify on any weak areas and focus your attention on them. But unless you are under a huge time crunch, you should work through this whole chapter to be the best prepared for your nursing school entrance exam. While reading, it is a good idea to have index cards and a notebook nearby so that you can record topics to study later and make flash cards; there are many shortcuts you will be able to take on your exams if you do some memorization beforehand.

Each section of this chapter has practice problems. You will find the solutions at the end of the chapter. Once you are finished with the chapter, build your test-taking confidence by taking the two Mathematical Ability Practice Tests in Chapter 10 of this book. Before you take those or any other math tests, here are some test-taking tips to keep in mind:

- **Show your work.** No, you will not get partial credit if you get something wrong, but writing everything down helps you keep track of what you are doing and makes it easier to catch your mistakes.
- **Do the easy stuff first.** Do the things that are least challenging to you first so that the stress of working harder problems will not make you mess up on the easier problems. Some exams are arranged in a rough order of difficulty, but what really matters is what is easy or hard to you, so do not be afraid to skip around. And be sure to mark any problems you skip with a large symbol, such as a star, so that you come back to them at the end.
- **Estimate.** Sometimes you can get a problem right—or at least make an educated guess if you are running out of time—just by estimating, ballparking, or eyeballing (whatever you want to call it). For example, if you are asked to subtract $7,348 - 5,492$, you can estimate that the correct answer will be just less than 2,000. How much will this help on the actual test? That depends on the answer choices. If the numbers in the choices vary widely, then estimating is an easy to way eliminate wrong answers. If the choices are closer together, there is still a good chance that you can eliminate one or more of them. This builds you a little bit of a "safety net" when you are doing the math, because you have already eliminated answers that simply cannot be correct.
- **Neatness counts!** No one is going to see your test paper, but you will do yourself a big favor if you keep everything organized as you work. We will show you examples as we approach the different problem types.

Ready to begin your review? Good! Let us get started.

INTEGERS

Most of the numbers you will deal with on your entrance exams are integers, which are undoubtedly the ones that you are most used to dealing with day to day. Integers are divisible by one, so they do not have anything after the decimal. You may round things to the nearest integer at the grocery store to keep track of how much you are spending without having to do a lot of mental math. They are the numbers you use to count things that are not divisible, such as cars, marbles, and children.

You may think of the term *whole number* when you hear or read *integer* if it is easier for you. (Technically, *whole numbers* do not include negative numbers, whereas *integers* do, but that is the only difference and it will not be tested on nursing school entrance exams.) We are going to use the word *integer* so that we do not get a lot of mail, but *whole number* is used more in everyday speech, so go ahead and substitute it if you wish.

The Number Line, Positive Numbers, Negative Numbers, and Zero

There may be questions on the test that deal with the concept of a number line, which is basically just a line with numbers on it, like this:

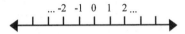

Generally number lines are divided up in increments of 1, so they show you the integers close to and including 0. All numbers to the right of 0 are positive and all numbers to the left of 0 are negative. This means that anything greater than 0—even the fractions and decimals between 0 and 1—is positive. And the same is true for anything less than 0: even between 0 and –1, it is all negative.

So what does that make 0? It is neither positive nor negative. But it is an integer, and it does have a place on the number line.

Absolute Value

Whenever you see a number with vertical lines on either side of it, such as |–3|, you are being asked to figure out the *absolute value* of that number. Absolute values are positive numbers only, so the absolute value of –3 is 3. Or, to put it in math terms, |–3| = 3.

If there is a positive number inside the symbols, such as |2|, then the absolute value is just equal to that same number: |2| = 2. So when you see the absolute value signs, remember that everything goes on the right, or positive, side of the number line. (Yes, it really is that easy. We are going to trust that mathematicians had a very good reason for giving this simple concept a fancy name and unfamiliar symbols, but whatever that reason is, you are not going to need to know it for your entrance exams. You are going to be tested only on the basics.)

Another way to think of absolute value is *distance from 0,* and distances are always positive. For example, –5 is *five* tick marks from *0* on the number line, so |–5| = 5.

Place Value

It's good to brush up on this terminology for your tests, and it will also help keep things straight when we review computation. The digit farthest to the right (unless there are digits after a decimal, but we will get to that later) is called the *ones* or *units* digit. Moving further to the left, you have the *tens*, *hundreds*, *thousands*, and *ten thousands* digits in order. So the number 36,827 has a 7 in the ones place, a 2 in the tens place, an 8 in the hundreds place, a 6 in the thousands place, and a 3 in the ten thousands place.

COMPUTATION

No matter which entrance exam you take, you will definitely be tested on your basic computation skills (addition, subtraction, multiplication, and division), and most tests will not allow the use of a calculator. That sounds like bad news, but it is not entirely; it means that there is a very definite cap on the difficulty level of the math you will be required to do. So it is time to brush off those grade school basics such as "borrowing ten and carrying the one."

Addition

Many addition problems simply line up two numbers and ask you to add them, like this:

$$\begin{array}{r} 497 \\ +362 \end{array}$$

Other addition problems may present information in a word problem, which we will get to later. But word problems are really the same thing; you just need to write down the numbers yourself so that they look like the above problem. And remember—neatness counts!

So how to solve this problem? In bite-sized pieces. Make sure the numbers are lined up in neat columns, and start on the right:

$$\begin{array}{r} 497 \\ +362 \\ \hline 9 \end{array}$$

Now on to the middle column.

$$\begin{array}{r} 497 \\ +362 \\ \hline 159 \end{array}$$

Well, unfortunately you cannot fit both the 1 and the 5 in the same column, so you leave the 5 there and *carry* the 1 over to the left column. Now your left column looks like this:

$$\begin{array}{r} 1 \\ 497 \\ +362 \\ \hline 859 \end{array}$$

So your total is 859.

Ready for another one? Try this one first, and the explanation will follow.

$$2847$$
$$+5463$$

Okay, here is how to do it, starting with the first column on the right. Adding up the far right column you get 10; leave the 0 there and carry the 1.

$$1$$
$$2847$$
$$+5463$$
$$\overline{0}$$

Adding up the second column you get 11; leave a 1 there and carry a 1.

$$1$$
$$2847$$
$$+5463$$
$$\overline{10}$$

Adding up the third column you get 13; leave a 3 there and carry a 1.

$$1$$
$$2847$$
$$+5463$$
$$\overline{310}$$

Adding up the fourth column you get 8, so your answer is 8,310.

Subtraction

Subtraction is very similar; you still line up the numbers in columns and deal with them one column at a time, starting with the right, even if the test writers do not line up the numbers for you. There is no carrying in subtraction; however, if the number you are subtracting in a column is larger than the number you are subtracting from, you may have to borrow from the column to the left.

For example:

$$527$$
$$-335$$

Starting with the first column on the right, you can simply subtract $7 - 5$.

$$527$$
$$-335$$
$$\overline{2}$$

In the next column over, you cannot really subtract $2 - 3$, so you *borrow* from the column to the left. Borrowing lets you add 10 to the current number you are subtracting from, so now you can subtract $12 - 3$ instead:

$$4\ 1$$
$$\cancel{5}27$$
$$-335$$
$$\overline{92}$$

Now all you have left is the last column, the hundreds.

$$
\begin{array}{r}
\mathbf{4}1 \\
\cancel{5}27 \\
-335 \\
\hline
192
\end{array}
$$

So your answer is 192.

Multiplication

In multiplication problems, you still want to be very aware of lining your numbers up properly. Multiplying several-digit numbers is always a matter of multiplying smaller numbers several times.

For example:

$$
\begin{array}{r}
424 \\
\times\ 31 \\
\hline
\end{array}
$$

Because there are two digits in the number on the second line, you actually work two smaller multiplication problems. First, multiply everything in the first line by 1 (because you are starting from the right).

$$
\begin{array}{r}
\mathbf{424} \\
\times\ \mathbf{31} \\
\hline
\mathbf{424}
\end{array}
$$

Then move one column to the left and multiply everything in the top line by the 3. Notice how you shift over when writing your answer. Also, if you end up with a two-digit number, you can carry to the next column to the left, just like in addition. Then just add that carried number after you multiply the original first and second line.

$$
\begin{array}{r}
\mathbf{1} \\
\mathbf{424} \\
\times\ \mathbf{31} \\
\hline
424 \\
\mathbf{1272}
\end{array}
$$

Now you have two numbers, 424 and 1,272. Keeping them in their current columns, you add to get the final result:

$$
\begin{array}{r}
424 \\
+\ 1272 \\
\hline
13144
\end{array}
$$

And your final answer is 13,144.

Division

Division is a bit different. Division problems may be presented like this:

$$3\overline{)21}$$

. . . or like this:

$$21 \div 3$$

. . . or even like this:

$$\frac{21}{3}$$

All of these mean the same thing. You would say "21 divided by 3" or, as a question, "How many times does 3 go into 21?" We will talk about fractions later, but for now, let us focus on long division, which means if you are given a problem such as $21 \div 3$, you will write it out as $3\overline{)21}$.

Unlike in addition, subtraction, and multiplication, you are going to start division problems on the left inside the division sign. But just as you did with the other operations, you are still going to keep things in neat columns.

Let us take $3\overline{)21}$. Starting at the left, ask: Is 2 divisible by 3? No, because 2 is smaller than 3. So then you include the next column to the right, as well: Is 21 divisible by 3? Yes, and the result is 7, so you put the 7 above the 1:

$$3\overline{)\overset{7}{21}}$$

. . . and that is your answer.

What if the problem were $3\overline{)210}$ instead? You just keep going; 21 is divisible by 3, and the result is 7, then 0 is divisible by 3, and the result is 0.

$$3\overline{)\overset{70}{210}}$$

Not all numbers divide evenly, however. Sometimes the *dividend* (the number inside the division sign) will have something left over when you divide it by the *divisor* (the number to the left of the division sign). Then you have a *quotient* (the result), and you also have a *remainder*. The remainder is the integer that is left over when you have divided out as many digits of the divisor as you can.

What if you are asked to divide $3\overline{)212}$? The first 2 is not divisible by 3, so you move on to $3\overline{)21}$. That gives you 7. The last 2 is not divisible by 3 either, so you put a 0 above the 2:

$$3\overline{)\overset{70}{212}}$$

However, that is not the whole story. You still have that 2 that is not represented in the answer, so it becomes your remainder, and you write that as 70r2.

To check your math, you can multiply the quotient by the divisor, then add the remainder, and you should come up with the dividend: $70 \times 3 + 2 = 212$. The math works, so 70r2 is the correct answer.

Let us try one more problem with a remainder:

$$6\overline{)45} = ?$$

First, does 6 go into 4? No, so you include both columns in the divisor. Does 6 go into 45? Yes, 7 times.

$$6\overline{)45}^{\,7}$$

However, 7×6 is only 42, so you have a remainder of 3. Written out, $45 \div 6 = 7r3$.

Time for some practice on computation. Use scratch paper and remember to work carefully. Solutions are at the end of the chapter.

DRILL: ADDITION, SUBTRACTION, MULTIPLICATION, AND DIVISION

1. $1473 + 582 =$	5. $2381 - 963 =$	9. $521 \times 47 =$
2. $5391 + 6729 =$	6. $768 - 529 =$	10. $709 \div 4 =$
3. $12,843 + 5928 =$	7. $408 \times 52 =$	11. $341 \div 3 =$
4. $3609 - 1727 =$	8. $823 \times 7 =$	12. $672 \div 16 =$

Factors

Factors are the sets of numbers that other numbers can be divided by. In the division problems you just did, the quotient and divisor are *factors* of the dividend. Some problems may require you to find factor pairs of numbers, and the process is pretty simple. For example, if you are asked to find the factors of 12, you just draw a *factor T*, like this:

$$\frac{12}{\vert}$$

At first you will not know how many factor pairs the number will have, so leave some room for your factor T to grow downward.

The first pair of factors in the factor T should be 1 and the number itself:

$$\frac{12}{1 \vert 12}$$

Then continue counting and fill in a pair every time you find a number that the original number is divisible by. (By the way, if this is new or challenging, we're about to review how you can tell if a number is divisible by another number.) The number 12 is also divisible by 2, so you add 2 to the list along with the result of $\frac{12}{2}$, or 6.

$$\begin{array}{r|l} & 12 \\ \hline 1 & 12 \\ \hline 2 & 6 \end{array}$$

The number 12 is also divisible by 3, so you can add 3 and the result of $\dfrac{12}{3}$, or 4.

$$\begin{array}{r|l} & 12 \\ \hline 1 & 12 \\ \hline 2 & 6 \\ \hline 3 & 4 \end{array}$$

Now you could go on to add the next number that 12 is divisible by, which is 4, but 4 is already in the list, meaning that all of 12's factors are in the factor T and you are done. The factors of 12 are 1, 2, 3, 4, 6, and 12.

Now it is your turn to find all the factors of the following numbers. Solutions are at the end of the chapter.

DRILL: FACTORS

1. 18 3. 30 5. 42
2. 27 4. 36 6. 45

Divisibility

When finding factors, dividing, reducing fractions, solving equations, and doing many other tasks, it's good to be able to tell quickly and easily if one number is divisible by another. To do this, memorize the rules of divisibility below. Do you have your flashcards ready?

If a Number Is Divisible By ...	How to Tell ...	Examples ...
2	It's even.	0, 2, 52
3	It has digits that add up to 3 or a multiple of 3.	3, 42, 5418
4	The last 2 digits (if there are that many) are divisible by 4.	16, 132, 2596
5	It ends in 0 or 5.	10, 25, 9845
6	It is both even and divisible by 3.	12, 36, 972
8	The last 3 digits (if there are that many) are divisible by 8.	64, 128, 5256
9	The digits add up to 9 or multiples of 9.	27, 549, 7875
10	It ends in 0.	20, 500, 7000

A few other notes on divisibility:

- Numbers that are divisible by other numbers are called *multiples*. For instance, 36 is a multiple of 3. It is also a multiple of 1, 2, 4, 6, 9, 12, 18, and 36.
- If you noticed that the numbers listed above are the factors of 36, you are right. Any number has *many* *m*ultiples, but probably only a *few* *f*actors.
- Negatives that meet the divisibility requirements are also divisible. For example, –5,256 is also divisible by 8.
- Zero is divisible by any number; the result is 0.
- There are no easy divisibility rules for 7. If you need to determine whether a number is divisible by 7 or a number larger than 10 (or if you forget the divisibility rules for any of the above numbers), just divide it out. If there is a remainder, the number is not evenly divisible.

Order of Operations

When solving any equation or making any calculation that has more than one operation to perform, the order in which you perform the operations has an effect on what answer you will get. For example, in the expression $5 + 4 \times 2$, if you perform the addition first and then the multiplication, you get a result of 18. If you perform the multiplication first and then the addition, you get 13. So which is correct? Although many people just perform the operations from left to right, there is an order of operations that must be followed to get the math right. The order can be remembered with the acronym PEMDAS, which stands for:

- **P**arentheses
- **E**xponents
- **M**ultiplication and **D**ivision (from left to right)
- **A**ddition and **S**ubtraction (from left to right)

So anything that is in parentheses takes precedence and is calculated first, then exponents, and so on. That means that in the problem above, the multiplication should be done first and then the addition, giving you 13. Try the order of operations on the following drill; solutions are at the end of the chapter.

DRILL: ORDER OF OPERATIONS

1. $3 + 2 \times 4 =$ 3. $4 \times 3 - 5 =$ 5. $(9 + 2) \times 2 =$
2. $(10 - 4) \div 3 =$ 4. $15 - 8 \div 2 =$ 6. $3 \times 4 \div 2 + 5 =$

Prime Numbers

A prime number is a number that has exactly two different factors: itself and one. So prime numbers cannot be negative numbers, 0, or 1; none of those fits the definition. It is a good idea to memorize the first six or so prime numbers so that you do not have to spend time figuring these out on the test. Any primes after the first six generally do not appear, even on tests that test much harder math, so these are your safest bet. Do you have some index cards ready to make flash cards? The six smallest six prime numbers are 2, 3, 5, 7, 11, and 13.

If you forget these and have to figure out whether a number is prime on the test, follow these steps:

1. Remember that negative numbers, 0, and 1 are not prime.
2. Check whether the number is even (divisible by 2). No prime numbers except 2 are even, so if the number is greater than 2 and even, it is not prime.
3. Check whether the number is divisible by 3. Remember, all numbers that are divisible by 3 have numerals that add up to something that is divisible by 3.
4. It is not really necessary to check divisibility by 4 because anything divisible by 4 is also divisible by 2 (which you took care of in step 2). So check whether the number is divisible by 5. Do you remember the rule to find numbers that are divisible by 5?
5. Keep checking divisibility with higher numbers until you reach half the value of the number in question. If it is not divisible by a number half its size, it is not going to be divisible by anything larger. So if you have not found factors other than the number and one by this point, you have found a prime number.

Let us try this out a few times. If a number is prime, circle Prime. If it is not, circle Not Prime and list which factors it has other than itself and 1. Solutions are at the end of the chapter.

DRILL: PRIME NUMBERS

1. 17   Prime   Not Prime: _____
2. 23   Prime   Not Prime: _____
3. 39   Prime   Not Prime: _____
4. 45   Prime   Not Prime: _____
5. 54   Prime   Not Prime: _____
6. 67   Prime   Not Prime: _____

Prime Factors

Sometimes you will need to calculate the *prime factors* of a number, which are all of the prime numbers that are multiplied together to create that number. Each number only has one *prime factorization*, or way that it can be divided into prime factors. You may be asked specifically to find prime factors, or you may have to find them as part of another problem, such as finding square roots or calculating the diagonal of a rectangle.

To find prime factors, it helps to make what is called a factor tree. Let us use 60 as an example. Start by writing down the number.

Then you need to determine whether it is divisible by the first prime number, which is 2. If it is, draw two branches leading from the number, one for 2 and one for the result of $\frac{60}{2}$, or 30. It should look something like this:

The 2 is there to stay, and now you are going to do the same for 30. It is divisible by 2, so you draw a branch for 2 and branch for $\frac{30}{2}$, or 15.

The 15 is not divisible by 2, so you move on to the next prime number, which is 3. But the 15 is divisible by 3, so you draw a branch for 3 and a branch for $\frac{15}{3}$, or 5.

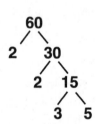

Now you are done, because the tips of the branches are all prime numbers: 2, 2, 3, and 5. So the prime factors of 60 are 2, 2, 3, and 5, and therefore, $2 \times 2 \times 3 \times 5 = 60$.

Ready to try some on your own? Solutions to the drill are at the end of the chapter.

DRILL: PRIME FACTORS

1. 36	3. 45	5. 81
2. 42	4. 92	6. 75

EXPONENTS

Exponents are very easy to recognize: Whenever you see a superscript number (like this: 3^2), you are working with exponents. Just for the sake of simplicity in this section, we are going to give some terminology; *exponents* themselves are the numbers in superscript, whereas the number being raised to an exponent is called a *base*. So in 5^2, 5 is the base and 2 is the exponent. Exponents are sort of shorthand for multiplication; they tell you how many times the same number is being multiplied together. For example, if you see 2^4, that is the same as $2 \times 2 \times 2 \times 2$, or 2 multiplied four times.

$$2 = 2^1$$
$$2 \times 2 = 2^2$$
$$2 \times 2 \times 2 = 2^3$$
$$2 \times 2 \times 2 \times 2 = 2^4$$

. . . and so on.

Just to solidify your familiarity with exponents, let us do a short drill. If you see the exponent (with a superscript number, such as 2^4), write out the multiplication (such as $2 \times 2 \times 2 \times 2$). If you see the multiplication, write the exponent. Solutions are at the end of the chapter.

DRILL: EXPONENTS 1

1. $3^5 =$ 3. $2^3 =$ 5. $3 \times 3 =$
2. $4^3 =$ 4. $6 \times 6 \times 6 \times 6 =$ 6. $8 \times 8 \times 8 \times 8 =$

Now that you have refamiliarized yourself with the concept of exponents, let us review how to work with them. Whenever you have exponents that are being multiplied, divided, or raised to other exponents, there are a few rules to follow. Let us look at some examples.

- **Multiplication:** If a problem has exponents of the same base being multiplied, such as $3^2 \times 3^5$, you combine or *add* the exponents to get 3^7.
- **Division:** If a problem has exponents of the same base being divided, such as $4^7 \div 4^5$, you *subtract* the exponents to get 4^2.
- **Exponents:** If an exponent is raised to another exponent, such as $(3^2)^4$, you *multiply* the exponents to get 3^8.

Warning: It is *really* easy to confuse multiplication of exponents and raising exponents to exponents, so be careful! Also, you need to be aware that if you are dealing with two different bases, you cannot combine the exponents in any way—by adding, subtracting, multiplying, or dividing. For example, 4^3 and 3^2 cannot be combined, because their bases (4 and 3) are not the same. (And yes, technically there is an exception to this, and that is when one base can be raised to an exponent to equal the other base. But you are extremely unlikely to see that situation on nursing school entrance exams, so we are not going to spend time on it here.)

Now it is time for some more practice. In each of the following, combine the exponents using the above rules, or write "cannot be combined" if the bases are unequal. You do not need to actually calculate the result. Solutions are at the end of the chapter.

DRILL: EXPONENTS 2

1. $3^2 \times 3^3 =$
3. $2^7 \div 2^3 =$
5. $(2^5)^4 =$
2. $4^5 \times 5^5 =$
4. $x^8 \div x^3 =$
6. $(y^2)^3 =$

Squares

You may have also heard the phrase "two squared" or "five squared"; *squared* means that you raise the base to an exponent of 2. There are a few squares that you really need to memorize, to save yourself a lot of math during the exams. Flash card time!

$1^2 = 1$	$7^2 = 49$	$13^2 = 169$
$2^2 = 4$	$8^2 = 64$	$14^2 = 196$
$3^2 = 9$	$9^2 = 81$	$15^2 = 225$
$4^2 = 16$	$10^2 = 100$	$20^2 = 400$
$5^2 = 25$	$11^2 = 121$	$25^2 = 625$
$6^2 = 36$	$12^2 = 144$	

ROOTS

Roots are the opposite of exponents; they generally ask you which number has been multiplied by itself to get a number. For the purposes of nursing school entrance exams, we will only deal with calculating *square roots*, which means finding which numbers have been raised to an exponent of 2. For example, if you need to calculate the square root of 25, it will look something like this:

$$\sqrt{25} = ?$$

One huge help when dealing with square roots is to know your *squares* from the Exponents section above. If you have those memorized, you know that $5^2 = 25$, and therefore $\sqrt{25} = 5$ We call 25 a *perfect square,* because it is the result of squaring a single integer. But if you are not dealing with a perfect square or you forget one of the squares you memorized, you can still calculate the square root. For example:

$$\sqrt{12} = ?$$

Remember calculating prime factors? Those skills are going to come in handy now. To calculate the square root of 12, find its prime factors.

Notice how the prime factor tree has two 2s and one 3. Circle the 2s. For any pair of prime factors, you are going to bring *just one* factor outside of the root sign. So $\sqrt{12} = 2\sqrt{3}$. The 3 has to stay inside, because it is not part of a pair. And that is it!

Let us try another:

$$\sqrt{200} = ?$$

The prime factor tree looks like this:

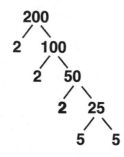

Now you have two 5s and three 2s. The pair of 5s can go outside of the root sign and so can a pair of 2s, but one 2 has to stay inside because it has no partner. When you find more than one pair of factors, you multiply the factors that come outside. So you would multiply 5 and 2 (remember, just one from each pair), which gives 10 on the outside; a 2 stays on the inside. So

$$\sqrt{200} = 10\sqrt{2}.$$

Ready to try some on your own? Just simplify the roots as much as possible; you do not need to do any calculation past what we have done above. Solutions are at the end of the chapter.

DRILL: CALCULATING ROOTS

1. $\sqrt{125} =$ 3. $\sqrt{72} =$ 5. $\sqrt{75} =$

2. $\sqrt{64} =$ 4. $\sqrt{147} =$ 6. $\sqrt{80} =$

DECIMALS

Decimals are one way to express parts of numbers. You have seen decimals all over the place—in price tags, paychecks, and digital scales. Everything after the decimal point is smaller than 1, and the place values have their own names: tenths, hundredths, thousandths, ten thousandths, and so on. So in the number 123.456, 4 is in the *tenths* place, 5 is in the *hundredths* place, and 6 is in the *thousandths* place.

Addition with decimals is exactly the same as it is with whole numbers; you just have to be sure to line up the decimals (remember—neatness counts!). So if a problem asks you to add 123.456 and 789.8099, you would line up the decimals with each other and get:

$$123.456$$
$$+789.8099$$

Adding each column, you get 913.2659.

Subtracting with decimals is also exactly the same; just line up the decimals and subtract, borrowing as you need to.

$$25.64$$
$$-19.72$$
$$\overline{5.92}$$

You only get into new rules when you start multiplying and dividing with decimals. With multiplication, you do not really have to deal with the decimals and the multiplication at the same time—you just have to remember to add an extra step on the end. For example, if a problem asks you to multiply 14.6 and 2.1, you can ignore the decimals and treat it as a regular multiplication problem:

$$146$$
$$\times 21$$
$$\overline{3,066}$$

Now it is time for the extra step. Go back to your original numbers, 14.6 and 2.1, and count the number of digits after the decimal. There is one in each number, or two total. That means your answer has to have two digits after the decimal. So 3,066 becomes 30.66. That is it. Having said that, you *must* be sure to include that last step, or you will definitely get the problem wrong (and the test writers may even include 3,066 in the answer choices so that you do not know you have made a mistake and therefore will not correct yourself). Tricky, but that is what the test creators like to do.

Let us try another one: 3.49 × 6.8. First, ignore the decimals and line them up like a regular multiplication problem:

$$349$$
$$\times 68$$
$$\overline{23,732}$$

Then count the digits after the decimals: There are two in 3.49 and one in 6.8, giving you three total. So your answer also must have three digits after the decimal: 23.732. Done!

With division, the rules change a little bit, which is both good news and bad news. The good news is that you do not have to worry about remainders;

remainders and decimals just do not mix. The better news is that dividing with decimals is usually kept pretty straightforward on these tests. Really, the only (kind of) bad news is that sometimes, you have to pay a little extra attention to what you are doing.

When dividing with decimals, you can ignore the decimals again, just like with multiplication. So if the problem says $4.8 \div 1.6$, you would put those numbers into our regular long division format: $1.6 \overline{)4.8}$

When you divide, you get 3. Here is the part where you have to pay attention to what you are doing: To determine how many digits are behind the decimal, you take the number of digits behind the decimal in the dividend (4.8) and subtract the number of digits behind the decimal in the divisor (1.6). Because there is one digit behind the decimal in each of these numbers, you have $1 - 1$, which equals 0. That means there are zero digits after the decimal in the answer (or we move the decimal zero places), so the answer remains 3.

Now try some problems with decimals. Solutions are at the end of the chapter.

DRILL: DECIMALS

1. $4.2 + 1.83 =$ 4. $2.4 - 1.99 =$ 7. $1.45 \div 0.5 =$
2. $0.95 + 1.28 =$ 5. $0.12 \times 0.27 =$ 8. $2.06 \div 0.4 =$
3. $82.4 - 7.93 =$ 6. $6.23 \times 0.4 =$

FRACTIONS

Fractions express the same kind of idea as decimals—basically, you are dealing with some parts smaller than one. The top of the fraction is called the *numerator* and the bottom is the *denominator*. The denominator tells you how many pieces the whole is being divided into, and the numerator tells you how many of those pieces you are dealing with. For example, if Scott has $\frac{2}{3}$ of a candy bar, the candy bar has been divided up into three pieces, and he has two of them. If Joanne counts 10 marbles in a bag and 7 of them are blue, $\frac{7}{10}$ of the marbles in the bag are blue.

Of course, sometimes fractions represent larger numbers than they seem to. Perhaps Heather tells you that $\frac{2}{5}$ of the employees in her office manage at least one other person. You know that Heather works in a large office, so she is probably talking about more than literally two people out of five in the whole office. The fraction is one way to present "two in every five." But how did she come up with that number? Perhaps there are 1,000 people who work in her office, and she heard a statistic that 400 of them are managers. That means the fraction was originally $\frac{400}{1000}$. Those are pretty big numbers to manipulate, so we reduce fractions to make them more manageable. Also, on exams, you generally will have to reduce any fractions you work with because the correct answers are reduced as much as they can be, which means they have had as much as possible divided out of both the numerator and denominator—whatever you divide out of one of them, you must do with the other, as well. (By the way, you probably learned in school to reduce by finding the greatest common factor, but we are going to do it a different way. Sometimes it takes a few more steps, but each step is much less stressful and therefore better for your test scores overall.)

Let us reduce $\frac{400}{1000}$. The first thing you should look for to reduce is whether there are 0s at the end of both the numerator and the denominator. In this case, there are two 0s in the numerator and three 0s in the denominator. Remember, you cannot do something to one part that you could not do to the other part, so in this case you can remove just two 0s from both parts. (It is actually not just removing 0s, of course; it is dividing by 100. This applies only to 0s; you could not just remove 3s on the end of both the numerator and denominator!)

Now your fraction is $\frac{4}{10}$. After removing 0s (i.e., a dividing by 10 or 100 or 1,000), you look for other numbers to divide by. Remember the divisibility rules you reviewed in the Integers section? Those really come in handy here. Two is always a good one to check toward the beginning of the process; if both the numerator and the denominator are even, divide them both by 2 as many times as you can.

In this case, the numerator and the denominator are divisible by 2, so your fraction is now $\frac{2}{5}$. You cannot divide by 2 again because 5 is odd. You cannot divide by 3 either, because neither 2 nor 5 is divisible by 3. This is kind of similar to checking possible factors and trying to determine whether a number is prime; once you have reached halfway to the larger number, you can stop. The fraction $\frac{2}{5}$ is reduced as much as it can be. (One other way to tell that it is reduced is that both numbers are prime. Not *all* reduced fractions have two primes, but if you do have two primes, you know the fraction is reduced.) Let us try some more reducing:

What is the most reduced form of $\frac{96}{32}$? This problem does not let you divide by 10 or 100 because there are no 0s at the end, so let us go straight to 2. Both the numerator and the denominator are divisible by 2, giving you $\frac{48}{16}$.

Again, you can divide by 2, giving you $\frac{24}{8}$. Divide again by 2 to get $\frac{12}{4}$. And dividing *again* by 2 gives you $\frac{6}{2}$. Divide again and you have $\frac{3}{1}$ or just 3. One more:

What is the most reduced form of $\frac{15}{130}$? Again, you do not have 0s at the end, but this time you do not have two even numbers either. Checking divisibility for 3, you see that 15 is divisible but 130 is not. There is no reason to check for 4, because 15 is not even (and all numbers divisible by 4 are definitely even). Both are divisible by 5, so divide. Your new numerator is $15 \div 5 = 3$. Your new denominator is $130 \div 5 = 26$. The fraction must be reduced now because you know you cannot divide by 3 or anything smaller than 3. So your answer is $\frac{3}{26}$.

It is your turn to reduce some fractions. Solutions are at the end of the chapter.

DRILL: REDUCING FRACTIONS

1. $\frac{40}{55} =$ 3. $\frac{64}{16} =$ 5. $\frac{12}{54} =$

2. $\frac{81}{45} =$ 4. $\frac{72}{28} =$ 6. $\frac{321}{243} =$

Adding and Subtracting Fractions

You may have learned in school that to add and subtract fractions, you need to find the least common multiple of the denominators or something to that effect. That is a good method, but we are going to use a shortcut method called the bowtie for our purposes. This method has three steps and it can be used on any two fractions, no matter whether you are adding or subtracting.

Let us try an example:

$$\frac{1}{2}$$

The first step of the bowtie is to multiply following the arrows below:

$$\frac{1}{2} \diagdown\!\!\!\!\!\diagup \frac{1}{3} = ?$$

So now you have $3 \times 1 = 3$ and $2 \times 1 = 2$. The second step is to add or subtract your new numbers, based on the operator in the problem. Here you have an addition sign, so you add: $3 + 2 = 5$. The result, 5, is the numerator of your answer. The third step is to multiply the denominators to get the denominator of your answer. In this case, $2 \times 3 = 6$, so your answer is $\frac{5}{6}$.

Let us try another:

$$\frac{5}{8} - \frac{3}{5}$$

Step 1 involves multiplying across in the direction of the arrows.

$$\frac{5}{8} \diagdown\!\!\!\!\!\diagup \frac{3}{5} = ?$$

$$5 \times 5 = 25 \text{ and } 8 \times 3 = 24$$

Step 2 involves adding or subtracting, according to the operation sign, to get the numerator of the correct answer.

$$25 - 24 = 1$$

Step 3 involves multiplying denominators to get the denominator of the correct answer.

$$8 \times 5 = 40$$

So the correct answer is $\dfrac{1}{40}$.

Now it is time to try a few on your own. The solutions to the drill are at the end of the chapter.

DRILL: ADDING AND SUBTRACTING FRACTIONS

1. $\dfrac{4}{5} + \dfrac{3}{4} =$ 4. $\dfrac{5}{2} + \dfrac{6}{7} =$ 7. $\dfrac{8}{9} - \dfrac{2}{3} =$

2. $\dfrac{1}{3} + \dfrac{5}{7} =$ 5. $\dfrac{4}{5} - \dfrac{1}{2} =$ 8. $\dfrac{2}{3} - \dfrac{1}{5} =$

3. $\dfrac{2}{9} + \dfrac{3}{5} =$ 6. $\dfrac{7}{5} - \dfrac{3}{4} =$

Multiplying and Dividing Fractions

Multiplying fractions, by comparison, is pretty easy. All you have to do is multiply the numerators, then multiply the denominators. For example:

$$\frac{3}{2} \times \frac{2}{5} = ?$$

The calculation $3 \times 2 = 6$ makes 6 the numerator of the fraction. The calculation $2 \times 5 = 10$ makes 10 the denominator. So your new fraction is $\dfrac{6}{10}$, but that needs to be reduced to be a correct answer on most tests; you can reduce it to $\dfrac{3}{5}$.

Dividing fractions is almost the same, but there is one step to add at the beginning: You must flip the second fraction first, and then you can just multiply straight across as you did for multiplying fractions. So if you start with this problem:

$$\frac{3}{10} \div \frac{5}{4} = ?$$

You would just flip the second fraction so that your new problem looks like this:

$$\frac{3}{10} \times \frac{4}{5} = ?$$

Multiply straight across and you get $3 \times 4 = 12$ for the numerator and $10 \times 5 = 50$ for the denominator. $\dfrac{12}{50}$ reduces to $\dfrac{6}{25}$, so that is your answer.

One thing to note: Sometimes you may see fraction division problems expressed this way:

$$\frac{\frac{3}{10}}{\frac{5}{4}} = ?$$

A line separating a numerator from a denominator is essentially a division sign, so this is really the same as $\frac{3}{10} \div \frac{5}{4}$. Feel free to rewrite it that way first if it makes things easier to work!

Now it is your turn. Solutions are at the end of the chapter.

DRILL: MULTIPLYING AND DIVIDING FRACTIONS

1. $\frac{1}{5} \times \frac{3}{10} =$ 4. $\frac{4}{9} \times \frac{1}{7} =$ 7. $\frac{8}{3} \div \frac{5}{6} =$

2. $\frac{1}{2} \times \frac{4}{5} =$ 5. $\frac{3}{8} \div \frac{1}{2} =$ 8. $\frac{4}{5} \div \frac{3}{10} =$

3. $\frac{2}{3} \times \frac{5}{6} =$ 6. $\frac{6}{7} \div \frac{3}{1} =$

Comparing Fractions

You can use the bowtie method to compare two fractions as well, and the process is even shorter than for adding and subtracting. Given two fractions side-by-side, just multiply in the direction of the arrows again.

$$\frac{3}{8} \quad \diagup\hspace{-1.2em}\diagdown \quad \frac{1}{4}$$

In this example, you end up with 12 on the left and 8 on the right, which means that the fraction on the left is larger than the fraction on the right.

Mixed Numbers

Occasionally, you will see numbers such as $1\frac{3}{4}$ or $3\frac{5}{6}$. These are called *mixed numbers*—numbers that are fractions but larger than 1. To add, subtract, or otherwise manipulate them, you must convert them to improper fractions, which are fractions that have a larger numerator than denominator. To convert a mixed number to an improper fraction requires two steps.

Let us take $3\frac{5}{6}$ as an example. Step 1 is to multiply the integer (in this case, 3) by the denominator (in this case, 6), which works out to $3 \times 6 = 18$. Step 2 is to add the result to the numerator, which is 5. So that looks like $\frac{18 + 5}{6}$, which solves as $\frac{23}{6}$. Done!

How about $1\frac{3}{4}$? Multiply the integer in front by the denominator ($1 \times 4 = 4$), then add it to the numerator $\frac{4 + 3}{4} = \frac{7}{4}$. And you are done; $1\frac{3}{4} = \frac{7}{4}$.

Once a mixed number is converted to an improper fraction, you can treat it exactly the same as a regular fraction; follow the same rules for adding, subtracting, multiplying, dividing, reducing, and anything else you can think of to do to a fraction.

Ready to try a few more? Solutions are at the end of the chapter.

DRILL: CONVERTING MIXED NUMBERS TO IMPROPER FRACTIONS

1. $2\frac{2}{3} =$ 3. $3\frac{3}{5} =$ 5. $2\frac{3}{7} =$

2. $1\frac{5}{6} =$ 4. $4\frac{1}{3} =$ 6. $4\frac{5}{8} =$

One final note on fractions: Any integer can be converted into a fraction by making it the numerator with 1 as the denominator, so if you need to subtract a fraction from an integer, it is a good idea to take that quick step first.

PERCENTAGES

You almost certainly deal with (or at least see) percentages every single day. If you think about it, there is a good chance that you have seen one or all of the following examples on a regular basis:

- Sales tax of 7% on your purchase
- Clearance sales offering 75% off the lowest marked price
- A 3% increase in inflation
- Annual interest of 19.99% on a credit card balance
- A 15% gratuity at a restaurant

So even if percentages were not a frequent topic on nursing school entrance exams (which they are), it would make your everyday life easier to know how to deal with them well.

First, you need to know that *percent* means *out of one hundred*. So if you are paying a 15 percent gratuity, you are paying 15 cents for every 100 cents (or one dollar) you have already paid. Have you ever heard the expression "pennies on the dollar"? Well, it is the same as saying *percent*—if you are paying only a few pennies on the dollar, you are paying only a few *percent* of the original price. (Of course, ads that say you are paying pennies on the dollar could well mean you will pay 80 pennies on the dollar, but the impression they want to give is that you are paying only a few percent.)

CONVERTING FRACTIONS, DECIMALS, AND PERCENTS

One of the most important things to know about percentages is how to convert fractions, decimals, and percents. In fact, some exams have sections dedicated to these conversions, but the lucky thing is that you can memorize the most common conversions, and learn a basic formula to calculate the rest. Ready with your index cards?

Percent	Fraction	Decimal
5%	$\frac{1}{20}$	0.05
10%	$\frac{1}{10}$	0.1 or 0.10
15%	$\frac{3}{20}$	0.15
20%	$\frac{1}{5}$	0.2 or 0.20
25%	$\frac{1}{4}$	0.25
30%	$\frac{3}{10}$	0.3 or 0.30
35%	$\frac{7}{20}$	0.35
40%	$\frac{2}{5}$	0.4 or 0.40
45%	$\frac{9}{20}$	0.45
50%	$\frac{1}{2}$	0.5 or 0.50
55%	$\frac{11}{20}$	0.55
60%	$\frac{3}{5}$	0.6 or 0.60
65%	$\frac{13}{20}$	0.65
70%	$\frac{7}{10}$	0.7 or .70
75%	$\frac{3}{4}$	0.75
80%	$\frac{4}{5}$	0.8 or 0.80
85%	$\frac{17}{20}$	0.85
90%	$\frac{9}{10}$	0.9 or 0.90
95%	$\frac{19}{20}$	0.95
100%	$\frac{1}{1}$ or 1	1 or 1.0 or 1.00

Percent	Fraction	Decimal
12.5%	$\frac{1}{8}$	0.125
37.5%	$\frac{3}{8}$	0.375
62.5%	$\frac{5}{8}$	0.625
87.5%	$\frac{7}{8}$	0.875

Should you come across a problem that is unfamiliar on one of your exams (or you blank out, as even the best test-takers do from time to time), remember that you can always follow these steps to convert from one system to another:

- **From percents to decimals.** Take off the percent sign and move the decimal two places to the left.
  75% becomes 0.75
  500% becomes 5.0

- **From decimals to percents.** Do the opposite; move the decimal two places to the right and add a percent sign.
  0.345 becomes 34.5%
  0.6 becomes 60%
  2.6 becomes 260%

- **From fractions to percents.** Treat the fraction as a division problem; actually move the numbers into a division sign and work the math. Then move the decimal two places to the right and add a percent sign at the end.
  $\frac{4}{5}$ becomes 0.8, or 80%
  $\frac{3}{8}$ becomes 0.375, or 37.5%

- **From percents to fractions.** Remove the percent sign and make the number the numerator of a fraction, with 100 on the bottom. Reduce, and you are done. (And if you need to brush up on reducing, see the section on fractions.)
  65% becomes $\frac{65}{100}$, which reduces to $\frac{13}{20}$
  120% becomes $\frac{120}{100}$, which reduces to $\frac{6}{5}$

- **From fractions to decimals.** Treat the fraction as a division problem; actually move the numbers into a division sign and work the math. This time you do not have to convert to percents, so you are done!
  $\frac{1}{4}$ becomes 0.25
  $\frac{11}{20}$ becomes 0.55

- **From decimals to fractions.** Move the decimal two places to the right and make the number the numerator of a fraction, with 100 on the bottom. Reduce and you are done.

0.75 becomes $\dfrac{75}{100}$, which reduces to $\dfrac{3}{4}$

0.60 becomes $\dfrac{60}{100}$, which reduces to $\dfrac{3}{5}$

Changing a percent or decimal to a fraction is less common than the other four types of conversions, but should you need to do it in the context of any problem type, there is your guide. One note on converting from fractions: If a problem asks you to convert from a ratio to a decimal or percent, it is the exact same as converting from a fraction; just take the ratio and change it into a fraction (for example, 3:2 becomes $\dfrac{3}{2}$).

Ready for some practice on your own? Solutions are at the end of the chapter.

DRILL: CONVERTING FRACTIONS, DECIMALS, AND PERCENTS

1. What is 27.5% as a decimal?

2. What is 33% as a decimal?

3. What is 0.425 as a percent?

4. What is 3.9 as a percent?

5. What is $\dfrac{12}{15}$ as a decimal?

6. What is $\dfrac{8.75}{10}$ as a percent?

Calculating Percentages Using Fractions or Decimals

As you may have noticed from the examples at the beginning of this section, you really never deal with percentages alone; a percent is only significant when it is a percent *of something else*. That means that you are always multiplying the percent times another number. So if you are calculating 7 percent sales tax on a $20 purchase, you multiply 7% × 20. You do that by converting the percentage to either a fraction or a decimal, whichever you prefer, and multiplying out:

$$0.07 \times 20 = 1.4$$

or

$$\frac{7}{100} \times 20 = \frac{140}{100} = 1.4$$

Either way, you end up with 1.4, or $1.40 in sales tax.

Let us take another example. You find a shirt on clearance and it is marked at 75% off the original price of $40. How do you find 75% of $40? With decimals, that is $0.75 \times 40 = 30$. With fractions, that is $\dfrac{75}{100} \times 40 = \dfrac{3000}{100} = 30$.

So 75% of $40 is $30. But remember what you are calculating; the item is 75% *off,* which is the same as saying $30 off. The clearance price of the item is $40 – $30, or $10. A little ballparking will take you a long way toward the correct answer on these problems; if an item is 75% off, that is *more than half* off, so the final price should be *less than half* of the original.

One more: The bill at a restaurant is $80 and you want to leave a 15 percent gratuity. What is 15% of 80? With decimals, that is $0.15 \times 80 = 12$. With fractions, that is $\frac{15}{100} \times 80 = \frac{1200}{100} = 12$. Either way, you are leaving a $12 tip. By the way, what if the problem asked you to calculate the entire bill, including gratuity? You would just add $12 to the $80 you already had, giving you a $92 total.

Okay, now it is your turn for some practice. Solutions are at the end of the chapter.

DRILL: CALCULATING PERCENTAGES

1. What is 75% of 120?   4. What is 45% of 80?
2. What is 40% of 75?   5. What is 25% of 30?
3. What is 80% of 90?   6. What is 65% of 160?

Translating Word Problems Involving Percents

Some problems are set up as word problems and they appear as if you have to make up an equation to solve them. But actually, you do not have to make up that equation yourself. In fact, all it takes is some translation to take the problem directly from English into equation form. That is great news, because setting up the equation correctly is at least half the battle toward getting that question right.

For example, take the following question:
The number 5 is what percent of 4?

This type of question is extremely common, but do not worry—each word in the question has a direct correlation in math-speak (and the numbers stay the same). So here is the same sentence, translated into a mathematical equation:

$$5 = x\% \times 4$$

You know from your experience with percentages that *percent* means *out of one hundred* or *over one hundred,* so you can do a little bit of manipulating and get $5 = \frac{x}{100} \times 4$, which is the same as $5 = \frac{4x}{100}$. Now you can just solve the equation $5 = \frac{4x}{100}$.

Multiply each side by 100, which gives $500 = 4x$. Then divide each side by 4, which gives $\dfrac{500}{4} = \dfrac{4x}{4}$. And solve: $125 = x$.

If you do not remember how to manipulate the equation, do not worry. We will take it step by step and go into all of the "whys" in the algebra section.

Let us try another translation question:

80 percent of what number is 4?

First, you translate: $\dfrac{80}{100} \times x = 4$. That is the same as $\dfrac{80x}{100} = 4$. Multiply each side by 100 to get $80x = 400$. Divide each side by 80 to get $\dfrac{80x}{80} = \dfrac{400}{80}$. And solve: $x = 5$.

Ready to put these skills to the test? Translate and calculate percentages on the following drill. The solutions are at the end of the chapter.

DRILL: TRANSLATING WORD PROBLEMS INVOLVING PERCENTS

1. 49 is what percent of 140?
2. 21 is what percent of 70?
3. 36 is what percent of 45?
4. 15% of what number is 12?
5. 80% of what number is 40?
6. 20% of what number is 12?

Other Shortcuts

Now that you have learned how to approach most percent problems on your entrance exams, here are some other shortcuts to help out in a pinch (on tests and in real life). If you do not like multiplying by 15 or 12.5, you can use the hints to "brute force" your way through percentage problems when your math muscles just are not in shape.

- **You can calculate 10% of anything.** Calculating 10% is just moving the decimal one place to the left, so 10% of 50 is 5, 10% of 0.3 is 0.03, and 10% of 873 is 87.3. This alone can help you ballpark if, say, you are asked to take 12% of a number; just find 10% and pick the one that is a little bit more.
- **You can calculate 1% of anything.** Calculating 1% is just moving the decimal *two* places to the left, so 1% of 400 is 4, 1% of 62 is 0.62, and 1% of 0.4 is 0.004. Again, helpful for ballparking on its own, but when you combine it with your ability to take 10%, you are able to add or subtract 1% and zoom in on the correct answer with ease.
- **You can calculate 5% of anything.** Remember how you can calculate 10% of anything? Well, calculating 5% of that number is the same as calculating 10% of the same number, then dividing it by two. Between now and your test, practice calculating tips such as this: Take 10% of the bill (and write it down if you wish), then take half of that and add it to the 10% you wrote down. Voila—you have just calculated a 15% gratuity.

MEAN, MEDIAN, AND MODE

Mean, median, and mode are ways of interpreting (or finding the significance of) a set of related numbers. On exams, you may be asked to calculate them based simply on some given numbers, or based on data that is presented in a chart or graph. Before calculating them, be sure you know which one the problem is asking for. It is important to know the difference between mean, median, and mode, based on what each one measures.

Mean

Mean is basically another word for average. When you are calculating a grade based on several tests, or a batting average based on many at-bats, you are calculating a mean. Calculating a mean involves adding and dividing. You are generally given a list of numbers—such as 8, 11, 4, 17, and 5—and asked to find their mean.

To do this, add up the list of numbers: $8 + 11 + 4 + 17 + 5 = 45$. Then divide by the number of numbers in the original list, which in this case is 5. The expression $\frac{45}{5} = 9$. And you are done! The average of 8, 11, 4, 17, and 5 is 9.

Now it is your turn to find the means of the following number sets. Solutions are at the end of the chapter.

DRILL: MEAN

1. 2, 6, 9, 4, 14
2. 9, 2, 5, 11, 18
3. 7, 21, –5, 8, 4
4. –2, 9, –5, 6

Median

A *median* is simply the number in the middle in an ordered list. Calculating a median involves less math—it is really just putting numbers in order and eliminating some of them.

For example, if you are asked to find the median of the list 8, 11, 4, 17, and 5, you would start by putting them in numerical order: 4, 5, 8, 11, 17. And then choose the number in the middle. For a short list such as this one, you can probably see that 8 is in the middle; however, to check yourself or to find the middle of a longer list, start eliminating the pairs on the ends. That means the 4 and the 17 are first—just cross them out. Then the 5 and 11.

When you are left with one only number, that is your median (in this case, 8). Another good reason to eliminate end pairs is to make sure that you do not actually have two numbers left in the middle. If that happens, you just take the mean of those two numbers, and that is your median.

Ready to try finding medians by yourself? Solutions are at the end of the chapter.

DRILL: MEDIAN

1. 3, 5, 2, 7, –2
2. 4, 8, 2, 7, 3
3. –3, 5, 1, 9
4. –5, 3, 2, 10, 2

Mode

The *mode* is the number that appears most frequently in the list. As with medians, it is a good idea to put the list of numbers in order first, because that makes the repeated numbers tend to stand out.

Let us take this list: 11, 8, –4, 11, 4, 17, and 5. First, you would carefully put the numbers in order. (It is a good idea to cross out numbers as you go, and remember, a negative number never has the same value as a positive—so it is not the same number!) Your ordered list looks like this: –4, 4, 5, 8, 11, 11, 17.

If you want, feel free to cross off numbers that only appear once after you have made your list. So you would cross off –4, 4 (remember, they are not the same), 5, 8, and 17. That just leaves two 11s, so 11 is your mode.

You are unlikely to run into this scenario, but in case you do find two different values that appear the most, both of them are modes. You do not "average" them by finding their mean; they stay as they are. For example, in the list –4, 4, 5, 5, 8, 11, 11, and 17, 5 and 11 are the modes.

It is your turn to find the modes. Solutions are at the end of this chapter.

DRILL: MODE

1. 2, 10, –2, 3, 8, 2
2. 3, 5, 3, –5, 0
3. 4, –2, 2, –3, 5, –3
4. 5, 12, 11, 11, 9, 12, 11

ALGEBRA

Algebra is usually one of the most intimidating topics for people who have not been to math class for a long time. It is easy to freeze up when you see letters instead of the numbers that you are used to working with. But before you resolve to just skip all of the algebra questions, remember these things:

1. Nursing school entrance exams only test basic algebra at most, so a little review goes a long way.
2. If x and y make you freeze up, you can rewrite any algebra problem so that it uses blanks or symbols that are more friendly.

Let us look at a traditional math problem:

$$2 + 4 = \underline{\quad}$$

In this problem, there is an unknown. It is represented by a ____. What is the value of the ____? If you answered 6, you are correct.

Algebra problems are just a little different. Algebra problems essentially say this instead:

$$2 + \underline{\hspace{1cm}} = 6.$$

What is the value of the blank now? If you said 4, you are correct. But how did you know that? You probably have this sum memorized, or you may not have even noticed that you quickly and automatically performed an operation in your head. If you did not get it, that is okay, too. To figure out the value of the blank, you need to figure out how many are between 2 and 6, which is just another way to say the *difference* between 2 and 6. So you would subtract 2 from 6 to get 4.

Solving for *x*

Luckily though, you really do not have to go through this process of figuring that stuff out. Most algebra test questions have to do with solving for the unknown, usually called *x*, and there are very straightforward rules to follow to do this. Basically, they go like this:

1. Get *x* alone. The main goal is to get *x* on one side of the equal sign and everything else on the other. That's because you want to end up with a statement that says, *x equals this*. When you get that, you have solved for *x*.

2. Do not play favorites. In the process of getting *x* alone, whatever you do to one side of the equation, you have to do the same thing to the other side. Think of it this way: When you see an equation, it is like seeing this:

The scales are perfectly balanced right now, because the two sides are equal. If you were to add something to one side but not the other, the scales would tip and you would no longer have an equation, and that is not good.

Let us see how those rules work out in the above example, $2 + \underline{\hspace{1cm}} = 6$, which can be rewritten as $2 + x = 6$. The *x* is the variable, (also called an unknown), which could also be represented as a blank space, question mark, smiley face, or whichever other symbol you want to use. According to rule 1, you need to get x alone, which means you need to get rid of that 2 that is being added to it. The rules for this are also very straightforward:

1. If a variable has a number *added* to it, *subtract* to get rid of the number.
2. If a variable is being *multiplied* by a number, *divide* to get rid of the number.

The other two rules are exactly the same, just reversed:

3. If a variable has a number *subtracted* from it, *add* to get rid of the number.
4. If a variable is being *divided* by a number, *multiply* to get rid of the number.

In $2 + x = 6$, the variable has a 2 added to it. So you would subtract the 2 to get the x alone. But you cannot just subtract it from the right side of the equation; that would be playing favorites. You must also subtract it from the left side. So your equation looks like this:

$$2 - 2 + x = 6 - 2$$

Now you have $0 + x = 4$, or just $x = 4$. You have solved for x.

Let us solve another problem together, and then you can solve a few problems on your own.

$$4x = 12$$

In case you do not remember from algebra class, $4x$ is another way of saying 4 times x. You could also see it written as $4(x)$, but it all means the same thing: 4 multiplied by x. When a number is multiplied by a variable, you divide by that number to get the variable alone. Dividing by 4 on both sides gives you: $\frac{4x}{4} = \frac{12}{4}$. So $x = \frac{12}{4}$, which means $x = 3$.

Ready to try some on your own? Here's a short drill. Solutions can be found at the end of the chapter.

DRILL: SOLVING FOR X

1. $3 + 2x = 7$
2. $3x - 10 = 5$
3. $5 + \dfrac{x}{2} = 12$
4. $4x + 3 = 15$
5. $2x + 8 = 4$
6. $\dfrac{4x}{5} + 7 = 15$

Combining Terms

Some algebra problems will not ask you to solve for x at all; in fact, solving for x will not even be possible. These problems just ask you to simplify as much as possible. For example, you could see a problem that asks

$4x - 2x + 3x =$
  (A) $9x$
  (B) $5x$
  (C) $3x$
  (D) $-x$

See how all of the answer choices include x? That is a giveaway that the correct answer includes x (makes sense, right?), so you will not actually solve for x and get rid of it. All you have to do is combine terms that are alike. The $4x$, $2x$, and $3x$ are alike, because they all include the x. That means you can add and subtract them just as if they were regular numbers. So $4x - 2x + 3x = 5x$, just like $4 - 2 + 3 = 5$. Remember though, that if the test-makers had thrown in a term that was not multiplied by x, you could not have combined that term with the others. So $4x - 2x + 3x + 6$, for example, would equal $5x + 6$.

Even when a problem requires solving for x, you may still need to combine terms to do it. For example:

If $2x + 3x = 15$, what is the value of x?

(A) $\dfrac{5}{2}$

(B) 3

(C) 5

(D) $\dfrac{2}{5}$

Clearly, you are going to be solving for x because the problem asks for the value of x. But you cannot get x alone on one side until the terms have been combined. Both terms are alike, so you can simply add $2x$ and $3x$ to get $5x$. Now you have $5x = 15$. What else do you need to do to get x alone? Because it is multiplied by 5, you need to divide each side by 5:

$$\frac{5x}{5} = \frac{15}{5}$$

Once you reduce, $x = 3$ (choice B).

Translating Algebra Word Problems

Some algebra problems really just involve translating from English into math, as you did with percentages. For example: If $10x$ is equal to 42 more than $28x$, what is the value of x?

Although you are unlikely to see percents in algebra translation, you still have a few translations that you have seen before:

- "Of" translates to $\times$ (multiplication).
- "Is" (as well as *has, have, do, does, equals,* and some other words) translates to $=$ (equal sign).
- "Number" translates to x or any variable of your choosing.

You are also more likely to see these words:

- "More than" means you need to add.
- "Less than" means you need to subtract the number *before* the "less than."
- "Divided by" or "multiplied by" means you need to divide or multiply.

Let us try a couple together, shall we?

If 8 more than a certain number is the same as three times that number, what is the number?

Translation:

$$8 + x = 3x$$

And then solve. The most direct way to get x alone is to remove the x from the left side.

$$8 + x - x = 3x - x$$
$$8 = 2x$$
$$\frac{8}{2} = \frac{2x}{2}$$
$$4 = x$$

And you're done! Try another:

If 2 less than 3 times a certain number is 13, what is the value of that number?

Translation: $3x - 2 = 13$. And then solve:

$$3x - 2 + 2 = 13 + 2$$
$$3x = 15$$
$$\frac{3x}{3} = \frac{15}{3}$$
$$x = 5$$

Done!

Ready to try a few on your own? Solutions are at the end of the chapter.

DRILL: TRANSLATING ALGEBRA WORD PROBLEMS

1. If 10 more than a certain number is the same as 3 times that number, what is the number?
2. When a certain number is multiplied by 5, that's the same as increasing its value by 8. What is the value of that number?
3. A certain number is 4 less than 5 multiplied by 10. What is the value of that number?
4. A certain number divided by $\frac{3}{4}$ is equal to 40. What is the value of that number?

Last Notes on Translating Algebra Problems

You could also see questions that cannot be solved completely, where the point is just to translate from English to math. These can be identified pretty easily by looking at the answer choices, because the answer choices have full equations instead of single numbers. Typically, these equations also have more than one variable (which is why you cannot solve them completely; it takes more than one equation to solve for more than one variable). Here are some example phrasings for these problems.

Sandra has 3 less than 4 times the number of marbles that Marla has.
Mr. Geary is 5 years more than twice his daughter Kelly's age.
As of today, Abbey has worked at the hospital half as long as Lauren has.

Remember, all you have to do on problems such as these is translate, and maybe do a little bit of rearranging to make the equation look like one of the answer choices (and as long as you do the same thing on each side of the equation, that is fine).

Systems of Equations

Occasionally you will run into problems that ask you to "solve for a system of equations" or "make both of these mathematical statements true." Although the terminology sounds fancy, these problems really are not hard to do. You will be presented with two equations, and each answer choice will contain a pair of values for the variables in the equations. All you have to do is select the answer choice that satisfies both equations, and you can tell just by substituting the answers into the equations. Be careful to check both equations! Here's an example:

Solve this system of equations:
$2x + 3y = 19$
$3x + 2y = 21$
  (A) $x = 3, y = 5$
  (B) $x = 5, y = 3$
  (C) $x = 3, y = 2$
  (D) $x = 2, y = 3$

There are more complex mathematical ways to solve, but why not just use the values given in the answer choices instead? Let us start with answer choice A and substitute the value into the first equation:

$$2(3) + 3(5) = 19$$

That gives you $6 + 15 = 19$, so choice A is clearly incorrect. Move on to choice B.

$$2(5) + 3(3) = 19$$

$10 + 9 = 19$ . . . that works! But before you pick it, you also have to make sure it works for the second equation.

$$3(5) + 2(3) = 21$$
$$15 + 6 = 21$$

Again, that works, so you do not even have to look at the remaining answers; B is correct.

Factoring

You may see a question or two on your exams that ask you to factor an algebraic expression. Basically, this means "divide out as much as you can" from each of the expression. For instance, if you are asked to factor $2x^2 + x^3$, it is your job to find the common numbers and exponents in each term being added. The only thing these terms have in common is x, and you want to divide out as many of them as you can from each term. You can only divide out x^2 from the first term, so that's your limit from the second term, as well. The factored expression looks like this: $x^2(2 + x)$.

CHARTS, GRAPHS, AND TABLES

Charts, graphs, and tables appear in some way on almost every exam you could take for nursing school admission. Luckily, they tend to be fairly straightforward as long as you know what to look for. They also tend to fall into very predictable types, so let us review each type of chart or graph that you are likely to see.

Column Charts

A column chart generally compares categories of information, such as a car model's sales revenue in different regions, numbers of adoptions of different dog breeds, or the number of people who went to see a particular movie by age range. The "columns" in column charts make it easy to compare amounts, because the taller the column, the larger the amount. Here's an example:

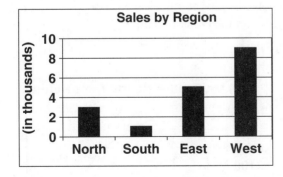

Notice the lines on the bottom and left of the chart. Those are called *axes*. Each axis contains a different kind of information. Generally in a column chart, the *x-axis* (or the line across the bottom) is labeled according to the categories of information (regions where a car was sold, breeds of dog that were adopted, age ranges of people going to see a movie). The axis on the left side of the columns generally displays numbers that represent how many cars were sold, dogs were adopted, or people went to see the movie. This is called the *y-axis*. Sometimes, the *y-axis* displays very large numbers, so to save space, the makers of the chart tell you that every unit or "1" on the chart actually represents tens, hundreds, thousands, or even millions. The above chart does that, using the label (*in thousands*).

Occasionally, you could see a column chart that looks like this:

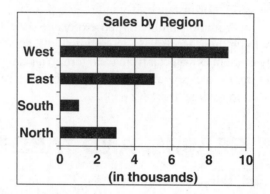

But it is really the same chart, just on its side. The numbers are going to run along the length of the columns to show you "how many" each column represents, so do not be thrown off by the chart being on its side.

Line Graphs

Line graphs are very similar to column charts, but they tend to be used to track progress over time. For example, a line chart may track the closing value of a stock day by day, a patient's temperature hour by hour, or a country's gross domestic product from year to year. Again, the labels across the bottom tell you which categories or units of time you are viewing, and the numbers on the left tell you the values at each point, which may be expressed in larger units. Line graphs look like this:

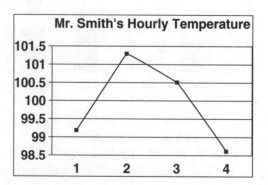

Pie Charts

Pie charts are different from column charts and line graphs in two major ways: First, they have no axes. Second, they do not necessarily have any real values. Instead, pie charts make it easy for you to see percents of a whole. For example, you may see a pie chart that shows the percentage of males versus females in a certain nursing program, the percentage of students who make As, Bs, Cs, Ds, and Fs in a freshman-level class, or the percentage of cars sold that are economy, mid-size, or luxury. For example, take this pie chart:

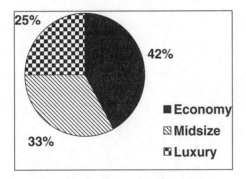

You can easily tell that more economy cars were sold than mid-size, and more mid-size than luxury, but you cannot tell the actual numbers of cars sold in any particular category or in total.

Pie charts are usually labeled with the percentage that each "slice" represents, and the category that is being measured by each slice may be labeled on the pie as well, or the labels might be in a legend (also called a key) near the chart.

Tables

Finally, there are tables, which are just ways to organize numeric data. They are not as visual as charts and graphs, but they can make it easier to display large amounts of data in a small amount of space. They also make it possible to see exact numbers for calculations, whereas using charts and graphs often just allows you to ballpark and compare. Tables look like this:

Movie Ticket Sales		
	Big Blockbuster	Romantic Comedy II	Animated Flick
Kids	973	287	3,492
Adults	4,729	2,841	1,134
Seniors	582	1,397	1,052

Stem-and-Leaf Plots

Stem-and-leaf plots are just a kind of table that, again, makes it easier to display larger amounts of data in limited space. In this case, it replaces a list of numbers and makes it easier to see patterns in the list. These will probably be the least familiar type of chart, graph, or table of all that you will see in this lesson. Here is an example of a stem-and-leaf plot:

Stem	Leaf
4	3 5 8 9 9
5	0 3 8
6	2

Remember your place values? The numbers in the "stem" category (on the left) represent the tens place (and sometimes hundreds or more, but that is rare on these exams). The "leaves" on the right represent the units digits for each stem. So the list represented by this stem-and-leaf plot is:

43, 45, 48, 49, 49, 50, 53, 58, 62

Answering Questions with Charts, Graphs, and Tables

When you see any of these on your test, be sure to check for a few things before you get started with the problem:

1. How many questions refer to it? Usually there are two, sometimes even three questions that refer to one chart, graph, or table, so noting how many questions are involved before you get started can save you some time and confusion. Typically, if there are two questions or more, there is a note above the chart, graph, or table that looks something like this: *Use the chart below to answer questions 9 and 10.*
2. Read the labels. It may sound obvious, but most chart, graph, and table problems become a lot easier when you go into the problem already knowing what information you're given. So be sure to read the title, the category, and value labels on the axes, the legend (if there is one), and any other notes that have been added. Also, note the units on the *y*-axis!
3. Note any trends. Is one column significantly taller than all the other ones? Does the line in a line graph generally point up or down? Is there one tiny slice in a pie chart? Are there more leaves for one stem than any of the others? Do not do any math here; just take a second to notice the data being presented.

Now you are ready to look at some questions.

Use the chart below to answer the following two questions.

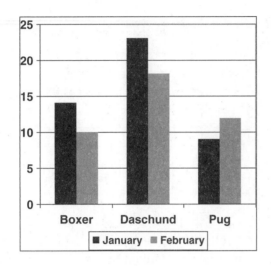

What is the best approximation of the number of dachshunds adopted in both months combined?

    (A) 18

    (B) 23

    (C) 40

    (D) 46

Approximately how many more boxers than pugs were adopted in January?

    (A) 5

    (B) 9

    (C) 12

    (D) 14

Start with the first question, *What is the best approximation of the number of dachshunds adopted in both months combined?* In January, the column for dachshunds is in the middle, either 22 or 23. In February, it is also in the middle, either 17 or 18. So you know the number of dachshunds adopted is between 39 and 41, making choice C the clear winner.

Then answer the second question, *Approximately how many more boxers than pugs were adopted in January?* This time you are focusing on just the January numbers, in black. It looks like the boxers column is almost all the way to the 15 line, so call it 14. The pugs column is almost all the way to the 10 line, so call it 9, giving you a difference of about 5, which is choice A; no other answer comes close.

Are you ready to try some on your own? The solutions to this drill are at the end of the chapter.

DRILL: CHARTS, GRAPHS, AND TABLES

Use the following graph for questions 1–2.

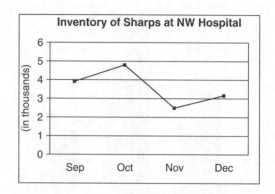

1. Which of the following is the best approximation of the percent decrease in sharps inventory from October to November?

(A) 25
(B) 50
(C) 75
(D) 100

2. If 500 sharps were used between the inventory counts in September and October, approximately how many were purchased in the same time period?

(A) 500
(B) 1,000
(C) 1,500
(D) 2,500

Use the following table for questions 3–4.

Stem	Leaf
1	0 4 4 5
2	2 3 5 6 7 9
4	3 5 8

3. What is the mode of the numbers in the above stem-and-leaf plot?

(A) 10
(B) 14
(C) 25
(D) 26

4. What is the difference between the largest and smallest numbers represented?

(A) 10
(B) 25
(C) 38
(D) 48

GEOMETRY

Geometry is probably one of the more dreaded topics for people who have not been in a math class for a long time, but there is good news. First, there are very few geometry problems on nursing school entrance exams. Second, there are no proofs or theorems, as you might remember from math classes. Third, you are going to be tested only on basic concepts and application. Fourth, geometry is a very concrete topic; most of it deals with shapes and measurements that you can easily see, rather than letters that stand in for numbers. (Okay, there are a *few* letters that stand for numbers in the geometry we are going to cover, but it is still far less abstract than algebra.) We will start with a basic review of the geometric shapes you are likely to see on the exams.

Angles

Okay, angles are not shapes, but they are important. Any time two lines or line segments connect, they form an angle, and that angle can be measured in degrees. Some of the important degree measurements to know are:

- 180 degrees: This is really a straight line.
- 90 degrees: This is probably the most common angle measurement that you will see. Lines that cross each other at a 90-degree angle are *perpendicular* lines. You will see 90-degree angles in right triangles and rectangles (including squares). When you see an angle with a little box where the lines meet, that means it is a 90-degree angle.

That's pretty much it for angles for right now.

Rectangles

Rectangles are four-sided figures and by definition, they have to have four right angles. In fact, "rectangle" is Latin for right angle. (Go ahead, look it up, we'll wait.) Because all four of the angles are "right" angles (meaning they are 90 degrees each), the total degree measure is 360 degrees.

To obtain the *perimeter* of a rectangle (which is the measurement around the outside), you add up the lengths of all of the sides. Hint: There are always two pairs of sides, so if you know the length of one side, you know the length of the side directly opposite. To obtain the *area* of a rectangle, you multiply one side by another side that is *adjacent* to (or right beside) it. The sides are

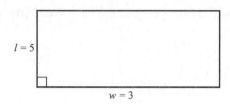

known as *l* and *w* for length and width, but it really does not matter which is which. Here are the formulas:

Perimeter: $P = 2l + 2w$

Area: $A = lw$

What is the perimeter of the rectangle above? _____ (all answers to the questions in this section are at the end of the shapes review, before the drill.)

What is the area of the rectangle above? _____

The word *rectangle* is usually used to mean the kind of shape shown above, where the height is different from the length. But technically, rectangles include squares.

Squares

Squares follow all the same rules that rectangles do, but they have one additional requirement: All sides have to be the same length. So a square is just a rectangle (a four-sided, 360-degree, all–right-angle shape) with all sides the same length.

Because all sides are the same length, squares have some shortcuts once you know one of the sides (abbreviated as *s*): You can multiply by four to get the perimeter or square one side (raise it to an exponent of two) to get the area. Here are the formulas:

Perimeter: $P = 4s$

Area: $A = s^2$

What is the perimeter of the square above? _____

What is the area of the square above? _____

Triangles

Triangles are three-sided figures with angles that add up to 180 degrees. That does not necessarily mean that each angle is 60 degrees; the angles can have any combination of measurements. The triangles that you will deal with most on your entrance exams are *right triangles,* which are triangles that have one right angle. Right triangles look like this:

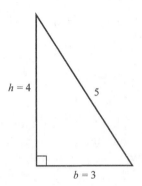

It is good news that you will see mostly right triangles on your exams, because you can figure out the perimeter and area of these triangles much more easily than with other kinds of triangles. Here are the formulas for area and perimeter of a triangle:

Perimeter: $P = s_1 + s_2 + s_3$ (just add up all the sides)

Area: $A = \dfrac{1}{2}bh$

What is the perimeter of the triangle above? _____

What is the area of the triangle above? _____

(In a later section, we will review a couple ways to calculate the third side of a triangle, because you will usually need to calculate it—it will not be given to you.)

Circles

Circles have no sides, but they do have some measurements you need to review. First, they have 360 degrees total, just like a rectangle or square. They have a center, and the measurement from the center to any part of the outside edge is called the *radius.* Any radius within one circle is equal to all others. The radius is the most important measurement because if you have it, you can find many other measurements. Double the radius and you get the *diameter,* the longest measurement across the circle. Multiply the radius by 2π and you get the *circumference,* which is kind of like a perimeter; it is the measurement around the outside of the circle. Square the radius and multiply it by π (pi), and you get the area of the circle.

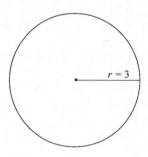

Here are the formulas for diameter, circumference, and area of a circle.

Diameter of a circle: $d = 2r$

Circumference of a circle: $C = 2\pi r$

Area of a circle: $A = \pi r^2$

What is π again? It is a Greek letter that stands in for 22/7, or 3.14. It just turns out that this measurement figures in to both the circumference and the area of circles, no matter how big or small the circle is. Do not worry, you will not have to deal with π much. You can think of it like any other variable because it follows the same rules.

What is the diameter of this circle? _____
What is the circumference of this circle? _____
What is the area of this circle? _____

Basic Geometric Shapes Quick-Fact Sheet

Before going on to the drill, take a few moments to review this quick-fact sheet about basic geometric shapes. If you're having trouble remembering any of this information, it's time to make flash cards, because you don't want to waste time trying to recall it during the test. Also if you had trouble figuring out any of the above measurements, the solutions to the drill are more step-by-step.

- Angle measure of a straight line: 180 degrees
- Angle measure of a right angle: 90 degrees
- A word that describes two lines that meet at a right angle: *perpendicular*
- A word that describes two lines on the same plane that never touch: *parallel*
- Total degree measure in a rectangle: 360 degrees
- Formula for perimeter of a rectangle: $P = 2l + 2w$
- Formula for area of a rectangle: $A = lw$
- Total degree measure in a square: 360 degrees
- Formula for perimeter of a square: $P = 4s$
- Formula for area of a square: $A = s^2$
- Only difference between rectangles and squares: *All sides are equal in a square.*

- Total degree measure in a triangle: 180 degrees
- Formula for perimeter of a triangle: $P = s_1 + s_2 + s_3$
- Formula for area of a triangle: $A = \frac{1}{2}bh$
- Total degree measure in a circle: 360 degrees
- Formula for diameter of a circle: $d = 2r$
- Formula for circumference of a circle: $C = 2\pi r$
- Formula for area of a circle: $A = \pi r^2$

Ready for the answers to the questions in this section? Here they are:

Rectangle:
perimeter: 16
area: 15
Square:
perimeter: 20
area: 25

Triangle:
perimeter: 12
area: 6
Circle:
diameter = 6
circumference = 6π
area = 9π

Now it is time for some practice. Solutions are at the end of the chapter.

DRILL: RECTANGLES, SQUARES, TRIANGLES, AND CIRCLES

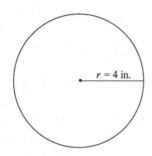

1. What is the circumference of the above circle?

(A) 8 in
(B) 16 in
(C) 8π in
(D) 16π in

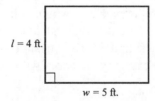

2. What is the perimeter of the above rectangle?

(A) 9 ft
(B) 18 ft
(C) 20 ft
(D) 22 ft

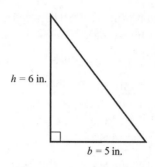

$h = 6$ in.

$b = 5$ in.

3. What is the area of the above triangle?

    (A) 11 in^2
    (B) 15 in^2
    (C) 17 in^2
    (D) 30 in^2

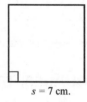

$s = 7$ cm.

4. What is the area of the above square?

    (A) 7 cm^2
    (B) 14 cm^2
    (C) 28 cm^2
    (D) 49 cm^2

Now that you have covered the basic geometric shapes, let us review a few other geometry topics that tend to come up on nursing school entrance exams.

Calculating Hypotenuse and Diagonals

These questions tend to be phrased two different ways: Either you are asked to calculate the diagonal of a rectangle (which is the line from one corner to the opposite corner), or you are asked to calculate the hypotenuse of a right triangle (which is the longest line in a right triangle—the one across from the 90-degree angle). The trick is, they are actually the same thing. See?

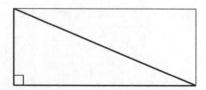

And by the way, there are two diagonals in a rectangle, one connecting each pair of opposite angles, but they always have the same length, so it does not matter which one you calculate.

There are two ways to calculate the diagonal/hypotenuse. One is called the Pythagorean theorem, which is a fancy term you may have heard of in school before but probably do not remember. Not to worry; the Pythagorean theorem says that the two legs of the triangle (or the two sides of the rectangle) are a and b, and the diagonal/hypotenuse is c. The formula is:

$$a^2 + b^2 = c^2$$

If you know your squares from the Exponents section and you are comfortable working with roots, this gets quite a bit easier than it would be otherwise.

Let us try some examples.

What is the length of a diagonal of a rectangle with sides 4 and 6?

The problem tells you that $a = 4$ and $b = 6$, so it is good to write that out or even draw a rectangle and label the sides. That serves as a quick resource in case you need to go back and rework the problem. (And it does not really matter whether you draw things to scale, as long as you are using a somewhat realistic figure.) Now let us plug your numbers into the Pythagorean theorem:

$$4^2 + 6^2 = c^2$$

Now it's just a matter of solving for c.

$$16 + 36 = c^2$$
$$52 = c^2$$
$$\sqrt{52} = \sqrt{c^2}$$
$$\sqrt{52} = c$$

And that's it, $c = \sqrt{52}$.

Try another one:

What is the length of the hypotenuse of a right triangle with sides of length 3 and 5?

Remember to draw your triangle and jot down your measurements:

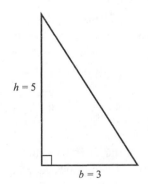

And now you plug the numbers into the Pythagorean theorem and solve:

$$3^2 + 5^2 = c^2$$

$$9 + 25 = c^2$$

$$34 = c^2$$

$$\sqrt{34} = \sqrt{c^2}$$

$$\sqrt{34} = c$$

In this case, that is as far as you can go; the prime factors of 34 are 2 and 17, neither of which has a partner.

Now here is a twist: The problem could give you the length of one side and the hypotenuse/diagonal, and ask you to figure out the length of the other side. Take a moment to think about how that would make the equation look.

Okay, try it:

Find the length of the base of a triangle that has a height of 4 and hypotenuse of 5.

This time the problem gives you a (or b; it really doesn't matter which one you choose as the base and which one you choose as the height) and c, the hypotenuse. So you would draw:

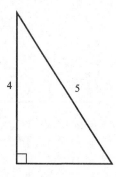

And your equation looks like this:

$$4(2) + b(2) = 5(2)$$

Solve!

$$16 + b(2) = 25$$
$$16 - 16 + b(2) = 25 - 16$$
$$b(2) = 9$$
$$\sqrt{b(2)} = \sqrt{9}$$
$$b = \sqrt{9}$$
$$b = 3$$

The following drill has two of the three measurements filled in for you; your job is to find the third. Remember to draw the appropriate shape, label it, and fill the numbers you know into the equation.

DRILL: CALCULATING HYPOTENUSE AND DIAGONALS

1. $a = 6$, $b = 3$, $c = ?$ 3. $a = 4$, $b = ?$, $c = 8$
2. $a = 4$, $b = 7$, $c = ?$ 4. $a = ?$, $b = 5$, $c = 6$

Pythagorean Shortcuts

If you did not love doing all that math, it is time to pull out your flash cards again. Did you notice how, when you found a diagonal/hypotenuse, it ended up as a noninteger? Well, there are a few sets of sides that show up often on standardized tests, probably because they are all integers and therefore easier to calculate. If you memorize them, you will save yourself from having to use any math at all! Here are the sides to memorize:

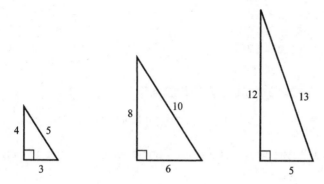

Notice that it matters which lengths are designated as a and b (the sides), and which one is c (the diagonal/hypotenuse). If you are given two sides of length 3 and 5, the hypotenuse is *not* going to be 4 (it is going to be $\sqrt{34}$, as you saw in an earlier problem). A good way to check yourself on this is once you have done the math, make sure that your hypotenuse is always longer than the other two sides.

By the way, did you notice that 3, 4, and 5 is really the same as 6, 8, and 10? You just multiply each side by 2 to get the second triangle. That is the way it works with Pythagorean shortcuts; any multiple of one of these triangles is another Pythagorean shortcut. So 60, 80, and 100 is also a Pythagorean shortcut; so is 50, 120, and 130.

More about Circles

You may need to use your knowledge of circles to solve questions about pie charts. Pie charts are circles, and like all circles, they have 360 degrees. They are usually divided into "slices," with the size of each slice dependent on what percent of the whole the slice represents. So each slice has a certain degree measure, based on that percentage. Some questions ask you to calculate how many degrees a certain slice encompasses (although the questions may refer to a slice as a "central angle" instead). For example:

> If a family's monthly expenses are shown in a pie chart and their mortgage encompasses 40 percent of their monthly expenses, how many degrees is the central angle representing their mortgage payment?

To solve this question, just take the percentage that the slice represents and multiply it by 360.

$$40\% \times 360 = \frac{40}{100} \times 360 = \frac{40 \times 360}{100} = \frac{4 \times 36}{1} = 144$$

As a quick point of reference, if you want to be able quickly to estimate the answer, here is a guide to memorize:

5% of 360 = 18
10% of 360 = 36
25% of 360 = 90
50% of 360 = 180
75% of 360 = 270

DRILL: MORE ABOUT CIRCLES

1. What is the measure of a central angle encompassing 90 percent of a pie chart?
2. What is the measure of a central angle encompassing 15 percent of a pie chart?

Coordinate Geometry

To give yourself an extra edge, you need to be familiar with at least the basics of coordinate geometry. First, there is the coordinate plane:

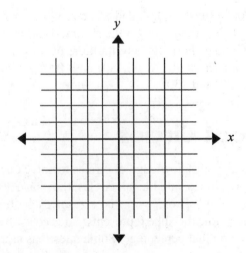

POINTS

Each point on the coordinate plane has two coordinates: one that tells how far up or down the point is, and one that tells how far left or right the point is. The two coordinates are known as x and y, after the axes they relate to. (See how each axis is labeled on the coordinate plane above?) So the x-coordinate tells you how far the point is to the left or right, and the y-coordinate tells you how far the point is up or down. The two coordinates are always written in this order: (x, y).

The x-axis has positive numbers on the right and negative numbers on the left, just like a number line. The y-axis is like a number line turned on its side, with positive numbers going up and negative numbers going down. So to plot the point $(2, -3)$ you would start where the axes cross; this is also known as the *origin*, or $(0, 0)$, and count two units to the *right*, then three units *down*—like this:

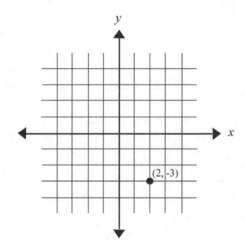

Now you try. Using the above coordinate plane, plot each of the following points. Solutions are at the end of the chapter.

DRILL: PLOTTING POINTS

1. $(1, -4)$ 3. $(-3, -2)$ 5. $(2, 4)$
2. $(4, 2)$ 4. $(0, -3)$ 6. $(-3, 3)$

Of course, points are not the only things that can be plotted on a coordinate plane. Lots of other shapes and figures can be plotted, including circles, rectangles, ellipses, parabolas, and so on. But for our purposes, we are only going to discuss points and lines.

LINES

Lines are basically what you would think of when you think of the word "line"; they are straight and connect any two points on the plane, and they go on forever in either direction. To be able to draw a line on the coordinate plane, you basically need to know two things: where it is and what direction it is pointed. "What direction it's pointed" is known more formally as *slope*.

There are several ways to figure out slope. The first is called the *rise-over-run* method. This method is helpful if there is a picture on which you can see the coordinates for two points. Starting at one point, you just count how many units up or down to the other point (the *rise*) and write it down as the top of your fraction. (Remember: up means positive, and down means negative.) Then count how many units left or right to get to the other point (again: left is negative, and right is positive). Write that down as the bottom of your fraction. Now you have $\dfrac{rise}{run}$.

SLOPE FORMULA

If you know any two points on the line, you can figure out the slope even without a picture. The formula to use is:

$$S = \frac{y_2 - y_1}{x_2 - x_1}$$

Now, do not let the subscripts throw you off; the only reason they are important is to remind you that the first number in both the numerator and the denominator belong to one point, whereas the second number in both the numerator and the denominator belong to the other point. So make sure you do not get them mixed up when filling in the formula with the numbers you know.

Try this a couple of times. Let us say you have two points on a line, (0, 5) and (2, 4), and you want to find the slope. Take one point and plug it in to the formula in its appropriate place:

$$S = \frac{5 - y_1}{0 - x_1}$$

Then take the other point and plug it in:

$$S = \frac{5 - 4}{0 - 2}$$

And then solve:

$$S = \frac{1}{-2}$$

The result is $-\dfrac{1}{2}$.

One more try: The points are (−2, −3) and (4, 6). Plug in one point:

$$S = \frac{-3 - y_1}{-2 - x_1}$$

Then another:

$$S = \frac{-3 - 6}{-2 - 4}$$

And solve:

$$S = \frac{-9}{-6}$$

And your result is $\frac{3}{2}$.

Here are a few for practice on your own. Solutions are at the end of the chapter.

DRILL: SLOPE FORMULA

1. (0, 1) and (2, 3)
2. (3, 2) and (−4, −2)
3. (4, 5) and (2, −1)
4. (−2, 3) and (4, 0)

SLOPE-INTERCEPT FORMULA

Another formula you may see on some exams is the slope-intercept formula. It follows this format:

$$y = mx + b$$

Luckily, you will not have to do a lot of manipulation, but you do need to know what the parts stand for. The *m* in the formula stands for the slope, like the ones you just found in the last drill. The *b* stands for the point at which the line crosses the *y*-axis. Of course, you just learned that all points have two coordinates, an *x* and a *y*. So how come this point only has *b*? Because *b* is the *y*-coordinate and the *x*-coordinate is always 0; you know that because it is right on the *y*-axis.

So that leaves *x* and *y*, which are the coordinates of any other point on the line. Here is a sample problem:

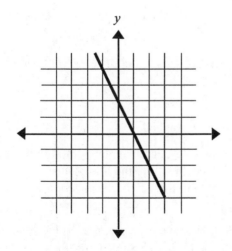

Which of the following equations represents the line drawn in the coordinate plane on the previous page?

(A) $y = 2x + 3$

(B) $y = \frac{1}{2}x + 3$

(C) $y = -2x + 2$

(D) $y = -\frac{1}{2}x + 2$

One of the easiest things in the equation to determine just by looking at the chart is the y-intercept, or where the line crosses the y-axis. In this case, the line crosses at 2, so you can eliminate answer choices A and B without even looking at them further.

A quick $\frac{rise}{run}$ on any two points on the line shows that the slope is -2, so the correct answer must be choice C.

BALLPARKING

Want to be even faster at estimating slope? It is also handy to know a bit about ballparking so that you can check yourself and make sure you did not forget a negative sign or something when you calculated slope. Here are the ballparking basics:

- A positive slope will always point up and to the right.
- A negative slope will always point down and to the right.
- A slope of 0 runs parallel to the x-axis.

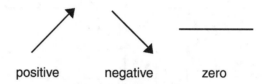

positive   negative   zero

To become even more advanced:

- A slope of 1 makes a 45-degree angle, pointing up.
- The greater the slope, the more the line points up.
- A line that is parallel to the y-axis has no slope, and it will not be tested on the exams.

Now you know that the slope is greater than 1, because the line in the picture points up more than a 45-degree angle does. So you can eliminate choice A, and the answer must be choice B!

Do you want to become a ballparking whiz? Here are some good ranges to know:

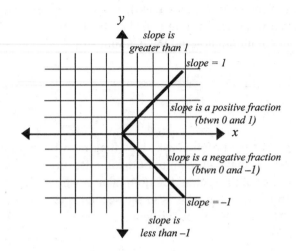

PROPORTIONS AND RATIOS

Proportion and ratio problems both deal with conversions. They are essentially the same kind of problem and they are set up similarly, but they have a little different terminology.

Proportions

Proportions compare two parts, such as miles and gallons or cents and oranges. They are usually presented like this:

> If Ben can type 5 pages in 12 minutes, how long will it take him to type 15 pages?
> If apples cost 50 cents for 3, how many apples can you buy with $2?
> If it takes 2 cans of paint to cover a wall, how many walls can be covered with 8 cans of paint?

Essentially, proportions ask you to convert one pair of numbers. They are easy to miss if you are not being careful or if you are making up a method on the spot, but there are very predictable ways to set them up properly. Once you realize you are working with a proportion problem, draw two blank fractions, like this:

$$\frac{\rule{2cm}{0.4pt}}{\rule{2cm}{0.4pt}} = \frac{\rule{2cm}{0.4pt}}{\rule{2cm}{0.4pt}}$$

Be sure to remember the equal sign, because they *will* actually be equal fractions. Now it is time to fill in the information that you know.

For example, let us take the first problem above:

> If Ben can type 5 pages in 12 minutes, how long will it take him to type 15 pages?

The first part of the problem tells you that Ben can type 5 pages in 12 minutes. So fill that information in to your first blank fraction, making sure that you label both the numerator and the denominator.

$$\frac{5 \text{ pgs}}{12 \text{ mins}} = \underline{}$$

The second part of the problem asks how long it will take to type 15 pages. Because "pages" is in the numerator of the first fraction, you are going to put it in the numerator of the second fraction—that is why it is important to label. You do not know what the time is in the second fraction—that is what you are trying to figure out—so you will put an x there.

$$\frac{5 \text{ pgs}}{12 \text{ mins}} = \frac{15 \text{ pgs}}{X}$$

Now there are two ways to solve. First, you can cross-multiply, which will work in any situation. Cross-multiplication is a lot like comparing fractions using the bowtie method; just multiply diagonally and upward. Cross-multiply here:

$$5x = 15 \times 12$$
$$5x = 180$$
$$x = \frac{180}{5}$$
$$x = 36$$

So 36 is your answer; it takes Ben 36 minutes to type 15 pages.

There is another way to do the math, and it does not work in every situation, but when it does, it can save you some calculation. Starting from filling in the fractions:

$$\frac{5 \text{ pgs}}{12 \text{ mins}} = \frac{15 \text{ pgs}}{X}$$

If you happen to notice that a number in one fraction is easily divisible by a number directly across from it, for example, 15 and 5, you can use that as a shortcut. The number 5 multiplied by 3 is 15, so you would also multiply 12 by 3 to get the value of x. It is just like finding the multiplier in a ratio problem. Because $12 \times 3 = 36$, again, Ben can type 15 pages in 36 minutes.

Try another:

If apples cost 50 cents for 3, how many apples can you buy with $2?

First, fill in your fractions:

$$\frac{50 \text{ cents}}{3 \text{ apples}} = \frac{\$2}{X}$$

Now, you may notice that when you fill in 50 cents and $2, they are not in the same units and therefore, the math really is not going to be accurate. The easiest way to deal with this is to convert dollars to cents, or change the $2 to 200 cents.

$$\frac{50 \text{ cents}}{3 \text{ apples}} = \frac{200 \text{ cents}}{X}$$

That's better. Now you can either cross-multiply or find the multiplier. If you cross-multiply:

$$3 \times 200 = 50x$$
$$600 = 50x$$
$$\frac{600}{50} = x$$
$$12 = x$$

You can buy 12 apples for $2. Or, you may recognize a multiplier; $50 \times 4 = 200$. Therefore you can multiply 3 by 4 to get 12, the number of apples that can be bought for $2.

One more:

> If it takes 2 cans of paint to cover a wall, how many walls can be covered with 8 cans of paint?

The only trick in this problem is that it does not appear to give you two numbers to put into the first fraction, but it does: *2* cans of paint and *1* wall. You may see the same situation if the problem tells you something can be done *per* minute, *per* gallon, or *per* mile. Just think of that as *per 1* minute, *1* gallon, *1* mile, and so on. So your fractions look like this:

$$\frac{2 \text{ cans}}{1 \text{ wall}} = \frac{8 \text{ cans}}{X}$$

Cross-multiplying, you get:

$$8 \times 1 = 2x$$
$$8 = 2x$$
$$\frac{8}{2} = x$$
$$4 = x$$

It takes 4 cans of paint to cover 8 walls. Or you may see that 2 and 8 have a multiplier of 4, and $4 \times 1 = 4$ cans of paint.

Ratios

Ratios are also comparisons of numbers, and if you have ever doubled or halved a recipe, you have worked with ratios. Probably the best news about ratios is that they are pretty easy to spot; they usually have the word "ratio" right there in the problem. Ratio problems do not tend to be very complex; you will usually have two parts to deal with. For example:

> The ratio of minivans to sedans in the parking lot is 3:2. If there are 69 minivans in the parking lot, how many sedans are there?

Time for the good news: You can deal with these problems in exactly the same way as you dealt with proportions. So start by setting up two equal fractions, this time with the parts of the ratio (3 and 2) making up one fraction:

$$\frac{3 \text{ mvans}}{2 \text{ sedans}} = \frac{69 \text{ mvans}}{X}$$

Then cross-multiply:

$$3x = 2 \times 69$$

And solve:

$$3x = 138$$
$$\frac{3x}{3} = \frac{138}{3}$$
$$x = 46$$

Another way ratios can be expressed is even closer to proportions.

> The ratio of the base to height of two triangles is equal. If one triangle has a base of 4 and a height of 7, and the second triangle has a base of 6, what is the height of the second triangle?

Set up fractions:

$$\frac{4 \text{ base}}{7 \text{ height}} = \frac{6 \text{ base}}{X}$$

Cross-multiply:

$$4x = 42$$

And solve:

$$\frac{4x}{4} = \frac{42}{4}$$
$$x = 10.5$$

And now it is time for you to attack a few ratio and proportion problems on your own. Solutions are at the end of the chapter.

DRILL: PROPORTIONS AND RATIOS

1. If long-distance telephone calls are billed at a rate of $0.13 per minute, how many minutes can Jorge talk for $6.50?
2. Sally's lemonade stand charges $0.15 for a glass of lemonade. How many glasses can Charlie buy for $1.80?
3. Ferdinand paid $0.25 for 3 marbles. How much would it cost him to buy 15 marbles?
4. If the ratio of women to men in the debate club is 5:4 and there are 40 women in the club, how many men are in the club?

CONVERTING U.S. AND METRIC UNITS

Remember how proportions and ratios really just deal with conversions? Well, you can use the same setup to handle unit conversions for fluid, mass/weight, and length. Sometimes you will be asked to convert from U.S. unit to U.S. unit (such as pounds to ounces), or metric unit to metric unit (such as meters to centimeters), or you may even be asked to approximate between U.S. and metric units. Memorizing the following values will help with these conversions.

U.S. Measurements

FLUID

8 ounces = 1 cup
2 cups = 1 pint
2 pints = 1 quart
4 quarts = 1 gallon

WEIGHT

16 ounces = 1 pound
2000 pounds = 1 ton

LENGTH

12 inches = 1 foot
3 feet = 1 yard
5280 feet = 1 mile

Metric Measurements

MASS

1 gram =

- 1,000 milligrams
- 100 centigrams
- 10 decigrams
- $\frac{1}{10}$ decagrams (1 decagram = 10 grams)
- $\frac{1}{100}$ hectograms (1 hectogram = 100 grams)
- $\frac{1}{1000}$ kilograms (1 kilogram = 1,000 grams)

LENGTH

The scale for length is the same as for mass, except the base unit is the meter instead of the gram. So a meter is equal to 1,000 millimeters or 100 centimeters, and a kilometer is equal to 1,000 meters.

FLUID

The scale for fluid is the same, except the base unit is the liter.

Metric/U.S. Conversions

Here are some approximate conversions between the U.S. and metric systems. Remember to use your ballparking skills; although you may or may not be given conversions on the test, it will usually be enough to know that a yard is slightly bigger than a meter, a quart is slightly bigger than a liter, and so on.

1 meter	1.09 yards
2.54 centimeters	1 inch
28 grams	1 ounces
1 kilogram	2.2 pounds
1 liter	1.06 quarts

Now that you have conversion rates, you can use them to set up a proportion to do any conversion. For example, if a problem asks you to approximate how many kilograms are in 11 pounds, you would set up two fractions just as if you were doing a proportion problem, then cross-multiply and solve.

Cross-multiplication gives $11 \times 1 = 2.2x$. Once you divide by 2.2 on both sides, you get $5 = x$.

Fahrenheit/Celsius Conversions

These conversion rates are normally given to you within a problem, but it is good to be prepared for them ahead of time, because they require a slightly different process than the proportional conversions you have been doing.

- **To convert degrees Fahrenheit to degrees Celsius:** subtract 32, then multiply by $\frac{5}{9}$.

- **To convert degrees Celsius to degrees Fahrenheit:** multiply by $\frac{9}{5}$, then add 32.

To convert 100 degrees Fahrenheit to degrees Celsius:

$$(100 - 32) \times \frac{5}{9}$$

$$68 \times \frac{5}{9} = \frac{68 \times 5}{9} = \frac{340}{9} = \text{approximately } 37.8°C$$

To convert 20 degrees Celsius to degrees Fahrenheit:

$$20 \times \frac{9}{5} + 32$$

$$\frac{20 \times 9}{5} + 32 = \frac{180}{5} + 32 = 36 + 32 = 68°F$$

Ready to try some conversions on your own? The answers are at the end of the chapter.

DRILL: UNIT CONVERSIONS

1. Convert 77°F to degrees Celsius.
2. How many millimeters is 32 meters?
3. If Kara is carrying an empty one-gallon container, approximately how many liters of fluid could she pour into it?
4. A five-pound brick weighs how many ounces?

APPLIED MATH

Most of this chapter is about specific mathematical skills, such as multiplying decimals or calculating percentages. This section is about a skill that is probably tested more than any other, which is your ability to interpret a word problem and decide which of those other mathematical skills to use on any problem. For example, you already know how to subtract fractions such as $6 - 2\frac{4}{5}$. Many problems on your entrance exams may test the same math, but in a context that looks like this:

> A certain beaker can hold 6 ounces of fluid without running over. If there is $2\frac{4}{5}$ ounces already in the beaker, how much can be added without overflowing the beaker?

This kind of problem adds an extra step: You have to decide which operations to perform. The translation skills you have learned in the Percentages and Algebra sections will be helpful in this process, and this section will add a few helpful hints and lots of practice.

One of the best things you can do if you do not know where to begin on a word problem is to start drawing. If your mind is freezing up, it may be because it cannot deal concretely with the information it is given, and particularly if you are a visual learner, drawing a picture can help you start to deal with the information. Do not worry; you do not have to be an expert artist. Even the most basic shapes can represent the information you are given.

For example, for the beaker problem above, you might draw something that looks like this:

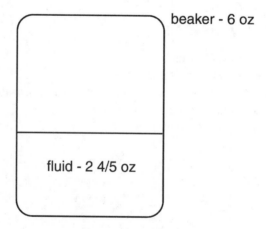

From there, you can even write out questions or emphasize areas that represent the amount you are trying to find. For example:

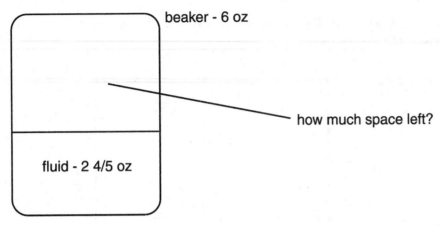

beaker - 6 oz

how much space left?

fluid - 2 4/5 oz

You can see that to find the missing quantity, you would have to subtract $2\frac{4}{5}$ from the whole. So set up the problem:

$$6 - 2\frac{4}{5}$$

$$= \frac{6}{1} - \frac{14}{5}$$

Multiplying across gives you $30 - 14$ for the numerator and 5 for the denominator, so that is a complete fraction of $\frac{16}{5}$ or, if the question has mixed numbers in the answers, $3\frac{1}{5}$.

Try another one.

> Labels will be cut from a sheet of paper that measures 9 inches by 12 inches. If each label needs to be $2\frac{1}{4}$ inches by $1\frac{1}{3}$ inches, how many labels can be cut from that sheet of paper?

This is another good one to draw, just so that you do not have to deal with all of this in your head.

12

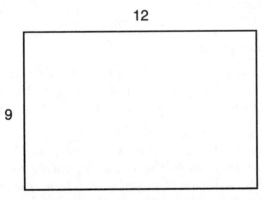

9

A problem like this does not require you to arrange each label; you just need to decide which side of the paper divides most neatly into sections of the size you need. Is 9 divisible by $2\frac{1}{4}$? Yes, but 12 is not, so it is a good bet that you are going to be dividing up the 9-inch side into $2\frac{1}{4}$-inch sections; $2\frac{1}{4}$ divides into 9 four times:

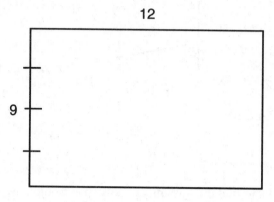

Now how many times does $1\frac{1}{3}$ go into 12? Some quick calculation tells you 9, so you will have 4×9 labels on the sheet of paper, which multiplies out to 36. Again, draw out as much as you need to help with the problem, label as much as you can, be neat, and do not waste time trying to make it perfect.

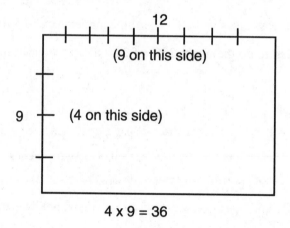

$$4 \times 9 = 36$$

On the other hand, sometimes you will not have much to draw, but you still will have words in the problem that will give you clues of what to do.

Here is another example:

> Mrs. Aziz walks two miles per day at the beginning of a fitness program. Exactly five months later, she is walking four miles per day. On average, how much per month has she increased her daily walk?

You can tell by the word "average" that this is an average/mean problem. Normally, you would be given a list of numbers to add up and divide, but does this problem have another way of telling you the total that you need to divide by? Well, you know that Mrs. Aziz's walk went from two to four miles, so that is an increase of two; that is your total. Because the increase happened over five months and you are being asked for a monthly average, you would divide by five. So she increased her daily walk an average of $\frac{2}{5}$ of a mile per month.

Try one more.

> A certain hospital has 24 beds in the emergency room. If 25 percent of the beds are currently occupied, how many more patients can the emergency room accept before all beds are full?

Whether you draw this one is up to you; it might be a good idea just to remind you of what you're looking for.

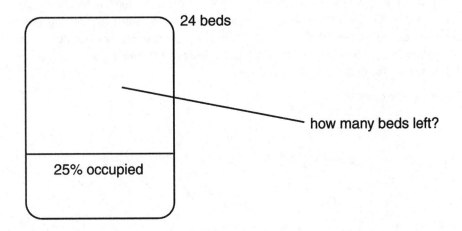

Now you need to do the math; 25% of 24 = 6. That means 6 beds are occupied, and 24 − 6 = 18 beds are available in the emergency room.

Be careful on problems like these to focus on what the problem is asking (how many beds are available) instead of the first calculation you need to do (how many beds are occupied). Drawing a quick picture can help keep you focused on the correct part of the problem.

Now it is your turn to try a few. Solutions are at the end of the chapter.

DRILL: APPLIED MATH

1. A patient is taking 150 mg of a certain prescription every day. How much of the prescription will the patient take during one week?
2. Marci is planning to sell all her shares of a certain stock if their value falls to $30 per share. If the value of the stock is now $45 per share, by what percent would they have to fall for Marci to sell?
3. A banquet room that measures 100 feet by 200 feet is being arranged for a party. If a space measuring 20 feet by 20 feet is needed for each table, what is the maximum number of tables that can be arranged in the room?
4. A certain barrel can hold 50 gallons of liquid. If Tom has to fill it using a one-quart container and he fills the container up completely each time, how many times will he have to pour the container into the barrel?
5. If Sara's current salary is $25,000 per year and she is due to get a 3 percent raise this year in addition to a 2 percent cost of living increase, how much will her salary be after these increases take effect?
6. If a family's total income is spent on the following expenses: one-fourth for the mortgage, one-eighth for car payments, one-eighth for groceries,

two-fifths on other expenses, and the rest to savings, what fraction of the family's total income goes toward savings?

SPATIAL RELATIONS

This final section is for questions that are not quite geometry but do deal with shapes. Spatial relations questions ask you to draw a relationship between two shapes. Given a third shape, you are to choose a fourth shape that best completes the same relationship. Sometimes, the correct answer does not complete the relationship in entirely the same way; however, your job is to choose the one that fits better than the rest.

Here is an example:

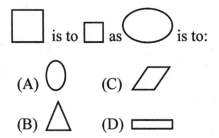

On spatial relation questions, start by describing what happened to turn the first shape into the second shape. In this case, it might be, "The shape got smaller." Then go to the third shape and apply the same to it. In this case, when the third shape gets smaller, the closest fit for it is answer choice A. It is not a perfect completion of the relationship, but clearly choices B, C, and D are worse.

Try another one:

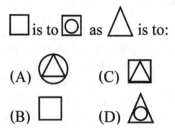

In this problem, the shape stays pretty much the same but a triangle is added to it. Choice D is pretty much the same thing; there is not much room for interpretation on this one.

Now try a couple on your own. Answers are at the end of the chapter.

 $\square$O$\diagup$ is to ● as △$\square$O is to:

(A) ◉ (C) ▣

(B) ◉ (D) ◮

$\square$ is to ▯ as △ is to:

(A) ▱ (C) ◿

(B) ○ (D) △

Congratulations, you have worked through the math you need to prepare for your nursing school entrance exams! But the fun is not over yet; there are two Mathematical Ability practice tests in Chapter 10 of this book to provide further practice. We recommend taking one, then going back and studying any area that you need to brush up on further before taking the second one.

Good luck!

SOLUTIONS

Addition, Subtraction, Multiplication, and Division

1. $1{,}473 + 582 = 2{,}055$
2. $5{,}391 + 6{,}729 = 12{,}120$
3. $12{,}843 + 5{,}928 = 18{,}771$
4. $3{,}609 - 1{,}727 = 1{,}882$
5. $2{,}381 - 962 = 1{,}419$
6. $768 - 529 = 239$
7. $408 \times 52 = 21{,}216$
8. $823 \times 7 = 5{,}761$
9. $521 \times 47 = 24{,}487$
10. $709 \div 4 = 177 \text{ r}1$
11. $341 \div 3 = 114 \text{ r}2$
12. $672 \div 16 = 42$

Factors

1. 18: 1, 2, 3, 6, 9, 18
2. 27: 1, 3, 9, 27
3. 30: 1, 2, 3, 5, 6, 10, 15, 30
4. 36: 1, 2, 3, 4, 6, 9, 12, 18, 36
5. 42: 1, 2, 3, 6, 7, 14, 21, 42
6. 45: 1, 3, 5, 9, 15, 45

Order of Operations

1. $3 + 2 \times 4 = 11$. Multiply 2 and 4, and then add 3.
2. $(10 - 4) \div 3 = 2$. Subtract 4 from 10 first because these numbers are inside parentheses, and then divide by 3.
3. $4 \times 3 - 5 = 7$. Multiply 4 and 3, and then subtract 5.
4. $15 - 8 \div 2 = 11$. Divide 8 by 2, and then subtract the result from 15.
5. $(9 + 2) \times 2 = 22$. Add 9 and 2 first because these numbers are inside parentheses, and then multiply the result by 2.
6. $3 \times 4 \div 2 + 5 = 11$. Multiply 3 and 4, then divide by 2, and then add 5.

Prime Numbers

1. 17: Prime
2. 23: Prime
3. 39: Not prime—3, 13
4. 45: Not prime—3, 5, 9, 15
5. 54: Not prime—2, 3, 6, 9, 18, 27
6. 67: Prime

Prime Factors

1. 36: 2, 2, 3, 3
2. 42: 2, 3, 7
3. 45: 3, 3, 5
4. 92: 2, 2, 23
5. 81: 3, 3, 3, 3
6. 75: 3, 5, 5

Exponents 1

1. $3^5 = 3 \times 3 \times 3 \times 3 \times 3$
2. $4^3 = 4 \times 4 \times 4$
3. $2^3 = 2 \times 2 \times 2$
4. $6 \times 6 \times 6 \times 6 = 6^4$
5. $3 \times 3 = 3^2$
6. $8 \times 8 \times 8 \times 8 = 8^4$

Exponents 2

1. $3^2 \times 3^3 = 3^5$
2. $4^5 \times 5^5$ cannot be combined.
3. $2^7 \div 2^3 = 2^4$
4. $x^8 \div x^3 = x^5$
5. $(2^5)^4 = 2^{20}$
6. $(y^2)^3 = y^6$

Calculating Roots

1. $\sqrt{125} = 5\sqrt{5}$ The prime factors of 125 are 5, 5, and 5.
2. $\sqrt{64} = 8$. The prime factors of 64 are 2, 2, 2, 2, 2, and 2.
3. $\sqrt{72} = 6\sqrt{2}$. The prime factors or 72 are 2, 2, 2, 3, and 3.
4. $\sqrt{147} = 7\sqrt{3}$. The prime factors of 147 are 3, 7, and 7.

5. $\sqrt{75} = 5\sqrt{3}$. The prime factors of 75 are 3, 5, and 5.

6. $\sqrt{80} = 4\sqrt{5}$. The prime factors of 80 are 2, 2, 2, 2, and 5.

Decimals

1. $4.2 + 1.83 = 6.03$

2. $0.95 + 1.28 = 2.23$

3. $82.4 - 7.93 = 74.47$

4. $2.4 - 1.99 = 0.41$

5. $0.12 \times 0.27 = 0.0324$

6. $6.23 \times 0.4 = 2.492$

7. $1.45 \div 0.5 = 2.9$

8. $2.06 \div 0.4 = 5.15$

Reducing Fractions

1. $\dfrac{40}{55} = \dfrac{8}{11}$

2. $\dfrac{81}{45} = \dfrac{9}{5}$

3. $\dfrac{64}{16} = 4$

4. $\dfrac{72}{28} = \dfrac{18}{7}$

5. $\dfrac{12}{54} = \dfrac{2}{9}$

6. $\dfrac{321}{243} = \dfrac{107}{81}$

Adding and Subtracting Fractions

1. $\dfrac{4}{5} + \dfrac{3}{4} = \dfrac{31}{20}$

$16 + 15 = 31$ for the numerator and $5 \times 4 = 20$ for the denominator makes $\dfrac{31}{20}$.

2. $\dfrac{1}{3} + \dfrac{5}{7} = \dfrac{22}{21}$

$7 + 15$ for the numerator and 3×7 for the denominator makes $\dfrac{22}{21}$.

3. $\dfrac{2}{9} + \dfrac{3}{5} = \dfrac{37}{45}$

$10 + 27$ for the numerator and 9×5 for the denominator makes $\dfrac{37}{45}$.

4. $\dfrac{5}{2} + \dfrac{6}{7} = \dfrac{47}{14}$

$35 + 12$ for the numerator and 2×7 for the denominator makes $\dfrac{47}{14}$.

5. $\dfrac{4}{5} - \dfrac{1}{2} = \dfrac{3}{10}$

$8 - 5$ for the numerator and 5×2 for the denominator makes $\dfrac{3}{10}$.

6. $\dfrac{7}{5} - \dfrac{3}{4} = \dfrac{13}{20}$

$28 - 15$ for the numerator and 5×4 for the denominator makes $\dfrac{13}{20}$.

7. $\dfrac{8}{9} - \dfrac{2}{3} = \dfrac{2}{9}$

$24 - 18$ for the numerator and 9×3 for the denominator makes $\dfrac{6}{27}$, which reduces to $\dfrac{2}{9}$.

8. $\dfrac{2}{3} - \dfrac{1}{5} = \dfrac{7}{15}$

$10 - 3$ for the numerator and 5×3 for the denominator makes $\dfrac{7}{15}$.

Multiplying and Dividing Fractions

1. $\dfrac{1}{5} \times \dfrac{3}{10} = \dfrac{3}{50}$

2. $\dfrac{1}{2} \times \dfrac{4}{5} = \dfrac{4}{10} = \dfrac{2}{5}$

3. $\dfrac{2}{3} \times \dfrac{5}{6} = \dfrac{10}{18} = \dfrac{5}{9}$

4. $\dfrac{4}{9} \times \dfrac{1}{7} = \dfrac{4}{63}$

5. $\dfrac{3}{8} \div \dfrac{1}{2} = \dfrac{3}{8} \times \dfrac{2}{1} = \dfrac{6}{8} = \dfrac{3}{4}$

6. $\dfrac{6}{7} \div \dfrac{3}{1} = \dfrac{6}{7} \times \dfrac{1}{3} = \dfrac{6}{21} = \dfrac{2}{7}$

7. $\dfrac{8}{3} \div \dfrac{5}{6} = \dfrac{8}{3} \times \dfrac{6}{5} = \dfrac{48}{15} = \dfrac{16}{5}$

8. $\dfrac{4}{5} \div \dfrac{3}{10} = \dfrac{4}{5} \times \dfrac{10}{3} = \dfrac{40}{15} = \dfrac{8}{3}$

Converting Mixed Numbers to Improper Fractions

1. $2\dfrac{2}{3} = \dfrac{8}{3}$

2. $1\dfrac{5}{6} = \dfrac{11}{6}$

3. $3\dfrac{3}{5} = \dfrac{18}{5}$

4. $4\dfrac{1}{3} = \dfrac{13}{3}$

5. $2\dfrac{3}{7} = \dfrac{17}{7}$

6. $4\dfrac{5}{8} = \dfrac{37}{8}$

Converting Fractions, Decimals, and Percents

1. 27.5% as a decimal = 0.275
2. 33% as a decimal = 0.33
3. 0.425 as a percent = 42.5%
4. 3.9 as a percent = 390%
5. $\dfrac{12}{15}$ as a decimal = 0.8
6. $\dfrac{8.75}{10}$ as a percent = 87.5%

Calculating Percentages

1. 90
   0.75×120
   $75 \times 120 = 9{,}000$, then move the decimal two places to the left.
2. 30
   0.40×75
   $40 \times 75 = 3{,}000$, then move the decimal two places to the left.
3. 72
   0.80×90
   $80 \times 90 = 7{,}200$, then move the decimal two places to the left. (Or you can start with 0.8×90, calculate $8 \times 90 = 720$, and move the decimal 1 place to the left. You end up in the same place, and the same is true for question 2 above.)
4. 36
   0.45×80
   $45 \times 80 = 3{,}600$, then move the decimal two places to the left.
5. 7.5
   0.25×30
   $25 \times 30 = 750$, then move the decimal two places to the left.
6. 104
   0.65×160
   $65 \times 160 = 10{,}400$, then move the decimal two places to the left.

Translating Word Problems Involving Percents

1. 35

   Translation: $49 = \dfrac{x}{100} \times 140$

$$49 = 49 = \frac{140x}{100}$$

$$4900 = 140x$$

$$\frac{4900}{140} = \frac{140x}{140}$$

$$35 = x$$

2. 30

Translation: $21 = \frac{x}{100} \times 70$

$$21 = \frac{x}{100}$$

$$2100 = 70x$$

$$\frac{2100}{70} = \frac{70x}{70}$$

$$30 = x$$

3. 80

Translation: $36 = \frac{x}{100} \times 45$

$$36 = \frac{45x}{100}$$

$$3600 = 45x$$

$$\frac{3600}{45} = \frac{45x}{45}$$

$$80 = x$$

4. 80

Translation: $\frac{15}{100} \times x = 12$

$$\frac{15x}{100} = 12$$

$$15x = 1,200$$

$$\frac{15x}{15} = \frac{1200}{15}$$

$$x = 80$$

5. 50

Translation: $\frac{80}{100} \times x = 40$

$$\frac{80x}{100} = 40$$

$$80x = 4,000$$

$$\frac{80x}{80} = \frac{4000}{80}$$
$$x = 50$$

6. 60

Translation: $\dfrac{20}{100} \times x = 12$

$$\frac{20x}{100} = 12$$
$$20x = 1{,}200$$
$$\frac{20x}{20} = \frac{1200}{20}$$
$$x = 60$$

Mean

1. $(2 + 6 + 9 + 4 + 14) \div 5 = 7$
2. $(9 + 2 + 5 + 11 + 18) \div 5 = 9$
3. $(7 + 21 + -5 + 8 + 4) \div 5 = 7$
4. $(-2 + 9 + -5 + 6) \div 4 = 2$

Median

1. The median of ordered list -2, 2, 3, 5, and 7 is 3.
2. The median of ordered list 2, 3, 4, 7, and 8 is 4.
3. The median of ordered list -3, 1, 5, and 9 is 3 (the mean of 1 and 5).
4. The median of ordered list -5, 2, 2, 3, and 10 is 2.

Mode

1. The mode of ordered list -2, 2, 2, 3, 8, and 10 is 2.
2. The mode of ordered list -5, 0, 3, 3, and 5 is 3.
3. The mode of ordered list -3, -3, -2, 2, 4, and 5 is -3.
4. The mode of ordered list 5, 11, 11, 11, 12, and 12 is 11.

Solving for *x*

1. $x = 2$
   Translation: $3 + 2x = 7$
   $$3 - 3 + 2x = 7 - 3$$
   $$2x = 4$$
   $$\frac{2x}{2} = \frac{4}{2}$$
   $$x = 2$$
2. $x = 5$
   Translation: $3x - 10 = 5$
   $$3x - 10 + 10 = 5 + 10$$
   $$3x = 15$$
   $$\frac{3x}{3} = \frac{15}{3}$$
   $$x = 5$$

3. $x = 14$

Translation: $5 + \dfrac{x}{2} = 12$

$5 - 5 + \dfrac{x}{2} = 12 - 5$

$\dfrac{x}{2} = 7$

$\dfrac{x}{2} \times 2 = 7 \times 2$

$x = 14$

4. $x = 3$

Translation: $4x + 3 = 15$

$4x + 3 - 3 = 15 - 3$

$4x = 12$

$\dfrac{4x}{4} = \dfrac{12}{4}$

$x = 3$

5. $x = -2$

Translation: $2x + 8 = 4$

$2x + 8 - 8 = 4 - 8$

$2x = -4$

$\dfrac{2x}{2} = \dfrac{-4}{2}$

$x = -2$

6. $x = 10$

Translation: $\dfrac{4x}{5} + 7 = 15$

$\dfrac{4x}{5} + 7 - 7 = 15 - 7$

$\dfrac{4x}{5} = 8$

$\dfrac{4x}{5} \times 5 = 8 \times 5$

$4x = 40$

$\dfrac{4x}{4} = \dfrac{40}{4}$

$x = 10$

Translating Algebra Word Problems

1. $x = 5$

Translation: $10 + x = 3x$

$10 + x - x = 3x - x$

$10 = 2x$

$\dfrac{10}{2} = \dfrac{2x}{2}$

$5 = x$

2. $x = 2$

Translation: $5x = x + 8$

$5x - x = x - x + 8$

$4x = 8$

$\dfrac{4x}{4} = \dfrac{8}{4}$

$x = 2$

3. $x = 46$

Translation: $x = 5 \times 10 - 4$

$x = 50 - 4$

$x = 46$

4. $x = 30$

Translation: $x \div \dfrac{3}{4} = 40$

$x \times \dfrac{4}{3} = 40$

$\dfrac{4x}{3} = 40$

$\dfrac{4x}{3} \times 3 = 40 \times 3$

$4x = 120$

$\dfrac{4x}{4} = \dfrac{120}{4}$

$x = 30$

Charts, Graphs, and Tables

1. B

   If you are starting from about 5,000 and going to about 2,500, that is a decrease of about 2,500, which is a percent decrease of about $\dfrac{2500}{5000}$, or 50%.

2. C

   The inventory of sharps increased from about 3,000 to about 4,000 during that period, so if 500 were discarded, a total of 1,500 must have been added to replace them and increase the inventory by 1,000.

3. B

   The list of numbers represented by the diagram is 10, 14, 14, 15, 22, 23, 25, 26, 27, 29, 43, 45, and 48. The number 14 is the only one that appears more than once; therefore, it must be the mode.

4. C

   The number 10 is the smallest number represented and 48 is the largest; $48 - 10 = 38$.

Rectangles, Squares, Triangles, and Circles

1. C

   The radius of the circle is 4 in. When you plug that into the formula for circumference, you get $C = 2\pi(4)$ or $C = 8(\pi)$.

2. B

   The formula for perimeter of a rectangle is $P = 2l + 2w$. When you plug in the values from the picture, you get $P = 2 \times 4 + 2 \times 5$, which equals 18. Be careful to calculate perimeter, not area!

3. B

   The formula for area of a triangle is $A = A = \dfrac{1}{2}bh$, and when you plug in the base of 5, and the height of 6, you get $A = \dfrac{1}{2} \times 5 \times 6$, which equals 15.

4. D

   Each side of the square is $7 \, \text{cm}$, so you just need to square that to get a value of $49 \, \text{cm}^2$.

Calculating Hypotenuse and Diagonals

1. $a = 6, b = 3, \ c = 3\sqrt{5}$

   $$6^2 + 3^2 = c^2$$
   $$36 + 9 = c^2$$
   $$45 = c^2$$
   $$\sqrt{45} = \sqrt{c^2}$$
   $$3\sqrt{5} = c$$

2. $a = 4, b = 7, c = ?$
   $$4^2 + 7^2 = c^2$$
   $$16 + 49 = c^2$$
   $$65 = c^2$$
   $$\sqrt{65} = \sqrt{c^2}$$
   $$\sqrt{65} = c$$

3. $a = 4, b = 4\sqrt{3}, c = 8$
   $$4^2 + b^2 = 8^2$$
   $$16 + b^2 = 64$$
   $$b^2 = 48$$
   $$\sqrt{b^2} = \sqrt{48}$$
   $$b = 4\sqrt{3}$$

4. $a = \sqrt{11}, b = 5, c = 6$
   $$a^2 + 5^2 = 6^2$$

$$a^2 + 25 = 36$$
$$a^2 + = 11$$
$$\sqrt{a^2} = \sqrt{11}$$
$$a = \sqrt{11}$$

More about Circles

1. 324

$$90\% \text{ of } 360 = \frac{9}{10} \times 360 = 324$$

2. 54

$$15\% \text{ of } 360 = \frac{3}{20} \times 360 = 54$$

Plotting Points

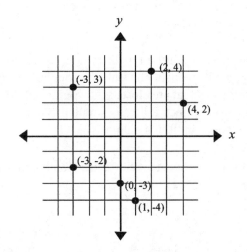

Slope Formula

1. (0, 1) and (2, 3) create a line with a slope of 1.

$$S = \frac{1-3}{0-2} = \frac{-2}{-2} = 1$$

2. (3, 2) and (−4, −2) create a line with a slope of $\frac{4}{7}$.

$$S = \frac{2-(-2)}{3-(-4)} = \frac{4}{7}$$

3. (4, 5) and (2, −1) create a line with a slope of 3.

$$S = \frac{5-(-1)}{4-2} = \frac{6}{2} = 3$$

4. $(-2, 3)$ and $(4, 0)$ create a line with a slope of $-\dfrac{1}{2}$.

$$S = \frac{3-0}{-2-4} = \frac{3}{-6} = -\frac{1}{2}$$

Proportions and Ratios

1. 50
2. 12
3. $1.25
4. 32

Unit Conversions

1. 25°C

   The process for converting to Celsius is to subtract 32, then multiply by $\dfrac{5}{9}$.

   $77 - 32 = 45$, and $45 \times \dfrac{5}{9} = 25$.

2. 32,000

   There are 1,000 millimeters in one meter, so 32 meters would have 32,000 millimeters.

3. About 4

   Because a liter is a little less than a quart and there are 4 quarts in a gallon, 4 will probably be a close enough answer. If there are two answer choices that are close, you would want to pick the one that is more than 4, since a liter is smaller than a quart and therefore more of them can fit in a gallon.

4. 80

   There are 16 ounces in a pound; therefore, there are 80 ounces in 5 pounds.

Applied Math

1. 1,050

   The patient is taking 150 mg per day over 7 days, so you need to multiply to get the total amount taken during that period; $150 \times 7 = 1,050$.

2. $33\dfrac{1}{3}\%$.

   Because the problem asks "by what percent" a change is made, you are dealing with percent change. The original is 45, and a drop to 30 would represent a difference of 15; this would make the fraction

   $\dfrac{15}{45}$, which reduces to $\dfrac{1}{3}$, or $33\dfrac{1}{3}\%$.

3. 50

   It may help to draw this one out if you are having trouble visualizing it. Twenty can fit into the 100-ft side five times and into the 200-ft side ten times. When you multiply 5×10, you get 50.

4. 200

This is essentially a proportions problem. There are four quarts in a gallon, and the question is asking how many quarts there are in 50 gallons. The fraction on the left should have 4 (quarts) on the top and 1 (gallon) on the bottom, and the fraction on the right should have 50 (gallons) on the bottom and x on top. Cross-multiply and solve, and you get 200.

5. $26,250

This problem is asking you to calculate a certain percentage of 25,000. The two percentages total up to 5%, and 5% of 25,000 is 1,250. Add this to 25,000 and you get 26,250.

6. $\dfrac{1}{10}$

To complete this problem, you need to add up the fractions. You can do this by using the bowtie method on individual fractions or by combining fractions using any shortcuts you can find. For example,

$\dfrac{1}{8} + \dfrac{1}{8} = \dfrac{2}{8}$, which reduces to $\dfrac{1}{4}$. Then, $\dfrac{1}{4} + \dfrac{1}{4} = \dfrac{2}{4}$, which you can

bowtie with $\dfrac{2}{5}$ to get $\dfrac{9}{10}$. If $\dfrac{9}{10}$ is spent on other expenses and the

rest is saved, then $\dfrac{1}{10}$ is saved.

Spatial Relations

1. In the first pair, one of the shapes grows larger and encompasses one of the other shapes, which turns black. Choice B shows the same relationship. Choice D is incorrect because the parallelogram is not part of the second group.

2. Choice C is the correct answer; in the first pair, the shape halves and choice C is the only answer choice that reproduces this. It may look as if the initial square gets narrower, but because none of the answers correspond to that, you must consider the possibility that it is cut in half instead.

CHAPTER 9

Science Review

Read this chapter to learn

• What science questions test

• The biological sciences facts and terms you need to know

• The physical sciences facts and terms you need to know

REVIEW OF BIOLOGICAL SCIENCES

CELL STRUCTURE

Cell Theory

The cell is considered to be the basic unit of life. It can take on a variety of functions, depending on the organism and the tissue in which the cell is located. Although early scientists were able to see various parts of the cell, they did not understand the processes that took place within the cell. From what was known in the early 1900s, the cell theory was formed:

• All cells arise from preexisting cells.
• Cells can carry out the processes of life.
• Organisms are made of cells that function together.

Prokaryotes versus Eukaryotes

There are two basic types of cells, called prokaryotic cells and eukaryotic cells. Single-celled organisms such as bacteria are examples of prokaryotes, whereas multicellular organisms such as plants and animals are examples of eukaryotes. Both have deoxyribonucleic acid (DNA) as the material that carries the genetic code, but a prokaryotic cell does not have a nucleus. Although both have a cell membrane, only some eukaryotes have a cell wall, whereas all prokaryotes have a cell wall. Today we know a great deal about cells and their functions.

Cell Structure and Organelles

The cell can be considered to be the basic unit of life. Within the cell there are a number of organelles that help the cell carry out certain functions. They can be compared to the organs within your body that perform certain processes to keep you alive. Below is a diagram of a eukaryotic cell and table of the organelle functions.

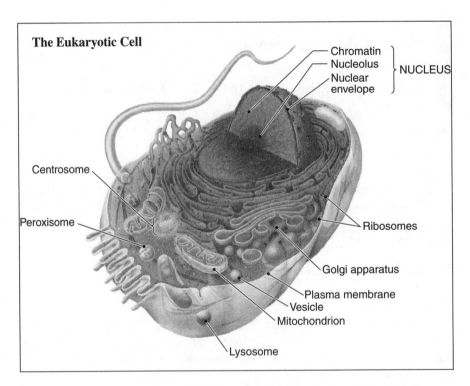

SOURCE: From Stephanie Zinn, ed., *McGraw-Hill's SAT Subject Test: Biology*, McGraw-Hill, 2006; reproduced with permission of The McGraw-Hill Companies.

Organelle	Function
Nucleus	The nucleus of the cell is responsible for the activities of the cell regarding DNA, including the transcription of DNA to messenger RNA. The nucleus has its own membrane, which allows for the passage of materials and proteins needed for DNA replication.
Ribosomes	The two-subunit ribosome is responsible for the production of proteins. Ribosomes can be free and not bound to any membrane, or they can be bound to the outer membrane of the endoplasmic reticulum.
Endoplasmic Reticulum (ER)	There are two types of endoplasmic reticulum, smooth and rough. The rough endoplasmic reticulum has ribosomes attached to the outer surface, while the smooth endoplasmic reticulum does not have ribosomes attached. The rough endoplasmic reticulum produces proteins, while the smooth endoplasmic reticulum works to transport proteins out of the cell.
Golgi Bodies	After modifying and packaging proteins and other macromolecules in the cell, the Golgi apparatus can take on the process of exocytosis so that materials can be secreted from the cell.
Lysosomes	Lysosomes are often termed the "suicide sacs of the cell" because of their involvement with digestion within the cell. Besides digesting proteins, the lysosome will also use its digestive enzymes to break down parts of the cell that are no longer of any use to the cell.
Vacuoles	Most known for their ability to store materials, vacuoles are sacs within the cell that house a range of materials for later use.
Mitochondria	The mitochondria can be thought of as the "powerhouses" of the cell because of their ability to produce the energy needed for life. This is accomplished by carrying out the process of aerobic respiration. Mitochondria have an inner membrane and outer membrane. The folds in the inner membrane are called cristae and are packed with the proteins needed for the electron transport chain to carry out its function so that the mitochondria can continuously produce ATP.
Chloroplasts	Present in plants, the chloroplast contains a substance called chlorophyll to carry out the process of photosynthesis.
Cytoskeleton	Much the way our skeletal system helps give us shape and structure, the cytoskeleton has a number of microtubule fibers to provide shape and structure to the cell. These tubules and fibers are made of protein.
Cilia/Flagella	These structures are not present within the cell. Instead they are located outside of the cell and allow the cells to move.
Cell Membrane	Not considered to be an organelle, this lipid bilayer contains both hydrophobic and hydrophilic portions to keep watery environments in and out of the cell as needed. The cell membrane is selective in which materials enter and exit the cell (selectively permeable). Also present are proteins (some for transport) and carbohydrates (for cell identification).
Cell Wall	Present in plant cells, the cellulose-containing cell wall helps give the plant cell rigidity.

Transport Across the Plasma Membrane

Consider a tea bag placed into a hot cup of water. Without any stirring, the water eventually becomes colored due to the tea moving throughout the cup of water. Particles naturally move from an area of high concentration (the tea bag) to an area of low concentration (the clean, boiled water). This process is called *diffusion*. Diffusion also explains why you can smell an odor from across a room. Concentrations of solutes inside and outside of a cell also cause these substances to diffuse through the cell membrane. Oxygen and carbon dioxide are excellent examples of substances that can diffuse through the membrane based on their concentrations both inside and outside the cell.

Water can also diffuse across a membrane in a process called *osmosis*. By doing so, the water dilutes a solution that is inside or outside of a cell in an attempt to equalize the concentrations. In an *isotonic solution,* the concentrations inside and outside the cell are the same. In a *hypotonic solution,* the solution outside the cell has a lower concentration of solutes than the solution inside the cell. Water moves from the outside solution into the cell in an attempt to dilute the concentrations in the cell. This causes the cell to swell and/or burst. In a *hypertonic solution,* the outside solution has a higher concentration of solute than the cell. Water leaves the cell in an effort to dilute the outside solution. This causes the cell to shrivel and shrink.

Transport across the cell membrane can be passive or active. *Passive transport* is transportation that occurs from a high concentration to a low concentration naturally and without any additional energy input. *Active transport* takes place when materials need to be moved from an area of low concentration to one of higher concentration. Because this works against the natural process, the cell must use energy to carry out active transport.

Biochemistry

The molecules needed for life to carry out its functions can be classified as being both *organic* (carbon-based) and *inorganic* (without carbon). Some organic compounds include lipids, carbohydrates, proteins, and nucleic acids. Some inorganic substances include ions, iron, calcium, and water. Water is considered to be the universal solvent and can dissolve a range of substances that are *polar* or contain ions. Water molecules are polar and can attract other water molecules via cohesive forces (forces between the same molecules). Water molecules can also attract other polar molecules via adhesive forces (forces between different molecules).

Carbohydrates are organic compounds that contain carbon, oxygen, and hydrogen. They are major sources of energy in the body. The simplest sugars are called monosaccharides; examples are glucose and fructose. The combination of monosaccharides to form disaccharides and starches occurs with the removal of water via a *dehydration synthesis*. *Hydrolysis* is the opposite process, in which larger starches or polysaccharides have water added to them to break them down into simple sugars for use by cells.

Proteins contain carbon, hydrogen, oxygen, and nitrogen. Proteins are long chains of amino acids joined via a dehydration synthesis. The amine group of one molecule reacts with the carboxylic acid group of another amino acid to form a dipeptide. The bond that is formed from this reaction is called the *peptide bond.* Besides an amine group and a carboxylic acid group, each one of the 20 amino acids has a special "R" group that makes it one of the distinct amino acids.

Proteins make complex structures by organizing themselves at different levels. The primary sequence of proteins is the order in which amino acids have formed peptide bonds. This sequence causes the protein to form an alpha helix or a beta pleated sheet, creating its secondary structure. The three-dimensional shaping of a protein is called its tertiary structure. This structure can be held together with hydrogen bonds and disulfide "bridges." A quaternary structure is made of many tertiary structures held together. Hemoglobin, with its four peptide chains held together, is an example of this.

Enzymes are examples of complex proteins that function to regulate the rate at which reactions occur. Enzymes are catalysts that aim to lower the amount of energy it takes for a reaction to occur. Once the activation energy of the reaction has been lowered, the reaction can take place at a faster rate. Each enzyme has a specific substrate on which it acts. Because of this, the fitting of a substrate into the active site of an enzyme is often compared to a lock and a key. The induced fit hypothesis tells a slightly different story, dictating that an enzyme changes the shape of its active site slightly to accommodate a substrate. Because enzymes can be denatured by certain temperatures and pH values, different structures of enzymes can function in various parts of the body and under different conditions. Outside of its ideal conditions, an enzyme can have its shape altered dramatically and become denatured.

Lipids are made of carbon, hydrogen, and oxygen (very little oxygen in comparison to carbohydrates). They are made from the dehydration synthesis of a glycerol molecule and three fatty acid molecules. Fats can contain carbon chains that contain single or double bonds. If a fat chain contains all single bonds, the fat is classified as saturated. If there is a double bond in the fat chain, the fat is classified as unsaturated. Lipids are stored by the body as an energy reserve, and they can provide about twice as much energy per gram as proteins or carbohydrates. Fats can also provide our bodies with insulation, preventing heat loss.

Nucleic acids are the building blocks of DNA and ribonucleic acid (RNA). Nucleic acids contain carbon, hydrogen, and oxygen, along with nitrogen and phosphorus atoms as well. Each nucleic acid contains a phosphate group, a five-carbon sugar, and a nitrogen base. The phosphate groups are what join the nucleic acids in a chain. The nitrogen bases can pair up with a complementary base to form the double-stranded DNA.

Pathways for Energy Synthesis

Energy is needed by all living things so that the processes of life can be carried out. The molecule that supplies energy is called adenosine triphosphate (ATP). The steps that the cells of an organism take to produce this needed energy can occur in a variety of ways. Some methods for producing energy require oxygen (*aerobic*), whereas some do not (*anaerobic*). The table below compares four processes for producing energy:

Glycolysis	Glycolysis is an anaerobic process that splits a six-carbon glucose molecule into two three-carbon pyruvic acid molecules. Two ATP molecules are needed to start the process, but four ATP molecules are produced, yielding a net of two ATP molecules. Also formed are two molecules of $NADH_2$, which can be used to form more ATP, provided it enters an aerobic process.
Fermentation	After glycolysis has taken place, the pyruvic acid can be further used to carry out anaerobic processes. Yeast, for example, changes the pyruvic acid to carbon dioxide (which causes bread dough to rise) and ethyl alcohol: $C_6H_{12}O_6 \rightarrow 2C_2H_5OH + 2CO_2$
Aerobic respiration	After pyruvic acid is formed, the mitochondria of the cell work to convert it to acetyl-CoA. Acetyl-CoA enters the Krebs cycle, in which one ATP molecule is produced each time the cycle is performed (two ATP formed per glucose molecule). Finally, the $NADH_2$ and $FADH_2$ work with the electron transport chain to pass the hydrogen atoms present to free oxygen. During this process 32 ATP molecules are formed along with water. The overall reaction is: $C_6H_{12}O_6 + 6O_2 \rightarrow 6CO_2 + 6H_2O + 36ATP$ (energy).
Photosynthesis	Photosynthesis is carried out in the chloroplasts of the plant cell. The overall equation is similar to that of aerobic respiration: $6CO_2 + 6H_2O + light$ $energy \rightarrow C_6H_{12}O_6 + 6O_2$. The light reactions of photosynthesis take place in the grana of the chloroplast, whereas the dark reactions take place in the stroma of the chloroplast.

Genetic Material

Deoxyribonucleic acid, or *DNA,* is the macromolecule in cells that codes for how amino acids form proteins. DNA is a double-stranded helix that has complementary nucleic acids that are hydrogen bonded to each other. These pairings are thymine with adenine and guanine with cytosine. The nucleic acids can be classified as purines (adenine and guanine) or pyrimidines (cytosine and thymine). The fact that the nitrogen bases are hydrogen bonded to each other, and not covalently bonded, makes it easy for a segment of a DNA molecule to "unzip" and replicate without having to overcome strong covalent bonds.

Ribonucleic acid, or *RNA,* exists as messenger RNA (mRNA), transfer RNA (tRNA), or ribosomal RNA (rRNA). Each of these types of RNA has a function:

mRNA	Copies DNA's genetic code via a process called transcription
tRNA	Complements mRNA via an anticodon that corresponds to an amino acid that tRNA will carry
rRNA	Is found as part of ribosomes and helps in the formation of polypeptides

RNA has nitrogen bases that match up to the nucleic acids for DNA with one exception: RNA does not have the nitrogen base thymine and pairs up uracil opposite the adenine nitrogen base of DNA. Also, while DNA is double-stranded, RNA exists as a single strand.

In the environment there are factors that can alter or damage genetic material. Radioactive isotopes, radiation, and carcinogens can alter or damage the sequence of nucleic acids in our genetic material. This is called a *mutation*. Mutations can lead to a number of disorders and/or cancers.

Cell Reproduction

There are two processes by which new cells are formed. One, called *mitosis*, is the process by which most new cells are produced in eukaryotes. At the completion of mitosis, two new daughter cells are produced from one preexisting cell. The other process, which produces sex sells (sperm and egg), is called *meiosis*. Let us examine mitosis first. The steps of mitosis are shown in the table and figure that follow.

Steps in Mitosis	
Interphase	Between mitotic cycles, the cell is said to be in interphase. During this phase, the cell is carrying on activities other than reproduction.
Prophase	Chromosomes that replicated during interphase now become visible as they coil to form chromatids. The chromatids are connected by a centromere.
Metaphase	With the help of centrioles, asters, and spindle fibers, the chromatids line up near the equator of the cell.
Anaphase	The chromosomes now move to the opposite poles of the cell via help from the spindle fibers. Now there are two separate sets of identical chromosomes on opposite poles of the cell. Cytokinesis, the division of the cytoplasm, begins with the "pinching" of the cell membrane.
Telophase	Telophase begins with the uncoiling of the chromosomes as they begin to look like chromatin again. The spindle fibers and asters are no longer visible. The cell then forms two daughter cells as the nuclear membrane becomes visible again. In plants, telophase is completed with the formation of a cell plate between the daughter cells, which is followed by the formation of a new cell wall.

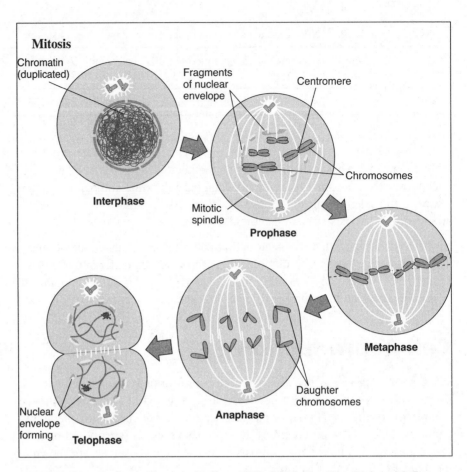

SOURCE: From Stephanie Zinn, ed., *McGraw-Hill's SAT Subject Test: Biology*, McGraw-Hill, 2006; reproduced with permission of The McGraw-Hill Companies.

Meiosis is the process by which cell division takes place so that the sex cells, sperm and egg, are produced. Although meiosis is similar to mitosis, you should note the number of divisions involved and the number of chromosomes present in each cell. While the human cell has 46 chromosomes, the sex cell needs to be produced so that each sex cell has just 23 chromosomes—all single chromosomes, no pairs. These cells are termed *haploid*. When a sperm cell and an egg cell join, the resulting zygote now has 46 chromosomes (*diploid*). The steps of meiotic division are shown in the table that follows.

Gametogenesis is different for males and females. In spermatogenesis, the primary spermatocyte develops into four sperm. In oogenesis, just one egg cell is formed from the oocyte along with three polar bodies.

Steps in Meiosis

Prophase I	Chromosomes have replicated and have produced two chromatids. Pairs of chromatids then pair up via synapsis to form a tetrad.
Metaphase I	Centromeres of the tetrads line up in the cell.
Anaphase I	Disjunction takes place and the homologous chromosomes separate.
Telophase I	The cytoplasm divides and two daughter cells are formed.
Prophase II	Spindles form to separate chromosomes. No replication of the chromosomes has occurred in this phase.
Metaphase II	The double-stranded chromosomes are lined up along the equator and become attached to spindle fibers at the centromere.
Anaphase II	The two chromatids separate and become single-stranded chromosomes as they move to opposite sides of the cell.
Telophase II	The cells divide again forming four cells, each with a haploid number of chromosomes.

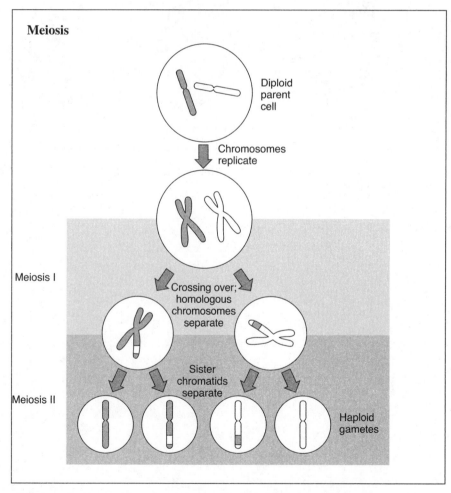

Meiosis

Diploid parent cell

Chromosomes replicate

Meiosis I

Crossing over; homologous chromosomes separate

Sister chromatids separate

Meiosis II

Haploid gametes

SOURCE: From Stephanie Zinn, ed., *McGraw-Hill's SAT Subject Test: Biology*, McGraw-Hill, 2006; reproduced with permission of The McGraw-Hill Companies.

Spermatogenesis and Oogenesis

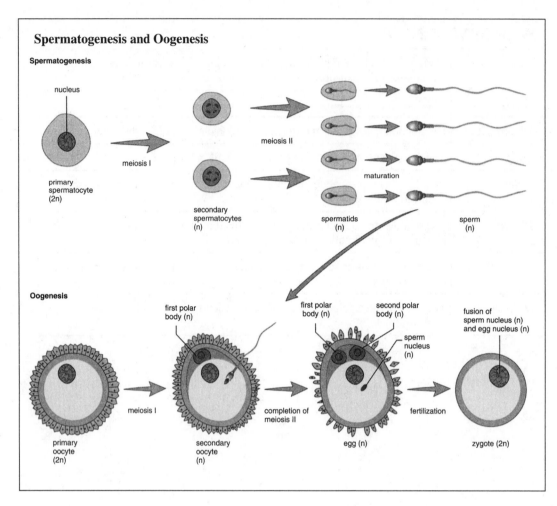

SOURCE: From Sylvia S. Mader, *Biology*, eighth edition, McGraw-Hill, 2004; reproduced with permission of the McGraw-Hill Companies.

CELL STRUCTURE QUIZ

1. Match the organelle on the left with the role the organelle takes on the right.

(A) Mitochondrion   _____ Provides storage space
(B) Vacuole   _____ Site of protein synthesis
(C) Nucleus   _____ Is selectively permeable
(D) Cell membrane   _____ Site of energy production
(E) Ribosome   _____ Holds the DNA of the cell

2. Enzymes

(A) are catalysts that are made from lipids.
(B) are made of proteins and can speed up reactions.
(C) form long chains to make double strands of DNA.
(D) cannot be denatured.

3. A cell is in a solution in which the concentration of solutes is higher inside the cell than outside the cell. The cell will likely

(A) swell up and possibly burst.
(B) shrivel and shrink.
(C) maintain its size.
(D) grow a cell wall for support.

4. Yeast is used to make bread rise because

(A) the yeast engages in photosynthesis, which produces oxygen gas.
(B) carbon dioxide forms while the yeast carries out photosynthesis.
(C) the yeast carries out fermentation, which produces ethanol and carbon dioxide.
(D) yeast breathes in oxygen and produces carbon dioxide as aerobic respiration takes place.

5. Which statement below does not have the same truth value as the others?

(A) RNA is single-stranded.
(B) RNA contains uracil.
(C) DNA codes for proteins.
(D) DNA cannot be altered.

6. Which of the following is a way in which mitosis differs from meiosis?

(A) Mitosis takes place to form sex cells.
(B) Meiosis creates cells with half the number of chromosomes than the original cell.
(C) Telophase does not take place in mitosis.
(D) Spermatogenesis and oogenesis occur via mitosis.

ORGAN SYSTEM ANATOMY

Locating the Organs

Because of the complexity of the organ systems located within the human body, a set of adjectives is used to locate the organs with reference to other parts of the body. Here is a brief summary of some of these terms:

Anterior: areas that are near the front of the body	*Posterior*: areas that are near the back of the body
Superior: areas that are near the upper end of the body	*Inferior*: areas that are closer to the lower parts of the body
Medial: areas that are more toward the middle of the body	*Lateral*: areas that are more toward the outer portions of the body
Proximal: areas that are closer to the body's trunk	*Distal*: areas of the body that are not near the body's trunk
Superficial: areas near the body's surface	*Deep*: areas that are away from the body's surface

Digestive System

Digestion, a process that takes approximately 24 hours, includes both chemical and mechanical means. At certain times during its travel through the digestive system, food is acted on by enzymes, acid, and other substances. At other times, food is chewed and churned to help break it down and continuously increase its surface area. The following table outlines the chemical and mechanical mechanisms for this breakdown as food moves through the digestive system.

The Digestive System		
Organ	**Mechanical Digestion**	**Chemical Digestion**
Mouth	Teeth grind food as the tongue helps mix food with saliva.	Saliva moistens the food as salivary amylase breaks down starches.
Epiglottis	This structure prevents food from entering the larynx as the food is swallowed. The food can enter only the esophagus.	
Esophagus	Muscles in the esophagus push food into the stomach via the process of peristalsis.	
Stomach	Churning helps break down food and mix it with gastric juices to form chyme.	Hydrochloric acid breaks down the food and kills bacteria. Pepsin breaks down proteins.

(continued)

Organ	Mechanical Digestion	Chemical Digestion
Small intestine	Villi and microvilli increase the surface area of the small intestine and greatly increase the level of absorption of nutrients.	Pancreatic juice containing amylase, proteases, and lipase is secreted from the pancreas. Bile, produced by the liver and stored in the gallbladder, is released to emulsify fats and oils. Intestinal secretions also help continue the breakdown of fats, carbohydrates, and proteins.
Large intestine	Water is reabsorbed along with vitamins.	
Rectum	Stores fecal matter before being defecated via the anus.	

The Digestive System

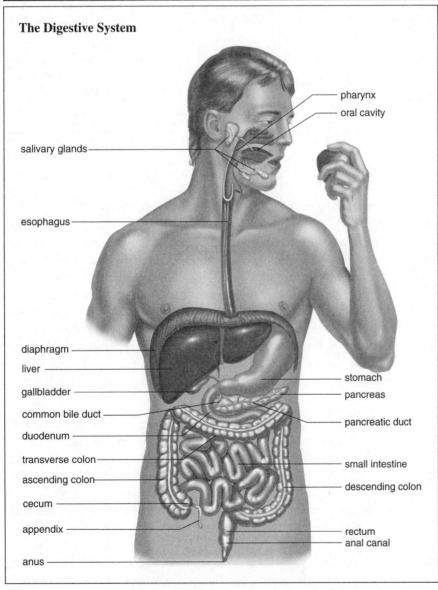

SOURCE: From Sylvia S. Mader, *Biology*, 8th ed., McGraw-Hill, 2004; reproduced with permission of The McGraw-Hill Companies.

Circulatory System

The circulatory system provides transport for a variety of substances throughout the body. Every single cell in the body needs to remove wastes, take in nutrition, and be defended against foreign matter. The circulatory system takes on this huge task and can adjust the rate at which it performs to help maintain homeostasis.

There are three types of blood vessels responsible for transporting the blood. They are arteries, capillaries and veins. A comparison is made in the chart that follows.

Arteries	Veins	Capillaries
• Carry blood away from the heart • Are elastic and thick	• Return blood to the heart • Are thin and less elastic • Use valves to prevent blood backflow	• Have walls that are one cell thick to allow for materials to pass through • Connect arteries to veins

A major concern regarding the American diet is the consumption of high levels of fat and cholesterol. Cholesterol is known to cause a buildup of a plaque in the arteries causing atherosclerosis. The hardening of the arteries as they close can lead to a heart attack. The *heart,* made almost entirely of muscle, works to pump blood through the body. The muscle cells present are tightly locked together to provide contractions strong enough to force the blood to all areas in the body. The heart contains four chambers, the upper two being labeled *atria* (singular: *atrium*) and the bottom two labeled *ventricles.* The *septum* is a wall that separates the left and right sides of the heart, whereas valves ensure that the blood flows in only one direction through the heart, to and from the lungs, and throughout the body.

There are two periods of one beat of the heart. The time during which the heart is contracting is called the *systole,* whereas the time during which the heart relaxes is called the *diastole.* Deoxygenated blood enters the heart via the right atrium by flowing through the inferior vena cava and superior vena cava. Most of the blood will then flow into the right ventricle when the heart is relaxed and the atrioventricular (AV) valve is open. Next, the right atrium contracts slightly. The right ventricle then contracts, which forces the blood to flow through the *pulmonary* (pertaining to the lungs) artery. On return to the heart from the lungs, the blood once again enters into an atrium; however, this time it enters the left atrium. The blood is now oxygenated and ready to provide this oxygen to the rest of the body. After a relaxation allows the

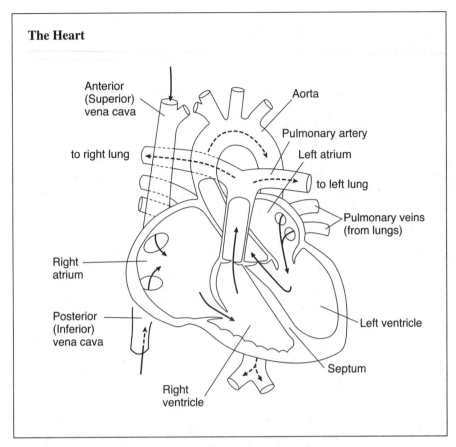

The Heart

Anterior (Superior) vena cava

Aorta

Pulmonary artery

to right lung

Left atrium

to left lung

Pulmonary veins (from lungs)

Right atrium

Left ventricle

Posterior (Inferior) vena cava

Septum

Right ventricle

SOURCE: From Stephanie Zinn, ed., *McGraw-Hill's SAT Subject Test: Biology*, McGraw-Hill, 2006; reproduced with permission of The McGraw-Hill Companies.

blood to enter the left ventricle, a contraction in the left atrium and then in the left ventricle pushes the blood through the aorta and to the rest of the body.

The cardiac cycle is regulated by autorhythmic cells in the heart, the sinoatrial (SA) node (pacemaker), and the AV node. The SA node is responsible for starting the cardiac cycle by contracting both atria and by sending a signal that causes the AV node to signal to contract the ventricles.

The *lymphatic system* is another passageway by which fluids and wastes can be delivered into the circulatory system. The lymphatic system is composed of veins and capillaries in which lymph can travel via contractions of the muscles surrounding the veins. These veins, just like the ones that carry blood, contain valves that prevent the backflow of lymph. Finally, the lymph is cleaned and filtered by lymph nodes. Inside the lymph nodes, the body's immune system works to respond to and defend against foreign invaders.

Blood is composed of plasma, red blood cells, white blood cells, and platelets. The red blood cells (erythrocytes) are responsible carrying oxygen via the hemoglobin present in the cells. White blood cells (leukocytes) defend the body against foreign invaders such as bacteria and viruses. Platelets are responsible for helping the blood clot and seal breaks in the walls of blood vessels.

Immune System

The body takes a number of measures to prevent infection. The body's primary defenses against infection include the skin, tears, stomach acid, urine, sweat, mucus, and saliva. By having this range of both physical and chemical defenses, the body is able to defend against a range of pathogens.

Secondary defenses bring about *inflammation*. The swelling, redness, and warmth of the infected area cause the body to call in macrophages and neutrophils to consume the bacteria. If the pathogen is a virus, interferon is produced so that other cells in that region of the body can block the virus from attacking any healthy cells.

The body's third line of defense is the way the body remembers specific pathogens and their structures. If the pathogen enters the body again, the body's response will be much quicker than the first time the pathogen invaded the body. Antibodies, specific to each pathogen, are ready to respond should this occur. The memorization and production of antibodies is called *active immunity*. In *passive immunity* the antibodies have been obtained from outside the body, either from another animal or person.

A number of cells are involved in combating the invasion of viruses and bacteria. *B cells* have antigen receptors and antibodies, and they work to fight off bacteria. B cells can form plasma cells and memory cells. The plasma cells produce antibodies that bind to antigens, whereas the memory B cells form new plasma cells if the bacteria enter the body again. *T cells* are responsible for recognizing nonself cells. On engagement with nonself cells, they produce killer T cells and memory T cells. The killer T cells have the task of binding to cells that have been infected by viruses. The memory T cells are ready to produce more killer T cells if the virus enters the body again. In both cases, bacterial and viral infections, helper T cells are available to recognize the antigens that have been ingested and displayed by macrophages.

Respiratory System

The respiratory system allows for gases to enter and exit as needed by the body. The rate at which respiration occurs is governed by the level of carbon dioxide present in the body. Higher levels will trigger the body to increase breathing rate to dispose of this excess carbon dioxide.

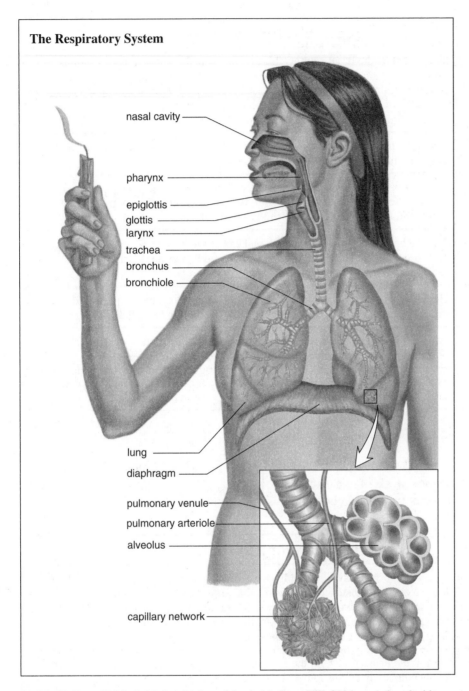

The Respiratory System

- nasal cavity
- pharynx
- epiglottis
- glottis
- larynx
- trachea
- bronchus
- bronchiole
- lung
- diaphragm
- pulmonary venule
- pulmonary arteriole
- alveolus
- capillary network

SOURCE: From Sylvia S. Mader, *Biology*, 8th ed., McGraw-Hill, 2004; reproduced with permission of The McGraw-Hill Companies.

The movement of air into the lungs first starts with the movement of the diaphragm downward. Because the chest cavity is sealed from air, the downward movement of the diaphragm creates a vacuum that causes air to flow into the respiratory system and fill this available space. The pathway of the airflow is shown in the following table.

The Respiratory System	
Nose	The air enters the nasal cavities through the nostrils. There, mucous linings and cilia work to trap particles and bacteria. The mucus is also responsible for moistening the air. The nasal cavity is also responsible for warming the air before it reaches the lungs. Should inhalation be carried out through the mouth, the air is not filtered and treated as much before it reaches the lungs.
Pharynx	The pharynx (throat) is the next step after the nasal cavity. It connects the nasal cavity to the larynx.
Larynx	The larynx (voice box), which is mostly made of cartilage, contains the vocal cords that can vibrate to produce sounds. Also present is the epiglottis to prevent solids and liquids from entering the larynx while swallowing.
Trachea	The trachea (windpipe) connects the larynx to the bronchi. The trachea uses cilia and mucus to further trap foreign matter before it goes any further into the respiratory tract.
Bronchi	Here is where the trachea separates into two pathways, one going toward each lung. The bronchi further divide and "branch out" into bronchial tubes.
Bronchioles	Eventually, the bronchial tubes have divided and branch out so much that they become very small tubes called bronchioles which reach the alveoli.
Alveoli	The bronchioles arrive at a group of tiny air sacs called alveoli. These one-cell-thick air chambers are thin and moist to allow for maximum gas exchange.

Excretory System

The fatal buildup of toxins and waste in our bodies is countered by the continuous work of the excretory system. Again, a number of organs work together to maintain homeostasis in the body.

The Excretory System	
Liver	Not part of the urinary system, the liver works to detoxify the blood. It does so by working to convert substances into forms that are less toxic or altogether harmless. For example, the liver works to convert excess amino acids into other substances and ammonia. Because the ammonia is toxic, the liver converts ammonia into urea that can later be excreted by the urinary system.
Skin	Not part of the urinary system, the skin also has a function in the excretion of excess heat. When the body begins to overheat, the blood vessels in the skin widen, allowing more blood to flow through the capillaries and more heat to be lost through the skin. The skin also removes heat from the body by producing sweat. When sweating produces moisture on the skin, the moisture absorbs heat and evaporates.
Kidneys	The kidneys work to produce urine. It is the one million or so nephrons in each kidney that do the filtering. Present in the nephrons are the Bowman's capsules and glomeruli.
Ureter	The ureter is responsible for taking urine from the kidneys to the urinary bladder.
Bladder	The bladder stores urine until it is ready to be excreted.
Urethra	This passageway takes urine from the bladder to outside the body.

The urinary system can be diagrammed as follows:

The Urinary System

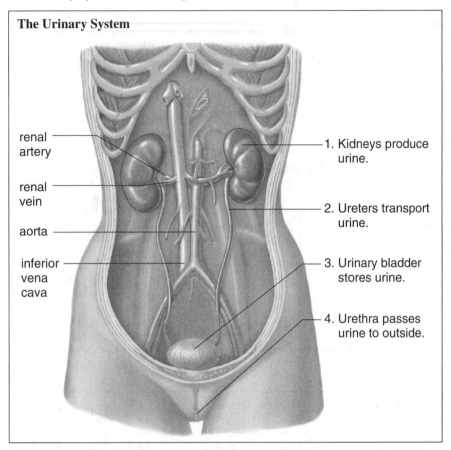

renal artery

renal vein

aorta

inferior vena cava

1. Kidneys produce urine.

2. Ureters transport urine.

3. Urinary bladder stores urine.

4. Urethra passes urine to outside.

SOURCE: From Sylvia S. Mader, *Biology*, 8th ed., McGraw-Hill, 2004; reproduced with permission of The McGraw-Hill Companies.

The Kidney

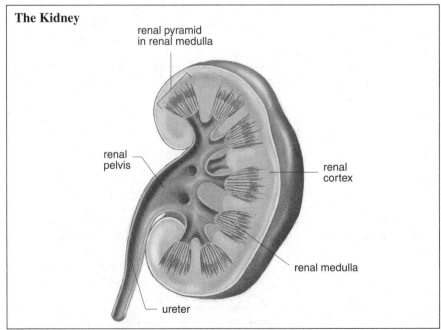

renal pyramid in renal medulla

renal pelvis

renal cortex

renal medulla

ureter

SOURCE: From Sylvia S. Mader, *Biology*, 8th ed., McGraw-Hill, 2004; reproduced with permission of The McGraw-Hill Companies.

Endocrine System

The endocrine system contains a number of endocrine glands that secrete *hormones* that regulate a range of processes in the body. The rate at which hormones are released is determined by the needs of the body at a given time. In a *positive feedback mechanism,* a change in a hormone's concentration causes the same kind of change in some other substance. In a *negative feed-*

The Endocrine System

Gland	Location	Hormone	Effect on the Body
Anterior pituitary	Hypothalamus	Growth hormone/ Thyroid-stimulating hormone	• Controls growth • Controls thyroxine release
Posterior pituitary	Hypothalamus	Oxytocin/ Vasopressin	• Affects uterine contractions • Affects water reabsorption in nephrons
Thyroid gland	Below larynx, in front of trachea	Thyroxine	• Regulates rate of metabolic activities
Parathyroid	Behind the thyroid gland	Parathormone	• Regulates calcium and phosphate metabolism
Islets of Langerhans	Pancreas	Insulin/Glucagon	• Lowers and raises blood glucose levels
Adrenal medulla	Adrenaline gland on kidney	Epinephrine/ Norepinephrine	• Increases rate of metabolism • Causes liver to release glucose
Adrenal cortex	Adrenaline gland on kidney	Cortisol	• Governs rate of metabolism for fats, proteins, and carbohydrates
Testes	Scrotum	Testosterone	• Affects development of male reproductive system and secondary sex characteristics
Ovaries	Female reproductive system	Estrogen/ Progesterone	• Affects development of female reproductive system and secondary sex characteristics • Regulates menstrual cycle
Thymus	Chest	Thymosin	• Produces lymphocytes during childhood years

back mechanism, a change in the concentration of a hormone causes a change in the concentration of another substance opposite to the change in the concentration of the hormone.

There are a number of glands that can release hormones into the blood, each with its own function. The chart on page 232 outlines some of the major glands and hormones that regulate our body's processes.

Nervous System

The nervous system is composed of a network of nerve cells that allow nerve impulses to travel throughout the body. *Neurons* (nerve cells) are made of a cell body that contains a nucleus. A number of branched fibers called *dendrites* receive impulses that are carried through the *axon*. The axon is covered by a fatty substance called the myelin sheath. The final destination of the impulse after traveling the axon is the terminal branches and synaptic knobs. The impulses then reach a gap between neurons called a *synapse* where neurotransmitters cross the gap and transmit the impulse to another neuron.

Nerve impulses travel at high speeds and are conducted via a sodium-potassium pump in the nerve cell membrane. Impulses travel along axons because the ions that are pumped cause a reverse in the polarity of the membrane.

There are a number of divisions in the nervous system, each with its own purpose and area of control in the body. The *central nervous system* is composed of the brain and the spinal cord. The *brain* is composed of the cerebrum, cerebellum, and medulla oblongata. The *cerebrum* is responsible for activities such as speech, memory, olfaction, and movement. The *cerebellum* controls voluntary movements and some involuntary movements. The *medulla oblongata* is responsible for involuntary commands.

The *spinal cord* runs along the spinal column and connects the peripheral nervous system to the brain (an electroencephalogram can be taken to measure the brain's activity). The spinal cord also allows for certain automatic reflex responses. The *peripheral nervous system* is composed of sensory neurons that transmit nerve impulses toward the central nervous system, along with motor neurons that transmit impulses from the central nervous system.

Motor neurons can be further classified as part of the somatic nervous system or the autonomic nervous system. The *somatic nervous system* guides the actions of skeletal muscles, whereas the *autonomic nervous system* guides the actions of organs and involuntary muscles. The autonomic nervous system controls actions that raise the body's level of activity. The *parasympathetic nervous system* guides the actions of the body that calm the body down.

The Nephron

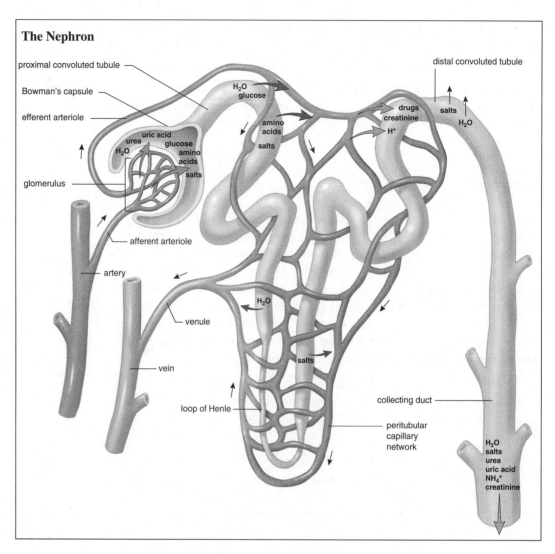

proximal convoluted tubule

Bowman's capsule

efferent arteriole

glomerulus

afferent arteriole

artery

venule

vein

loop of Henle

H_2O
glucose

uric acid
urea
H_2O
glucose
amino
acids
salts

amino
acids
salts

H_2O

salts

drugs
creatinine

H^+

distal convoluted tubule

salts
H_2O

collecting duct

peritubular
capillary
network

H_2O
salts
urea
uric acid
NH_4^+
creatinine

SOURCE: From Sylvia S. Mader, *Biology*, 8th ed., McGraw-Hill, 2004; reproduced with permission of The McGraw-Hill Companies.

A Nerve Cell

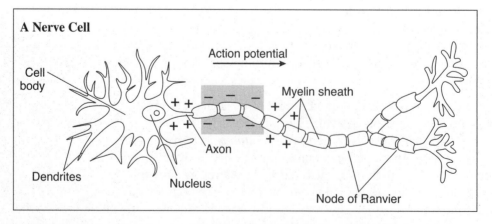

Action potential

Cell
body

Myelin sheath

Axon

Dendrites

Nucleus

Node of Ranvier

SOURCE: From Stephanie Zinn, ed., *McGraw-Hill's SAT Subject Test: Biology*, McGraw-Hill, 2006; reproduced with permission of The McGraw-Hill Companies.

Musculoskeletal System

The human musculoskeletal system provides structure, and the muscles provide the strength and ability to move. Bones, besides providing structure, also provide protection for internal organs. The *marrow* of the bone is where red blood cells are formed along with white blood cells. Some parts of our bodies contain *cartilage* instead of bone, an example being the ear. Cartilage is flexible but serves the same purpose as bone, as a type of connective tissue. Cartilage allows for some degree of movement so that bones can bend easily at the joints. Cartilage also allows for some protection against impacts.

Of the parts of the skeletal system, *the axial skeletal system* includes the breastbone, skull, ribs, and vertebrae (organisms with a spine are called vertebrates). The *appendicular skeleton* includes the legs, arms, shoulder blades, collar bones, and the pelvic bone and girdle. The point where one bone meets another is called a *joint.* Movable joints have *ligaments,* keeping the bones held together. Ligaments should not be confused with *tendons,* which connect bones to muscle.

The element calcium is a metallic element, which accounts for the hardness of bones and teeth. Calcium needs to be obtained from foods to keep bones strong and healthy. Vitamin D also helps with the body's uptake of calcium to maintain overall health in the bones.

There are three types of muscle present in the body: smooth, skeletal, and cardiac. As its name suggests, *cardiac muscle* is present in the heart. *Skeletal muscle* is attached to the skeleton of the body and is used for voluntary movements. *Smooth muscle* is used involuntarily and is present in the diaphragm, digestive system, and arteries. Some muscles cause the joints in the body to flex and are called flexors, whereas other muscles extend joints of the body and are called *extensors.*

The Human Skeletal System

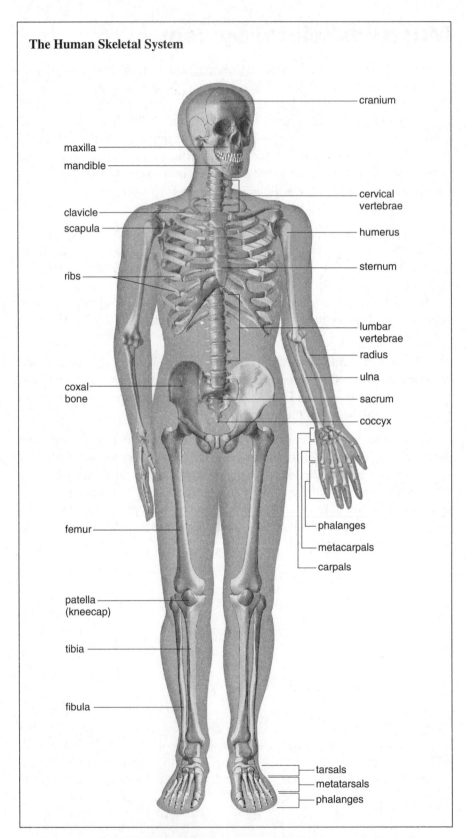

SOURCE: From Sylvia S. Mader, *Biology*, 8th ed., McGraw-Hill, 2004; reproduced with permission of The McGraw-Hill Companies.

Human Reproductive Systems

Human reproduction takes place internally, where sperm and egg join inside the female reproductive system. (In many other species, eggs are fertilized and develop outside of body.) Before getting into the details of reproduction and development, let us first review the parts of the human reproductive systems.

Human Male Reproductive System

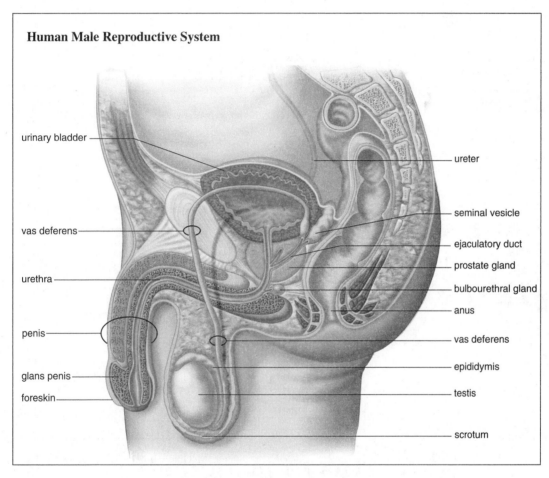

SOURCE: From Sylvia S. Mader, *Biology*, 8th ed., McGraw-Hill, 2004; reproduced with permission of The McGraw-Hill Companies.

In the male, the *testes* are located in the scrotum. After sperm are produced in the testes, they are then stored in the epididymis where they mature. On leaving the epididymis, the sperm travel through the vas deferens. These two passageways lead the sperm into the urethra. As the sperm travel through the vas deferens, a number of glands, including the seminal and prostate glands, secrete fluids to create semen. The process by which semen exits the penis is called ejaculation.

In the female, eggs are produced in the *ovaries* and on maturation, move with their follicles to the surface of the ovary. The process of ovulation is the point where the egg is released from its follicle. The egg is then moved through the

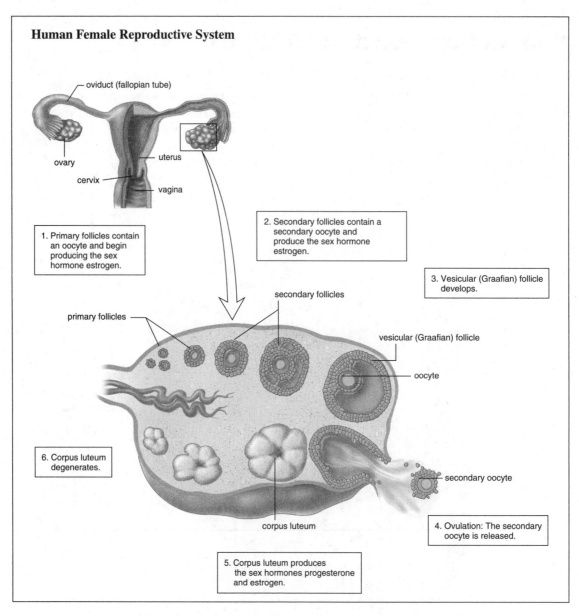

Human Female Reproductive System

- oviduct (fallopian tube)
- ovary
- uterus
- cervix
- vagina

1. Primary follicles contain an oocyte and begin producing the sex hormone estrogen.

2. Secondary follicles contain a secondary oocyte and produce the sex hormone estrogen.

3. Vesicular (Graafian) follicle develops.

- primary follicles
- secondary follicles
- vesicular (Graafian) follicle
- oocyte
- secondary oocyte
- corpus luteum

4. Ovulation: The secondary oocyte is released.

5. Corpus luteum produces the sex hormones progesterone and estrogen.

6. Corpus luteum degenerates.

SOURCE: From Sylvia S. Mader, *Biology*, 8th ed., McGraw-Hill, 2004; reproduced with permission of The McGraw-Hill Companies.

fallopian tube (oviduct) via the action of cilia. If a sperm is present, it meets the egg in the fallopian tube. The egg then passes into the uterus. If the egg is fertilized, it remains at the uterine wall to develop into a fetus. The fetus then passes through the birth canal (vagina) during birth.

Upon *fertilization,* the sperm and egg become a *zygote,* which begins a number of cell divisions called *cleavage.* The cells do not grow during this time; instead they continue to divide. The cells form a ball of cells called a *morula,* then a hollow ball called a *blastula.* A second layer of cells forms, and the resulting cells make a *gastrula.* The germ layers then form what are called the *ectoderm, mesoderm,* and *endotherm.* These layers will develop into the different organs and organ systems in the body.

As the development continues in the uterus, the fetus receives nutrients from the mother via the umbilical cord, which is attached to the placenta. The fetus continues to develop while surrounded by amniotic fluid.

Senses

The *ear,* besides allowing humans to hear sounds, helps humans keep their equilibrium and balance. Each part of the ear has a number of organs working together to convert air compressions into a sound that can be interpreted. These parts are shown in the following diagram:

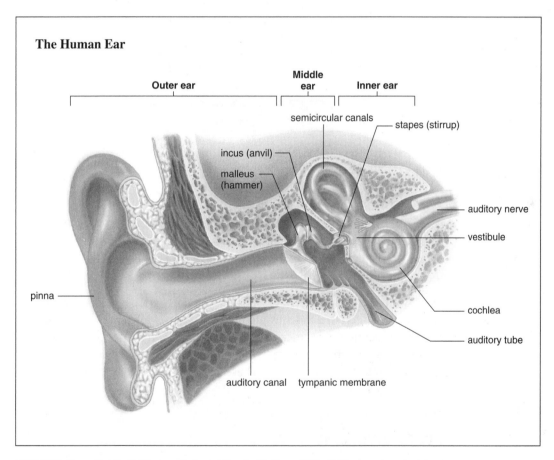

The Human Ear

SOURCE: From Sylvia S. Mader, *Biology,* 8th ed., McGraw-Hill, 2004; reproduced with permission of The McGraw-Hill Companies.

The *eye* features the *cornea,* allowing light into the eye. Light then passes through the *iris* (the colored portion of the eye). The iris has an opening called the *pupil,* which can become larger or smaller depending on how much light is present. The *lens* then focuses the light on the retina, which is

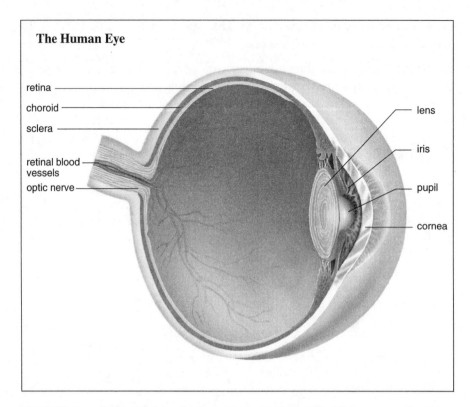

The Human Eye

retina
choroid
sclera
retinal blood vessels
optic nerve

lens
iris
pupil
cornea

SOURCE: From Sylvia S. Mader, *Biology*, 8th ed., McGraw-Hill, 2004; reproduced with permission of The McGraw-Hill Companies.

attached to the *optic nerve*. A layer of light-sensitive cells called the *cones* and *rods* make up one of the layers of the retina. Individuals with defects to this portion of the eye are color-blind and usually cannot see shades of greens and/or reds.

The *nose* and *tongue* also have sensory nerves. Inside the nose, olfactory cells are embedded in a mucous membrane. When odors enter the nose, they enter this mucous lining, causing the olfactory nerves to be stimulated and then be interpreted by the brain. On the tongue, taste buds pick up tastes that are sweet, sour, bitter, and salty. These sensory nerve fibers are located on four regions of the tongue.

ORGAN SYSTEMS QUIZ

Circle the letter of your choice.

1. The ribs are _____ to the lungs in the human body.

(A) medial
(B) distal
(C) anterior
(D) deep

2. Which of the following statements is true?

   (A) The digestive system can do its job without the use of accessory organs.
   (B) The digestive system uses sphincters to contain substances being digested at certain points of the digestive tract.
   (C) Mechanical digestion is more important than chemical digestion.
   (D) The juices that are used to digest food can be effective at any point along the digestive tract.

3. The heart and veins have valves to ensure that

   (A) blood flows in only one direction.
   (B) oxygen and carbon dioxide can be exchanged.
   (C) lymph can be directed through the arteries.
   (D) platelets do not clot at the site of a wound.

4. Of the processes below, which one is a different level of defense from the other three?

   (A) a low pH in the stomach
   (B) cilia present in the trachea
   (C) cells within the body recognizing a pathogen
   (D) mucus present in the nasal cavity

5. The movement of air through the respiratory system depends on

   (A) the movements of the diaphragm.
   (B) how hard the muscles in the trachea contract.
   (C) how hard the lungs push air out of the body.
   (D) cilia along the respiratory tract pushing air in and out of the body.

6. Which pathway/order is correct?

   (A) sperm: testes, epididymis, vas deferens, urethra
   (B) egg: vagina, uterus, ovary, fallopian tube
   (C) development: morula, blastula, zygote, egg
   (D) development: fertilization, ovulation, ejaculation

7. Which of the following statements is false?

   (A) Vitamin D and calcium are needed for strong healthy bones.
   (B) Ligaments keep bones joined together.
   (C) Skeletal muscle is needed for voluntary movements.
   (D) Cartilage's rigidity helps maintain structure.

8. Which of the following statements is false?

(A) The autonomic nervous system allows humans to decide how to use involuntary muscles.
(B) The brain and the spinal cord are part of the central nervous system.
(C) Nerve impulses can send signals faster than chemical signals traveling through the blood.
(D) Neurotransmitters are needed to help send signals between nerves.

9. Inside the kidney one does not find

(A) nephrons.
(B) Bowman's capsules.
(C) glomeruli.
(D) ureters.

10. The purpose of the endocrine system is to

(A) send nerve impulses throughout the body.
(B) aid in digestion.
(C) release chemical signals into the body to regulate functions.
(D) act as a primary defense against foreign invaders.

PLANTS

The structure of plants includes roots, leaves, stem, and flowers. The *roots* hold the plant in place and provide an enormous surface area for increased water uptake along with the uptake of minerals from the soil. This is made possible by capillary action and root pressure. From there, the water and minerals are carried up through the plant via a plant tissue called *xylem*. Another vascular tissue that plants have is *phloem,* which carries food and other materials both up and down in the plant. The *leaves* are where light is captured by the plant. This is why the leaves usually have a large surface area and develop in all directions around the plant. On the leaves are holes called *stomates* that can be opened and closed by guard cells. The opening and closing of the stomates allows for carbon dioxide, oxygen, and water vapor to be exchanged with the air.

Plants have the ability to capture light and convert it into chemical energy. This is accomplished by carrying out *photosynthesis*. Because plants can make their own food, they are classified as *autotrophs*. It is the *chloroplasts* that contain the chlorophyll to help with this conversion. Chlorophyll absorbs light best when the wavelength of the light is approximately 430 nm (blue) and 660 nm (red). Plants have more than just one type of chlorophyll, and they also contain other pigments as well. This helps give plants additional wavelengths in which they can absorb light optimally. Besides this, plants also have the ability to carry out *phototropism*. This process allows them to bend toward a light source so that they can obtain the maximum amount of the available light.

The *flowers* of the plant are responsible for the sexual reproduction that many plants carry out. The *stamen* (composed of a filament and anther) is the male

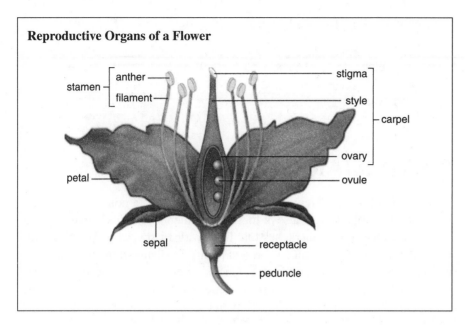

Reproductive Organs of a Flower

SOURCE: From Sylvia S. Mader, *Biology*, eighth edition, McGraw-Hill, 2004; reproduced with permission of the McGraw-Hill Companies.

reproductive organ, whereas the *pistil* (composed of the ovary, style, and stigma) is the female reproductive organ. When pollen from the anther is transferred to a stigma, the two gametophytes form a zygote and develop a seed with an embryo inside. The ovaries of the pistil contain ovules. These ovules develop the seed and the ovary of the plant becomes a fruit. The fruit holds the seeds and protects them. This is why tomatoes are classified as fruits and *not* vegetables.

PLANTS QUIZ

1. Plant cells are different from animal cells because plant cells

(A) have a nucleus.
(B) divide to form daughter cells.
(C) have a cell wall.
(D) have no need for chloroplasts.

2. The roots of a plant are not

(A) needed to uptake water.
(B) responsible for carrying out photosynthesis.
(C) responsible for anchoring the plant into the soil.
(D) needed to uptake minerals from the soil.

3. Which wavelength of light is best absorbed by chlorophyll?

(A) 500 nm
(B) 550 nm
(C) 660 nm
(D) 485 nm

4. Which part of the plant reproductive system is of a different "gender" from the other three?

(A) stamen
(B) pistil
(C) stigma
(D) style

MENDELIAN GENETICS

The Austrian botanist Gregor Mendel (1822–1884) is famous for his experiments with pea plants. Because of these experiments, humans began to understand the expression of the genes that living organisms carry. When Mendel crossed a tall pea plant with a short pea plant, the plants in the resulting generation, the F_1 generation, were all tall. The F_1 generation of pea plants is said to be a *hybrid* because it contains the genes for both tallness and shortness. The genes that are carried by an organism make up its *genotype.*

But why were the genes for tallness expressed and the genes for shortness were not? This refers to the organism's *phenotype,* the physical traits that are actually expressed by an organism. Because the genes for tallness were the only ones expressed, Mendel described them as *dominant.* The genes for shortness that were not expressed (or "hidden") he described as *recessive.* From these results, Mendel deduced that genes exist in varied forms called *alleles.* For each trait, an organism inherits two alleles, one from each parent. The resulting allele pair determines how the trait is expressed in the organism. According to *Mendel's law of segregation*, these allele pairs separate (or segregate) during gamete formation and then randomly unite at fertilization. The new allele pair then determines how the trait is expressed in the new organism. This process can be diagrammed using what is called a *Punnett square.*

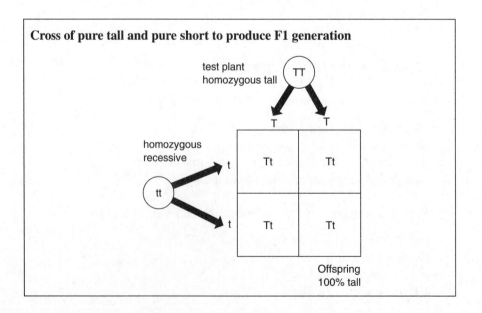

Cross of pure tall and pure short to produce F1 generation

The Punnett square above shows Mendel's experiment. The tall pea plant is said to be *homozygous* because it has two alleles for tallness (TT). The short pea plant is also homozygous, with two alleles for shortness (tt). However, the offspring are *heterozygous,* with alleles for both tallness and shortness. All of the offspring are tall because tallness is dominant. But each offspring also carries an allele for shortness that is not expressed.

When seeds from this F_1 generation were crossed, in the F_2 generation approximately three-fourths of the plants were tall and one-fourth of the plants were short. The short plants, a phenotype that was not expressed in the F_1 generation, thus appeared again but in only 25 percent of the plants of the F_2 generation.

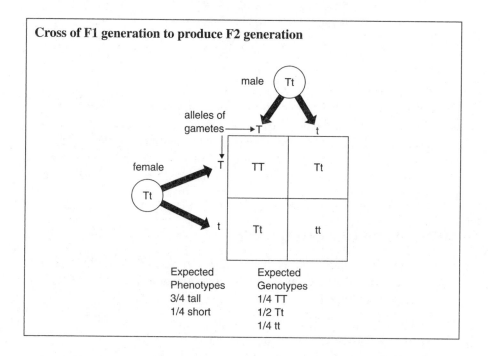

Cross of F1 generation to produce F2 generation

The cross between a male and a female shows that a couple has a 50 percent chance of having either a boy or a girl. Because the female always provides X chromosomes, it is the male who determines the sex of the child because the male can provide either an X chromosome or a Y chromosome. The Y chromosome is dominant. Although the Punnett square below shows more X chromosomes, it is the dominance of the Y chromosome that keeps the chance of producing a male at 50 percent.

Some traits are controlled by genes that are found on the sex chromosomes. These are called *sex-linked traits.* Sometimes diseases and conditions such as color blindness are the results of these traits being passed on to offspring. A sex-linked trait (allele) on an X sex chromosome, for example, is shown as X'. For color blindness to occur in an individual, all of the X chromosomes must have the allele for color blindness. For females to have the condition, both X chromosomes must have this allele (X'X'). For males, it is just the one X chromosome (X'Y). That is why color blindness occurs more often in males, whereas females can be carriers of the disorder without expressing it in their phenotype.

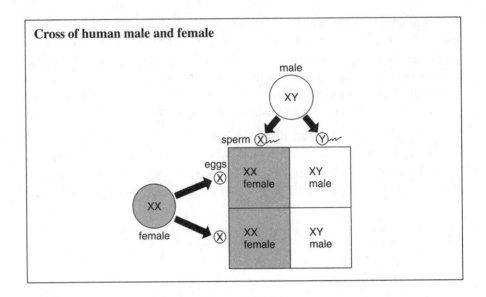

Cross of human male and female

Recessive defective alleles on chromosomes can lead to other disorders such as sickle cell anemia, cystic fibrosis, and Tay-Sachs disease. Many people can carry these disorders and not show signs of the illness because they have a dominant allele that is expressed instead of the recessive one. However, should two carriers produce offspring, they have a 25 percent chance of having a child with the disorder.

MENDELIAN GENETICS QUIZ

1. A short pea plant that is homozygous recessive for tallness (tt) is crossed with a tall pea plant which is heterozygous for tallness (Tt). The expected outcome is

   (A) 25 percent of the plants will be short.
   (B) 75 percent of the plants will be short.
   (C) 50 percent of the plants will be tall.
   (D) 100 percent of the plants will be tall.

2. A male who is color-blind (X'Y) produces offspring with a female carrier of the same disorder (X'X). Which of the following is expected?

   (A) All of the children will be color-blind.
   (B) None of the children will be color-blind.
   (C) The male offspring will be color-blind.
   (D) The offspring have a 50 percent chance of being color-blind.

ECOLOGY

Ecology is the study of relationships between organisms and between organisms and their surroundings. A number of factors can affect an organism and its surroundings. These can be classified as biotic or abiotic. *Abiotic* factors are the factors that are not living, such as amounts of light available, temperature, amounts of water available, and levels of minerals present in the soil. *Biotic* factors are factors that are living.

Many organisms live in *symbiosis,* a relationship in which two or more organisms live close to each other and at least one of them benefits from the relationship. If both organisms benefit, the relationship is called *mutualism.* *Commensalism* is a symbiotic relationship in which one organism benefits and the other is not affected. *Parasitism* is a symbiotic relationship in which an organism benefits while harming another.

A group of organisms of the same type living together is called a *population;* for example, the population of humans in the United States is roughly 360 million people. A *community* includes many different organisms living in the same area. An *ecosystem* includes a community and the biotic and abiotic factors that govern the exchange of living and nonliving parts within that ecosystem. *Biomes* are large regions inhabited by ecologically similar communities of living organisms. Terrestrial (land-based) biomes include deserts and tropical rainforests. Aquatic (water-based) biomes include oceans and lakes. Different biomes have different animal and plant life as well as different climates and weather patterns.

Within ecosystems, materials are passed from one organism to another. Repeated patterns of materials being exchanged are called *cycles.* Cycles exist for water, oxygen, carbon dioxide, and nitrogen. Producers and consumers also pass materials to one another in a *food chain.* For example, grass (producer) might be consumed by a mouse (primary consumer), which could then be consumed by a snake (secondary consumer). Because many animals can consume a range of living organisms, we can combine the many food chains together to produce a *food web.*

One other important member of the ecosystem is the *decomposer.* Decomposers break down the remains of dead animals and plants. By doing so, they release substances into the ecosystems that can be reused by other organisms. Examples of decomposers are bacteria, fungi, and detritivores (earthworms, for example).

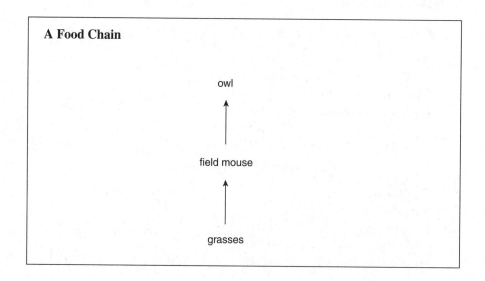

A Food Chain

owl

↑

field mouse

↑

grasses

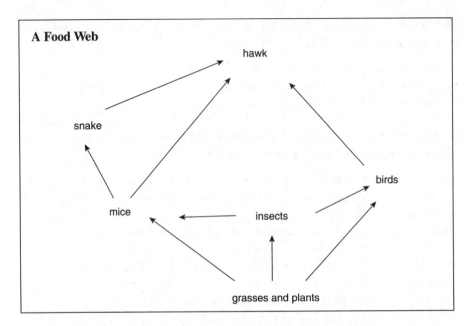

A Food Web

Humans have had a tremendous impact on the Earth and the environment. The Earth's population of humans is believed to be more than 6 billion people. Because of this, humans have urbanized areas that once belonged to other species. In addition, pollution of the water, air, and soil has made living conditions harsh for many organisms. Places on Earth that were once habitable by organisms can no longer support life. Efforts to combat the problem include recycling, use of renewable energy sources, pollution control laws, and conservation.

ECOLOGY QUIZ

1. Two organisms live in a symbiotic relationship from which both benefit. This is best described as

(A) mutualism.
(B) parasitism.
(C) commensalism.
(D) conservation.

2. Which of the following is not helpful in protecting the environment?

(A) recycling plastic, glass, and paper
(B) making use of solar energy
(C) burning fossil fuels
(D) driving hydrogen fuel cell cars

3. This question is based on the following:

Grass → Insect → Bird → Hawk

This diagram shows
(A) a food web.
(B) a food chain.
(C) decomposers in action.
(D) what happens when sunlight is not available.

4. Examples of biomes do not include

(A) deserts.
(B) tundra.
(C) tropical rainforests.
(D) neighborhoods in a city.

DIVERSITY OF LIFE

Evolution has produced millions and millions of different types of organisms over a few billion years. Only a fraction of all of the organisms that have ever made an appearance on Earth still exist today. Fossils within rocks, amber, and ice provide the remains of organisms that were once on earth but are now extinct. In addition to providing fossils and clues about the past, rock layers provide clues to the relative ages of fossils and the sequence of which they were once living organisms. Methods of radioactive dating and measuring the decay of certain isotopes can provide a better estimate of the age of a fossil. The isotopes usually used are C-14 for living organisms and U-235 for rocks.

The English naturalist Charles Darwin (1809–1882) proposed the theory of *natural selection* and described it in his book *On the Origin of Species* in the mid-1800s. According to this theory, all organisms compete for food and survival. Only the organisms that possess the best genes to survive live to reproduce and pass on those "best survival genes" to their offspring. Those organisms that cannot compete die off and are not able to pass on genes that are not favorable to survival. The term *natural selection* is sometimes described as "survival of the fittest."

Because of the vast number of organisms that are alive today or that have lived in the past, scientists use a system of *taxonomy* for classifying organisms. In this system, each organism is classified as a member of a kingdom, phylum, class, order, family, genus, species, and subspecies. To name organisms, scientists use a binomial system that includes the organism's genus and species. Because the diversity of life is so great and new species are being discovered all the time, the classifications of many organisms have changed over the years.

DIVERSITY OF LIFE QUIZ

1. The scientific name for a house cat is *Felis catus*. This indicates the house cat's

(A) kingdom and family.
(B) order and subspecies.
(C) phylum and class.
(D) genus and species.

2. Which of the following statements is false?

   (A) The exact age of a fossil can be determined by examining rock layers.
   (B) Radioisotope dating can help determine the approximate age of a fossil.
   (C) It is possible to determine the approximate age of a rock.
   (D) Just a small number of organisms that ever lived on Earth are alive today.

3. Natural selection does not include the idea that

   (A) only the genes of the best fit organisms will be passed on.
   (B) all organisms have a fair and equal chance of surviving.
   (C) only the fittest organisms survive.
   (D) there is a competition between organisms for survival.

ANSWERS TO BIOLOGICAL SCIENCES QUIZZES

CELL STRUCTURE

1. Correct choices in order: B, E, D, A, C.
Mitochondria are the sites of energy production. Vacuoles provide storage space in the cell. The nucleus holds the DNA of the cell. The cell membrane is selectively permeable and allows only certain substances to pass through. Ribosomes are the sites of protein synthesis.

2. The correct choice is B.
Enzymes are proteins and catalysts that can speed up a reaction.

3. The correct choice is A.
Because the cell is in a solution where the concentration of solutes is higher inside the cell than outside the cell, water is expected to flow into the cell to dilute the concentration of solutes inside the cell. This causes the cell to swell up and possibly burst.

4. The correct choice is C.
The products of fermentation are ethanol and carbon dioxide. It is the carbon dioxide that causes the dough to rise.

5. The correct choice is D.
"DNA cannot be altered" is a false statement because DNA can be mutated and changed. The other answer choices are true statements.

6. The correct choice is B.
Mitosis creates cells that are exact copies of each other, including the number of chromosomes in the cell. Meiosis, which creates sex cells, forms cells with half the number of chromosomes in the original cell.

ORGAN SYSTEMS

1. The correct choice is C.
The ribs are in front of the lungs in the human body, making them closer to the front of the body. This is best described as being anterior.

2. The correct choice is B.

Sphincters help keep food in the stomach while being digested, and the anus is a sphincter that holds fecal matter from being eliminated until the organism is ready to do so.

3. The correct choice is A.

The heart and veins have valves to ensure that the blood flows in only one direction.

4. The correct choice is C.

A low pH in the stomach, cilia present in the trachea, and mucus present in the nasal cavity are primary defenses. Cells within the body recognizing a pathogen are a third line of defense.

5. The correct choice is A.

The movement of air through the respiratory system depends on the movements of the diaphragm. It is the movement of this muscle that creates a void space, allowing air to rush in.

6. The correct choice is A.

Sperm are produced in the testes, stored in the epididymis, and then travel through the vas deferens and urethra.

7. The correct choice is D.

Cartilage is a soft type of bone that lacks rigidity. This is why you are able to bend your ears.

8. The correct choice is A.

The autonomic nervous system guides the actions of organs and involuntary muscles. However, because involuntary muscles are involved, you cannot control those actions.

9. The correct choice is D.

The ureter, although part of the excretory system, is not part of the kidney.

10. The correct choice is C.

The purpose of the endocrine system is to release hormones (chemical signals) into the body to regulate the body's functions.

PLANTS

1. The correct choice is C.

Plant cells are different from animal cells because plant cells have cell walls and contain chloroplasts to carry out photosynthesis.

2. The correct choice is B.

The roots of a plant are not responsible for carrying out photosynthesis. This is the job of the chloroplasts.

3. The correct choice is C.

Red and blue light are best absorbed by chlorophyll. This corresponds to wavelengths of 660 nm and 430 nm, respectively.

4. The correct choice is A.

The stamen is considered to be a male part of the plant reproductive system, whereas the pistil, stigma, and style (and ovary) are considered to be female parts of the plant reproductive system.

MENDELIAN GENETICS

1. The correct choice is C.

Fifty percent of the plants will be tall because, as a Punnett square would show, two of the new allele sets will be Tt and the other two will be tt.

2. The correct choice is D.

If a Punnett square is created showing the cross between a color-blind male (X'Y) and a female carrier (X'X), the resulting combinations will be X'X', X'Y, X'X, and XY. The underlined offspring are color-blind.

	X'	Y
X'	X'X' Color-blind female	X'Y Color-blind male
X	X'X Carrier female	XY Normal male

ECOLOGY

1. The correct choice is A.

Mutualism is a relationship in which two organisms live symbiotically and both benefit.

2. The correct choice is C.

The burning of fossil fuels has raised levels of carbon dioxide, a greenhouse gas, in the atmosphere. This is believed to be the cause of global warming.

3. The correct choice is B.

This example shows a food chain because only one pathway of energy transfer has been diagramed. A food web would show multiple pathways by which the energy from an organism could be passed along.

4. The correct choice is D.

Biomes are large regions inhabited by ecologically similar communities of living organisms. Examples are deserts, the tundra, and tropical rainforests. A city neighborhood is not a biome.

DIVERSITY OF LIFE

1. The correct choice is D.

The scientific name of an organism reflects its genus and species.

2. The correct choice is A.

Finding the exact age of a fossil by examining a rock layer is impossible. A rock layer can, however, can give an approximate age of a fossil.

3. The correct choice is B.

The idea that all organisms have a fair and equal chance of surviving is not the case. Organisms must compete for survival and resources. Only those that survive can pass on their genes to offspring, and those genes will produce physical characteristics that aid survival.

REVIEW OF PHYSICAL SCIENCES:
CHEMISTRY
SCIENTIFIC NOTATION AND THE METRIC SYSTEM

Because science often deals with measurements that are much larger or smaller than our usual measurements, scientists use scientific notation to express those measurements.

Scientific Notation

Suppose you wanted to express the number of carbon atoms in one mole of carbon. One way is to say that there are 602,000,000,000,000,000,000,000 atoms of carbon present. But it is much easier to write that number in *scientific notation* as follows: 6.02×10^{23}. In scientific notation, the number is simplified. The zeros are replaced by a power of 10, which indicates the number of places to move the decimal point left or right to write the actual number. Note the use of powers of 10 in the following examples:

$1 \times 10^0 = 1$

$1 \times 10^2 = 100$

$1 \times 10^4 = 10,000$

$1 \times 10^{-1} = 0.1$

$1 \times 10^{-3} = 0.001$

When you write a very large or very small number, count the number of zeros or decimal places in the number and use a power of 10 to express the number in scientific notation.

The Metric System

When expressing measurements in the *metric system,* often you can indicate powers of ten by adding common prefixes to the base units. Some examples are shown below:

Power of Ten	Prefix	Symbol	Example Applied to a Base Unit
10^3	Kilo	K	1 kilogram (1 kg) = 10^3 grams (1,000 g)
10^{-2}	Centi	C	1 centimeter (1 cm) = 10^{-2} meters (0.01 m)
10^{-3}	Milli	M	1 millimeter (1 mm) = 10^{-3} meters (0.001 m)
10^{-6}	Micro	μ	1 microliter (1 μL) = 10^{-6} L (0.000001 L)
10^{-9}	Nano	N	1 nanosecond (1 ns) = 10^{-9} s (0.000000001 s)

SCIENTIFIC NOTATION AND THE METRIC SYSTEM QUIZ

1. The number 1,000,000 is what power of 10?

(A) 10^{-6}
(B) 10^6
(C) 1^6
(D) 0.000001

2. The quantity 6,180 meters can be rewritten as

(A) 6.180×10^3 meters.
(B) 6,180 kilometers.
(C) $6,180 \times 10^3$ meters.
(D) 180×10^3 meters.

3. How many millimeters are there in one centimeter?

(A) 10,000
(B) 1,000
(C) 100
(D) 10

ATOMIC STRUCTURE
Dalton's Atomic Theory

A number of theories about the structures of the atom have been proposed over the years. At one time it was thought that an atom was the point where a piece of matter could no longer be divided. Hence, atoms were named after the Greek word *atomos*, meaning "indivisible."

The English chemist John Dalton (1766–1844) first developed the modern atomic theory. His theory, which summarized what was known about the atom in his time, was as follows:

1. All elements/matter are composed of atoms.
2. All atoms of the same element are exactly alike.
3. Atoms of different elements are different.
4. Compounds are formed by the joining of atoms in different ratios, and chemical reactions cause atoms to rearrange into different compounds.

Elements, Compounds, and Allotropes

Elements are substances that cannot be broken down chemically. Elements can bond together to form *compounds*. The bond that forms can later be broken so that the atoms can rearrange again to form new compounds. Here is an example:

$$CH_4 + 2O_2 \rightarrow 2H_2O + CO_2$$

In this example, the elements carbon (C), hydrogen (H), and oxygen (O) are present. The reactants (CH_4 and O_2) and products (H_2O and CO_2) are composed of the same elements. However, rearrangement of these elements has formed different compounds.

Allotropes are different forms of the same element. For example, oxygen can be found as diatomic oxygen, O_2, or ozone, O_3. Allotropes of carbon include diamonds, graphite, or buckminsterfullerene.

Subatomic Particles

Although the atom is considered the basic unit of matter, it is composed of three smaller subatomic particles. These are called protons, neutrons, and electrons, and they can be summarized as follows:

Subatomic particle	Proton	Electron	Neutron
Mass	1 atomic mass unit (AMU)	1/1836 AMU	1 AMU
Charge	+1	−1	0
Location in the atom	Nucleus	Principal Energy Levels	Nucleus

The Nucleus of the Atom

The nucleus of an atom contains the element's protons and neutrons. The chemical symbol for the atom will tell you how many of each are present. Here is an example using the symbol for oxygen (O):

$$^{16}_{8}O$$

This symbol gives you the mass number (16) and the atomic number (8). The *atomic number* is the number of protons in the nucleus of the atom. In an atom of neutral charge, the number of electrons is the same as the number of protons. The *mass number* is the total number of nucleons (protons plus neutrons) in the nucleus of the atom. In the example above, there are eight protons in the nucleus of the oxygen atom. The number of neutrons is also eight (16 nucleons − 8 protons = 8 neutrons).

Isotopes

Even though Dalton's atomic theory states that all atoms of a given element are alike, this idea has been modified by later discoveries. Consider two atoms of chlorine: chlorine-35 and chlorine-37. Let us compare them with respect to their subatomic particles in the table that follows.

	Chlorine-35	Chlorine-37
Mass number	35	37
Number of protons/Atomic number	17	17
Number of neutrons	18	20

Note that the two atoms have different numbers of neutrons present. As a result, they have different mass numbers. Yet because the two atoms have the same number of protons, they are both the element chlorine. We say that atoms like these, which have the same number of protons but different numbers of neutrons and thus different mass numbers, are *isotopes* of each other.

Mass Number Compared to Atomic Mass

Do not confuse mass number with atomic mass. Although the mass number indicates the number of protons and neutrons for one particular isotope, the *atomic mass* accounts for all of the isotopes of an element. For example, the atomic mass of chlorine is 35.45. This is because the atomic mass takes into account the relative amounts of Cl-35 and Cl-37. A similar pattern holds true for bromine. The atomic mass of bromine 79.90 takes into account its two most abundant isotopes, Br-81 and Br-79.

Nuclear Reactions

Although the root meaning of *atom* is "indivisible," by no means is the atom indivisible. Nuclear reactions can cause transmutations (changes in the nucleus). A *fusion reaction* is a nuclear reaction in which the nuclei of atoms are joined. An example is the joining of hydrogen nuclei in the sun to produce heavier elements and energy. A *fission reaction* is a nuclear reaction in which a nucleus or nuclei is/are split. Energy is released in this type of reaction as well. Fission and fusion reactions take place in atomic weapons and nuclear reactors.

Radioactive Nuclear Decay

Some atomic nuclei are unstable and lose energy by emitting radioactive *alpha* or *beta particles* or *gamma rays*. This process is called *radioactive decay,* and when it takes place, the atom is transformed from one type to another. The rate of transformation is called the *half-life* (the time it takes for half of a sample of a radioactive substance to decay), and it is different for each radioactive isotope of an element. Below are three examples of radioactive decay. In each case, a different radioactive particle or ray is emitted. Note the formulas and symbols used to denote each of the two types of particles as well as the gamma radiation.

Alpha $^{226}_{88}Ra \rightarrow ^{222}_{86}Rn + ^{4}_{2}He$ (alpha particle, α)

Beta $^{214}_{82}Pb \rightarrow ^{214}_{83}Bi + ^{0}_{-1}e^-$ (beta particle, β^-)

Gamma $^{99}_{43}Tc \rightarrow ^{99}_{43}Tc + \gamma$ (gamma radiation, γ)

Uses for Radioisotopes

Certain radioactive isotopes (*radioisotopes*) have medical uses. These substances are used by the body as usual because the body cannot distinguish between isotopes of elements. Once in the body, they can be used via a scan to create pictures of the body's internal organs. In addition, the radioactive particles emitted by radioisotopes can be used to fight cancer. Examples are radioactive "seeds" that are placed in the prostate to fight prostate cancer and radiation therapy that is used to counter a tumor.

Electron Configurations

The electrons are located in regions around the nucleus called *orbitals* and are arranged in a series of principal energy levels (PELs). Each PEL can hold up to a certain maximum number of electrons. You can calculate each maximum using the formula $2n^2$, where n is the number of the PEL. Thus the maximum numbers of electrons in the first four PELs are as follows:

PEL number	1	2	3	4
Maximum number of electrons	2	8	18	32

To picture how the electrons are arranged, you can imagine them filling the PELs starting with the level 1. When each level is filled to its maximum, the electrons begin filling the next level until all the electrons are in place. If you were to write the electron configuration of an atom of sulfur (sixteen electrons) it would look like this: 2-8-6. In other words, the sulfur atom has two electrons in the first PEL, eight in the second, and six in the third. Here is the electron configuration of nitrogen with its seven electrons: 2-5.

Atoms versus Ions

As atoms interact with each other, they sometimes gain or lose electrons. As a result, the number of electrons in the atom will be different from the number of protons. An atom of this kind is called an *ion*. An ion with more electrons than protons has a negative change and is called an *anion*. An atom with more protons than electrons has a positive charge and is called a *cation*. For example, an atom of nitrogen normally has seven protons and seven electrons. But it may gain three electrons to form N^{3-}, an ion with seven protons (7 positive charges) but ten electrons (10 negative charges), giving a total charge of −3. An ion with a positive charge is the sodium ion Na^{1+}. This ion has lost one electron and now has eleven protons (11 positive charges) but only ten electrons (10 negative charges), giving a total charge of +1.

ATOMIC STRUCTURE QUIZ

1. Explain how isotopes are inconsistent with Dalton's theory that "all atoms of the same element are alike."

   _____
   _____
   _____
   _____
   _____

Circle the letter of your choice.

2. Which isotope below contains the greatest number of neutrons?

   (A) $^{35}_{17}Cl$
   (B) $^{18}_{8}O$
   (C) $^{40}_{18}Ar$
   (D) $^{41}_{20}Ca$

3. Aluminum (Al) has 13 protons in its nucleus. What is the number of electrons in an Al^{3+} ion?

   (A) 13
   (B) 10
   (C) 16
   (D) 3

4. How many electrons can be held in the third PEL of an atom?

   (A) 2
   (B) 8
   (C) 18
   (D) 32

5. Fill in the chart below.

Element	# of Protons	# of Electrons	# of Neutrons
$^{18}_{8}O$			
$^{14}_{6}C$			

6. An atom with more protons in its nucleus has _____ an atom with fewer protons in its nucleus.

(A) a lesser nuclear charge than
(B) a greater nuclear charge than
(C) the same nuclear charge as
(D) no nuclear charge compared to

7. The half-life of a certain radioactive isotope is 5 days. How much of a 100-gram sample of this radioactive isotope will remain after 10 days?

(A) 25
(B) 50
(C) 75
(D) 100

8. What is the name of particle X in the following reaction?

$$^{232}_{90}\text{Th} \rightarrow ^{228}_{88}\text{Ra} + \text{X}$$

(A) deuterium
(B) gamma radiation
(C) beta particle
(D) alpha particle

9. The electron configuration for neon is

(A) 2-5.
(B) 2-8.
(C) 2-18.
(D) 2-10.

THE PERIODIC TABLE

In the *periodic table,* the different elements are shown in order by increasing atomic number. The table is configured in such a way that different locations on the table correspond to different properties of the elements. As you move from one location to another on the table, the elements possess or lack different properties, or possess those properties to a greater or lesser extent. That is why the table is said to show "trends" among the elements. By knowing the location of an element on the periodic table, you can tell the properties of that element.

Each horizontal row in the periodic table is called a *period.* The periods correspond to the PELs that are filled by increasing numbers of electrons as you move from one element to the next across the row from left to right. The vertical columns are called *groups* or *families.* Each one contains elements with similar properties.

Periodic Table of the Elements

1	2	3	4	5	6	7	8	9	10	11	12	13	14	15	16	17	18
1 H 1.0079																	2 He 4.0026
3 Li 6.941	4 Be 9.0122											5 B 10.81	6 C 12.011	7 N 14.007	8 O 15.999	9 F 18.998	10 Ne 20.179
11 Na 22.989	12 Mg 24.305											13 Al 26.981	14 Si 28.086	15 P 30.974	16 S 32.06	17 Cl 35.453	18 Ar 39.948
19 K 39.098	20 Ca 40.08	21 Sc 44.956	22 Ti 47.88	23 V 50.941	24 Cr 51.996	25 Mn 54.938	26 Fe 55.847	27 Co 58.933	28 Ni 58.69	29 Cu 63.546	30 Zn 65.38	31 Ga 59.72	32 Ge 72.59	33 As 74.922	34 Se 78.96	35 Br 79.904	36 Kr 83.80
37 Rb 85.468	38 Sr 87.62	39 Y 88.906	40 Zr 91.22	41 Nb 92.905	42 Mo 95.94	43 Tc (98)	44 Ru 101.07	45 Rh 102.91	46 Pd 106.42	47 Ag 107.87	48 Cd 112.41	49 In 114.82	50 Sn 118.69	51 Sb 121.75	52 Te 127.60	53 I 126.90	54 Xe 131.29
55 Cs 132.91	56 Ba 137.33	57 * La 138.90	72 Hf 178.49	73 Ta 180.95	74 W 183.85	75 Re 186.21	76 Os 190.2	77 Ir 192.22	78 Pt 195.08	79 Au 196.97	80 Hg 200.59	81 Tl 204.38	82 Pb 207.2	83 Bi 208.98	84 Po (209)	85 At (210)	86 Rn (222)
87 Fr (223)	88 Ra 226.0	89 # Ac 227.03	104 Rf (261)	105 Db (262)	106 Sg (263)	107 Bh (262)	108 Hs (265)	109 Mt (266)	110 Uun (269)	111 Uuu (272)	112 Uub (277)						

* Lanthanides

58 Ce 140.12	59 Pr 140.91	60 Nd 144.24	61 Pm (145)	62 Sm 150.36	63 Eu 151.96	64 Gd 157.25	65 Tb 158.92	66 Dy 162.50	67 Ho 164.93	68 Er 167.26	69 Tm 168.93	70 Yb 173.04	71 Lu 174.97

Actinides

90 Th 232.03	91 Pa 231.03	92 U 238.03	93 Np 237.05	94 Pu (244)	95 Am (243)	96 Cm (247)	97 Bk (247)	98 Cf (251)	99 Es (254)	100 Fm (257)	101 Md (257)	102 No (255)	103 Lr (256)

Metals, Nonmetals, and Semimetals

Metals make up about two-thirds of the elements in the periodic table. They are mainly located on the left and center areas of the table (hydrogen, a non-metal, is an exception; it is located on the left). On the upper right side of the table are the nonmetals. In between are the semimetals: B, Si, As, Te, At, Ge, and Sb. Note how they form a "staircase" that separates the metals from the nonmetals. The properties of metals and nonmetals are outlined below.

Properties of Metals	Properties of Nonmetals
• Shiny • Malleable • Ductile • Conduct heat • Conduct electricity	• Lack luster • Brittle • Poor conductor of heat • Poor conductor of electricity

Atomic Radius

As you move from left to right across a period on the table, each element has a smaller atomic radius (distance from the nucleus to the outermost electron) than the one before. For example, in period two, lithium (Li) on the left side of the table has a larger atomic radius than fluorine (F), which is located on the right side of the periodic table. As you proceed from top to bottom in a group/family, the atomic radius increases as well.

Ionization Energy

The *ionization energy* of an atom is the energy required to remove the outermost electron from the atom. This energy is needed to overcome the attraction between the positively charged protons and negatively charged electrons. As you proceed from left to right in a period, the ionization energy of the elements increases, indicating their greater ability to attract or "hold on to" electrons. As you proceed from top to bottom in a group/family, the ionization energy of the elements decreases and electrons are lost more easily.

Electronegativity

The ability to attract electrons is called an element's *electronegativity*. As you proceed from left to right in a period, the electronegativity of the elements increases. As you proceed down a group/family, the electronegativity of the elements decreases. One element to keep in mind is fluorine (top right corner of the periodic table) because it has the highest electronegativity of all of the elements. Use it as a reference for trends in electronegativity.

Groups and Families

The elements in the groups or families (vertical columns) of the periodic table exhibit similar chemical properties. That is because they have similar electron configurations, form ions of the same charge, and react in a similar fashion. For example, fluorine and chlorine each have seven electrons in their outermost PELs, 2-7 and 2-8-7, respectively. This places fluorine and chlorine in the same family. Both atoms will also form ions with the same charge of 1−. The names and properties of some selected families are shown in the following chart.

Name of Group/Family	Location	Properties
Alkali metals	Group 1	Metals with one outermost electron. Form 1+ ions.
Alkaline earth metals	Group 2	Metals with two outermost electrons. Form 2+ ions.
Transition metals	Groups 3-10	Metals that usually form colored ions and solutions. Have multiple oxidation states.
Halogens	Group 17	Nonmetals with seven outermost electrons. Form 1− ions.
Noble gases	Group 18	Nonmetal gases that do not react because they have full outermost PELs.

PERIODIC TABLE QUIZ

Circle the letter of your choice.

1. The arrangement of the modern periodic table is based on atomic

    (A) mass.
    (B) number.
    (C) radius.
    (D) electronegativity.

2. Where on the periodic table are the nonmetals located?

    (A) upper right
    (B) upper left
    (C) lower right
    (D) lower left

3. Which two elements have chemical properties that are similar?

    (A) H and He
    (B) Fe and W
    (C) Li and Be
    (D) Mg and Ca

4. Which element has the lowest electronegativity?

(A) F
(B) Cl
(C) Br
(D) I

5. Which of the following elements has the greatest atomic radius?

(A) strontium
(B) fluorine
(C) neon
(D) cobalt

6. Which statement below is false?

(A) Hydrogen is a nonmetal.
(B) Aluminum is a semimetal.
(C) Calcium is a metal.
(D) Argon is a gas at room temperature.

BONDING

Covalent Bonds and Ionic Bonds

Bonds between atoms can be formed when electrons are transferred or shared. The types of atoms involved in the bond also determine what type of bond will form. Two kinds of bonds are covalent bonds and ionic bonds. The differences between these two types are outlined in the chart on the next page.

Covalent Bonding	Ionic Bonding
• Electrons are shared between two nonmetals.	• Electrons are transferred from a metal to a nonmetal, causing ions to form. • Oppositely charged ions attract one another.

Examples of covalently bonded substances are H_2O (water), CH_4 (methane), and NH_3 (ammonia). Ionic substances are salts such as NaCl (sodium chloride), KI (potassium iodide), and $CaCl_2$ (calcium chloride). Noting the types of elements present in the covalent compounds and the ionic compounds, you see that covalently bonded substances have all nonmetal atoms while the ionic substances contain metals and nonmetals.

If you further examine the electron configuration of Na and Cl before bonding and after bonding, you see that when one electron is transferred, each atom ends up with the full quota of eight electrons in its outermost principal energy level (this is the "*octet rule*").

| Before | Na | 2-8-**1** | Cl | 2-8-**7** |
| After | Na | 2-**8** (Na^+) | Cl | 2-8-**8** (Cl^-) |

If you look at covalent bonding in ammonia (NH_3), you see how two non-metals share electrons. The three hydrogen atoms each have one electron in their outermost PEL, and nitrogen has five electrons in its outmost PEL. After they bond, there will be eight electrons around the nitrogen atom, again fulfilling the octet rule and becoming more stable due to the eight electrons present.

If two atoms of the same nonmetal element, such as the two hydrogen atoms in H_2, should bond, then the covalent bond is termed *nonpolar*. The easy way to identify nonpolar bonds is in diatomic molecules where there is no difference in electronegativity between the elements. Examples of these diatomic molecules are O_2, F_2, and Br_2. If the elements in the covalent bond have different electronegativity values, the unequal sharing of electrons causes the bond to be *polar*. Familiar substances that have polar covalent bonds are H_2O, NH_3, and HCl.

Formation of Covalent Bonds in Ammonia

$$\cdot \overset{\cdot \cdot}{N} \cdot \; + \; 3\,H \cdot \quad \longrightarrow \quad H : \overset{\cdot \cdot}{\underset{H}{N}} : H$$

Types of Reactions

Reactions between substances do not cause matter to be created or destroyed. Instead, new compounds are formed by the rearrangement of atoms. There are four general categories of reactions, depending on how the substances involved rearrange. (As you study more chemistry, you will learn that there are also names for many specific types of chemical reactions.) The four basic categories are as follows:

Synthesis	$A + B \rightarrow AB$	$C + O_2 \rightarrow CO_2$
Decomposition	$AB \rightarrow A + B$	$CaCO_3 \rightarrow CaO + CO_2$
Single replacement	$AB + C \rightarrow AC + B$	$2NaI + Cl_2 \rightarrow 2NaCl + I_2$
Double replacement	$AB + CD \rightarrow AD + CB$	$AgNO_3 + NaCl \rightarrow NaNO_3 + AgCl$

Endothermic versus Exothermic Reactions

As discussed earlier, there are reactions, such as fusion and fission reactions, that can release energy. These reactions are classified as *exothermic* reactions (literally, "exit heat"). Reactions or processes that absorb heat are classified as *endothermic* reactions (literally, "enter heat"). Placing a cold pack on an injured leg is an example of an endothermic process because the ice pack allows the heat from the leg to enter the ice pack.

But what is it that causes the absorption or release of heat energy? It all comes back to the breaking or formation of bonds. Breaking bonds causes energy to be absorbed, whereas the formation of bonds causes energy to be released. What makes a reaction exothermic or endothermic is the overall amount of energy that is needed to break and create bonds; one process is sure to involve more heat than the other. This heat energy can be measured in *calories* or *joules*.

BONDING QUIZ

Circle the letter of your choice.

1. Which compound contains a bond with **no** ionic character?

  (A) CO
  (B) CaO
  (C) K_2O
  (D) Na_2O

2. When K bonds with I, the

  (A) electrons are shared.
  (B) potassium gains electrons which are lost by iodine.
  (C) two elements form a covalent compound.
  (D) potassium loses one electron to iodine.

3. Which compound below has a nonpolar bond in which the electrons are being shared equally?

  (A) H_2O
  (B) NH_3
  (C) Cl_2
  (D) CH_4

4. Which of the following processes is endothermic?

  (A) ice melting
  (B) a piece of paper burning
  (C) a bomb exploding
  (D) an organism's metabolism producing a certain amount of heat

5. Which sentence best describes the following reaction?

$$2H_2(g) + O_2(g) \rightarrow 2H_2O(l) + heat$$

  (A) It is an endothermic reaction.
  (B) It is an exothermic double replacement reaction.
  (C) It is a synthesis reaction that is also exothermic.
  (D) It is a decomposition reaction that is also endothermic.

PHASES OF MATTER
Temperature Scales

Temperature is the measure of the average kinetic energy of a sample. In other words, temperature measures the amount of motion of a sample's molecules. In the United States, *Fahrenheit* is the temperature scale that is used. In this scale, 32 degrees, or 32°F, is the freezing point of water, and 212 degrees, or 212°F, is the boiling point of water. Elsewhere, the Celsius scale is generally used. The *Celsius* temperature scale is based on the freezing and boiling points of water; 0 degrees Celsius, or 0°C, is the freezing point of water, and 100 degrees Celsius, or 100°C, is the boiling point of water. There is also a third scale, the Kelvin scale. In the Kelvin scale, water freezes at 273°K and water boils at 373°K. The *Kelvin* scale is based on the fact that a temperature below absolute zero cannot be achieved. Kelvin is the preferred scale for calculations involving temperature because there cannot be a negative number for the temperature. The relationship between Kelvin and Celsius is $K = C + 273$.

Gases, Liquids, and Solids

The three phases of matter are gas, liquid, and solid. As energy is added to or removed from a sample, its phase can change. The following table compares the three phases.

Gases	Liquids	Solids
• Have no definite shape • Have no definite volume • Have molecules far apart	• Have no definite shape • Have a definite volume • Have molecules touching but not fixed in position	• Have a definite shape • Have a definite volume • Have molecules in a fixed position

You can also outline the processes of changes in phases as follows:

Phase Change	Name of Change	Energy Change
Liquid to gas	Vaporization	Energy added/endothermic
Gas to liquid	Condensation	Energy removed/exothermic
Solid to liquid	Melting	Energy added/endothermic
Liquid to solid	Freezing	Energy removed/exothermic
Solid to gas	Sublimation	Energy added/endothermic
Gas to solid	Deposition	Energy removed/exothermic

A phase change diagram can help you understand how energy affects changes in phase and changes in temperature. The phase change diagram below is also called a heating curve. In this curve, you are examining the effect of heat on phase and temperature as you follow a sample from its solid state to its gaseous state. A few points should be noted as you follow the curve upward:

- As the temperature (average kinetic energy) of the sample increases, the phase remains the same.
- As the phase of the sample changes (change in potential energy), the temperature remains the same.
- Two phases can exist at the same temperature (in equilibrium with each other).

With regard to the vaporization of liquids, liquids that evaporate at a very high rate, given the same temperature, are called *volatile*.

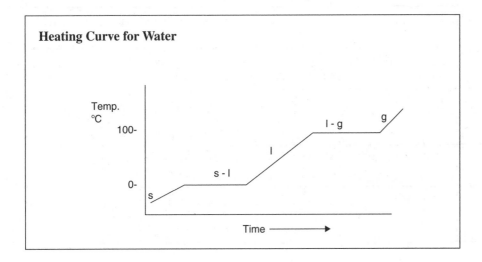

Heating Curve for Water

Density of Solids, Liquids, and Gases

Consider 1.0 kilograms of lead and 1.0 kilograms of feathers. Which one makes for more fun at a pillow fight? Should there be a difference if both samples have the same mass of 1.0 kilograms? The clear difference is in the density of the materials in question. When calculating the density of a solid or liquid, the mass of the sample is divided by the volume of the sample. This shows how much mass is "packed" into a certain amount of space. The equation for the density of solids and liquids is D = mass/volume. The units are in grams/milliliters. When determining the density of a gas, a larger volume needs to be considered because of the nature of gases. The density of a gas is calculated by dividing its gram formula mass (GFM, from the periodic table) by 22.4 liters giving D_{gas} = GFM/22.4 L. The density of water is 1 g/mL. This is helpful in determining if another liquid or solid will sink or float once placed in water.

The Gas Laws

Gases, because of their compressibility, behave according to a number of specific laws. Although it would be too much to look at each one in depth, a general outline helps review the major concepts. These laws are summarized in the chart below.

The Gas Laws		
Gas Law	**Equation**	**Relationship**
Boyle's Law	$P_1V_1 = P_2V_2$	Pressure and volume are inversely proportional.
Charles' Law	$V_1/T_1 = V_2/T_2$	Volume and temperature are directly proportional.
Gay-Lussac's Law	$P_1/T_1 = P_2/T_2$	Pressure and temperature are directly proportional.
Combined Gas Law	$P_1V_1/T_1 = P_2V_2/T_2$	Combines the three laws above.
Dalton's Law of Partial Pressure	$P_1 + P_2 + P_3 \ldots = P_T$	The total pressure of a system is equal to the sum of pressures of the individual gases inside.
Graham's Law of Diffusion	$\dfrac{(\text{Diffusion rate B})^2}{(\text{Diffusion rate A})^2} = \dfrac{\text{Ml. weight A}}{\text{Ml. weight B}}$	Lighter/less dense gases travel at greater speeds.
Ideal Gas Equation	$PV = nRT$	Relates pressure, volume, and temperature to the number of moles of a gas present.

PHASES OF MATTER QUIZ

Circle the letter of your choice.

1. Which one of the following substances can be compressed the most?

   (A) $NaCl(aq)$
   (B) $O_2(g)$
   (C) $H_2O(s)$
   (D) $Br_2(l)$

2. Definite shape and definite volume best describes a sample of

   (A) $I_2(s)$.
   (B) $Br_2(l)$.
   (C) $Cl(g)$.
   (D) $F_2(g)$.

3. In which part of the heating curve below do water and ice exist at the same time?

(A) AB
(B) BC
(C) CD
(D) DE

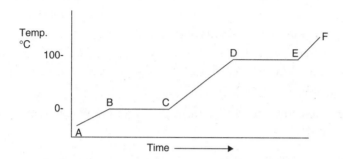

4. Which gas law below involves a variable not present in the other three?

(A) Boyle's Law
(B) Charles' Law
(C) Graham's Law
(D) Combined Gas Law

THE MOLE

Moles Related to Mass and Volume

The *mole* is another name for Avogadro's number. Just as the word *dozen* refers to 12 of something, the mole has its own value, which is equal to 6.02×10^{23}. But more important is what the mole can do for you when working quantitatively in chemistry. One important mole concept to remember is that one mole of atoms of any element has a weight equal to its atomic mass. For example, if you have 12.011 grams of carbon, then you have one mole of carbon atoms. If you were to weigh out 55.8 grams of iron, you would have a sample of 6.02×10^{23} atoms of iron or one mole of iron atoms.

Another concept that relates to the mole is that one mole of gas particles at 0°C (273°K) at 1 atmosphere (standard temperature and pressure, or STP) will occupy a volume of 22.4 liters. For example, 1 mole of nitrogen gas molecules, N_2, occupies 22.4 liters, whereas 1 mole of neon gas molecules also occupies 22.4 liters, provided that both samples are at STP.

Percent Composition

If you were to look at a molecule of methane, CH_4, you might think that because the hydrogen atoms outnumber the carbon atom, the hydrogen makes up more of the molecule. But if you consider the atomic masses of the elements, you see that the opposite is true. You can set up a simple fraction to find the percent composition of each element. First, there are four hydrogen atoms present, and each one has an atomic mass of 1.0 gram (from the periodic table). There is only one carbon atom, and it has an atomic mass of 12.0 grams. Summarizing and calculating, you get:

Hydrogen	4 atoms	×	1.0	=	4.0 grams
Carbon	1 atom	×	12.0	=	12.0 grams
					16.0 grams total

Because the hydrogen atoms make up 4.0 of the 16.0 grams, the amount of hydrogen by mass in methane is 4.0/16.0 = 0.25, or 25%. Because the carbon atom makes up 12.0 of the 16.0 grams, the amount of carbon by mass in methane is 12.0/16.0 = 0.75, or 75%.

A similar calculation can be performed to find the percent composition of potassium in $KHCO_3$:

Potassium	1 atom	×	39.0	=	39.0 grams
Hydrogen	1 atom	×	1.0	=	1.0 grams
Carbon	1 atom	×	12.0	=	12.0 grams
Oxygen	3 atoms	×	16.0	=	48.0 grams
					100.0 grams total

The percent potassium in the sample is 39.0/100.0 = 0.39, or 39%.

Moles Quiz

Circle the letter of your choice.

1. What is the molar mass (the mass of one mole of a substance) of ammonia, NH_3?

    (A) 10
    (B) 17
    (C) 8
    (D) 15

2. What is the molar mass of calcium oxide, CaO?

    (A) 56
    (B) 28
    (C) 640
    (D) 320

3. Given one mole of O_2 gas at STP, what is the mass of this sample?

    (A) 8 grams
    (B) 16 grams
    (C) 32 grams
    (D) 64 grams

4. Exactly 2.0 moles of an element weigh 8.0 grams. Which of the following is true?

(A) One mole of the element weighs 16.0 grams, and the element is sulfur, S.
(B) The element in question is beryllium, Be.
(C) One mole of the element also weighs 8.0 grams, and the element is oxygen, O.
(D) One mole of the element weighs 4.0 grams, and the element is helium, He.

5. Given 3.0 moles of krypton gas, $Kr(g)$, how many liters will this sample occupy at STP?

(A) 11.2
(B) 22.4
(C) 44.8
(D) 67.2

6. What is the percent of oxygen in H_2O?

(A) 11.1
(B) 33.3
(C) 88.9
(D) 100.0

SOLUTIONS

Solute and Solvents

A *solution* is a homogeneous mixture that combines a solute and a solvent. A *solute* is the substance that dissolved in the *solvent.* A solute changes phase when dissolved, whereas the solvent does not change its phase. Salt water, $NaCl(aq)$, is an excellent example of this. The water is the solvent because it did not change its phase, but the salt changes its phase and is no longer visible as a white solid.

Molarity

As its name suggests, *molarity* makes use of the mole in calculating the concentration of a solution. To find the molarity of the solution, divide the number of moles of solute by the total volume of the solution:

M = Moles of solute/Liters of solution

For example, if 2.0 moles of KI (332 grams of KI) are dissolved in enough water to make 3.0 liters of solution, what is the molarity of this solution? Dividing 2.0 moles/3.0 liters gives a molarity of 0.67 M KI(aq).

Dilutions

If your glass of iced tea is too strong, one quick remedy is to add more water. By adding more water, the volume increases while the number of moles of tea mix in the drink does not change. What you have done is *diluted* the tea by increasing the total number of liters of solution. Dividing by this larger number causes the molarity of the iced tea to decrease. To calculate changes in molarity, use the equation:

$$M_1V_1 = M_2V_2$$

Tinctures and Emulsifications

Solutions do not necessarily have to involve water. Although water is termed the "universal solvent," it is not the only substance in which other substances can be dissolved. When alcohol is used as a solvent, the solution is termed a *tincture*. An example of this is an iodine tincture, which is used to kill bacteria and prevent infection at the site of a wound.

Emulsifications are formed when two substances that have opposite polarities are mixed. For example, a detergent can emulsify the oils and grease on a shirt with the water in a washing machine. Normally, water and oils do not mix, but because the detergent works to emulsify the oils, the water and oils/grease can now mix together. Bile, formed in the liver and secreted from the gallbladder, works to emulsify fats while they are being digested.

Solubility of Gases and Solids

Temperature can affect the amount of a solid or gas that dissolves in a certain amount of solvent. Evidence of this can be seen in the purchase of a cold, bottled ice tea from a convenience store. One look at the bottom of the bottle and you see the extra tea mix (solute) that has settled out. Why? As the temperature of a solvent decreases, the solubility of a solid decreases because there is less space between the solvent molecules in which the solute can dissolve. The opposite holds true for gases. Gases are more soluble at colder temperatures and less soluble at higher temperatures. When you heat a pot of water, you notice the bubbles that appear on the inside of the pot because the gases that are dissolved in the water are becoming less soluble with the increase in temperature.

Colligative Properties

A winter storm blows in overnight and leaves a sheet of ice on the sidewalk in front of your house. The remedy? You quickly reach for the rock salt in your garage and spread it all over the ice. The result: a few minutes later the ice has melted! *Colligative properties* are properties that change with the addition of a solute to a solvent. Two of these properties are melting point and boiling point.

As a solute is added to a solvent, two things happen: the boiling point increases, making it harder for the solvent to boil. Also, the freezing point of the solvent decreases, so colder temperatures are needed for the solvent to freeze.

Consider antifreeze added to the radiator of a car. The ethylene glycol and water mixed together can lower the freezing point of the radiator to below 0°C and the boiling point to more than 100°C! If you live in the extreme cold or heat, you will be happy to have this protection rather than have your car break down in extreme climates.

SOLUTIONS QUIZ

Circle the letter of your choice.

1. Given a sample of $C_6H_{12}O_6$(aq), which of the following is true?

(A) The glucose is the solvent and water is the solute.
(B) The glucose is the solvent and water is the solvent.
(C) The glucose is the solute and water is the solute.
(D) The glucose is the solute and water is the solvent.

2. If 58.5 g of NaCl (1 mole of NaCl) are dissolved in enough water to make 0.500 L of solution, what is the molarity of this solution?

(A) 2.0 M
(B) 11.7 M
(C) 1.0 M
(D) The answer cannot be determined from the information above.

3. A salt solution has a molarity of 1.5 M. How many moles of this salt are present in 2.0 L of this solution?

(A) 1.5 moles
(B) 2.0 moles
(C) 3.0 moles
(D) 0.75 moles

4. As water is evaporated from a solution, the concentration of the solute in the solution will

(A) increase.
(B) decrease.
(C) remain the same.
(D) the answer cannot be determined from the information given.

5. Which substance shows a decrease in solubility in water with an increase in temperature?

(A) NaCl
(B) O_2
(C) KI
(D) $CaCl_2$

6. Salt is added to sample of water. Which of the following is true?

(A) The boiling point will increase and the freezing point will decrease.
(B) The boiling point will increase and the freezing point will increase.
(C) The boiling point will decrease and the freezing point will decrease.
(D) The boiling point will decrease and the freezing point will increase.

ORGANIC CHEMISTRY
Hydrocarbons

Organic compounds are the foundation for life as we know it. We are a carbon-based life form, and long carbon chains are the foundation of the molecules that make up life. Carbon atoms can form long and stable chains and can bond with other atoms such as oxygen and nitrogen to form various functional groups such as alcohols, carboxylic acids, and ketones. It is this variety of lengths, shapes, and functions of organic molecules that creates the incredible diversity of organic substances which, in turn, allows for diversity among living things.

Organic hydrocarbons are easily named depending on the number of carbon atoms present in the longest chain of the hydrocarbon. For example, if the longest carbon chain is three carbon atoms long, the prefix to the name is *prop-*. If the longest carbon chain is four carbon atoms long, the prefix to the name is *but-*. The following chart summarizes the prefixes for the longest carbon chains. The other factor that helps determine the name of a hydrocarbon is the presence of all single bonds, a double bond, or a triple bond. Hydrocarbons that have all single bonds end in *-ane*, whereas those that have double or triple bonds end in *-ene* or *-yne*, respectively.

Number of Carbon Atoms	Prefix	Example
One	Meth-	Methane
Two	Eth-	Ethene
Three	Prop-	Propane
Four	But-	Butane
Five	Pent-	Pentyne
Six	Hex-	Cyclohexane
Seven	Hept-	Heptene
Eight	Oct-	Octane
Nine	Non-	Nonene
Ten	Dec-	Decyne

Aromatics

Another class of organic compounds that are made of hydrogen and carbon are the *aromatics*. At the heart of these ringed compounds is a simple, six-carbon aromatic compound called benzene, C_6H_6.

Although benzene itself is a known carcinogen, many benzene derivatives are important compounds that we use on a daily basis. Two examples are phenol (a disinfectant) and naphthalene (mothballs).

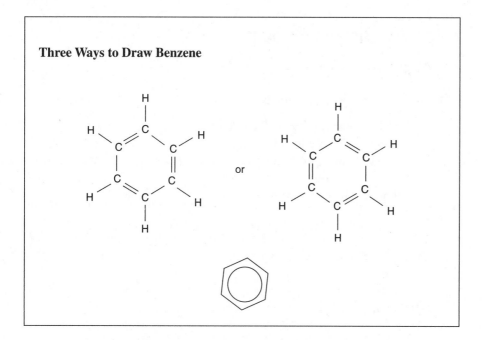

Three Ways to Draw Benzene

Oxygen, Nitrogen, and Sulfur

Although carbon and hydrogen are the elements most common in organic compounds, they are not the only ones. It is not uncommon to find an oxygen atom or nitrogen atom in the compound as well. Some popular functional groups containing these elements are:

Alcohols	R-OH		Carboxylic acids	R-COOH
Ketones	R-CO-R		Aldehydes	R-CHO
Esters	R-COOR		Ethers	R-O-R
Amines	R-NH$_2$		Amides	R-CO-NH$_2$

Although sulfur is not the most common element present in organic compounds, it is important in making disulfide bridges. These structures are needed to help proteins and enzymes maintain their structure.

Isomers

Many organic compounds contain the same number of certain elements but have different structures. Compounds that have the same molecular formula but different structures are termed *isomers*. For example, C_2H_6O is the molecular formula of ethyl (drinking) alcohol, but it is also the molecular formula for dimethyl ether. Comparing the two functional groups for these compounds, you see the different structures for these compounds, CH_3CH_2OH and CH_3OCH_3. The location makes all the difference as the ethyl alcohol can be consumed while the ether is highly toxic.

ORGANIC CHEMISTRY QUIZ

Circle the letter of your choice.

1. Organic compounds are the basis for life as we know it because

   (A) carbon-to-carbon bonds are strong.
   (B) carbon can form long chains.
   (C) carbon chains can include other elements to give rise to different functional groups.
   (D) all of the above are correct.

2. The name of the compound CH_3-CH_2-CH_2-CH_3 is most likely

   (A) cyclobutane.
   (B) butane.
   (C) butene.
   (D) butyne.

3. The compound CH_2=CH-CH_2-CH_2-CH_3 is an example of

   (A) a pentane.
   (B) a hexene.
   (C) an alkene.
   (D) an organic macromolecule.

4. An amino acid is expected to contain which two functional groups?

   (A) R-NH_2 and R-COOH
   (B) R-CHO and R-CO-NH_2
   (C) R-OH and R-COOR
   (D) R-O-R and R-COOH

5. Which element is most likely to be found in an organic compound?

   (A) carbon
   (B) oxygen
   (C) nitrogen
   (D) calcium

ACIDS AND BASES

Properties

Before examining acids and bases, it is important to first describe electrolytes. The Swedish chemist Arrhenius, who is famous for his definition of acids and bases, was actually an electrochemist. This makes sense because *electrolytes* conduct electricity in solution. This occurs because the mobile ions are able to carry an electrical current. The same occurs in a molten salt. Once the solid salt is heated to a liquid, the ions are able to move freely and conduct electricity. When a salt is in its solid state, its ions cannot conduct electricity. Reading on, you will see the connection between acids, bases, and electrolytes.

Acids and bases can be defined and identified in a number of ways. The operational definition relates to the properties that you can see, feel, or taste. These properties are as follows:

Properties of Acids	Properties of Bases
• Taste sour • Turn blue litmus paper red	• Taste bitter • Turn red litmus paper blue • Feel slippery

Chemically, *acids* are thought of as substances that produce H^+ ions (hydronium ions) in solution, whereas *bases* yield OH^- ions (hydroxide ions). Acidic substances are easily identified by their chemical formulas because they start with H, as in HCl and H_2SO_4. Basic substances have chemical formulas that usually end in OH, as in $NaOH$ or $Ca(OH)_2$. Some substances can act like an acid or a base, depending on the environment. Water is one of these substances, and it is termed *amphoteric* because of its ability to act as either an acid or a base.

Indicators

Indicators are substances that change color to indicate the presence of an acid or a base. Indicators can also be used to determine the pH of a substance. Common acid-base indicators are litmus and phenolphthalein. This chart shows their colors in acids and bases:

Indicator	In acid	In base
Litmus	Red	Blue
Phenolphthalein	Colorless	Pink/magenta

Reactions

The most common acid-base reaction that you will encounter is the neutralization reaction. In this reaction, an acid and a base react to form a salt and water. The water is formed from the combination of the hydronium ion from the acid and the hydroxide ion from the base. A simple reaction between hydrochloric acid (HCl) and sodium hydroxide (NaOH) demonstrates this:

$$HCl + NaOH \rightarrow NaCl + H_2O$$

You might see the equation written as $\underline{H}Cl + Na\underline{OH} \rightarrow NaCl + \underline{HOH}$ to emphasize the formation of the water.

Acids can also react with active metals to form hydrogen gas. Samples of this type of reaction feature zinc and magnesium:

$$2HCl(aq) + Zn(s) \rightarrow ZnCl_2(aq) + H_2(g)$$
$$2HCl(aq) + Mg(s) \rightarrow MgCl_2(aq) + H_2(g)$$

Not every metal undergoes this type of reaction. Metals such as gold and silver do not lose electrons to hydronium ions, which explains why gold and silver are able to resist tarnishing and reaction with other substances.

pH

The *pH* of a solution indicates just how acidic or basic a solution is. The pH scale ranges from 1 through 14, with the number 7 indicating a neutral solution. As the number of hydronium ions increases, the pH value decreases as the solution becomes more acidic. As the number of hydroxide ions increases, the pH value increases as the solution becomes more basic. The pH scale below summarizes these trends:

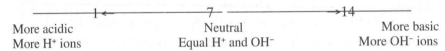

More acidic	Neutral	More basic
More H⁺ ions	Equal H⁺ and OH⁻	More OH⁻ ions

The calculation of pH requires that you understand the molarity of the hydronium ions in solution and also understand powers of ten. For starters, the equation for calculating the pH of a solution is $pH = -\log[H^+]$. Although this equation seems intimidating because of the use of logarithms, it is actually quite simple because logarithms are based on powers of ten. Bypassing the math involved, let us look at a solution with a pH of 2 and a solution with a pH of 4. Using the pH scale above, we should be able to see that the solution with a pH of 2 is more acidic than a solution with a pH of 4 and that there are more hydronium ions in the solution with a pH of 2. But just how much more acidic is the pH of 2 than the pH of 4? Your first reaction might be to answer "two" or "twenty." Keeping in mind that the pH scale is based on powers of 10, the pH of 2 is 100 (10^2) times more acidic than the pH of 4. Because they are two pH values apart, they are two powers of ten apart in their strength.

More intricate calculations involving pH can be accomplished by knowing the concentration of hydronium ions. When concentrations of hydronium ions are written in scientific notation, the exponent present in the number can give a clue as to what the pH of the solution will be. The equation $pH = -\log[H^+]$ can be rearranged to read $[H^+] = 1.0 \times 10^{-pH}$. This means that if you were to negate the exponent of the concentration, you would obtain the value for the pH. For example, if the concentration of the hydronium ion in a solution is 1.0×10^{-6} M, the pH would be 6 (the negation of the exponent). If you were to examine the concentration of hydronium ion for a solution with a pH of 7 (neutral), you would see that the concentration of $[H^+] = 1.0 \times 10^{-7}$ M. Because this solution is neutral, the concentration of hydroxide ions must be the same at this pH and $[OH^-]$ must also be equal to 1.0×10^{-7} M.

Buffers

Buffers are substances that are added to a solution so that the solution resists changes in pH. A number of medications are designed to have a buffer around them so that they do not upset the lining of the stomach with a change in the pH of the stomach on ingestion. Also, the blood contains carbonic acid and bicarbonate working as buffers to help the blood maintain its pH at approximately 7.4.

Titration

Titrations are performed to determine the concentration of an acidic or a basic solution. During this process, an acid or a base is added to the solution so that the acid and base neutralize each other. Before the experiment is started, an indicator is added to the solution being titrated. As the acid or base is added drop by drop, the indicator changes color. This indicates the endpoint of the titration. At this point the number of moles of acid is equal to the number of moles of base present in solution.

A calculation involving the number of milliliters of acid and base used along with a known concentration of either the acid or base will provide the concentration of the acidic or basic solution. This calculation follows the equation $M_a V_a = M_b V_b$.

ACIDS AND BASES QUIZ

Circle the letter of your choice.

1. Blue litmus paper turns red when the pH of a solution is

    (A) 12.
    (B) 8.
    (C) 6.
    (D) 7.

2. When an acid reacts with an active metal such as zinc, the products are

    (A) water and salt.
    (B) an acid and a base.
    (C) neutralized.
    (D) a salt and $H_2(g)$.

3. Which of the following substances is most likely to taste sour?

(A) NaOH
(B) NaCl
(C) NH_3
(D) $HC_2H_3O_2$

4. Which reaction below demonstrates a neutralization reaction?

(A) $^{232}_{90}Th \rightarrow ^{228}_{88}Ra + ^4_2He$
(B) $NaCl + H_2O \rightarrow HCl + NaOH$
(C) $2HNO_3 + Mg(OH)_2 \rightarrow 2H_2O + Mg(NO_3)_2$
(D) $CH_4 + 2O_2 \rightarrow CO_2 + 2H_2O$

5. How many times stronger is an acid with a pH of 3 than an acid with a pH of 6?

(A) A pH of 3 is three times as strong.
(B) A pH of 3 is one thousand times as strong.
(C) A pH of 3 is thirty times as weak.
(D) A pH of 3 is one thousand times as weak.

6. Which of the following is true for a basic solution?

(A) The hydroxide concentration equals zero.
(B) The hydronium concentration equals the hydroxide concentration.
(C) The hydronium concentration is less than the hydroxide concentration.
(D) The hydronium concentration is greater than the hydroxide concentration.

Rates of Reaction

The rate (or speed) at which a reaction proceeds can depend on a number of factors. As we have already examined, enzymes are catalysts that can alter the speed of a reaction. But how do they do this? All reactions need energy to get the reaction started. This energy is called the *activation energy*. Enzymes and catalysts work to lower the activation energy of a reaction. Because this energy barrier has been lowered, it is easier and less time consuming to put in enough energy to start the reaction.

Besides enzymes and catalysts, other factors can also modify reaction rates. These factors:

• Cause molecules to collide more frequently
• Cause molecule to collide with more energy

The factors that affect rates of reaction are as follows:

Temperature	Higher temperatures cause molecules to collide more frequently and with more energy as to initiate the reaction faster.
Surface area	Having substances chopped up into finer powders exposes more of the surface area of the substance. The reaction then takes place faster than if the substance were in one piece.
Concentration	Higher concentrations cause the molecules to collide more frequently.
Pressure	Although not effective for solids or liquids, increasing the pressure on a gas causes the gas molecules to collide more frequently as they are packed more tightly together.

RATES OF REACTION QUIZ

Circle the letter of your choice.

1. A reaction takes place between an acid and 0.5 grams of solid magnesium ribbon. Another reaction takes place between an acid and 0.5 grams of powdered magnesium. Which statement is true?

   (A) The powdered magnesium reacts faster because the activation energy has been lowered.
   (B) The magnesium strip reacts faster because it has a higher concentration of magnesium.
   (C) The powdered magnesium reacts faster because it has a greater surface area.
   (D) The magnesium strip reacts faster because it will create a higher temperature once the reaction starts.

2. Two different solutions, A and B, are in separate beakers. These solutions are mixed together into a third beaker that contains pure water. Which statement is true?

   (A) The two solutions would have reacted faster if they were mixed together directly and not with water.
   (B) The two solutions would react faster if they were under higher pressure.
   (C) The two solutions would react faster if they had a greater activation energy.
   (D) The two solutions would react faster after being mixed with water because their surface area will be increased.

ANSWERS TO CHEMISTRY QUIZZES

SCIENTIFIC NOTATION AND THE METRIC SYSTEM

1. The correct choice is B.
The number 1,000,000, or 1 million, has six zeros, making it 10^6.
2. The correct choice is A.
The number 6,180 meters can be rewritten as 6.180×10^3 meters.

3. The correct choice is D.

The prefix *milli-* means one-thousandth and *centi-* means one-hundredth. The prefixes differ by one power of ten. Because the prefix *milli-* is a smaller unit than *centi-*, ten millimeters are in one centimeter.

ATOMIC STRUCTURE

1. According to Dalton's atomic theory, "All atoms of the same element are alike." This is inconsistent with the concept of isotopes because the same element can differ in its mass number or number of neutrons. This explains why carbon can exist as three isotopes: C-12, C-13, and C-14.

2. The correct choice is C.

The atomic number of Ar is 18. Subtracting 18 protons from its mass number of 40 gives 22; Ar-40 has 22 neutrons in its nucleus.

3. The correct choice is B.

Aluminum as an atom has thirteen electrons. The aluminum ion with a positive three charge indicates that the atom lost three electrons and now has ten electrons.

4. The correct choice is C.

Eighteen electrons can be held in principal energy level number three.

5. Correct choice: see chart. Subtracting the number of protons from the mass number gives the number of neutrons: 10 for oxygen and 8 for carbon.

Element	# of Protons	# of Electrons	# of Neutrons
$^{18}_{8}O$	8	8	10
$^{14}_{6}C$	6	6	8

6. The correct choice is B.

Atoms with more protons in the nucleus have a greater nuclear charge than atoms with fewer protons.

7. The correct choice is A.

The initial sample starts with 100 grams. Because the half-life is five days, every five days only half of the sample will remain. After the first five days only 50 grams will remain. Because the problem calls for the mass after ten days, in another five days only 25 grams of the original sample will remain. This process can be outlined as follows:

100 grams – 5 days → 50 grams – 5 more days (10 days total) → 25 grams

8. The correct choice is D.

The reaction, $^{232}_{90}Th \rightarrow {^{228}_{88}}Ra + X$ shows that a particle was produced as a result of nuclear decay. This transmutation shows an original mass number of 232 before the reaction and 228 after the reaction. This is a loss of 4 AMU. The number of protons before the decay was 90 and it became 88 after the decay, resulting in a net loss of two protons.

9. The correct choice is B.

Neon has 10 electrons. This is a configuration of 2-8.

PERIODIC TABLE

1. The correct choice is B.
The modern periodic table is arranged by atomic number.
2. The correct choice is A.
The nonmetals are located in the upper right of the periodic table.
3. The correct choice is D.
Elements in the same group/family are chemically similar. Mg and Ca are in the same group on the periodic table.
4. The correct choice is D.
Fluorine has the highest electronegativity. Because iodine (I) is the element farthest from fluorine (F), it has the lowest electronegativity of the choices.
5. The correct choice is A.
Fluorine and neon are nonmetals and are expected to have smaller atomic radii because they are located next to each other on the periodic table. Because strontium is located on the lower left of the periodic table, it has a larger atomic radius than cobalt.
6. The correct choice is B.
Aluminum is a metal. Further proof lies in the aluminum pan in your kitchen, which is shiny and conducts heat.

BONDING

1. The correct choice is A.
The compound CO is formed from two nonmetals and is a covalent compound.
2. The correct choice is D.
Potassium (K) is a metal, and iodine (I) is a nonmetal. This means that an ionic compound forms. To do this, the metal K loses an electron to the nonmetal I.
3. The correct choice is C.
All of the compounds listed are covalently bonded because they contain all nonmetals. The equal sharing occurs when the electronegativity of the elements is the same.
4. The correct choice is A.
The melting of ice requires the ice to absorb heat, an endothermic process.
5. The correct choice is C.
The reaction synthesizes water from hydrogen and oxygen. The reaction also indicates the release of heat energy—an exothermic reaction.

PHASES OF MATTER

1. The correct choice is B.
Oxygen has been labeled as a gas, which is the phase that is most easily compressed.
2. The correct choice is A.
The compound $I_2(s)$ indicates solid iodine, which has a definite shape and volume.
3. The correct choice is B.
Portion BC of the graph shows a phase change and no temperature change. Because it is occurring at the melting point of the substance, this is where the solid and liquid phase will exist together.

4. The correct choice is C.

Graham's Law takes into account masses of gases and their speed. The other three choices all take into account the volume, pressure, and temperature of a sample of gas.

MOLES

1. The correct choice is B.

The atomic mass of nitrogen is 14.0 and the atomic mass of a hydrogen atom is 1.0. Because there are three hydrogen atoms, it is necessary to add 14.0 and 3.0, which gives 17.0.

2. The correct choice is A.

CaO has a gram formula mass of 56 because the atomic mass of Ca is 40 and the gram atomic mass of oxygen is 16.

3. The correct choice is C.

One mole of a substance weighs its gram formula mass. Because there are two oxygen atoms (16 grams each) present, the weight is 32.0 grams per mole.

4. The correct choice is D.

Because 2 moles weigh 8.0 grams, 1 mole of the substance will weigh 4.0 grams. The weight of one mole of a substance is its gram atomic mass. This corresponds to helium, He.

5. The correct choice is D.

The volume of 1 mole of a gas at STP is 22.4 liters, and 3 moles of the gas is three times the molar volume, or which is 67.2 liters.

6. The correct choice is C.

The gram formula mass of water is 18 grams per mole. The weight of the oxygen present makes up 16 of 18 grams per mole. Dividing 16 by 18 gives 0.888 or 88.9%.

SOLUTIONS

1. The correct choice is D.

The glucose is the solute and water is the solvent because the glucose changes its phase and the water does not.

2. The correct choice is A.

There are 58.5 grams of NaCl in 1 mole of NaCl. Setting up to calculate the molarity of the solution, you divide 1.0 moles by 0.500 liters: 1.0 moles/0.500 liters = 2.0 M.

3. The correct choice is C.

Using the equation for molarity, the number of moles divided by 2.0 liters equals 1.5. If 3.0 moles are dissolved in the 2.0 liters of solution, the concentration is 1.5 M.

4. The correct choice is A.

As water is evaporated from a solution, the concentration of the solute in the solution increases because there is less water present.

5. The correct choice is B.

Gases show a decrease in solubility in water with an increase in temperature. The other three choices are salts, and they show an increase in solubility as temperature increases.

6. The correct choice is A.
As a solute is added to a solvent, the solvent undergoes a freezing point depression and a boiling point elevation.

ORGANIC CHEMISTRY

1. The correct choice is D.
The ability of carbon to form strong bonds and long chains and to have various functional groups allows for millions of organic compounds that are essential to life.

2. The correct choice is B.
The compound CH_3-CH_2-CH_2-CH_3 has four carbon atoms that are joined by single bonds. This makes for a molecule of butane.

3. The correct choice is C.
The compound CH_2=CH-CH_2-CH_2-CH_3 has five carbon atoms (pent-) and it has a double bond present as well (-ene). Because pentene is not a choice, this compound is an alkene.

4. The correct choice is A.
An amino acid has an amine and a carboxylic acid group present. These are represented by R-NH_2 and R-$COOH$.

5. The correct choice is A.
Organic chemistry is the study of carbon.

ACIDS AND BASES

1. The correct choice is C.
Blue litmus paper turns red when the pH of a solution is acidic. The number 6 corresponds to this type of pH.

2. The correct choice is D.
A salt and H_2 gas form when an acid reacts with an active metal.

3. The correct choice is D.
$HC_2H_3O_2$ is acetic acid, the major ingredient in vinegar. It is an acid and tastes sour, the way citric acid can make lemons taste sour.

4. The correct choice is C.
The reactions are labeled as shown below:

$^{232}_{90}Th \rightarrow\, ^{228}_{88}Ra + ^{4}_{2}He$ Nuclear decay

$NaCl + H_2O \rightarrow HCl + NaOH$ Hydrolysis ("opposite"
                                        of neutralization)

$2HNO_3 + Mg(OH)_2 \rightarrow 2H_2O + Mg(NO_3)_2$ Neutralization

$CH_4 + 2O_2 \rightarrow CO_2 + 2H_2O$ Combustion

5. The correct choice is B.
A pH of 3 is one thousand times as strong as a pH of 6 because the pH scale works on powers of ten. Three pH units means a difference of 10^3 or 1,000 times.

6. The correct choice is C.
A basic solution has fewer hydronium ions and more hydroxide ions.

RATES OF REACTION

1. The correct choice is C.
Because the powdered magnesium has a greater surface area, it reacts faster than one solid strip of magnesium.

2. The correct choice is A.
Because water can dilute a solution, adding water lowers the concentration of the substances. This would cause the reactants to react slowly. Instead, it would have been better to mix the reactants directly.

REVIEW OF PHYSICAL SCIENCES: PHYSICS

KINEMATICS

As its name suggests, kinematics involves objects that are in motion (kinetic). We will start with the basics, distance and displacement, before looking into the rates at which objects move.

Distance and Displacement

A car travels one mile east on on a highway. After traveling one mile east, the car then makes a U-turn and continues two miles west. The car has traveled a total of three miles, but it has also traveled only one mile from its starting point. Both views are correct, depending on whether you are considering the car's displacement or its distance. The car did travel a distance of three miles, as its odometer would indicate. However, because the car ended up only one mile from its starting point, the displacement (distance of final destination from the starting point) is one mile west. The distance is said to be a *scalar* quantity because it involves just a number, three miles total. The displacement is said to be a *vector* quantity because it involves a direction, one mile west.

Speed, Velocity, and Acceleration

The rate of motion at which an object travels in a certain amount of time is called the object's *speed*. Speed is calculated using the formula $s = d/t$, and the units are usually measured in meters per second (m/s). When traveling by car, the units are usually measured in kilometers per hour (km/h) or miles per hour (mph). Because speed does not indicate a direction, it is a scalar quantity. Speed does have a magnitude (a number), but it lacks a direction, such as east or north.

Velocity, in contrast, takes into account speed and direction. The formula for velocity is the same as the formula for speed: $v = d/t$. But velocity also takes into account the direction in which the object travels. For example, if a car is heading east at 65 km/h, the speed of the car is 65 km/h, but the velocity of the car is 65 km/h east. Because velocity takes into account a magnitude (65 km/h) and a direction (east), velocity is said to be a vector quantity.

Acceleration calculates the change in an object's velocity over time. The formula is $a = \Delta v/t$. The delta symbol (Δ) is read as "change in." To calculate the change in velocity, you subtract the initial velocity from the final velocity. In other words, $\Delta v =$ (final velocity – initial velocity). An object that is increasing in velocity is said to be accelerating. An object that is decreasing in velocity is said to be decelerating. The unit of measure for acceleration is meters per second (m/s) per second (t). The units are written as m/s^2. Acceleration due to gravity (a_g or just g) has a value of $9.8 \, m/s^2$. This is the acceleration of an object near the Earth's surface, disregarding air friction. If two objects of different masses are in a vacuum (no air present to introduce friction), they will both fall with the same acceleration of $9.8 \, m/s^2$.

Momentum and Impulse

Compare a car traveling at a speed of 5 m/s with a bird flying at 10 m/s. Although the bird has a greater speed, the car has a greater momentum. The difference between the two is the masses involved. *Momentum* is calculated by multiplying the mass of an object by its velocity, $p = mv$.

An *impulse* is a force (we will discuss forces shortly) that is applied to an object over time, Ft. Impulse can also be thought of as a change in momentum, the mass times the change in velocity, $m(v_f - v_i)$. Because the two equations both represent impulse, we can set them equal to each other, $Ft = m\Delta v$.

NEWTONIAN MECHANICS

According to a (probably fictitious) story, the English physicist Sir Isaac Newton (1642–1727) once was sitting under a tree when an apple fell from the tree and hit him on the head. What Newton encountered in that story was the force of gravity and what it does to the motion of objects. Newton is most famous for his three laws of motion.

1. *Newton's First Law* involves *inertia,* a property of matter by which an object in motion tends to continue traveling in a straight line, whereas an object at rest stays at rest unless that object is acted on by a force. To put it simply, it takes a force to move an object or change its direction of motion.
2. *Newton's Second Law* concerns the relationship between the forces applied to an object and the acceleration of the object. The greater the force applied to the object, the greater is its acceleration. The equation that shows this relationship is $F = ma$. The unit of measure for force is the Newton (N). This unit is a derived unit, which comes from multiplying the unit of mass, kg,

by the unit of acceleration, m/s^2. Multiplying the two, you get kg·m/s^2. One caution: if an object is moving at a constant velocity ($\Delta v = 0$), then it is not being accelerated and the force needed to achieve this constant velocity is also equal to zero.

3. *Newton's Third Law* says that when one object applies a force to a second object, that second object applies an opposite and equal force to the first object. For example, if you were to push against a wall but neither you nor the wall moves as a result, then both you and the wall are applying an equal force to each other.

WORK AND ENERGY

The *work* done on an object is defined as the force applied to the object multiplied by the distance the object moves. The equation for calculating work is $W = Fd$. The unit of measure for force is the newton, etc., and the unit of measure for distance is the meter, so the unit of measure for work is the newton·meter (N·m). Power is related to work in that *power* is the amount of work done in a certain amount of time. The formula for calculating power is $P = W/t$. When you divide newton·meters by seconds, you get N·m/s (or the unit called the watt, W).

Energy is defined as the capacity to do work. Energy can be either potential or kinetic. *Potential energy* (PE) is energy that is stored within an object for later release. For example, a book held in the air above some surface such as a table top is considered to have PE (the energy that would be released when the book is dropped). *Kinetic energy* (KE) is energy that is in motion, The energy released when the book falls is KE. The amount of potential or kinetic energy an object has can be quantified. The formula for calculating gravitational PE (the kind stored up in the book in the example above) is $PE = mgh$ where m = mass, g = gravity, and h = the height of the object above a particular surface. The formula for calculating kinetic energy includes velocity (v) because the object is moving. The formula for calculating KE is $KE = \frac{1}{2}mv^2$. The unit of measure for both kinetic and potential energy is the *joule* (kg·m^2/s^2).

One important concept to remember is that energy is *conserved;* that is, it is never either created or destroyed. For example, consider a book that is held two meters above a table top. As you saw above, the book has PE. If the book is released, and starts falling, the PE is converted into KE. Once the book hits the table top, the KE is converted into sound energy (the noise made by the impact). In this example the energy has taken three forms: potential, kinetic, and sound. What does this show? It shows that although energy can never be created or destroyed, it can be converted from one form to another.

WAVES

Take a good look at a stadium full of fans who have started a "wave" as they cheer for the home team. What are they doing to create this "wave"? One group of people after another stands, and those around them remain seated. This pattern moves around the stadium, making it look as though a wave is rolling across the seats. This type of "wave" is similar to what we will discuss in this section.

Amplitude, Frequency, and Wavelength

Waves, which are continuous, as shown below, have an amplitude, frequency, and wavelength.

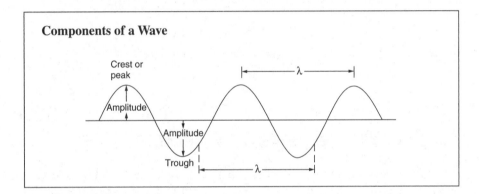

The highest and lowest points of a wave are called *crests* and *troughs*, respectively. The distance that crests and troughs are from the normal is called the *amplitude*. The distance between two crests (or two troughs, for that matter) is called the *wavelength* and is represented by the Greek letter lambda (λ). The wavelength is can also be thought of as the distance for one wave to be completed. The *frequency* is the number of complete waves that pass through a point over a given amount of time. Multiplying the frequency of a wave by its wavelength gives the velocity of the wave as shown by the formula $v = f\lambda$.

Longitudinal and Transverse Waves

The difference between transverse and longitudinal waves is shown below. *Transverse waves* have vibrations that are perpendicular (at right angles) to the direction in which the wave is moving. *Longitudinal waves* have vibrations that are moving in the same direction as the wave. In a longitudinal wave, there are no crests and troughs. Instead, there are areas of compression and expansion.

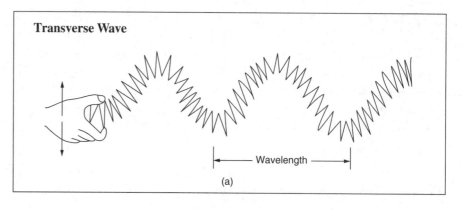

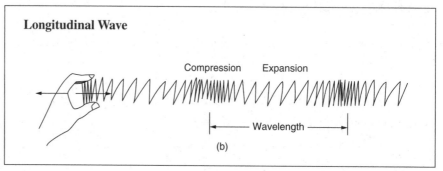

Light: Wave versus Particle

Light can be thought of as being either a wave or a particle because it exhibits the properties of both. This is called the "wave-particle duality of light." Light particles are called *photons,* and their existence helps explain why processes such as photosynthesis, the photoelectric effect, and the Compton effect can take place (no need to worry about this in detail).

Reflection, Diffraction, Dispersion, and Refraction

When light hits a surface, some of the light energy is absorbed by the object, some is reflected back, and if the object is transparent, some light passes through. Look into a mirror, at a shiny new car, at polished furniture, or into a still pool of water and you will see your reflection. These surfaces allow for the light to be *reflected* or "bounced back," because the surface allows the angle at which the light hits it to equal the angle at which the light is reflected. Rough surfaces do not allow you to see yourself in them because the angle at which the light hits the surface is different from the angle at which the light is "bounced back."

When light goes from one medium (air, for example) into another medium (water, for example), the velocity of the wave changes. If you fill a glass halfway with water and drop a spoon into it, you notice that the image of the spoon under the water looks different from the image of the spoon above the water—because of the *refraction* of the light.

Diffraction takes place when a wave that is spreading out hits an object and, as it continues to travel, bends around the object. This is not to be confused with *dispersion,* which is the breaking up of white light into its colors. Dispersion occurs when white light passes through a prism, which breaks it up into a range of colors.

ELECTRICITY
Charges

As explained earlier in the chemistry portion of this chapter in the section on ions, the transfer of electrons from one object to another causes the objects to become charged. The object that loses electrons becomes positively charged, and the one that gains electrons becomes negatively charged. Like charges repel each other. If two positive charges come near each other, they repel each other. The same holds true for two negative charges placed near each other. If a positive charge comes near a negative charge, the two unlike charges attract.

Current, Voltage, Resistance, and Power

Every day you take advantage of electricity flowing through wires to run appliances and other devices. When you were younger, you probably had fun with static electricity by rubbing a balloon against your hair and then watching as the balloon clung to a wall. Electricity is a flow of electrons through a wire. Static electricity results when electrons create a charge without having to flow.

A *current* (I) is a flow of charge from one terminal of a circuit to another. To be more specific, it is the amount of charge that passes through a point per second. The unit of measure for current is coulombs/second or just amperes (A). *Voltage* (V) is the electrical potential (stored energy) that a power source has. For example, air conditioners for your home can run on 110 volts, whereas others need a potential of 220 volts. *Resistance* (R) is the ability of a substance to stop the flow of a current. For example, copper wire has low resistance and is a good conductor of electricity, whereas rubber has high resistance and cannot conduct electricity. The unit of measure for resistance is the ohm (Ω). Ohm's law relates voltage, current, and resistance with this formula: $V = IR$. *Power,* which is measured in watts (W), can be calculated by multiplying the current by the voltage. The formula for calculating power is $P = IV$.

Series and Parallel Circuits

Some circuits have their components connected in series, and others have their components connected in parallel. The diagram below shows light bulbs connected in series on the left and in parallel on the right. In the series circuit, if one light bulb is removed, the entire set of lights goes out because of the break in the circuit. This can be countered by connecting the light bulbs in a parallel configuration. If one light goes out or is removed, the other light bulbs continue to glow. This configuration is appropriate for houses, buildings, and sets of lights that are usually used during the holiday season.

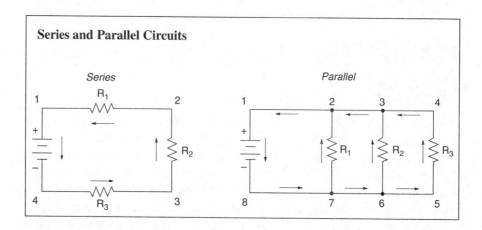

Series and Parallel Circuits

Physics Quiz

Circle the letter of your choice.

1. A car travels 3 miles north, 6 miles south, 2 miles east, 2 miles west, and then 3 miles north. Which of the following is true?

   (A) The displacement of the car is 16 miles, and the distance traveled is 0 miles.
   (B) The displacement of the car is 16 miles, and the distance traveled is 16 miles.
   (C) The displacement of the car is 0 miles, and the distance traveled is 0 miles.
   (D) The displacement of the car is 0 miles, and the distance traveled is 16 miles.

2. A car is traveling at 5 m/s. A squirrel jumps into the middle of the road, and the car comes to a screeching halt over 2.5 seconds. What is the car's acceleration over this time period?

   (A) $-2\,\text{m/s}^2$
   (B) $2\,\text{m/s}^2$
   (C) $1.25\,\text{m/s}^2$
   (D) $0\,\text{m/s}^2$

3. A car, starting from rest, accelerates at $10 \, \text{m/s}^2$ for 5 seconds. What is the velocity of the car after 5 seconds?

(A) 2 m/s
(B) 50 m/s
(C) 0 m/s
(D) The answer cannot be determined from the information given.

4. Which of these objects has the greatest momentum?

(A) a 1,250-kg car moving at 5 m/s
(B) a 0.5-kg rock moving at 40 m/s
(C) a 10-kg piece of meteorite moving at 600 m/s
(D) a 80-kg person running at 4 m/s

5. A 1.0-kg block on a table is given a push so that it slides along the table. If the block is accelerated at $6 \, \text{m/s}^2$, then what was the force applied to the block?

(A) 3 N
(B) 0 N
(C) 6 N
(D) The answer cannot be determined from the information above.

6. A box is moved by a 15 N force over a distance of 3 m. What is the amount of work that has been done?

(A) 45°C
(B) 5 J
(C) 45 W
(D) 45 N·m

7. Which of the following is true?

(A) The amplitude of a wave is the distance that one complete wave covers.
(B) The frequency of a wave is the distance the crests and troughs are from the normal.
(C) The wavelength of a wave is how many waves pass a point in a given amount of time.
(D) The velocity of a wave can be found by multiplying the frequency by the wavelength.

8. Pair up each term with its correct definition:

(A) Reflection _____ White light is broken into the colors of the rainbow.

(B) Dispersion _____ Light bounces back at the same angle at which it hit an object.

(C) Refraction _____ A wave hits an object and bends around the object.

(D) Diffraction _____ Light changes speed as it goes from one medium to another.

9. Referring to Ohm's law, you can conclude that

 (A) voltage and current are inversely proportional when the resistance is constant.
 (B) an electronic device that is connected to a 6-volt source and draws 3 amperes has a total resistance of 2 ohms.
 (C) resistance is measured in volts.
 (D) voltage is the amount of charge that passes through a point per second.

ANSWERS TO PHYSICS QUIZ

1. The correct choice is D.
If a car travels 3 miles north, 6 miles south, 2 miles east, 2 miles west, and then 3 miles north, it has traveled a total distance of 16 miles. But because of the directions the car has traveled in, it has ended up in the same place from which it started. This means that the displacement of the car is zero.

2. The correct choice is A.
Using the equation $a = \Delta v/t$, the car has a final velocity of 0 m/s and an initial velocity of 5 m/s. The change in velocity is −5 m/s. Dividing this by the time, 2.5 seconds, the acceleration is −2 m/s^2.

3. The correct choice is B.
The velocity of the car is equal to the time multiplied by the acceleration. Multiplying 5 seconds by 10 m/s^2, you get a velocity of 50 m/s.

4. The correct choice is A.
Momentum is calculated by multiplying mass and velocity, $p = mv$. Although the meteorite sounds intimidating, it is the car that has the greatest momentum at 6,250 kg·m/s.

5. The correct choice is C.
Applying Newton's Second Law, $F = ma$, a 1.0-kg block accelerated at 6 m/s^2 requires a 6-N force to move it.

6. The correct choice is D.
Work is the force that is applied to an object over a distance, $W = Fd$. The force is 15 N and the distance is 3 m, giving a total amount of work equal to 45 N·m.

7. The correct choice is D.
The equation of the velocity of a wave is $v = f\lambda$. This is the multiplication of frequency by wavelength.

8. Correct choices: B, A, D, C.
Reflection takes place when light bounces back at the same angle at which it hit an object. *Refraction* takes place when light changes speed as it goes from one medium to another. *Dispersion* takes place when white light is broken into the colors of the full spectrum. *Diffraction* is the bending of waves around obstacles in their path.

9. The correct choice is B.
Using the equation $V = IR$ or $R = V/I$, an electronic device connected to a 6-volt source drawing 3 amperes has a total resistance of 2 ohms.

Practice Tests

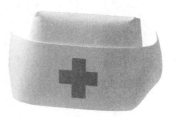

This chapter contains eight practice tests; two each in verbal skills, reading comprehension, mathematics, and science. The questions are modeled on the questions in real nursing school entrance exams. They cover the same topics and are designed to be at the same level of difficulty. Answer explanations are given at the end of each test.

These practice exams are intended to help you test your knowledge of each subject area and sharpen your test-taking skills. The real exam that you take will include questions from several different subject areas. It will also have its own specific organization and time limit. But no matter what the format of your real exam, these practice tests will prepare you for the questions you will face on test day.

Each test includes an Answer Sheet that you may want to remove from the book. Use this sheet to mark your answers. When you are finished with each test, carefully read the answer explanations, especially for any questions that you answered incorrectly. Identify any weak areas by determining the subjects in which you made the most errors. Then go back and review the corresponding chapters in this book. If time permits, you may also want to review your stronger areas.

These practice tests will help you gauge your test readiness if you treat each one as an actual examination. Here are some hints on how to take each one under conditions similar to those of the actual exam.

- Find a time when you will not be interrupted.
- Complete each test in one session, following the suggested time limit.
- If you run out of time on any test, take note of where you ended when time ran out. This will help you determine if you need to speed up your pacing.

Verbal Skills Test 1

ANSWER SHEET

1 (A) (B) (C) (D)
2 (A) (B) (C) (D)
3 (A) (B) (C) (D)
4 (A) (B) (C) (D)
5 (A) (B) (C) (D)
6 (A) (B) (C) (D)
7 (A) (B) (C) (D)
8 (A) (B) (C) (D)
9 (A) (B) (C) (D)
10 (A) (B) (C) (D)
11 (A) (B) (C) (D)
12 (A) (B) (C) (D)
13 (A) (B) (C) (D)
14 (A) (B) (C) (D)
15 (A) (B) (C) (D)
16 (A) (B) (C) (D)
17 (A) (B) (C) (D)
18 (A) (B) (C) (D)
19 (A) (B) (C) (D)
20 (A) (B) (C) (D)

21 (A) (B) (C) (D)
22 (A) (B) (C) (D)
23 (A) (B) (C) (D)
24 (A) (B) (C) (D)
25 (A) (B) (C) (D)
26 (A) (B) (C) (D)
27 (A) (B) (C) (D)
28 (A) (B) (C) (D)
29 (A) (B) (C) (D)
30 (A) (B) (C) (D)
31 (A) (B) (C) (D)
32 (A) (B) (C) (D)
33 (A) (B) (C) (D)
34 (A) (B) (C) (D)
35 (A) (B) (C) (D)
36 (A) (B) (C) (D)
37 (A) (B) (C) (D)
38 (A) (B) (C) (D)
39 (A) (B) (C) (D)
40 (A) (B) (C) (D)

41 (A) (B) (C) (D)
42 (A) (B) (C) (D)
43 (A) (B) (C) (D)
44 (A) (B) (C) (D)
45 (A) (B) (C) (D)
46 (A) (B) (C) (D)
47 (A) (B) (C) (D)
48 (A) (B) (C) (D)
49 (A) (B) (C) (D)
50 (A) (B) (C) (D)
51 (A) (B) (C) (D)
52 (A) (B) (C) (D)
53 (A) (B) (C) (D)
54 (A) (B) (C) (D)
55 (A) (B) (C) (D)
56 (A) (B) (C) (D)
57 (A) (B) (C) (D)
58 (A) (B) (C) (D)
59 (A) (B) (C) (D)
60 (A) (B) (C) (D)

VERBAL SKILLS TEST 1

60 questions

Time limit: 50 minutes

1. Which noun in the sentence below is the subject?

   The night nurse had to call Dr. Leon to let him know that his patients had been waiting for him for over an hour.

   (A) nurse
   (B) Dr. Leon
   (C) patients
   (D) hour

2. Read the sentence below. What is the subject?

   Remember that the charts have to be in place for the doctor before she can start her morning rounds.

   (A) charts
   (B) doctor
   (C) you
   (D) rounds

3. Which noun in the sentence below is the subject?

   Taking charge of the situation, Dr. Clemens immediately dispatched Sheila and me to the intensive care unit.

   (A) situation
   (B) Dr. Clemens
   (C) Sheila
   (D) unit

4. Read the sentence below. Which pronoun should be used to replace *the victims* in the second part of the sentence?

   The accident victims all arrived at the emergency ward at the same time, and the victims were treated in order according to degree of injury.

   (A) them
   (B) they
   (C) us
   (D) those

GO ON TO THE NEXT PAGE

5. Read the sentence below. Which pronoun should be used to replace *Mrs. Connors* following the comma?

> After Mrs. Connors signed the consent form, Mrs. Connors handed it to the nurse at the admissions desk.

(A) his
(B) hers
(C) he
(D) she

6. Read the sentence below. There is an error with the first verb. Which answer corrects that error?

> Even though the prescription drugs were ordering this afternoon, the patient is already complaining about the delay.

(A) had been ordering
(B) was ordering
(C) were ordered
(D) was ordered

7. Which verb fits in the blank space of the sentence below?

> When Dr. Carmine walked into the office this morning, I was already _____ to speak to him.

(A) waited
(B) wait
(C) waits
(D) waiting

8. Which word in the following sentence is an adjective?

> Calling frantically for some assistance, the distraught mother scanned the room for a nurse or doctor.

(A) calling
(B) frantically
(C) assistance
(D) distraught

9. Which two words in the following sentence are adjectives?

> While the electrical power went out unexpectedly, the hospital had to depend entirely on the unreliable generator.

(A) electrical/ unreliable
(B) out/unexpectedly
(C) depend/entirely
(D) power/generator

GO ON TO THE NEXT PAGE

10. Which word in the following sentence is an adverb?

The clinic's chief of staff did not remember that he had made an appointment.

(A) chief
(B) not
(C) remember
(D) made

11. Which two words in the following sentence are adverbs?

The patient was bleeding heavily, and our most immediate concern was maintaining her blood pressure.

(A) patient/concern
(B) bleeding/maintaining
(C) heavily/most
(D) our/pressure

12. Which of the following sets of words lists the adjective and adverb in the sentence below?

The comfort and elegance of the hospital's new lounge utterly amazed our staff.

(A) new/utterly
(B) elegance/lounge
(C) comfort/amazed
(D) lounge/staff

13. Which of the following sets of words lists the adjective and adverb in the sentence below?

The radiology equipment that arrived belonged solely to Dr. Olsen, Dr. Matthews, and Dr. Connors.

(A) equipment/belonged
(B) Olsen/Matthews
(C) arrived/Connors
(D) radiology/solely

14. What type of word is needed to repair the error in the sentence below?

The magnetic resonance imaging (MRI) tube so narrow that many people find it terribly claustrophobic and need medication to get through the exam.

(A) a verb
(B) a subject
(C) an adjective
(D) an adverb

GO ON TO THE NEXT PAGE

15. What type of word is needed to repair the error in the sentence below?

Noting the change in blood pressure reading, wrote a special note for the patient's physician.

(A) a verb
(B) a subject
(C) an adjective
(D) an adverb

16. All of the following corrections to the run-on sentence below are correct EXCEPT

Dr. Julien removed the oxygen mask the patient attempted to speak.

(A) Dr. Julien removed the oxygen mask; the patient attempted to speak.
(B) Dr. Julien removed the oxygen mask. The patient attempted to speak.
(C) Dr. Julien removed the oxygen mask, the patient attempted to speak.
(D) Dr. Julien removed the oxygen mask, and the patient attempted to speak.

17. All of the following corrections to the run-on sentence below are correct EXCEPT

Nurse Rodriguez agreed to take an additional shift Nurse Williams needed an extra sick day.

(A) Nurse Rodriguez agreed to take an additional shift; Nurse Williams needed an extra sick day.
(B) Nurse Rodriguez agreed to take an additional shift because Nurse Williams needed an extra sick day.
(C) Nurse Rodriguez agreed to take an additional shift or Nurse Williams needed an extra sick day.
(D) Nurse Rodriguez agreed to take an additional shift. Nurse Williams needed an extra sick day.

18. Which of the following coordinating conjunctions fits best in the sentence below?

The x-ray department will be shut down for the rest of the week, _____ patients will be sent to the telemetry department instead.

(A) nor
(B) yet
(C) because
(D) so

GO ON TO THE NEXT PAGE

19. Which of the following subordinating conjunctions fits best in the sentence below?

_____ the administration is willing to increase hourly pay rates, that concession alone is not enough to satisfy most of the staff.

(A) Even though
(B) Because
(C) Provided that
(D) Unless

20. Which of the following subordinating conjunctions fits best in the sentence below?

I agreed to be transferred to another city clinic _____ it was clear that the chief physician and I could not get along.

(A) as soon as
(B) before
(C) although
(D) wherever

21. An independent clause

(A) modifies an adjective.
(B) has no subject.
(C) modifies an adverb.
(D) stands on its own.

22. A dependent clause

(A) has only a verb.
(B) has only a noun.
(C) cannot stand alone.
(D) starts with a preposition.

23. What type of clause is used in the sentence below?

After Dr. Carlisle finished the surgery, she took a few minutes to sit down and relax.

(A) adverbial
(B) noun
(C) adjectival
(D) independent

24. Which of the following examples is a prepositional phrase?

(A) beneath the front desk
(B) where I was sitting
(C) because he was exhausted
(D) when she stated the time

GO ON TO THE NEXT PAGE

25. Which of the following is spelled correctly?

(A) beige
(B) sieze
(C) wieght
(D) cheif

26. Which of the following is the correct way to spell this word?

(A) acommodate
(B) accomodate
(C) accommodate
(D) accommidate

27. The word "allowed" is an example of what?

(A) homophone
(B) silent letter
(C) unstressed vowel
(D) missing consonant

28. The word "subtle" is an example of what?

(A) homophone
(B) silent letter
(C) unstressed vowel
(D) missing consonant

29. Which of the following is the correct way to spell this word?

(A) eligable
(B) eligble
(C) eligible
(D) elligible

30. Certain words are known as "spelling demons." All four of these words are examples. Which one is spelled correctly?

(A) guidence
(B) liason
(C) millenium
(D) prescription

31. Which of the following words is spelled incorrectly?

(A) ninety
(B) recommend
(C) specimen
(D) sufficent

GO ON TO THE NEXT PAGE

32. What punctuation is needed in this sentence to make it correct?

Exactly when will the information be released so that the board can make some decisions

(A) a period
(B) a question mark
(C) a comma
(D) an exclamation mark

33. What punctuation is needed in this sentence to make it correct?

The Lakeview Community Public Hospital opened the new wing today more than 2,000 people came to see it.

(A) a comma
(B) a semicolon
(C) a colon
(D) a question mark

34. Where should a comma be added in the following sentence?

Even though she was exhausted Mrs. Stone continued to sit patiently in the waiting room.

(A) after exhausted
(B) after Mrs. Stone
(C) after patiently
(D) No comma is needed.

35. Where should a comma be added in the following sentence?

The patient was so confused that she could not even fill out the admission forms.

(A) after confused
(B) after that
(C) after fill out
(D) No comma is needed.

36. What kind of punctuation is needed in this sentence?

The maternity ward is extremely busy tonight more babies are born during the full moon than any other time of the month.

(A) comma
(B) semicolon
(C) colon
(D) apostrophe

GO ON TO THE NEXT PAGE

37. Which word in the following sentence is missing an apostrophe?

The two patients were sharing a hospital room that used to be a nurses lounge.

(A) patients
(B) hospital
(C) room
(D) nurses

38. What kind of punctuation is missing in this sentence?

The orderly reported that the following items were missing bandages, oxygen masks, antiseptic wash, rubber gloves, and several types of medication.

(A) apostrophe
(B) question mark
(C) colon
(D) exclamation mark

39. Where should the missing quotation mark go in the following sentence?

"Dr. Palmer, please," cried Mr. Thompson. You have to fill out these papers before you go home tonight!"

(A) after Dr. Palmer
(B) after Mr. Thompson
(C) before You
(D) before tonight

40. Which punctuation mark is missing from the following sentence?

"Mrs. Wade, your little girl is going to be fine"

(A) a quotation mark
(B) an exclamation point
(C) a question mark
(D) an apostrophe

41. What punctuation should be used to show possession or a contraction?

(A) apostrophe
(B) semicolon
(C) parentheses
(D) comma

42. What is the purpose of parentheses?

(A) to highlight the most important information
(B) to set aside unnecessary details
(C) to introduce an unfamiliar term
(D) to speak directly to the reader

GO ON TO THE NEXT PAGE

43. What punctuation is needed when something is written with strong emotion?

(A) quotation mark
(B) semicolon
(C) exclamation point
(D) parentheses

44. His opinion of how to treat measles was the exact *antithesis* of mine. **Antithesis** means

(A) opposite.
(B) opinion.
(C) same.
(D) philosophy.

45. The lab test fortunately showed that the growth on her arm was completely *benign*. **Benign** means

(A) unfamiliar.
(B) foreign.
(C) typical.
(D) harmless.

46. Someone or something that indicates forthcoming bad news is called a

(A) debacle.
(B) harbinger.
(C) fetish.
(D) iconoclast.

47. It was clear from the way she sighed and blushed when the new intern entered the room that the nurse was totally

(A) dissident.
(B) enamored.
(C) laconic.
(D) maudlin.

48. Although I am completely innocent, I was still accused of *nefarious* behavior. **Nefarious** means

(A) wicked.
(B) bizarre.
(C) unkind.
(D) sarcastic.

49. I had been trying to *placate* the angry patients for several hours, but I was not very successful. **Placate** means

(A) inform.
(B) listen.
(C) calm.
(D) inspire.

GO ON TO THE NEXT PAGE

50. Which of the following words best fits in the blank below?

The _____ patron always gave generously to the hospital's fundraisers.

(A) altruistic
(B) cantankerous
(C) depraved
(D) ethereal

51. The physician was determined to *extricate* the splinter, but the task was proving difficult. **Extricate** means

(A) replace.
(B) bandage.
(C) remove.
(D) soften.

52. Which of the following words best fits in the blank below?

Although I appreciate your _____, I don't agree with your opinion on the matter at all.

(A) amity
(B) candor
(C) flippancy
(D) repugnance

53. Which of the following words is a synonym for the word *homogeneous?*

(A) assorted
(B) anonymous
(C) diverse
(D) standardized

54. The new head nurse was extremely *meticulous* and made us double-check every entry in our reports. **Meticulous** means

(A) irresponsible.
(B) careful.
(C) punctual.
(D) knowledgeable.

55. Which of the following means the opposite of *sagacity?*

(A) wisdom
(B) imprudence
(C) protocol
(D) stature

GO ON TO THE NEXT PAGE

56. Which of the following is a synonym for the word *affinity*?

  (A) kindness
  (B) leadership
  (C) resemblance
  (D) variation

57. Which of the following fits best in the blank in this sentence?

  The new administration keeps telling us that we have to cut costs, so we need to be _____.

  (A) impersonal
  (B) exuberant
  (C) frugal
  (D) contrite

58. In the following sentence, which word is the subject?

  Drop that sterile needle this second!

  (A) sterile
  (B) needle
  (C) you
  (D) second

59. In the following sentence, which word is the verb?

  The entire department from the janitors to the head nurse rushed to the front doors at once.

  (A) department
  (B) rushed
  (C) front
  (D) doors

60. In the following sentence, which word is the subject?

  The new oxygen mask fit perfectly across the patient's mouth.

  (A) oxygen
  (B) mask
  (C) patient's
  (D) mouth

**STOP. IF YOU HAVE TIME LEFT OVER,
CHECK YOUR WORK ON THIS SECTION ONLY.**

Verbal Skills Test 2

ANSWER SHEET

1 Ⓐ Ⓑ Ⓒ Ⓓ
2 Ⓐ Ⓑ Ⓒ Ⓓ
3 Ⓐ Ⓑ Ⓒ Ⓓ
4 Ⓐ Ⓑ Ⓒ Ⓓ
5 Ⓐ Ⓑ Ⓒ Ⓓ
6 Ⓐ Ⓑ Ⓒ Ⓓ
7 Ⓐ Ⓑ Ⓒ Ⓓ
8 Ⓐ Ⓑ Ⓒ Ⓓ
9 Ⓐ Ⓑ Ⓒ Ⓓ
10 Ⓐ Ⓑ Ⓒ Ⓓ
11 Ⓐ Ⓑ Ⓒ Ⓓ
12 Ⓐ Ⓑ Ⓒ Ⓓ
13 Ⓐ Ⓑ Ⓒ Ⓓ
14 Ⓐ Ⓑ Ⓒ Ⓓ
15 Ⓐ Ⓑ Ⓒ Ⓓ
16 Ⓐ Ⓑ Ⓒ Ⓓ
17 Ⓐ Ⓑ Ⓒ Ⓓ
18 Ⓐ Ⓑ Ⓒ Ⓓ
19 Ⓐ Ⓑ Ⓒ Ⓓ
20 Ⓐ Ⓑ Ⓒ Ⓓ

21 Ⓐ Ⓑ Ⓒ Ⓓ
22 Ⓐ Ⓑ Ⓒ Ⓓ
23 Ⓐ Ⓑ Ⓒ Ⓓ
24 Ⓐ Ⓑ Ⓒ Ⓓ
25 Ⓐ Ⓑ Ⓒ Ⓓ
26 Ⓐ Ⓑ Ⓒ Ⓓ
27 Ⓐ Ⓑ Ⓒ Ⓓ
28 Ⓐ Ⓑ Ⓒ Ⓓ
29 Ⓐ Ⓑ Ⓒ Ⓓ
30 Ⓐ Ⓑ Ⓒ Ⓓ
31 Ⓐ Ⓑ Ⓒ Ⓓ
32 Ⓐ Ⓑ Ⓒ Ⓓ
33 Ⓐ Ⓑ Ⓒ Ⓓ
34 Ⓐ Ⓑ Ⓒ Ⓓ
35 Ⓐ Ⓑ Ⓒ Ⓓ
36 Ⓐ Ⓑ Ⓒ Ⓓ
37 Ⓐ Ⓑ Ⓒ Ⓓ
38 Ⓐ Ⓑ Ⓒ Ⓓ
39 Ⓐ Ⓑ Ⓒ Ⓓ
40 Ⓐ Ⓑ Ⓒ Ⓓ

41 Ⓐ Ⓑ Ⓒ Ⓓ
42 Ⓐ Ⓑ Ⓒ Ⓓ
43 Ⓐ Ⓑ Ⓒ Ⓓ
44 Ⓐ Ⓑ Ⓒ Ⓓ
45 Ⓐ Ⓑ Ⓒ Ⓓ
46 Ⓐ Ⓑ Ⓒ Ⓓ
47 Ⓐ Ⓑ Ⓒ Ⓓ
48 Ⓐ Ⓑ Ⓒ Ⓓ
49 Ⓐ Ⓑ Ⓒ Ⓓ
50 Ⓐ Ⓑ Ⓒ Ⓓ
51 Ⓐ Ⓑ Ⓒ Ⓓ
52 Ⓐ Ⓑ Ⓒ Ⓓ
53 Ⓐ Ⓑ Ⓒ Ⓓ
54 Ⓐ Ⓑ Ⓒ Ⓓ
55 Ⓐ Ⓑ Ⓒ Ⓓ
56 Ⓐ Ⓑ Ⓒ Ⓓ
57 Ⓐ Ⓑ Ⓒ Ⓓ
58 Ⓐ Ⓑ Ⓒ Ⓓ
59 Ⓐ Ⓑ Ⓒ Ⓓ
60 Ⓐ Ⓑ Ⓒ Ⓓ

VERBAL SKILLS TEST 2

60 questions

Time limit: 50 minutes

1. Which noun in the sentence below is the subject?

> As soon as the last patient had been tucked in for the night, the nursing staff sat down to hot pizza and cold soda.

(A) patient
(B) staff
(C) pizza
(D) soda

2. Read the sentence below. What is the subject?

> Don't even think about taking your break until Dr. Hopman or your replacement gets here!

(A) break
(B) Dr. Hopman
(C) you
(D) replacement

3. Which noun in the sentence below is the subject?

> After adjusting the patient's arm band, the supervising nurse checked the chart to see the last recorded temperature and respiratory rate.

(A) patient's
(B) band
(C) nurse
(D) chart

4. Read the sentence below. Which pronoun should be used to replace "the doctor" everywhere except the first time it appears?

> The doctor started his rounds, but then the doctor remembered that the doctor had an appointment that the doctor could not miss.

(A) he
(B) she
(C) they
(D) him

GO ON TO THE NEXT PAGE

5. Read the sentence below. Which pronoun should be used to replace "Mrs. Lincoln's"?

> When Mrs. Lincoln returned from lunch, Mrs. Lincoln's husband had already been taken to surgery.

(A) she
(B) our
(C) her
(D) he

6. Read the sentence below. There is an error with the verb. Which answer corrects the error?

> Provided that you get here by 7:00 a.m. tomorrow, we were ready for you.

(A) we would have been ready
(B) we was ready
(C) we are ready
(D) we will be ready

7. Which of the following verbs fits in the blank space in the sentence below?

> When Dr. Carol arrived here yesterday, she _____ the doctor's report with her.

(A) brought
(B) is bringing
(C) will bring
(D) will be bringing

8. Which word in the following sentence is an adjective?

> After reading the test results, the doctor immediately called me with the news.

(A) test
(B) immediately
(C) me
(D) news

9. Which word in the following sentence is an adjective?

> The parking lot across the street fills up by 7:00 in the morning.

(A) parking
(B) lot
(C) up
(D) morning

GO ON TO THE NEXT PAGE

10. Which two words in the following sentence are adjectives?

When a dozen victims arrived all at once, the doctors went into emergency mode.

(A) victims/doctors
(B) arrived/went
(C) dozen/emergency
(D) When/mode

11. Which word in the following sentence is an adverb?

The cosmetic surgeon cautiously cut through the young victim's scar tissue.

(A) cosmetic
(B) cautiously
(C) young
(D) scar

12. Which two words in the following sentence are adverbs?

The staff lounge reeked terribly from the garlic pizza that the interns had foolishly ordered.

(A) staff/garlic
(B) reeked/ordered
(C) terribly/foolishly
(D) lounge/pizza

13. Which of the following sets of words list the adverb and adjective in the sentence below?

You can easily obtain the necessary prescriptions at their store as long as you arrive before 7:00 p.m.

(A) easily/necessary
(B) prescriptions/store
(C) obtain/arrive
(D) at/before

14. Which of the following sets of words lists the adjective and adverb in the sentence below?

As the clock chimed the hour, the modified ambulance roared noisily past our windows.

(A) clock/chimed
(B) hour/windows
(C) ambulance/roared
(D) modified/noisily

GO ON TO THE NEXT PAGE

15. What type of word is needed to repair the error in the sentence below?

The automatic defibrillator, the latest and most high-tech model the company had to offer.

(A) a verb
(B) a noun
(C) an adverb
(D) an adjective

16. What type of word is needed to repair the error in the sentence below?

Closed the curtains, trying to get some much-needed privacy for the patient's examination.

(A) a verb
(B) a subject
(C) an adverb
(D) an adjective

17. All of the following corrections to the run-on below are correct EXCEPT

None of the televisions on the fourth floor was working a repairman had been called.

(A) None of the televisions on the fourth floor was working; a repairman had been called.
(B) None of the televisions on the fourth floor was working, a repairman had been called.
(C) None of the televisions on the fourth floor was working, so a repairman had been called.
(D) None of the televisions on the fourth floor was working. A repairman had been called.

18. All of the following corrections to the run-on below are correct EXCEPT

The security guard's shift was over the new guard took her place.

(A) The security guard's shift was over, and the new guard took her place.
(B) The security guard's shift was over; the new guard took her place.
(C) The security guard's shift was over: the new guard took her place.
(D) The security guard's shift was over. The new guard took her place.

19. Which of the following coordinating conjunctions fits best in the sentence below?

Dr. Addison had been transferred to another department, _____ he kept coming back to check on his former colleagues.

(A) nor
(B) yet
(C) or
(D) so

GO ON TO THE NEXT PAGE

20. Which of the following coordinating conjunctions fits best in the sentence below?

The meatloaf on sale in the cafeteria is delicious, _____ it is nutritious.

(A) but
(B) nor
(C) and
(D) or

21. Which of the following subordinating conjunctions fits best in the sentence below?

_____ the administration is willing to hire additional part-time employees, the service in the maternity department is going to suffer.

(A) Even though
(B) Because
(C) Provided that
(D) Unless

22. Which of the following subordinating conjunctions fits best in the sentence below?

I decided to pursue my degree as a registered nurse _____ I still had enough time and energy to do so.

(A) after
(B) before
(C) how
(D) while

23. An independent clause is the same thing as a

(A) phrase.
(B) sentence.
(C) dependent clause.
(D) fragment.

24. A dependent clause

(A) is always missing a verb.
(B) always contains an adverb.
(C) never can stand alone.
(D) never contains a preposition.

25. Which of the following examples is a prepositional phrase?

(A) when she finally arrived
(B) below the telemetry unit
(C) listening to the lecture
(D) forgetting he was there

GO ON TO THE NEXT PAGE

---

26. What type of phrase is used in the sentence below?

Dr. Connors discovered the missing patient files under the nurse's desk.

(A) noun
(B) dependent
(C) adjectival
(D) prepositional

27. Which of the following words is spelled correctly?

(A) niether
(B) especaly
(C) fourty
(D) surrounded

28. Which of the following is the correct way to spell this word?

(A) arithmatic
(B) arithmatik
(C) arithmetic
(D) arithmetec

29. The word *mince* is an example of what?

(A) silent letter
(B) unstressed vowel
(C) missing consonant
(D) homophone

30. The word *handkerchief* is an example of what?

(A) homophone
(B) unstressed vowel
(C) silent letter
(D) missing consonant

31. Which of the following is the correct way to spell this word?

(A) cemetary
(B) cemetery
(C) cematery
(D) cemitary

32. Certain words are known as "spelling demons." All four of the following words are examples. Which one is spelled correctly?

(A) committed
(B) foriegn
(C) liason
(D) possesion

GO ON TO THE NEXT PAGE

33. Which of the following words is spelled incorrectly?

(A) believe
(B) conscience
(C) jewelry
(D) rhythum

34. What punctuation is needed in this sentence to make it correct?

The interns excuse is that he was never taught how to properly use the emergency equipment.

(A) comma
(B) question mark
(C) apostrophe
(D) semicolon

35. What punctuation is needed in this sentence to make it correct?

My doctor now sends her patients to Jefferson Memorial Hospital which opened two years ago.

(A) period
(B) colon
(C) comma
(D) apostrophe

36. Where does a comma need to be added in the following sentence?

Because the entire staff was out with the flu the department was terribly short-handed.

(A) after Because
(B) after staff
(C) after out
(D) after flu

37. To which word in the following sentence does an apostrophe need to be added?

All of the psychiatric patients and their families planned to attend the departments holiday parties.

(A) patients
(B) families
(C) departments
(D) parties

GO ON TO THE NEXT PAGE

38. What kind of punctuation is needed in this sentence?

Dr. Leopold is in charge tonight he is one of the strictest doctors on staff here.

(A) colon
(B) apostrophe
(C) semicolon
(D) parentheses

39. Which word in the following sentence is missing an apostrophe?

The hospitals answering machines were full of messages asking the doctors to call as soon as possible.

(A) hospitals
(B) machines
(C) messages
(D) doctors

40. What kind of punctuation is missing in this sentence?

The nurse told the police officer that several items were missing from the front desk scissors, a stapler, computer discs, stamps, envelopes, and mailing labels.

(A) apostrophe
(B) colon
(C) parentheses
(D) question mark

41. Where should the missing quotation mark go in the following sentence?

"Yes, Elaine," agreed Dr. Larson. "Those are the orders I left with the head nurse this morning. You should have known that.

(A) after Dr. Larson
(B) after morning
(C) after you
(D) after that

42. Which punctuation mark is missing from the following sentence?

"Nurse Higgins, this is an emergency"

(A) parentheses
(B) quotation mark
(C) question mark
(D) exclamation point

GO ON TO THE NEXT PAGE

43. What punctuation should be used to connect two complete sentences?

  (A) apostrophe
  (B) semicolon
  (C) parentheses
  (D) comma

44. What is the purpose of a colon?

  (A) to indicate unnecessary information
  (B) to show where a speaker would pause
  (C) to introduce a list
  (D) to point out a question

45. What punctuation is needed to indicate a speaker's actual words?

  (A) question marks
  (B) parentheses
  (C) quotation marks
  (D) apostrophe

46. I felt honored when Mrs. Rodriguez's children asked me to give her *eulogy.* ***Eulogy*** means

  (A) medication.
  (B) funeral speech.
  (C) recommendation.
  (D) nutrition advice.

47. If a patient's notes state that he is *corpulent,* it means that he is

  (A) overweight.
  (B) quite tall.
  (C) elderly.
  (D) masculine.

48. If the doctor finds out that the patient was living in *squalid* conditions, it means that the conditions were

  (A) filthy.
  (B) luxurious.
  (C) foreign.
  (D) dangerous.

49. The new clerk hoped to find an older, more experienced colleague who could give her career advice and act as her

  (A) mentor.
  (B) protégé.
  (C) delegate.
  (D) misnomer.

GO ON TO THE NEXT PAGE

50. Which of the following words is a synonym for *protocol?*

(A) ideas
(B) rules
(C) preferences
(D) obsessions

51. Which of the following words best fits in the blank below?

I did not write down the patient's comments word for word; instead I _____ them.

(A) emphasized
(B) underlined
(C) paraphrased
(D) imitated

52. Which of the following words means the opposite of *taciturn?*

(A) aloof
(B) generous
(C) outgoing
(D) puzzled

53. Dr. Parker was *reluctant* to say anything that might upset his patients. ***Reluctant*** means

(A) eager.
(B) anxious.
(C) happy.
(D) unwilling.

54. I was so nervous about my new job that I was sure I needed the *sedative* more than the patient did. ***Sedative*** means a medication that

(A) kills pain.
(B) calms emotions.
(C) cures illness.
(D) stops infection.

55. A person who worries that something bad is about to happen is said to be

(A) apprehensive.
(B) menial.
(C) laconic.
(D) protean.

GO ON TO THE NEXT PAGE

56. Which word has almost the same meaning as *sanction?*

    (A) authorize
    (B) define
    (C) inform
    (D) palpitate

57. A patient who is resting calmly can be described as

    (A) morose.
    (B) placid.
    (C) literal.
    (D) profane.

58. The credulous patient believed the stories he read about treatments that produced miracle cures. **Credulous** means

    (A) naive.
    (B) skeptical.
    (C) knowledgeable.
    (D) confused.

59. A person who is *infallible* never

    (A) puts things away.
    (B) leaves the house.
    (C) makes a mistake.
    (D) asks for help.

60. The three doctors decided to *collaborate* on the project. This means that they are going to

    (A) work as a team.
    (B) start over again.
    (C) stop work temporarily.
    (D) work harder.

**STOP. IF YOU HAVE TIME LEFT OVER,
CHECK YOUR WORK ON THIS SECTION ONLY.**

Reading Comprehension Test 1

ANSWER SHEET

1 (A) (B) (C) (D)   13 (A) (B) (C) (D)   25 (A) (B) (C) (D)
2 (A) (B) (C) (D)   14 (A) (B) (C) (D)   26 (A) (B) (C) (D)
3 (A) (B) (C) (D)   15 (A) (B) (C) (D)   27 (A) (B) (C) (D)
4 (A) (B) (C) (D)   16 (A) (B) (C) (D)   28 (A) (B) (C) (D)
5 (A) (B) (C) (D)   17 (A) (B) (C) (D)   29 (A) (B) (C) (D)
6 (A) (B) (C) (D)   18 (A) (B) (C) (D)   30 (A) (B) (C) (D)
7 (A) (B) (C) (D)   19 (A) (B) (C) (D)   31 (A) (B) (C) (D)
8 (A) (B) (C) (D)   20 (A) (B) (C) (D)   32 (A) (B) (C) (D)
9 (A) (B) (C) (D)   21 (A) (B) (C) (D)   33 (A) (B) (C) (D)
10 (A) (B) (C) (D)   22 (A) (B) (C) (D)   34 (A) (B) (C) (D)
11 (A) (B) (C) (D)   23 (A) (B) (C) (D)   35 (A) (B) (C) (D)
12 (A) (B) (C) (D)   24 (A) (B) (C) (D)

READING COMPREHENSION TEST 1

35 questions

Time limit: 40 minutes

Questions 1–5 are based on the following passage.

Over the years, acupuncture has become a more widely accepted type of alternative medicine. It is used for a wide variety of ailments, and if a recent study from Germany is valid, relieving menstrual pain can be added to the continuously growing list.

Traditionally nonsteroidal anti-inflammatory drugs (NSAIDs) are the typical treatment for menstrual discomfort. However, as many consumers and physicians are aware, NSAIDs have a number of side effects, including nausea, vomiting, rash, dizziness, headache, and drowsiness. Acupuncture rarely has any kind of side effects other than the occasional stinging sensation when the needle is inserted or a deep ache around it after it is in place.

Acupuncture has proven helpful with relieving a number of kinds of pain, so researchers at Charité University Medical Center in Berlin wanted to find out how effective it might be in combating cramps and other menstrual discomforts. More than 200 women were enrolled in the study, and after three months and approximately ten sessions, the women who were treated with acupuncture reported significantly less pain than those in the control group who received no treatment at all. They also reported a 33 percent improvement in their symptoms. Because of these findings, the researchers came to the conclusion that "acupuncture should be considered as a viable option in the management of these patients."

1. What is the best title for this passage?

   (A) A Miracle Cure for Cramps Discovered
   (B) Throw Away the Pills and Bring in the Needles
   (C) Acupuncture Holds Promise for Combating Menstrual Pain
   (D) Alternative Medicine Tries to Prove Itself Better than Traditional

2. Why were experts interested in finding an alternative treatment for menstrual discomfort?

   (A) The usual treatment may produce a number of side effects.
   (B) The usual treatment is not profitable enough.
   (C) The usual treatment has repeatedly been proved ineffective.
   (D) The usual treatment can be too expensive for some families.

GO ON TO THE NEXT PAGE

3. Why did experts believe that acupuncture may help with menstrual cramps?

   (A) Multiple studies suggested that acupuncture would help.
   (B) Acupuncture has been effective in treating other types of pain.
   (C) Repeated testimonials from patients convinced them.
   (D) Acupuncture is a technique that has been used for hundreds of years.

4. What is the main advantage that acupuncture has over NSAIDs?

   (A) It costs less.
   (B) It is easier to find.
   (C) It carries less risk.
   (D) It is more effective.

5. What conclusion is suggested by this study from Germany?

   (A) So far, acupuncture does not have much credibility as a treatment option.
   (B) Acupuncture can relieve women of all menstrual discomfort.
   (C) NSAIDs are generally more effective than acupuncture for treating cramps.
   (D) Acupuncture is a reasonable treatment choice for cramps.

Questions 6–10 are based on the following passage.

One of the most common stereotypes surrounding young teenage boys is that they are hostile, belligerent, and generally display "attitude." Some considered this just a phase in the maturing process, some thought it was a reflection of poor parenting skills, and others placed blame on everything from violent video games to too much television.

A recent study by a team of Australian and American researchers may prove all of those theories wrong. These researchers say that boys' aggressive behaviors may actually be due to overly large amygdalae in the boys' brains. The amygdala is a part of the brain found deep within the medial temporal lobes. It is intricately involved in emotional responses such as fear and anger.

As the researchers reported in an article for the *Proceedings of the National Academy of Science,* boys may show no ability to control their emotions because they literally do not have the brain development to do so until their early twenties. According to Nicholas Allen of the University of Melbourne's psychology department. "It's important to realize that . . . parts of the brain are still developing for these young people."

The study required 137 twelve-year-old boys and their parents to sit down and discuss emotionally sensitive issues such as homework, bedtime, and hours spent on the Internet. Afterwards, the boys' brains were scanned. Boys who had the largest amygdalae behaved more aggressively than other boys who had smaller ones. They also appeared to have smaller-than-usual prefrontal cortexes, the region of the brain that is involved with regulating emotions.

GO ON TO THE NEXT PAGE

The researchers concluded that those boys who had less brain development had a much stronger tendency to be negative and even hostile when they interacted with their parents. Just do not tell the teenage boys—it gives them a built-in excuse!

6. Which of these topics is the main focus of the passage?

(A) how best to discipline unruly young people
(B) why scientists think that the amygdala affects emotions
(C) how behavior may be linked to brain development
(D) why parents and teenage boys tend to have disagreements

7. According to the study, when is brain development sufficient for boys to control their emotions?

(A) by the time boys reach puberty
(B) by the time boys reach their mid-to-late teens
(C) by the time boys graduate from high school
(D) by the time boys reach their early twenties

8. Why does the author include a quote from Nicholas Allen?

(A) His son is one of the boys involved in the study.
(B) His credentials lend authority to the conclusions of the study.
(C) He himself was once an overly aggressive young man.
(D) He was the one who initiated the research study.

9. What physical tests were performed after the boys and their parents discussed sensitive issues?

(A) The boys' brains were scanned.
(B) The boys' blood was analyzed for elevated testosterone levels.
(C) The parents' blood pressure levels were measured.
(D) The boys were given MRIs.

10. What conclusion did researchers reach about boys with "attitude"?

(A) The boys would benefit from additional discipline from parents.
(B) Surgery and medication would be beneficial in controlling emotions.
(C) Brain development was the key to much of their overall behavior.
(D) Additional research is needed to find out how to prevent brain abnormalities.

Questions 11–15 are based on the following passage.

Lie out in the sun too much today—and get skin cancer 20 years from now. Smoke too many cigarettes now—and get lung cancer decades down the road. Now there is potentially a third danger to add to this list: be exposed to too much lead, pesticides, or mercury now and have your aging brain become seriously confused during your senior years.

GO ON TO THE NEXT PAGE

"We're trying to offer a caution that a portion of what has been called normal aging might in fact be due to ubiquitous environmental exposures like lead," says Dr. Brian Schwartz of Johns Hopkins University. "The fact that it's happening with lead is the first proof of the principle that it's possible."

A new area of medical research is one that studies how exposure to toxic elements in younger years can result in serious health problems in senior years. It is difficult to research these problems because the only way to do so is to observe people over many years to determine results.

Physicians test for lead amounts by seeing how much has accumulated in a person's shinbone. Testing the blood also often reveals amounts of lead, but that is a sign of recent, not lifelong, exposure. The higher the lifetime lead dose, according to the study, the worse the performance of mental functions, including verbal and visual memory and language ability.

11. What is the best title for this passage?

(A) There Is Lead Everywhere
(B) The Shins Tell a Story
(C) Toxins Today, Health Problems Tomorrow
(D) Avoid the Sun—and Cigarette Smoke

12. You might infer from this passage that

(A) people are exposed to lead more than they realize.
(B) doctors are increasingly concerned about what happens to the brain during aging.
(C) shin bones are good indicators of many health ailments or conditions.
(D) blood tests are the best way to measure individuals' lifetime lead exposure.

13. Why is the effect of lead exposure hard to study?

(A) Lead is difficult to trace in the body.
(B) Today, exposure to lead is no longer a problem.
(C) Lead is discarded from the body at too rapid a rate.
(D) Scientists have to observe lead exposure in subjects over a long time period.

14. Why does the author of the article include a quote from Dr. Brian Schwartz?

(A) to point out how exposure to several toxins can affect the brain
(B) to support the idea that some symptoms of aging might be due to lead exposure
(C) to introduce an idea that contradicts the main point of the article
(D) to demonstrate that all doctors are taking this new research on lead seriously

GO ON TO THE NEXT PAGE

15. What conclusion can be drawn from the fact that the shin bone is used for diagnosing lead levels?

    (A) Lead accumulates only in the shin bone.
    (B) The shin bone is very delicate.
    (C) Lead stays within the body for a long time.
    (D) It is easiest to test bones that are closer to the body's surface.

Questions 16–20 are based on the following passage.

When most people think about taking a nap, they typically envision being down for the count for at least an hour or two. A German study, however, has shown that if you really want to refresh your brain, a six-minute cat nap will do it. Not only will you feel better afterwards, but your ability to learn and remember will have improved as well.

As described in a recent article in the *Journal of Sleep Research,* students at the University of Düsseldorf participated in experiments in which they had to memorize a list of words and then either take a nap or play a video game. The ones who napped consistently scored higher than those who stayed awake.

The study may help scientists learn more about what happens when people go to sleep. They already know that the brain undergoes a number of significant changes in the process. "There are dramatic shifts in brain chemistry and electro-physiology," said Dr. Matthew Tucker, a researcher at Harvard University School of Medicine and the Center for Sleep and Cognition. "For example, we know that levels of the transmitter acetylcholine go down. And we think that when acetyl-choline gets to a low point, it should have an enhancing effect on memory."

Experts believe that sleeping is the brain's chance to decide which details and memories from the day need to be placed in permanent storage and which ones need to be thrown out. It has to do this because there is only so much room in the brain for information.

Of course, those catnaps may be wonderful but they can never replace the value of a solid eight hours of sleep. As Dr. Olaf Lahl, the study's lead author phrases it, "A regular sleep schedule still plays an important role in overall well-being and health."

16. What is the main idea of this passage?

    (A) Everyone has to have eight hours of sleep each night.
    (B) Brief naps are enough to help energize most people.
    (C) There is a limited amount of room in the brain for storage.
    (D) Memorizing lists of words is more difficult than you would think.

17. Sleeping apparently helps with everything EXCEPT

    (A) fatigue.
    (B) memory.
    (C) learning.
    (D) appetite.

GO ON TO THE NEXT PAGE

18. What happens when the level of acetylcholine decreases in the brain?

(A) A person gets sleepy.
(B) A person learns more slowly.
(C) A person's memory improves.
(D) A person's fatigue fades away.

19. What is one of the primary purposes of sleep, according to this passage?

(A) to allow a person mentally to sort out important and unnecessary information
(B) to let a person experience dreams and work out emotional issues
(C) to ensure that a person stays healthy and resists illness at all times
(D) to allow a person to experience dramatic changes in overall brain chemistry

20. Which of the following statements best states the conclusion of the passage?

(A) German studies about sleep deprivation are becoming scientifically accepted.
(B) Brain chemistry undergoes significant changes during the different stages of sleep.
(C) A solid night's sleep is not necessary if a person takes several naps each day.
(D) According to a study, cat naps are much more effective than you might think.

Questions 21–25 are based on the following passage.

The Centers for Disease Control and Prevention (CDC) is always busy monitoring health issues and sending out regular warnings to make sure people know of any impending threats. One of the most recent warnings, however, caught Americans by surprise. The CDC announced that one of today's most under-recognized public health problems is sleep loss. It is estimated that between 50 and 70 million Americans suffer from this problem.

Adequate sleep is essential to good mental and physical health. If you do not get enough sleep on a regular basis, you run an increased risk of obesity, diabetes, high blood pressure, stroke, cardiovascular disease, depression, cigarette smoking, and excessive drinking. Those are not minor health issues!

To find out how many Americans are not getting enough sleep, the CDC surveyed almost 20,000 adults in four states. Ten percent of the people studied reported not getting enough sleep every single day of the previous month, and 38 percent reported not getting enough in seven or more days in the previous month.

How much sleep is enough sleep? According to the National Sleep Foundation, adults need seven to nine hours each night, whereas children under

GO ON TO THE NEXT PAGE

twelve need nine to eleven hours and teenagers need between eight and a half and nine and a half hours. Unfortunately, instead of sleeping, however, many people stay up late at night to surf the Internet or watch television.

Along with the health risks that chronic sleep loss can bring, experts also believe it is responsible for the thousands of people who die on the road each year from accidents caused by sleepy drivers. There is no doubt that spending less time with eyes closed can make your days longer, your health worse, and your driving riskier.

21. The main idea of this passage is

    (A) the CDC keeps an eye out for new potentially threatening health issues.

    (B) children require several more hours of sleep per night than adults.

    (C) more people are staying up at night to surf the Internet or watch television.

    (D) a lack of adequate sleep is becoming a major national health problem.

22. According to the passage, the CDC wanted to know how many

    (A) hours of sleep children younger than 12 years of age need for proper development.

    (B) accidents are being caused each day by sleepy drivers.

    (C) Americans are not getting adequate amounts of sleep.

    (D) health risks are involved in people not getting enough sleep.

23. What does the word "surfing" mean as used in this passage?

    (A) spending time swimming in the ocean

    (B) looking at different Web sites on the Internet

    (C) watching too many hours of late-night television

    (D) writing homework and other assignments on the computer

24. All of the following are potential risks from inadequate sleep EXCEPT

    (A) cancer.

    (B) obesity.

    (C) diabetes.

    (D) depression.

25. According to the passage, how many hours of sleep does the average adult need per night?

    (A) 7 to 9

    (B) 8½ to 9½

    (C) 9 to 11

    (D) more than 12

GO ON TO THE NEXT PAGE

Questions 26–30 are based on the following passage.

Put a dozen parents together in a room, and you will most likely have a dozen different theories of parenting. One of the most debated issues in raising kids is how to discipline them, especially when it comes to the question of to spank or not to spank. Some moms and dads are sure that it is an integral part of showing their kids what is right and wrong. Others are equally sure that spanking is a cruel act of violence against kids. Which is it?

According to a new study reported at the American Psychological Association Summit Conference on Violence and Abuse in Relationships, spanking or other forms of corporal punishment apparently increase the risk of future sexual problems such as violent and/or coercive sex with partners.

Proving this new theory is tricky because with spanking, you cannot set up a double-blind or randomized study such as those used in testing medications. A number of other researchers in the field, however, tend to agree with this link between corporal punishment and sexual aggression. "The more children are spanked, the more aggressive they are and the more likely they are to engage in delinquent or at-risk behaviors," says Elizabeth Gershoff from the University of Michigan's School of Social Work. "Kids may learn that sometimes there's pain and fear involved in loving relationships."

Naturally, there are those who disagree as well. Some scientists believe that spanking two- to six-year-old children can be very helpful as long as parents are not angry or out of control emotionally. Human development researcher Robert Larzelere adds that parents simply must be able to differentiate between appropriate and inappropriate use.

Although opinion on spanking remains divided, research continues on this contentious issue. In the meantime, however, the American Academy of Pediatrics advises parents to use other methods of discipline.

26. What is the best title for this passage?

   (A) Parents Have Different Ideas on Punishment
   (B) Keeping Parental Emotions Under Control
   (C) A Smack on the Backside—Abuse or Appropriate?
   (D) A Double-Blind Study on Spanking Effectiveness

27. The word *integral* as used in the first paragraph of the passage can best be defined as

   (A) central.
   (B) initial.
   (C) trifling.
   (D) irrelevant.

GO ON TO THE NEXT PAGE

28. Which of the following best summarizes Gershoff's opinion about spanking?

(A) She is certain that corporal punishment will result in violent sexual encounters later.
(B) She believes that it can teach children some very negative lessons about relationships.
(C) She knows that as long as the parents' emotions are under control, it is quite effective.
(D) She believes that spanking is so abusive that it should be made illegal.

29. What can be inferred about spanking and future sexual problems?

(A) One leads directly to the other in every case.
(B) Spanking is a prelude to predatory sexual behavior and rape.
(C) The researchers who study this topic tend to have a bias against spanking.
(D) Studies have shown some correlation between the two.

30. What advice does the American Academy of Pediatrics give parents about spanking?

(A) Do it only if you are not feeling emotional.
(B) Find other alternatives to use before spanking.
(C) Try to limit spankings to once a week or less.
(D) Avoid it completely because it leads to other issues.

Questions 31–35 are based on the following passage.

It sounds contradictory, but here is some new advice for people who are feeling unusually tired: get out and get some exercise. Studies have shown that regular, low-impact workouts such as short strolls or brief bike rides can help increase overall energy levels by 20 percent and decrease fatigue levels by 65 percent. In other words, if you are feeling tired, the best way to feel more energetic is to get some exercise.

This advice is based on a study done by the University of Georgia's Exercise Pathology Lab. Three dozen people who did not get any kind of regular exercise yet consistently felt exhausted were divided into three groups. One group did not exercise at all. A second group worked out fairly intensively on an exercise bike three times a week. The third group also worked out but at a slower pace. Of the two groups that exercised, both reported a 20 percent increase in energy levels. However, the group that exercised at a more leisurely pace stated that they experienced far less fatigue than the high-intensity group.

This was not the first study to point out a link between regular exercise and energy levels. The same team that conducted it also published one several years ago that stated that low-impact exercise can also help reduce fatigue in patients with serious health conditions such as heart disease and cancer. Clearly, it is time to get off the couch and onto the track.

GO ON TO THE NEXT PAGE

31. What is the main idea of this passage?

    (A) Low-impact exercise is always better for people than intensive exercise.

    (B) The best way to address fatigue is get out and exercise hard every single day.

    (C) If people feel tired, they can best improve their energy levels by regular exercise.

    (D) Low-impact exercise helps people with serious conditions such as heart disease and cancer.

32. According to the passage, which group experienced the greatest benefit from this experiment?

    (A) the group that did not exercise at all

    (B) the group that rode exercise bikes intensively

    (C) the group that stuck to low-impact exercise

    (D) the group that took additional daily naps

33. What type of people participated in this study on fatigue and exercise?

    (A) athletes wanting to get more rest

    (B) sedentary people who were always tired

    (C) scientists interested in proving their various theories

    (D) patients with life-threatening diseases who were exhausted

34. The word *track* as used in the last paragraph of the passage can best be defined as

    (A) keep a record of.

    (B) a new attitude.

    (C) follow carefully.

    (D) a paved, circular path.

35. Based on this passage, what conclusion can best be drawn about the effect of exercise on chronic disease?

    (A) It helps patients heal much faster.

    (B) It improves the effectiveness of any medical treatment.

    (C) It helps manage a patient's overall weight during medical care.

    (D) It lessens the exhaustion that often accompanies disease conditions.

**STOP. IF YOU HAVE TIME LEFT OVER,
CHECK YOUR WORK ON THIS SECTION ONLY.**

Reading Comprehension Test 2

ANSWER SHEET

1 (A) (B) (C) (D)	13 (A) (B) (C) (D)	25 (A) (B) (C) (D)
2 (A) (B) (C) (D)	14 (A) (B) (C) (D)	26 (A) (B) (C) (D)
3 (A) (B) (C) (D)	15 (A) (B) (C) (D)	27 (A) (B) (C) (D)
4 (A) (B) (C) (D)	16 (A) (B) (C) (D)	28 (A) (B) (C) (D)
5 (A) (B) (C) (D)	17 (A) (B) (C) (D)	29 (A) (B) (C) (D)
6 (A) (B) (C) (D)	18 (A) (B) (C) (D)	30 (A) (B) (C) (D)
7 (A) (B) (C) (D)	19 (A) (B) (C) (D)	31 (A) (B) (C) (D)
8 (A) (B) (C) (D)	20 (A) (B) (C) (D)	32 (A) (B) (C) (D)
9 (A) (B) (C) (D)	21 (A) (B) (C) (D)	33 (A) (B) (C) (D)
10 (A) (B) (C) (D)	22 (A) (B) (C) (D)	34 (A) (B) (C) (D)
11 (A) (B) (C) (D)	23 (A) (B) (C) (D)	35 (A) (B) (C) (D)
12 (A) (B) (C) (D)	24 (A) (B) (C) (D)	

READING COMPREHENSION TEST 2

35 questions

Time limit: 40 minutes

Questions 1–5 are based on the following passage.

For years, aromatherapy has been touted as a safe and natural way to relax and even heal. Essential oils from a variety of scents have been added to candles and sprays to help people feel better. However, a recent study performed at Ohio State University says that these smells, as nice as they may be, do not do a thing to improve people's health.

To find out if aromatherapy actually works, the researchers tested two of the most popular scents: lemon and lavender. First, test subjects had their heart rate, blood pressure, stress hormones, and immune function measured and noted. Next, they were subjected to mild stressors and then told to sniff one of the scents to see if the scent would help them relax. Finally, all the subjects were tested again to look for improvement. There were no significant changes noted—even in people who had previously stated they were true believers in the power of aromatherapy.

Of course, this does not necessarily prove that aromatherapy is worthless, either. It was just one small study, pitted against the opinions of thousands of consumers who swear by peppermint on their pillow for an upset stomach or vanilla for a headache. More tests will be done but, in the meantime, a whiff of lavender, lemon, or other scents will certainly do no harm—and can be quite pleasant at the same time.

1. What is the best title for this passage?

   (A) Lavender Help for Headaches
   (B) The Importance of Avoiding Aromatherapy
   (C) Great Aroma Yes, Health Boost No
   (D) The Benefits of Lemon Pillow Spray

2. Why did the researchers decide to test lemon and lavender?

   (A) They were the two easiest scents to find.
   (B) They were two of the most popular scents.
   (C) They were the two scents that helped with headaches.
   (D) They were the two least expensive scents available.

3. Why might being a "true believer" in aromatherapy be a factor in the test?

   (A) True believers would believe anything they were told.
   (B) True believers would be more apt to lie to support their ideas.
   (C) True believers had something to gain if they were proven right.
   (D) True believers would be more inclined to report a positive change.

GO ON TO THE NEXT PAGE

4. Which of the following is a likely reason why some people choose aromatherapy as a type of treatment?

(A) They believe it is a safe and natural way to treat a condition.
(B) They know that it is better than any kind of medication.
(C) They trust the traditional medical advice from their physicians.
(D) They fear that not using aromatherapy will make them worse.

5. Which of the following is a conclusion that you can draw from this passage?

(A) Aromatherapy is not a legitimate therapy by anyone's standards.
(B) Lemon and lavender are not healthy scents to inhale or use.
(C) More studies are needed to determine if aromatherapy is truly beneficial.
(D) Adding aromatherapy to regular treatment will help speed healing.

Questions 6–10 are based on the following passage.

Almost everyone knows, thanks to everything from newspaper articles to endless television commercials, that bone density is a major health concern for women. Osteoporosis has become a familiar term, and more and more women are scheduling bone density tests to make sure all is well underneath the skin. In all the hype, however, there are certain people who are being overlooked: men. It appears that older men need routine checks for bone thinning as well.

A new computerized tool sponsored by the World Health Organization is being used to identify the people most at risk for experiencing a broken bone. One of its findings is that men older than 70 years of age should have a bone mineral density x-ray test on a regular basis. This tool, called FRAX, calculates the risk of a person experiencing a hip, wrist, shoulder, or spine fracture within the next decade. Those tested were age 40 or older and either had osteoporosis or low bone mass. FRAX takes many different elements into consideration when figuring a person's risk level. It factors in diet, exercise, and exposure to sunlight, for example. It also looks at where people live, what genetic factors might be involved, as well as lifestyle factors such as smoking, heavy alcohol consumption, and the use of steroids.

The National Osteoporosis Foundation has used the FRAX predictions to create updated guidelines. Its new recommendations not only include bone density tests for men but also a stronger emphasis on the importance of weight-bearing and muscle-strengthening exercises and an increased amount of vitamin D supplementation.

6. What is the main idea of this passage?

(A) Osteoporosis is a terrible disease for women to have.
(B) A tool named FRAX measures the risk of osteoporosis.
(C) The World Health Organization is concerned about osteoporosis.
(D) New technology has shown that men are also at risk from osteoporosis.

GO ON TO THE NEXT PAGE

7. What conclusion can you draw from the first sentence of the passage?

    (A) Osteoporosis is more common than anyone previously imagined.
    (B) The media give a lot of overall coverage to osteoporosis.
    (C) Only women are at high risk for developing bone thinning.
    (D) Thinning bones is not considered a serious medical problem.

8. FRAX takes into account all of the following factors EXCEPT

    (A) lifestyle choices.
    (B) exposure to hazardous materials.
    (C) genetic heritage.
    (D) exposure to sunlight.

9. Which of the following is the most likely reason why smoking and alcohol intake are part of FRAX's calculations?

    (A) They may be factors leading to loss of bone mass.
    (B) They are both known to contribute to cancer risk.
    (C) They indicate a lack of concern about health care.
    (D) They are the main cause of severe bone thinning.

10. The FRAX results have resulted in

    (A) more research money for medical grants.
    (B) new techniques for testing men's bone density.
    (C) updated health guidelines and recommendations.
    (D) additional pressure to cure osteoporosis.

Questions 11–15 are based on the following passage.

Without a doubt, one of the biggest risks to the elderly today is falling. It is also one of the most common accidents that people age 65 and older experience. Some just receive a few bumps and bruises, while others are hurt so badly that they cannot ever fully recover.

U.S. health officials surveyed thousands of elderly people and found that approximately one in six Americans have fallen in the past three months. A third of these people sustained considerable injuries, including the most dreaded break of all, a hip fracture. Approximately 16,000 people even died from the injuries they suffered, whereas even more were left completely disabled. The Centers for Disease Control and Prevention (CDC) epidemiologist Judy Stevens stated, "It's a tremendous public health problem because so many older adults are affected."

It only takes one fall to completely steal an older person's self-confidence. According to a CDC report, "Even when those injuries are minor, they can seriously affect older adults' quality of life by inducing a fear of falling, which can lead to self-imposed activity restrictions, social isolation, and depression."

Along with an admonition to move slowly and carefully, the CDC also recommends that the elderly get enough gentle exercise or physical therapy to help strengthen their muscles and improve their balance. This not only will reduce the number of falls, but give a real boost to older adults' self-esteem.

GO ON TO THE NEXT PAGE

11. What is this passage primarily about?

   (A) Most falls experienced by the elderly are either disabling or fatal.
   (B) Falling is one of the biggest health risks for older people.
   (C) Elderly people's self-confidence is threatened by falling.
   (D) The CDC claims that regular exercise will prevent all falls.

12. Why does the author include a quote from a CDC report?

   (A) to support the basic idea of the passage
   (B) to provide a controversial point of view
   (C) to demonstrate current and relevant statistics
   (D) to show that treatment for falls is readily available

13. Why does the author refer to the hip fracture as the most dreaded break of all?

   (A) It is the hardest one of all to recover from.
   (B) It is the most expensive one to medically repair.
   (C) It is the one break that cannot be treated in any truly effective way.
   (D) It is so debilitating that it introduces the chance of additional health problems.

14. Gentle exercise is recommended to do all of the following EXCEPT

   (A) improve balance.
   (B) reduce the number of falls.
   (C) maintain proper weight.
   (D) boost overall self-esteem.

15. What conclusion did the CDC reach about the elderly?

   (A) They are too fragile to live on their own.
   (B) They should all be enrolled in physical therapy classes.
   (C) They are at a very high risk of serious injury if they fall.
   (D) They all are staying home because of a fear of falling.

Questions 16–20 are based on the following passage.

It is hard to imagine how the eating disorders anorexia and bulimia could be any worse than they already are, but somehow people have found a way. Known unofficially as *drunkorexia,* this condition is a blend of self-imposed starvation or binging and purging mixed with alcohol abuse. Anorexics use alcohol either to soothe their conscience for eating something they feel they should not, or as their only sustenance. Bulimics binge on alcohol for emotional reasons and then purge by vomiting all of it back up.

Our current culture's obsession with thinness, coupled with widespread acceptance of drug and alcohol abuse, have made this combination particularly attractive. Dr. Doug Bunnell, former president of the National Eating Disorders Association, said, "Binge drinking is almost cool and hip, and losing

GO ON TO THE NEXT PAGE

weight and being thin is a cultural imperative for young women in America," he said. "Mixing both is not surprising, and it has reached a tipping point in terms of public awareness."

Some experts are beginning to explore the possible psychological and neurological links between eating disorders and substance abuse. Does eating or binging somehow trigger the same pleasure centers as drugs or alcohol? Another avenue being explored is what to do if a person has both conditions. Treatment for addiction is abstinence, but no one can abstain completely from food. As Dr. Kevin Wandler, vice president for medical services at an eating disorders center, phrases it, "Eating normally would be an effective behavior, but it's easier to give up alcohol and drugs because you never need them again. If your drug is food, that's a challenge."

16. What is the best title for this passage?

(A) When Alcohol Meets Anorexia
(B) The Dangers of Binging and Purging
(C) The Pleasure Centers of the Brain
(D) Neurological Links in Eating Disorders

17. *Drunkorexia* refers to a combination of

(A) anorexia and bulimia.
(B) eating disorders and drug use.
(C) binging and purging.
(D) eating disorders and alcohol abuse.

18. According to this article, some experts believe there may be a link between eating disorders and

(A) substance abuse.
(B) low self-esteem.
(C) severe vomiting.
(D) chronic depression.

19. Which of the following problems with *drunkorexia* does the passage focus on?

(A) how to diagnose it
(B) how to treat it
(C) how to label it
(D) how to recognize it

20. Why does the author include a quote in the last paragraph?

(A) to emphasize a link between eating disorders and substance abuse
(B) to point out how "cool" binge drinking is for some people
(C) to introduce a totally contradictory viewpoint
(D) to highlight a new theory in eating disorders treatment

GO ON TO THE NEXT PAGE

Questions 21–25 are based on the following passage.

Millions of people all over the country choose to drink only bottled water because they are convinced that it is much better for them. In fact, according to the Beverage Marketing Corporation, the average person drinks 30 gallons of bottled water each year. Multiple companies are profiting from this new obsession, and the industry is currently worth $12 billion in the United States.

Bottled water and tap water have a lot in common, however. Both have set limits on how many chemicals or how much bacteria or radiation allowed to be in the water. Neither one of them, however, has any kind of limitation on acceptable levels of pharmaceuticals. Apparently, there are no U.S. standards set for pharmaceutical residue in any kind of water.

Without any limitations or laws in place guiding them, most bottled water companies do not even test their products for traces of pharmaceuticals. Kevin Mathews, director of health and environmental affairs for Nestlé Waters North America, Inc., says, "I don't think anybody could say anything is 'free' from pharmaceuticals."

The presence of pharmaceuticals in the water should be worrisome, but so far, no one is overly concerned. "The industry is monitoring it," says Bob Hirst, vice president of the International Bottled Water Association, "but we haven't seen anything to alarm us at this point."

21. What is the main topic of this passage?

   (A) The bottled water industry is currently worth $12 billion.
   (B) The average person drinks more than 30 gallons of water annually.
   (C) There need to be more laws regulating bottled water production.
   (D) There are some ingredients in all drinking water that may be dangerous.

22. All of the following ingredients in water are monitored carefully EXCEPT

   (A) pharmaceuticals.
   (B) chemicals.
   (C) bacteria.
   (D) radiation.

23. You might infer from this passage that

   (A) bottled water is far safer than tap water.
   (B) bottled water undergoes no testing at all.
   (C) tap water and bottled water are similar in content.
   (D) tap water has more pharmaceuticals than bottled water.

GO ON TO THE NEXT PAGE

24. What can you infer from the fact that the bottled water industry is monitoring pharmaceuticals?

    (A) The industry wants to make sure standards are being met.
    (B) The industry is concerned that pharmaceuticals may eventually be a problem.
    (C) The industry knows that pharmaceuticals are extremely dangerous.
    (D) The industry wants to have a position statement ready for the media.

25. What conclusion can be drawn from the fact that an expert in the field states that most likely nothing is free from pharmaceuticals?

    (A) The expert has not been properly informed.
    (B) It is impossible to remove pharmaceuticals from any product.
    (C) There are contaminants in products that most people don't know about.
    (D) Pharmaceuticals are clearly not toxic or harmful to any human beings.

Questions 26–30 are based on the following passage.

New mothers as well as mothers-to-be have known it for years, but scientists have just corroborated it: pregnant women do tend to suffer from forgetfulness. Occasionally, that short-term memory loss continues up to a full year after the birth of the child. It is not an obvious loss; it comes on gradually and subtly and seems especially prevalent when the woman is expected to do something new and demanding. For example, she is more likely to forget a telephone number she just learned but can still remember all the numbers she is familiar with.

What causes the loss is still unknown, although the Australian researchers who led this study suspect it is due to the hormonal shifts going on during pregnancy. The changes in lifestyle might account for some of it also. "You're going to have more difficulty sleeping," said Dr. Julie Henry, one of the study's authors. "And other studies have shown that sleep deficiency definitely disrupts cognitive performance. There's no reason to think it won't do so during pregnancy."

The results of this study were published in the *Journal of Clinical and Experimental Neuropsychology*. It was performed at Melbourne's Australian Catholic University and it looked at the memory performances of more than 1,000 women, including expectant women, new mothers, and nonpregnant women.

26. What is the best title for this passage?

    (A) The Threat of Long-Term Memory Loss
    (B) Pregnancy Hormones May Cause Memory Trouble
    (C) Mothers-to-Be Have Permanent Amnesia
    (D) Nine Months of Not Enough Sleep

GO ON TO THE NEXT PAGE

27. According to the article, to what do Australian researchers attribute memory loss?

(A) changes in lifestyle
(B) lack of sleep
(C) hormonal shifts
(D) excessive fatigue

28. This study included all types of women EXCEPT

(A) pregnant women.
(B) new mothers.
(C) nonpregnant women.
(D) women undergoing menopause.

29. What does the word *suspect* mean as used in the passage?

(A) suppose
(B) decide
(C) doubt
(D) conclude

30. Which of the following statements best states the conclusion of the passage?

(A) Pregnancy results in severe memory loss that can last up to a year.
(B) Lack of sleep is hard on everyone and especially pregnant women.
(C) Some women have a great deal of trouble remembering phone numbers.
(D) When women are pregnant, they may suffer from short-term memory loss.

Questions 31–35 are based on the following passage.

Almost anyone who lives in a place where the winter months are mostly dark and rainy or snowy knows what it is like to yearn longingly for "just a few rays." For some people, however, this feeling is much more than a simple longing; it is a physical and emotional need. These people suffer from seasonal affective disorder (SAD).

Although in the past the experience has been put down to nothing more than "winter blues," more and more physicians are recognizing the fact that for some, it is much more than a mood swing. Those with SAD not only get depressed, they struggle with lethargy and chronic fatigue, often to the point of impairing their daily lives. Other symptoms include anxiety, social withdrawal, appetite changes, weight gain, and insomnia.

Although more women than men are diagnosed with SAD, men seem to have the most severe symptoms. Those who live in the north and those with a family history of SAD are at highest overall risk.

GO ON TO THE NEXT PAGE

Currently SAD is considered a subtype of bipolar disorder and/or depression, and physicians rely on thorough psychological and physical examinations to determine if a patient actually has the condition. If left untreated, SAD can actually lead to complications such as substance abuse or even suicidal thoughts. Treatment focuses primarily on light therapy but may be supplemented with medications and psychotherapy.

31. What is the best title for this passage?

(A) Everyone Should Move to the Sunshine State
(B) The "Winter Blues" Are Exaggerated
(C) When Sadness Comes with the Season
(D) Men Get the Worst SAD Symptoms

32. What does the word *rays* mean as used in the passage?

(A) waves
(B) energy
(C) sunshine
(D) warmth

33. The word *lethargy* as used in the second paragraph of the passage can best be defined as

(A) sluggishness.
(B) irritability.
(C) energy.
(D) starvation.

34. According to the passage, one of the worst things that can happen if SAD is left untreated is that the patient may

(A) suffer depression.
(B) need medication.
(C) commit suicide.
(D) require therapy.

35. Based on this passage, what is the primary treatment for SAD?

(A) light therapy
(B) medication
(C) surgery
(D) psychotherapy

STOP. IF YOU HAVE TIME LEFT OVER, CHECK YOUR WORK ON THIS SECTION ONLY.

Mathematics Test 1

ANSWER SHEET

1 (A) (B) (C) (D)
2 (A) (B) (C) (D)
3 (A) (B) (C) (D)
4 (A) (B) (C) (D)
5 (A) (B) (C) (D)
6 (A) (B) (C) (D)
7 (A) (B) (C) (D)
8 (A) (B) (C) (D)
9 (A) (B) (C) (D)
10 (A) (B) (C) (D)
11 (A) (B) (C) (D)
12 (A) (B) (C) (D)
13 (A) (B) (C) (D)
14 (A) (B) (C) (D)
15 (A) (B) (C) (D)
16 (A) (B) (C) (D)
17 (A) (B) (C) (D)

18 (A) (B) (C) (D)
19 (A) (B) (C) (D)
20 (A) (B) (C) (D)
21 (A) (B) (C) (D)
22 (A) (B) (C) (D)
23 (A) (B) (C) (D)
24 (A) (B) (C) (D)
25 (A) (B) (C) (D)
26 (A) (B) (C) (D)
27 (A) (B) (C) (D)
28 (A) (B) (C) (D)
29 _____
30 (A) (B) (C) (D)
31 (A) (B) (C) (D)
32 (A) (B) (C) (D)
33 (A) (B) (C) (D)
34 (A) (B) (C) (D)

35 _____
36 (A) (B) (C) (D)
37 (A) (B) (C) (D)
38 (A) (B) (C) (D)
39 (A) (B) (C) (D)
40 (A) (B) (C) (D)
41 (A) (B) (C) (D)
42 (A) (B) (C) (D)
43 (A) (B) (C) (D)
44 (A) (B) (C) (D)
45 (A) (B) (C) (D)
46 (A) (B) (C) (D)
47 (A) (B) (C) (D)
48 (A) (B) (C) (D)
49 (A) (B) (C) (D)
50 (A) (B) (C) (D)

MATHEMATICS TEST 1

50 questions

Time limit: 50 minutes

Use the following chart for questions 1–2.

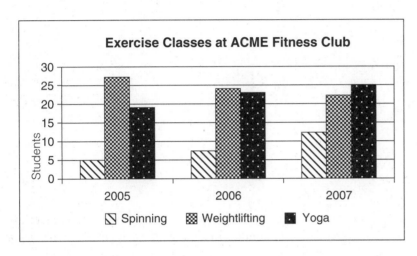

1. Which class or classes have seen participation increase over both years?

(A) both spinning and yoga
(B) weightlifting
(C) yoga
(D) both spinning and weightlifting

2. Which class has seen the largest change in participation (increase or decrease) from any year to the next?

(A) spinning
(B) weightlifting
(C) yoga
(D) both spinning and yoga

3. What is the average (mean) of 12, 5, 1, 0, and 7?

(A) 2
(B) 4
(C) 5
(D) 10

4. $769 + 351 =$

(A) 960
(B) 1,020
(C) 1,080
(D) 1,120

GO ON TO THE NEXT PAGE

5. If shirts at a garage sale cost $0.75 each, how many shirts can Abby buy for $15?

(A) 10
(B) 20
(C) 30
(D) 40

6. Express $\dfrac{60}{12}$ as a percentage.

(A) 0.5%
(B) 5%
(C) 50%
(D) 500%

7. How many centimeters are in 56 meters?

(A) 56
(B) 560
(C) 5,600
(D) 56,000

8. Jane started her stamp collection exactly one year ago, and in that time, she has collected 132 stamps. On average, how many stamps has she collected per month?

(A) 10
(B) 11
(C) 12
(D) 20

9. $2\dfrac{66}{84} =$

(A) $\dfrac{39}{14}$

(B) $\dfrac{22}{7}$

(C) $\dfrac{85}{21}$

(D) $\dfrac{113}{21}$

10. The measurement from the center to the rim of an economy car tire is 15 inches. How much road can this tire cover in one rotation?

(A) 30π in
(B) 180π in
(C) 225π in
(D) 360π in

GO ON TO THE NEXT PAGE

11. $\triangle$ is to $\wedge$ as $\diagup\!\!\!\diagup$ is to:

(A) $\bigodot$ (C) $\sqsubset$

(B) $\diagup\!\!\!\angle$ (D) $\triangle$

12. If the number of babies born in a certain maternity ward in January is five more than twice the number born in February, which of the following mathematical statements reflects this relationship?

(A) $J = 2 + 5F$
(B) $J = (5 + 2)F$
(C) $J = 5 + 2F$
(D) $J = (2 + 5)F$

13. $287 \times 36 =$

(A) 8,452
(B) 9,282
(C) 9,862
(D) 10,332

14. If the annual operating expenses of a corporation are graphed in a pie chart and building maintenance accounts for $33\frac{1}{3}\%$, what is the measure of the central angle that represents this percentage?

(A) 80 degrees
(B) 100 degrees
(C) 120 degrees
(D) 180 degrees

15. $3^{10} \div 3^2 =$

(A) 3^5
(B) 3^6
(C) 3^8
(D) 3^{12}

16. $3.902 \times 28 =$

(A) 1.09256
(B) 10.9256
(C) 109.256
(D) 1,092.56

GO ON TO THE NEXT PAGE

17. What is 60% of 70?

(A) 35
(B) 42
(C) 46
(D) 54

18. If a right triangle has a base of 30 feet and a height of 40 feet, what is the length of the hypotenuse?

(A) 45 feet
(B) 50 feet
(C) 60 feet
(D) 70 feet

Use the following chart for questions 19–20.

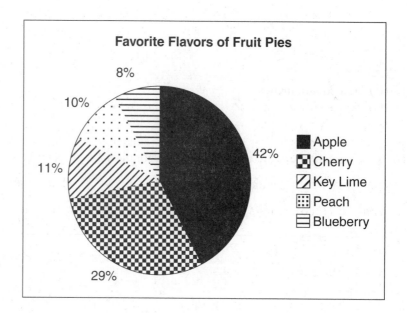

19. Which flavors of pies together are equal in popularity to cherry pie?

(A) apple, key lime, peach
(B) blueberry, peach, apple
(C) key lime, peach
(D) blueberry, peach, key lime

20. Which pies together are greater in popularity than apple?

(A) key lime, cherry
(B) blueberry, peach, key lime, cherry
(C) peach, key lime, cherry
(D) both B and C

GO ON TO THE NEXT PAGE

21. Which of the following is the smallest?

(A) $|-3|$
(B) -3
(C) $\dfrac{1}{3}$
(D) $-\dfrac{1}{3}$

22. $3,498 \div 26 =$

(A) 105r6
(B) 134r14
(C) 215r2
(D) 232r12

23. If a bowl is 8 inches across at its widest point, what is the area of the circle at the widest part of the bowl?

(A) 8π square inches
(B) 16π square inches
(C) 32π square inches
(D) 64π square inches

Stem	Leaf
3	5 6 9 9
4	0 1 2 8

24. Using the above diagram, write out the data set.

(A) 3, 4, 5, 6, 9, 9, 4, 0, 1, 2, 8
(B) 35, 36, 39, 39, 40, 41, 42, 48
(C) 35, 36, 39, 40, 41, 42, 48
(D) 8, 11, 12, 12, 4, 5, 6, 12

GO ON TO THE NEXT PAGE

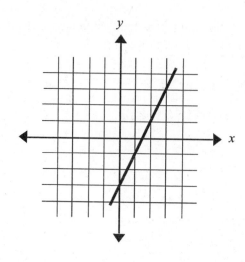

25. Which of the following mathematical statements accurately describes the above picture?

(A) $y = 2x - 3$

(B) $y = \dfrac{1}{2}x - 3$

(C) $y = 2x + 3$

(D) $y = \dfrac{1}{2}x + 3$

26. Linda is making a smoothie recipe that calls for five parts berries to four parts yogurt. If she is putting in 10 cups of yogurt for a big party, how many cups of berries will she need?

(A) 2.5

(B) 5

(C) 10

(D) 12.5

27. $329 \times 43 =$

(A) 11,347

(B) 12,947

(C) 14,147

(D) 15,237

28. Of the following numbers, which one is the only prime?

(A) 18

(B) 19

(C) 21

(D) 25

GO ON TO THE NEXT PAGE

29. 45 is 125% of what number? (Enter numeric value only. If rounding is necessary, round to the whole number.)

_____

30. Express $\dfrac{3}{5}$ as a decimal.

(A) 0.3
(B) 0.6
(C) 3.0
(D) 6.0

31. If the sides of a rectangular table are 18 feet by 12 feet, what is the area of the table's surface?

(A) 96 square feet
(B) 144 square feet
(C) 216 square feet
(D) 256 square feet

32. Express the ratio of 15:40 as a percentage.

(A) 15%
(B) 37.5%
(C) 62.5%
(D) 67.5%

33. 7,236 + 5,972 =

(A) 10,328
(B) 12,098
(C) 13,208
(D) 14,018

34. A package of 6 cookies is split between 2 children at snack time. How many cookies does it take to feed 12 children?

(A) 6
(B) 12
(C) 18
(D) 36

35. A certain number is three less than the product of 2 and 10. What is the value of that number? (Enter numeric value only. If rounding is necessary, round to the whole number.)

_____

GO ON TO THE NEXT PAGE

36. $673 - 375 =$

    (A) 298
    (B) 328
    (C) 398
    (D) 438

37. $\dfrac{7}{9} - \dfrac{1}{4}$

    (A) $\dfrac{19}{36}$

    (B) $\dfrac{3}{4}$

    (C) $\dfrac{37}{36}$

    (D) $\dfrac{5}{4}$

38. If the amount of rainfall in one week was measured in centimeters per day and recorded as 3, 4, 0, 2, 0, 3, 0, what was the mode of the rainfall?

    (A) 0
    (B) 2
    (C) 3
    (D) 4

39. What is the median of −8, 12, 3, 4, and −1?

    (A) 2
    (B) 3
    (C) 4
    (D) 8

40. If Sven ate three slices of a pizza divided exactly into eight slices, what is the degree measure of the central angle encompassing Sven's slices of pizza?

    (A) 45 degrees
    (B) 90 degrees
    (C) 135 degrees
    (D) 180 degrees

41. If the temperature of the water in a beaker is 60 degrees on the Celsius scale, approximately what is the temperature on the Fahrenheit scale?

    (A) 16°F
    (B) 32°F
    (C) 100°F
    (D) 140°F

GO ON TO THE NEXT PAGE

42. What is the sum of the prime factors of 75?

(A) 5
(B) 8
(C) 13
(D) 18

43. $8{,}751 - 832 =$

(A) 8,129
(B) 7,919
(C) 9,229
(D) 9,583

44. Which expression is the same as $\dfrac{y^7}{y^4}$?

(A) y^3
(B) $y^{7/4}$
(C) y^{11}
(D) y^{28}

45. $783 \div 27 =$

(A) 29
(B) 33
(C) 37
(D) 39

46. Fred is trying to determine the longest line that can be drawn on a presentation board, and he has determined that it must be the diagonal of the board. If the board is 4 feet by 6 feet, what is the length of its diagonal?

(A) $\sqrt{15}$

(B) $16\sqrt{3}$

(C) $2\sqrt{13}$

(D) $4\sqrt{5}$

47. Completely simplify $\sqrt{80}$.

(A) $2\sqrt{5}$

(B) $4\sqrt{5}$

(C) $2\sqrt{20}$

(D) $4\sqrt{20}$

GO ON TO THE NEXT PAGE

48. What is the smallest prime number greater than 45?

    (A) 46
    (B) 47
    (C) 48
    (D) 49

49. Michelle can paint two walls in 90 minutes. How long will it take her to paint six walls?

    (A) 30 minutes
    (B) 45 minutes
    (C) 180 minutes
    (D) 270 minutes

50. $5.31 \div 3 =$

    (A) 1.77
    (B) 1.79
    (C) 1.97
    (D) 1.99

**STOP. IF YOU HAVE TIME LEFT OVER,
CHECK YOUR WORK ON THIS SECTION ONLY.**

Mathematics Test 2

ANSWER SHEET

1 (A) (B) (C) (D)
2 (A) (B) (C) (D)
3 (A) (B) (C) (D)
4 (A) (B) (C) (D)
5 (A) (B) (C) (D)
6 (A) (B) (C) (D)
7 (A) (B) (C) (D)
8 (A) (B) (C) (D)
9 (A) (B) (C) (D)
10 (A) (B) (C) (D)
11 (A) (B) (C) (D)
12 (A) (B) (C) (D)
13 _____
14 (A) (B) (C) (D)
15 (A) (B) (C) (D)
16 (A) (B) (C) (D)
17 (A) (B) (C) (D)

18 (A) (B) (C) (D)
19 (A) (B) (C) (D)
20 (A) (B) (C) (D)
21 (A) (B) (C) (D)
22 (A) (B) (C) (D)
23 (A) (B) (C) (D)
24 (A) (B) (C) (D)
25 (A) (B) (C) (D)
26 (A) (B) (C) (D)
27 (A) (B) (C) (D)
28 (A) (B) (C) (D)
29 (A) (B) (C) (D)
30 _____
31 (A) (B) (C) (D)
32 (A) (B) (C) (D)
33 (A) (B) (C) (D)
34 (A) (B) (C) (D)

35 (A) (B) (C) (D)
36 (A) (B) (C) (D)
37 (A) (B) (C) (D)
38 (A) (B) (C) (D)
39 (A) (B) (C) (D)
40 (A) (B) (C) (D)
41 (A) (B) (C) (D)
42 (A) (B) (C) (D)
43 (A) (B) (C) (D)
44 (A) (B) (C) (D)
45 (A) (B) (C) (D)
46 (A) (B) (C) (D)
47 (A) (B) (C) (D)
48 (A) (B) (C) (D)
49 (A) (B) (C) (D)
50 (A) (B) (C) (D)

MATHEMATICS TEST 2

50 questions

Time limit: 50 minutes

Stem	Leaf
2	0 3 3 8 9
7	1 2 5 6

1. Using the diagram above, write out the data set.

(A) 2, 5, 8, 9, 10, 11, 12, 13
(B) 0, 1, 2, 3, 5, 6, 7, 8, 9
(C) 20, 23, 28, 29, 71, 72, 75, 76
(D) 20, 23, 23, 28, 29, 71, 72, 75, 76

2. If Andy receives 20% of the retail price on each of his published books, how much does he make on a book that retails for $35?

(A) $5
(B) $7
(C) $14
(D) $28

3. Express $\dfrac{60}{24}$ as a percentage.

(A) 25%
(B) 40%
(C) 250%
(D) 400%

4. If Jacob spends 45 minutes per day playing video games, how long does he play in one week?

(A) 3 hours, 45 minutes
(B) 4 hours
(C) 4 hours, 15 minutes
(D) 5 hours, 15 minutes

5. If a table measures 48 inches across, approximately how many centimeters is that?

(A) 20
(B) 50
(C) 60
(D) 120

GO ON TO THE NEXT PAGE

6. What is the average (mean) of 8, −4, 3, 9, and 4?

(A) 2.75
(B) 3
(C) 4
(D) 5.6

7. $2\dfrac{3}{4} \div \dfrac{7}{8} =$

(A) $\dfrac{15}{7}$

(B) $\dfrac{77}{32}$

(C) $\dfrac{22}{7}$

(D) $\dfrac{63}{16}$

8. What is the area of a circle that has a radius of 6 feet?

(A) 12π square feet
(B) 18π square feet
(C) 24π square feet
(D) 36π square feet

9. $15,829 + 1,302 =$

(A) 16,131
(B) 17,031
(C) 17,131
(D) 18,131

10. Which of the following mathematical statements best reflects this graph?

(A) $y = \dfrac{1}{3}x + 1$

(B) $y = \dfrac{1}{3}x - 1$

(C) $y = 3x + 1$

(D) $y = 3x - 1$

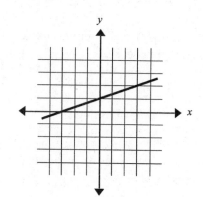

GO ON TO THE NEXT PAGE

11. A certain rectangle has a length of 12 inches and a width of 5 inches. What is the measurement of one of its diagonals?

    (A) 10 inches
    (B) 13 inches
    (C) 17 inches
    (D) 26 inches

12. After taking inventory at his grocery store, Harry realizes that 20 percent of the items in stock are in the produce category. If he were to represent this in a pie chart, what would be the degree measure of the central angle that represents this percentage?

    (A) 18 degrees
    (B) 20 degrees
    (C) 64 degrees
    (D) 72 degrees

13. Polly's scores on the first four tests in her English class were 94, 91, 88, and 95. If all the tests counted equally, what was the average of her scores on those four tests? (Enter numeric value only. If rounding is necessary, round to the whole number.)

_____

14. Which of the following expressions is the mathematical equivalent of $7^3 \times 7^5$?

    (A) 7^{-2}
    (B) 7^2
    (C) 7^8
    (D) 7^{15}

15. A recent census of wild animals in a state park showed that there was a ratio of 15:8 raccoons to coyotes. Which of the following is a possible actual number of raccoons and coyotes in the park?

    (A) 600:320
    (B) 300:180
    (C) 600:400
    (D) 450:240

16. What is the mean (average) of 3, 14, 10, and −7?

    (A) 4.5
    (B) 5
    (C) 7
    (D) 8.5

GO ON TO THE NEXT PAGE

17. Which of the following is the greatest prime number less than 30?

    (A) 26
    (B) 27
    (C) 28
    (D) 29

18. Which of the following has the largest value?

    (A) |−5.5|
    (B) −5.5
    (C) −7.2
    (D) |−7.2|

Use the following chart to answer questions 19–20.

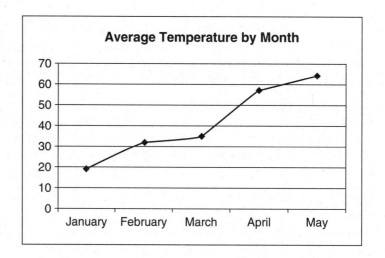

19. In the above chart, which month showed the smallest increase in temperature from the month before?

    (A) February
    (B) March
    (C) April
    (D) May

20. How many months show an increase of more than 10 degrees?

    (A) 1
    (B) 2
    (C) 3
    (D) 4

GO ON TO THE NEXT PAGE

21. $1,296 - 938 =$

    (A) 258
    (B) 358
    (C) 398
    (D) 428

22. If it is currently 90 degrees on the Fahrenheit scale outside, what is the approximate temperature on the Celsius scale?

    (A) 18°C
    (B) 32°C
    (C) 48°C
    (D) 64°C

23. Gail owns a compact disc (CD) store and has decided that as a special promotion, she will make each $15 CD one dollar more than half price. If x is the sale price of one of these CDs, which of the following mathematical statements represents this best?

    (A) $x = \dfrac{1}{2} \times 15 - 1$

    (B) $x = \dfrac{1}{2} \times 15 + 1$

    (C) $x = \dfrac{1}{2} \times 1 + 15$

    (D) $x = \dfrac{1}{2} \times 1 \times 15$

24. $593 \div 5 =$

    (A) 118r3
    (B) 118r6
    (C) 121r3
    (D) 121r6

25. $3.4 \div 0.2 =$

    (A) 0.17
    (B) 1.7
    (C) 17
    (D) 170

26. $782 \times 21 =$

    (A) 9,384
    (B) 15,640
    (C) 16,422
    (D) 17,204

GO ON TO THE NEXT PAGE

27. Which of the following lists is in order from smallest to largest?

(A) $\frac{1}{8}, \frac{2}{5}, \frac{1}{2}, \frac{3}{4}$

(B) $\frac{2}{5}, \frac{1}{8}, \frac{3}{4}, \frac{1}{2}$

(C) $\frac{3}{4}, \frac{1}{2}, \frac{2}{5}, \frac{1}{8}$

(D) $\frac{2}{5}, \frac{3}{4}, \frac{1}{2}, \frac{1}{8}$

28. What is the sum of the prime factors of 28?

(A) 7
(B) 11
(C) 14
(D) 28

29. $0.38 \times 2.35 =$

(A) 0.273
(B) 0.893
(C) 2.73
(D) 8.93

30. What is 60 percent of 60? (Enter numeric value only. If rounding is necessary, round to the whole number.)

_____

31. If donut holes cost 45 cents for two, how much does it cost to buy 10 donut holes?

(A) $0.90
(B) $1.45
(C) $2.25
(D) $4.50

32. What is the area of a triangle with a base of 10 inches and a height of 9 inches?

(A) 19 square inches
(B) 38 square inches
(C) 45 square inches
(D) 90 square inches

GO ON TO THE NEXT PAGE

33. □O△ is to △□O as O△⧄ is to:

(A) △□O   (C) △□⧄

(B) □⧄O   (D) O⧄△

34. Express $\dfrac{7}{8}$ as a decimal.

(A) 0.625

(B) 0.875

(C) 62.5

(D) 87.5

35. $14,985 + 3,806 =$

(A) 17,781

(B) 17,791

(C) 18,781

(D) 18,791

Use the following chart to answer questions 36 and 37.

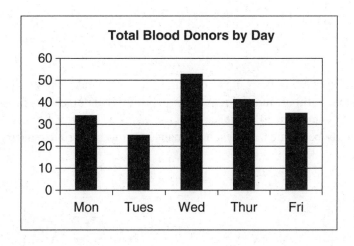

36. What is the approximate percent increase between the number of donors on Tuesday and the number of donors on Wednesday?

(A) 25%

(B) 50%

(C) 100%

(D) 200%

GO ON TO THE NEXT PAGE

37. Which day showed the largest decrease in the number of blood donors from the day before?

(A) Tuesday
(B) Wednesday
(C) Thursday
(D) Friday

38. $5,263 - 3,959 =$

(A) 1,304
(B) 1,394
(C) 1,404
(D) 1,494

39. What is the average (arithmetic mean) of 23, 8, 2, and 7?

(A) 4.5
(B) 7.5
(C) 8
(D) 10

40. Express $\dfrac{7}{35}$ as a decimal.

(A) 0.014

(B) 0.14

(C) 0.02

(D) 0.2

41. After surveying her fellow nursing school students, Amber has found that the ratio of students who want to be surgical nurses compared with those who want to be geriatric nurses is 5:2. If 30 of her classmates want to be surgical nurses, how many want to be geriatric nurses?

(A) 10
(B) 12
(C) 15
(D) 18

42. $583 \times 6 =$

(A) 3,480
(B) 1,758
(C) 3,378
(D) 3,498

GO ON TO THE NEXT PAGE

43. Which of the following expressions is the most simplified form of

$\sqrt{56}$?

(A) $2\sqrt{7}$

(B) $2\sqrt{14}$

(C) $4\sqrt{7}$

(D) $4\sqrt{14}$

44. Dora is three years younger than half the age of one of her regular patients, Mario. Which of the following mathematical statements reflects this relationship?

(A) $D = 2M + 3$

(B) $D = 2M - 3$

(C) $D = \dfrac{1}{2}M + 3$

(D) $D = \dfrac{1}{2}M - 3$

45. The number 5 is what percent of 40?

(A) 8

(B) 12.5

(C) 80

(D) 125

46. $7,314 \div 46 =$

(A) 159

(B) 159r4

(C) 262

(D) 262r6

47. A certain rectangular room has a length of 90 meters and a width of 85 meters. What is the area of the room?

(A) 350 square meters

(B) 1,250 square meters

(C) 3,825 square meters

(D) 7,650 square meters

GO ON TO THE NEXT PAGE

48. $3 - 1\dfrac{5}{6} =$

    (A) $\dfrac{1}{7}$

    (B) $\dfrac{1}{6}$

    (C) $\dfrac{6}{7}$

    (D) $\dfrac{7}{6}$

49. What is the most reduced form of $2x^5y^3 + 4x^4y^6$?

    (A) $x^4y^3(x + 2y^3)$
    (B) $x^3y^4(x + 2y^3)$
    (C) $2x^4y^3(x + 2y^3)$
    (D) $4x^4y^3(x + 2y^3)$

50. If Bob is paid \$5,000 less than the sum of Al and Carl's salaries, which of the following mathematical statements expresses this relationship?

    (A) $B = A + C - 5{,}000$
    (B) $B = A \times C - 5{,}000$
    (C) $B = A + C + 5{,}000$
    (D) $B = A \times C + 5{,}000$

STOP. IF YOU HAVE TIME LEFT OVER, CHECK YOUR WORK ON THIS SECTION ONLY.

Science Test 1

ANSWER SHEET

1 (A) (B) (C) (D)	21 (A) (B) (C) (D)	41 (A) (B) (C) (D)
2 (A) (B) (C) (D)	22 (A) (B) (C) (D)	42 (A) (B) (C) (D)
3 (A) (B) (C) (D)	23 (A) (B) (C) (D)	43 (A) (B) (C) (D)
4 (A) (B) (C) (D)	24 (A) (B) (C) (D)	44 (A) (B) (C) (D)
5 (A) (B) (C) (D)	25 (A) (B) (C) (D)	45 (A) (B) (C) (D)
6 (A) (B) (C) (D)	26 (A) (B) (C) (D)	46 (A) (B) (C) (D)
7 (A) (B) (C) (D)	27 (A) (B) (C) (D)	47 (A) (B) (C) (D)
8 (A) (B) (C) (D)	28 (A) (B) (C) (D)	48 (A) (B) (C) (D)
9 (A) (B) (C) (D)	29 (A) (B) (C) (D)	49 (A) (B) (C) (D)
10 (A) (B) (C) (D)	30 (A) (B) (C) (D)	50 (A) (B) (C) (D)
11 (A) (B) (C) (D)	31 (A) (B) (C) (D)	51 (A) (B) (C) (D)
12 (A) (B) (C) (D)	32 (A) (B) (C) (D)	52 (A) (B) (C) (D)
13 (A) (B) (C) (D)	33 (A) (B) (C) (D)	53 (A) (B) (C) (D)
14 (A) (B) (C) (D)	34 (A) (B) (C) (D)	54 (A) (B) (C) (D)
15 (A) (B) (C) (D)	35 (A) (B) (C) (D)	55 (A) (B) (C) (D)
16 (A) (B) (C) (D)	36 (A) (B) (C) (D)	56 (A) (B) (C) (D)
17 (A) (B) (C) (D)	37 (A) (B) (C) (D)	57 (A) (B) (C) (D)
18 (A) (B) (C) (D)	38 (A) (B) (C) (D)	58 (A) (B) (C) (D)
19 (A) (B) (C) (D)	39 (A) (B) (C) (D)	59 (A) (B) (C) (D)
20 (A) (B) (C) (D)	40 (A) (B) (C) (D)	60 (A) (B) (C) (D)

SCIENCE TEST 1

60 questions

Time limit: 50 minutes

1. To be isotopes, two atoms of the same element must have a different number of

   (A) neutrons.
   (B) protons.
   (C) electrons.
   (D) quarks.

2. Depending on its environment, a substance that can act as either an acid or a base is described as

   (A) amphoteric.
   (B) an isomer.
   (C) hydrolytic.
   (D) a polymer.

3. A certain substance is not broken down in a chemical reaction. The substance is most likely

   (A) a compound.
   (B) an aqueous solution.
   (C) an element.
   (D) a heterogeneous mixture.

4. A hydrogen ion concentration of 1×10^{-7} M in a solution is considered

   (A) basic.
   (B) alkali.
   (C) acidic.
   (D) neutral.

5. The radioactive isotope I-131 has a half-life of 8 days. What fraction of a sample of I-131 will remain after 24 days?

   (A) ¼
   (B) ¹⁄₁₆
   (C) ⅛
   (D) ½

6. Which of the following particles/rays is not a type of radioactive emanation?

   (A) alpha particle
   (B) beta particle
   (C) gamma ray
   (D) carbon-12

GO ON TO THE NEXT PAGE

7. The strongest acid can be found in which of the following pH ranges?

   (A) 11.1–12
   (B) 7.1–8.2
   (C) 4.5–5.7
   (D) 1.0–2.0

8. The symbol K on the periodic table stands for

   (A) potassium.
   (B) calcium.
   (C) carbon.
   (D) phosphorus.

9. Which of the following reactions releases heat energy?

   (A) double replacement
   (B) decomposition
   (C) endothermic
   (D) exothermic

10. Which gas law states that the volume of a gas is inversely proportional to the pressure?

    (A) Ideal Gas Law
    (B) Boyle's Law
    (C) Combined Gas Law
    (D) Charles' Law

11. What type of bond is created when bromine and magnesium are reacted to form $MgBr_2$?

    (A) polar covalent
    (B) metallic
    (C) ionic
    (D) nonpolar covalent

12. Which of the following wavelengths of visible light is best absorbed by chlorophyll?

    (A) 300 nm
    (B) 495 nm
    (C) 665 nm
    (D) 550 nm

13. The xylem vessels of a plant are responsible for carrying

    (A) water up through the plant.
    (B) light energy to the leaves.
    (C) chlorophyll to the leaves.
    (D) oxygen into the leaves.

GO ON TO THE NEXT PAGE

14. When placed in distilled water, a human red blood cell

(A) shrivels up.
(B) neither shrinks nor swells.
(C) takes up more salts to balance all concentrations.
(D) swells to a larger size.

15. During plant cell replication, the division of the cytoplasm is called

(A) cytohydrolysis.
(B) cytokinesis.
(C) plasmolysis.
(D) cytoplasmosis.

16. Which of the following are classified as animals that eat only meat?

(A) carnivores
(B) herbivores
(C) decomposers
(D) consumers

17. In which phase of mitosis do the chromosomes line up?

(A) interphase
(B) metaphase
(C) prophase
(D) anaphase

18. Digestive enzymes can be found in which cellular organelle?

(A) lysosomes
(B) mitochondria
(C) Golgi apparatus
(D) ribosomes

19. The process by which an enzyme acts on the substrate can be described by the

(A) lock-and-key model.
(B) enzyme-and-substrate model.
(C) enzyme folding model.
(D) catalytic model.

20. When an organism contains chloroplast in its cells, the color of the organism would most likely be

(A) orange.
(B) brown.
(C) yellow.
(D) green.

GO ON TO THE NEXT PAGE

21. In most living things, all of the following groups of chemicals can be found naturally EXCEPT

(A) lipids.
(B) synthetic polymers.
(C) nucleic acids.
(D) carbohydrates.

22. Carbohydrates and starches must be changed to _____ so that they can be used by cells.

(A) glucose
(B) glycerin
(C) sucrose
(D) fructose

23. The process of food traveling throughout the digestive system is known as

(A) defecation.
(B) contractions.
(C) reverse peristalsis.
(D) peristalsis.

24. Accumulation of cholesterol leads to the hardening of the arteries. This is called

(A) vasoconstriction.
(B) venipuncture.
(C) atherosclerosis.
(D) hypertension.

25. The stomach and mouth are connected by the

(A) anus.
(B) esophagus.
(C) spinal column.
(D) epiglottis.

26. Which of the following is not a type of muscle?

(A) nervous muscle
(B) smooth muscle
(C) skeletal muscle
(D) cardiac muscle

27. The heart is composed of which type of tissue?

(A) cardiac muscle
(B) ligaments
(C) smooth tendons
(D) cartilage

GO ON TO THE NEXT PAGE

28. The growth and development of bone is assisted by the use of vitamin D because vitamin D can

(A) help the body excrete excess salt.
(B) control sulfur and calcium levels in the blood.
(C) aid in the absorption of calcium.
(D) regulate levels of chloride ion.

29. Synapses are the gaps between

(A) nephrons.
(B) neurons.
(C) the cell membrane.
(D) protons and neutrons.

30. The small intestine contains a large quantity of villi that help

(A) absorb acids and salvia from the mouth.
(B) provide a greater surface for absorption of materials passing through the digestive tract.
(C) produce saliva.
(D) secrete hydrochloric acid to break down foods.

31. The process by which oxygen travels from the air into your lungs and then into your blood is called

(A) hypertonic.
(B) osmosis.
(C) diffusion.
(D) passive transport.

32. Which of the following are considered normal values for the measurements of a person's pulse and blood pressure?

(A) 72 beats per minute and 120 over 80 mm Hg
(B) 100 beats per minute and 140 over 100 mm Hg
(C) 160 beats per minute and 100 over 70 mm Hg
(D) 55 beats per minute and 75 over 60 mm Hg

33. The retina transmits nerve impulses to the brain via the

(A) optic nerve.
(B) cranial nerve.
(C) cardiac nerve.
(D) esophagus.

34. Which muscle pushes food through the digestive system?

(A) renal
(B) smooth
(C) cardiac
(D) rough

GO ON TO THE NEXT PAGE

35. A person gets hit in the face with a puck while playing a game of ice hockey and fractures a bone. Which bone is a most likely candidate for this fracture?

(A) mandible
(B) rib
(C) radius
(D) femur

36. The word *renal* refers to the

(A) liver.
(B) gallbladder.
(C) kidney.
(D) lung.

37. The bicuspid valve is found in the

(A) heart.
(B) veins.
(C) lymph nodes.
(D) anus.

38. Which of the following is not an accessory organ?

(A) liver
(B) pancreas
(C) gallbladder
(D) stomach

39. Bile is stored in the _____ and helps digest _____ via _____.

(A) liver . . . proteins . . . emulsification
(B) liver . . . fats . . . dehydration synthesis
(C) gallbladder . . . fats . . . emulsification
(D) gallbladder . . . proteins . . . proteases

40. If a salt is added to water, which of the following is likely to occur?

(A) The boiling point will increase and the freezing point will decrease.
(B) The boiling point will increase and the freezing point will increase.
(C) The boiling point will decrease and the freezing point will decrease.
(D) The boiling point will decrease and the freezing point will increase.

41. A 60-watt light bulb is powered by a 110-volt power source. What is the current being drawn?

(A) 1.83 amperes
(B) 0.55 amperes
(C) 50 amperes
(D) 6,600 amperes

GO ON TO THE NEXT PAGE

42. A transverse wave does not have

(A) a compression.
(B) an amplitude.
(C) a frequency.
(D) a wavelength.

43. A wave moves through its medium at $20\,\text{m/s}$ with a wavelength of $4\,\text{m}$. What is the frequency of the wave?

(A) $24\,\text{s}^{-1}$
(B) $5\,\text{s}^{-1}$
(C) $16\,\text{s}^{-1}$
(D) $80\,\text{s}^{-1}$

44. Light hits a smooth mirror at an angle of 45 degrees. At what angle will the light be reflected?

(A) 0 degrees
(B) 180 degrees
(C) 45 degrees
(D) 90 degrees

45. White light enters a prism and is broken up into the colors of the rainbow. This phenomenon is called

(A) reflection.
(B) diffraction.
(C) dispersion.
(D) refraction.

46. A laser beam of light is pointed through the air and then into a diamond. The beam of light then bends. This results from the process called

(A) reflection.
(B) diffraction.
(C) dispersion.
(D) refraction.

47. An atom becomes an ion that possesses a negative charge. The atom must have

(A) gained protons.
(B) lost protons.
(C) lost electrons.
(D) gained electrons.

GO ON TO THE NEXT PAGE

48. Which of the following is not correctly paired up with its unit of measure?

(A) current/ohms
(B) voltage/volts
(C) charge/coulombs
(D) power/watts

49. The symbol Ω represents

(A) current.
(B) resistance.
(C) amperes.
(D) power.

50. Which equation is written incorrectly, demonstrating a relationship that does not exist?

(A) $V = IR$
(B) $P = IV$
(C) $R = V/I$
(D) $I = R/V$

51. A set of lights decorates the window of a store. One of the light bulbs burns out, but the remaining light bulbs stay lit. The light bulbs are connected in

(A) parallel.
(B) series.
(C) short circuit.
(D) a 220-volt line.

52. What is the voltage required to deliver a current of 1.0 amps to a device that has a resistance of 1.5 ohms?

(A) 2.5 volts
(B) 1.5 volts
(C) 0.67 volts
(D) 0.5 volts

53. Electrical potential is measured in

(A) ohms.
(B) watts.
(C) amperes.
(D) volts.

54. A 110-volt appliance draws 2.0 amperes. How many watts of power does it require?

(A) 220 watts
(B) 55 watts
(C) 112 watts
(D) 108 watts

GO ON TO THE NEXT PAGE

55. A 110-volt hair dryer delivers 1,525 watts of power. How many amperes does it draw?

(A) 167,750 amperes
(B) 1,635 amperes
(C) 1,415 amperes
(D) 13.9 amperes

56. A force of 10 N is delivered to an object for 1.5 seconds. What is the impulse directed on the object?

(A) 15 N·s
(B) 8.5 N
(C) 11.5 s
(D) 6.7 N/s

57. A 10-kg object moving at 5 m/s has an impulse acted on it causing the velocity to change to 15 m/s. What was the impulse which was applied to the object?

(A) 10 kg·m/s
(B) 20 kg·m/s
(C) 15 kg·m/s
(D) 100 kg·m/s

58. An airplane travels 500 miles northeast and then, on the return trip, travels 500 miles southwest. Which of the following is true?

(A) The displacement of the plane is 1,000 miles and the distance traveled is 0 miles.
(B) The displacement of the plane is 1,000 miles and the distance traveled is 1,000 miles.
(C) The displacement of the plane is 0 miles and the distance traveled is 0 miles.
(D) The displacement of the plane is 0 miles and the distance traveled is 1,000 miles.

59. The reaction $2NaI + Cl_2 \rightarrow 2NaCl + I_2$ demonstrates a

(A) decomposition reaction.
(B) synthesis reaction.
(C) single replacement reaction.
(D) double replacement reaction.

GO ON TO THE NEXT PAGE

60. An electromagnet is holding a 1,500-kg car at a height of 25 m above the ground. The magnet then experiences a power outage, and the car falls to the ground (without injuring anyone). Which of the following is false?

(A) The car had a potential energy of 367.5 kJ.
(B) 367.5 kJ of potential energy is converted to kinetic energy.
(C) The car still has a potential energy of 367.5 kJ when it hits the ground.
(D) The potential energy is converted to kinetic energy and then converted to sound energy.

STOP. IF YOU HAVE TIME LEFT OVER, CHECK YOUR WORK ON THIS SECTION ONLY.

Science Test 2

ANSWER SHEET

1 Ⓐ Ⓑ Ⓒ Ⓓ	21 Ⓐ Ⓑ Ⓒ Ⓓ	41 Ⓐ Ⓑ Ⓒ Ⓓ
2 Ⓐ Ⓑ Ⓒ Ⓓ	22 Ⓐ Ⓑ Ⓒ Ⓓ	42 Ⓐ Ⓑ Ⓒ Ⓓ
3 Ⓐ Ⓑ Ⓒ Ⓓ	23 Ⓐ Ⓑ Ⓒ Ⓓ	43 Ⓐ Ⓑ Ⓒ Ⓓ
4 Ⓐ Ⓑ Ⓒ Ⓓ	24 Ⓐ Ⓑ Ⓒ Ⓓ	44 Ⓐ Ⓑ Ⓒ Ⓓ
5 Ⓐ Ⓑ Ⓒ Ⓓ	25 Ⓐ Ⓑ Ⓒ Ⓓ	45 Ⓐ Ⓑ Ⓒ Ⓓ
6 Ⓐ Ⓑ Ⓒ Ⓓ	26 Ⓐ Ⓑ Ⓒ Ⓓ	46 Ⓐ Ⓑ Ⓒ Ⓓ
7 Ⓐ Ⓑ Ⓒ Ⓓ	27 Ⓐ Ⓑ Ⓒ Ⓓ	47 Ⓐ Ⓑ Ⓒ Ⓓ
8 Ⓐ Ⓑ Ⓒ Ⓓ	28 Ⓐ Ⓑ Ⓒ Ⓓ	48 Ⓐ Ⓑ Ⓒ Ⓓ
9 Ⓐ Ⓑ Ⓒ Ⓓ	29 Ⓐ Ⓑ Ⓒ Ⓓ	49 Ⓐ Ⓑ Ⓒ Ⓓ
10 Ⓐ Ⓑ Ⓒ Ⓓ	30 Ⓐ Ⓑ Ⓒ Ⓓ	50 Ⓐ Ⓑ Ⓒ Ⓓ
11 Ⓐ Ⓑ Ⓒ Ⓓ	31 Ⓐ Ⓑ Ⓒ Ⓓ	51 Ⓐ Ⓑ Ⓒ Ⓓ
12 Ⓐ Ⓑ Ⓒ Ⓓ	32 Ⓐ Ⓑ Ⓒ Ⓓ	52 Ⓐ Ⓑ Ⓒ Ⓓ
13 Ⓐ Ⓑ Ⓒ Ⓓ	33 Ⓐ Ⓑ Ⓒ Ⓓ	53 Ⓐ Ⓑ Ⓒ Ⓓ
14 Ⓐ Ⓑ Ⓒ Ⓓ	34 Ⓐ Ⓑ Ⓒ Ⓓ	54 Ⓐ Ⓑ Ⓒ Ⓓ
15 Ⓐ Ⓑ Ⓒ Ⓓ	35 Ⓐ Ⓑ Ⓒ Ⓓ	55 Ⓐ Ⓑ Ⓒ Ⓓ
16 Ⓐ Ⓑ Ⓒ Ⓓ	36 Ⓐ Ⓑ Ⓒ Ⓓ	56 Ⓐ Ⓑ Ⓒ Ⓓ
17 Ⓐ Ⓑ Ⓒ Ⓓ	37 Ⓐ Ⓑ Ⓒ Ⓓ	57 Ⓐ Ⓑ Ⓒ Ⓓ
18 Ⓐ Ⓑ Ⓒ Ⓓ	38 Ⓐ Ⓑ Ⓒ Ⓓ	58 Ⓐ Ⓑ Ⓒ Ⓓ
19 Ⓐ Ⓑ Ⓒ Ⓓ	39 Ⓐ Ⓑ Ⓒ Ⓓ	59 Ⓐ Ⓑ Ⓒ Ⓓ
20 Ⓐ Ⓑ Ⓒ Ⓓ	40 Ⓐ Ⓑ Ⓒ Ⓓ	60 Ⓐ Ⓑ Ⓒ Ⓓ

SCIENCE TEST 2

60 questions

Time limit: 50 minutes

1. What term describes the electrons in the outermost principal energy level of an atom?

   (A) vector
   (B) core
   (C) kernel
   (D) valence

2. In the presence of a base, blue litmus paper is

   (A) clear.
   (B) blue.
   (C) pink.
   (D) red.

3. Which compound below contains the alcohol functional group?

   (A) $C_2H_5OCH_3$
   (B) C_3H_4
   (C) CH_3CH_2CHO
   (D) C_3H_7OH

4. Blood with pH of 7.4 indicates that the blood sample is

   (A) strongly acidic.
   (B) strongly basic.
   (C) weakly acidic.
   (D) weakly basic.

5. When one liquid evaporates much faster than another liquid, the first liquid is said to be more

   (A) volatile.
   (B) transient.
   (C) viscous.
   (D) evaporative.

6. Which compound is nonpolar and contains a nonpolar covalent bond?

   (A) F_2
   (B) HI
   (C) KCl
   (D) NH_3

GO ON TO THE NEXT PAGE

7. When solid iodine becomes gaseous iodine with no apparent liquid phase in between, the process is called

(A) evaporation.
(B) condensation.
(C) sublimation.
(D) precipitation.

8. What area of the periodic table shows the most nonmetallic elements?

(A) upper left
(B) upper right
(C) lower left
(D) lower right

9. Diamond and graphite are allotropes of

(A) oxygen.
(B) carbon.
(C) hydrogen.
(D) water.

10. The coefficient of O_2 after the following equation is balanced is

$$\_CH_4 + \_O_2 \rightarrow \_CO_2 + \_H_2O$$

(A) 1
(B) 2
(C) 3
(D) 4

11. Refer to the following chart:

Object	Density in g/mL
W	0.56
X	1.45
Y	1.91
Z	8.45

Which object floats in water?

(A) W
(B) X
(C) Y
(D) Z

GO ON TO THE NEXT PAGE

12. If 40 g of a radioactive substance naturally decays to 10 g after 16 days, what is the half-life of the substance?

(A) 40 days
(B) 8 days
(C) 16 days
(D) 10 days

13. A fertilized egg becomes a female fetus if the sperm contains which type of chromosome?

(A) YY
(B) XX
(C) XY
(D) X

14. In a food chain that contains producers, the original source of energy is most likely

(A) the sun.
(B) carbohydrates.
(C) chlorophyll.
(D) DNA.

15. Nitrogen bases, phosphate groups, and sugars containing five carbon atoms can be found in which of the following compounds?

(A) lipids
(B) proteins
(C) nucleic acids
(D) carbohydrates

16. Which process named below includes the other three choices?

(A) cellular respiration
(B) the Krebs cycle
(C) anaerobic usage of glucose
(D) electrons passing through the electron transport chain

17. Which color pairing of light is most beneficial for photosynthesis?

(A) green/yellow
(B) green/orange
(C) green/blue
(D) red/blue

18. The scientific nomenclature of an organism includes which of the following?

(A) family and order
(B) kingdom and phylum
(C) genus and species
(D) kingdom and class

GO ON TO THE NEXT PAGE

19. Of the organisms below, which is classified as a herbivore?

(A) snakes
(B) birds
(C) insects
(D) green plants

20. In pea plants, shortness is recessive and tallness is dominant. If 50 percent of the F_2 generation of pea plants are short, then the F_1 generation could have been

(A) tt x tt.
(B) Tt x tt.
(C) TT x Tt.
(D) Tt x Tt.

21. Which process does the following equation represent?

$$6CO_2 + \text{light energy} + 6H_2O \rightarrow C_6H_{12}O_6 + 6O_2$$

(A) glycolysis
(B) fermentation
(C) photosynthesis
(D) cellular respiration

22. Which of a plant's organs is responsible for sexual reproduction?

(A) phloem
(B) flower
(C) bark
(D) root

23. The smaller molecules that are responsible for the synthesis of starches are called

(A) lipids.
(B) monosaccharides.
(C) amino acids.
(D) nucleic acids.

24. Which of the following statements about catalysts is false?

(A) Catalysts speed up chemical reactions.
(B) Enzymes are catalysts.
(C) Catalysts are most effective at an optimum temperature and pH.
(D) Catalysts are destroyed while doing their job.

25. Chemical digestion does not occur in the

(A) mouth.
(B) small intestine.
(C) stomach.
(D) rectum.

GO ON TO THE NEXT PAGE

26. Separating the left and right sides of the heart is the

   (A) septum.
   (B) atrium.
   (C) aorta.
   (D) valve.

27. A secondary defense for the body against pathogens is

   (A) tears.
   (B) urine.
   (C) inflammation.
   (D) mucus.

28. The larynx is covered by the _____ so that food does not enter the trachea.

   (A) esophagus.
   (B) alveoli.
   (C) cilia.
   (D) epiglottis.

29. The organ that works to detoxify the blood and to produce bile is the

   (A) kidney.
   (B) liver.
   (C) pancreas.
   (D) gallbladder.

30. Which gland below is not paired up with a hormone that it produces?

   (A) testes/testosterone
   (B) adrenal medulla/estrogen
   (C) adrenal cortex/cortisol
   (D) pancreas/insulin

31. The brain and the spinal cord make up the

   (A) peripheral nervous system.
   (B) somatic nervous system.
   (C) autonomic nervous system.
   (D) central nervous system.

32. Ligaments hold

   (A) bone to bone.
   (B) bone to muscle.
   (C) tendons to bone.
   (D) cartilage to tendons.

GO ON TO THE NEXT PAGE

33. Which reproductive organ below belongs to a different system from the other three?

(A) follicle
(B) oviduct
(C) uterus
(D) epididymis

34. The iris and retina are part of the

(A) eye.
(B) ear.
(C) tongue.
(D) skin.

35. The kidneys are _____ to the small intestine.

(A) posterior
(B) superior
(C) anterior
(D) medial

36. A protease is an enzyme that works to digest

(A) lipids.
(B) proteins.
(C) carbohydrates.
(D) nucleic acids.

37. Which choice below is in a different category from the other three?

(A) antibody
(B) killer T cell
(C) virus
(D) phagocytes

38. Breathing occurs through of the actions of the

(A) lungs.
(B) nose.
(C) vocal cords.
(D) diaphragm.

39. Which of the following is not a function of the skin?

(A) providing protection against pathogens
(B) protecting the body's internal environment
(C) regulating heat loss
(D) assisting in the production of white blood cells

GO ON TO THE NEXT PAGE

40. Which of the following is not a physical part of a nerve cell?

(A) synapse
(B) axon
(C) dendrite
(D) myelin sheath

41. The alimentary canal is part of the

(A) endocrine system.
(B) nervous system.
(C) digestive system.
(D) reproductive system.

42. A scalar quantity and a vector quantity differ in that

(A) a scalar quantity has both magnitude and direction, and a vector does not.
(B) a scalar quantity has direction only, and a vector has only magnitude.
(C) a vector has both magnitude and direction, and a scalar quantity has only magnitude.
(D) a vector has only direction, and a scalar quantity has only magnitude.

43. Which of the following describes a vector quantity?

(A) five miles per hour due southwest
(B) five miles per hour
(C) five miles
(D) none of the above

44. An object moves 100 m in 10 s. What is the velocity of the object over this time?

(A) 1,000 m/s
(B) 90 m/s
(C) 110 m/s
(D) 10 m/s

45. An object is moving at 15 m/s. How far will it travel in 5 s?

(A) 75 m
(B) 20 m
(C) 3 m
(D) 15 m

46. An object has a constant velocity of 50 m/s and travels for 10s. What is the acceleration of the object?

(A) 500 m/s^2
(B) 0 m/s^2
(C) 5 m/s^2
(D) 60 m/s^2

GO ON TO THE NEXT PAGE

47. When calculating an object's acceleration, you must

(A) divide the change in time by the velocity.
(B) multiply the velocity and time.
(C) find the difference between the time and velocity.
(D) divide the change in velocity by the change in time.

48. Which of these objects has the least amount of momentum?

(A) a 1,250-kg car moving at 5 m/s
(B) a 0.5-kg rock rolling at 40 m/s
(C) a 10-kg piece of meteorite moving at 600 m/s
(D) a 80-kg person running at 4 m/s

49. Momentum is calculated using the formula

(A) $F = ma$.
(B) $p = mv$.
(C) $\frac{1}{2} mv^2$.
(D) $q = H_v m$.

50. The unit of measure of momentum is

(A) m/s.
(B) m/s^2.
(C) kg·m/s.
(D) N·m/s.

51. Newtons (N) are measured in

(A) m/s.
(B) watts.
(C) kg.
(D) kg·m/s^2.

52. Newton's first law describes

(A) inertia.
(B) acceleration.
(C) forces.
(D) apples.

53. Newton's second law describes

(A) inertia.
(B) acceleration.
(C) quantum mechanics.
(D) relativity.

GO ON TO THE NEXT PAGE

54. Newton's third law describes

    (A) inertia.
    (B) static friction.
    (C) forces.
    (D) string theory.

55. An object sliding along a table top will come to rest because of

    (A) a gain in potential energy.
    (B) a gain in kinetic energy.
    (C) a force of friction.
    (D) an increase in momentum.

56. A force of 3 N is applied to a box, causing it to move 5 m. What is the amount of work done?

    (A) 15 N·kg
    (B) 15 N/m
    (C) 15 N·m
    (D) $15 \, N \cdot m/s^2$

57. 100 N·m of work is done over 20 m. What force was applied to the object that was moved?

    (A) 120 N
    (B) 5 N
    (C) 80 N
    (D) 2000 N

58. A book is held six feet above the floor and then dropped. Which statement is true?

    (A) The potential energy of the book is converted to kinetic energy.
    (B) The potential energy of the book is destroyed.
    (C) Kinetic energy is created.
    (D) The total energy of the system will not be conserved.

59. The joule cannot be the unit for

    (A) potential energy.
    (B) kinetic energy.
    (C) heat energy.
    (D) height.

60. Which organ below has olfactory cells?

    (A) nose
    (B) ear
    (C) tongue
    (D) eye

STOP. IF YOU HAVE TIME LEFT OVER, CHECK YOUR WORK ON THIS SECTION ONLY.

Answer Key

Verbal Skills Test 1

1. A	21. D	41. A
2. C	22. C	42. B
3. B	23. A	43. C
4. B	24. A	44. A
5. D	25. A	45. D
6. C	26. C	46. B
7. D	27. A	47. B
8. D	28. B	48. A
9. A	29. C	49. C
10. B	30. D	50. A
11. C	31. D	51. C
12. A	32. B	52. B
13. D	33. B	53. D
14. A	34. A	54. B
15. B	35. D	55. B
16. C	36. B	56. C
17. C	37. D	57. C
18. D	38. C	58. C
19. A	39. C	59. B
20. A	40. B	60. B

Verbal Skills Test 2

1. B	21. D	41. D
2. C	22. D	42. D
3. C	23. B	43. B
4. A	24. C	44. C
5. C	25. B	45. C
6. D	26. D	46. B
7. A	27. D	47. A
8. A	28. C	48. A
9. A	29. D	49. A
10. C	30. C	50. B
11. B	31. B	51. C
12. C	32. A	52. C
13. A	33. D	53. D
14. D	34. C	54. B
15. A	35. C	55. A
16. B	36. D	56. A
17. B	37. C	57. B
18. C	38. C	58. A
19. B	39. A	59. C
20. C	40. B	60. A

Reading Comprehension Test 1

1. C	13. D	25. A
2. A	14. B	26. C
3. B	15. C	27. A
4. C	16. B	28. B
5. D	17. D	29. 36
6. C	18. C	30. B
7. D	19. A	31. C
8. B	20. D	32. C
9. A	21. D	33. B
10. C	22. C	34. D
11. C	23. B	35. 17
12. A	24. A	

Reading Comprehension Test 2

1. C	13. D	25. C
2. B	14. C	26. B
3. D	15. C	27. C
4. A	16. A	28. D
5. C	17. D	29. A
6. D	18. A	30. D
7. B	19. B	31. C
8. B	20. A	32. C
9. A	21. D	33. A
10. C	22. A	34. C
11. B	23. C	35. A
12. A	24. B	

Mathematics Test 1

1. A	18. B	35. 17
2. A	19. D	36. A
3. C	20. D	37. A
4. D	21. B	38. A
5. B	22. B	39. B
6. D	23. B	40. C
7. C	24. B	41. D
8. B	25. A	42. C
9. A	26. D	43. B
10. A	27. C	44. A
11. B	28. B	45. A
12. C	29. 36	46. C
13. D	30. B	47. B
14. C	31. C	48. B
15. C	32. B	49. D
16. C	33. C	50. A
17. B	34. D	

Mathematics Test 2

1. D	18. D	35. D
2. B	19. B	36. C
3. C	20. B	37. C
4. D	21. B	38. A
5. D	22. B	39. D
6. C	23. B	40. D
7. C	24. A	41. B
8. D	25. C	42. D
9. C	26. C	43. B
10. A	27. A	44. D
11. B	28. B	45. B
12. D	29. B	46. A
13. 92	30. 36	47. D
14. C	31. C	48. D
15. A	32. C	49. C
16. B	33. A	50. A
17. D	34. B	

Science Test 1

1. A	21. B	41. B
2. A	22. A	42. A
3. C	23. D	43. B
4. D	24. C	44. C
5. C	25. B	45. C
6. D	26. A	46. D
7. D	27. A	47. D
8. A	28. C	48. A
9. D	29. B	49. B
10. B	30. B	50. D
11. C	31. C	51. A
12. C	32. A	52. B
13. A	33. A	53. D
14. D	34. B	54. A
15. B	35. A	55. D
16. A	36. C	56. A
17. B	37. A	57. D
18. A	38. D	58. D
19. A	39. C	59. C
20. D	40. A	60. C

Science Test 2

1. D	21. C	41. C
2. B	22. B	42. C
3. D	23. B	43. A
4. D	24. D	44. D
5. A	25. D	45. A
6. A	26. A	46. B
7. C	27. C	47. D
8. B	28. D	48. B
9. B	29. B	49. B
10. B	30. B	50. C
11. A	31. D	51. D
12. B	32. A	52. A
13. D	33. D	53. B
14. A	34. A	54. C
15. C	35. A	55. C
16. A	36. B	56. C
17. D	37. C	57. B
18. C	38. D	58. A
19. C	39. D	59. D
20. B	40. A	60. A

EXPLANATIONS
Verbal Skills Test 1

1. The correct choice is A.
The sentence is about the nurse. Choices B, C, and D are all nouns but are not the focus of the sentence.

2. The correct choice is C.
This is an example of an implied subject, which is *you*. The other choices are nouns but are not the focus of the sentence.

3. The correct choice is B.
The sentence is about Dr. Clemens. *Sheila* (choice C) is the object of the verb, and *situation* (choice A) and *unit* (choice D) are objects of prepositions.

4. The correct choice is B.
Because the noun being replaced is plural and the subject of the sentence, the correct answer is *they.*

5. The correct choice is D.
Because the noun being replaced is singular, female, and not possessive, the correct answer is *she.*

6. The correct choice is C.
In the sentence, the patient is complaining about something that happened in the past, so the first verb needs to be in the past tense. It also needs to be plural to agree with the plural noun *drugs.* The only correct answer is choice C.

7. The correct choice is D.
The verb in the blank needs to be the participle form that is used with the helping verb *was.* The correct answer is *waiting,* choice D.

8. The correct choice is D.
Calling (choice A) is a participial verb, *frantically* (choice B) is an adverb, and *assistance* (choice C) is a noun.

9. The correct choice is A.
In choice B, both words are adverbs; in choice C, the first word is a verb and the second word is an adverb; and in choice D, both words are nouns.

10. The correct choice is B.
Chief (choice A) is a noun, *remember* (choice C) is a verb, and *made* (choice D) is also a verb.

11. The correct choice is C.
In choice A, both words are nouns. In choice B, both words are verbs. In choice D, the first word is a possessive pronoun and the second word is a noun.

12. The correct choice is A.
In choice B, both words are nouns; in choice C, the first word is a noun and the second word is a verb. In choice D, the first word is a possessive pronoun and the second word is a noun.

13. The correct choice is D.

In choice A, the first word is a noun and the second word is a verb. In choice B, both words are proper nouns. In choice C, the first word is a verb and the second word is a proper noun.

14. The correct choice is A.

This sentence is a fragment and is missing a verb.

15. The correct choice is B.

This sentence is a fragment and is missing a subject.

16. The correct choice is C.

Choice C adds a comma, which creates a comma splice and does not fix the sentence.

17. The correct choice is C.

Choice C adds the conjunction *or*, which does not fit the meaning of the sentence.

18. The correct choice is D.

Only choice D has a conjunction that fits the meaning of the sentence. *Nor* and *yet* indicate contrast, and *because* implies cause and effect.

19. The correct choice is A.

Choice B does not fit because it implies cause and effect. Neither choice C nor choice D would make sense.

20. The correct choice is A.

Choices B, C, and D do not retain the meaning of the sentence.

21. The correct choice is D.

An independent clause is the same thing as a complete sentence.

22. The correct choice is C.

A dependent clause has both a subject and a verb and does not need to start with a preposition. Its defining element is that it cannot stand alone.

23. The correct choice is A.

After Dr. Carlisle finished the surgery is an adverbial clause. It tells *when* she took a few minutes to sit down and relax.

24. The correct choice is A.

Only choice A begins with a preposition.

25. The correct choice is A.

Choices B, C, and D all reverse the correct order of *i* and *e*.

26. The correct choice is C.

Only choice C uses the right number of *m*'s and *c*'s.

27. The correct choice is A.

Allowed is a homophone of *aloud*. It is pronounced the same way but spelled differently.

28. The correct choice is B.

The word *subtle* includes a *b* that is silent; that is, it is not pronounced.

29. The correct choice is C.
Only choice C is the correct spelling

30. The correct choice is D.
All the other choices are spelled incorrectly.

31. The correct choice is D.
All the other choices are spelled correctly.

32. The correct choice is B.
Choice A is incorrect because this is a question and the same is true for choice D. Choice C would only create a comma splice.

33. The correct choice is B.
This question needs to end with a question mark. None of the other choices makes sense.

34. The correct choice is A.
The comma needs to follow the dependent clause, which ends after the word *exhausted.*

35. The correct choice is D.
No comma is needed in this sentence.

36. The correct choice is B.
This is a run-on sentence, so adding a comma (choice A) after *tonight* would create a comma splice. A colon (choice C) is used to introduce a list, and there are no contractions or possessives to need an apostrophe (choice D).

37. The correct choice is D.
Patients (choice A) is simply a plural noun; it does not need an apostrophe. *Hospital* (choice B) is a singular adjective and *room* (choice C) is a singular noun; neither needs an apostrophe. However, *nurses* (choice D) is a possessive plural; it should be written *nurses'.*

38. The correct choice is C.
There are no possessives or contractions that would need an apostrophe. The sentence is neither a question nor an exclamation. However, it does need a colon after *missing* to introduce the list.

39. The correct choice is C.
The only place where a quotation mark is needed is right before *You,* where the second part of the quote begins. Every other place where a quotation mark is needed already has one.

40. The correct choice is B.
This sentence conveys strong emotion and needs to end with an exclamation point. Both quotation marks are present, and the sentence is not a question. There are no contractions or possessives that need apostrophes.

41. The correct choice is A.
All the other options are punctuation marks that serve other functions.

42. The correct choice is B.
Parentheses are used only for the purpose in choice B.

43. The correct choice is C.
All the other choices are punctuation marks that serve other functions.

44. The correct choice is A.
Only *opposite* (choice A) has the same meaning as *antithesis*.

45. The correct choice is D.
Only *harmless* (choice D) has the same meaning as *benign*.

46. The correct choice is B.
Debacle (choice A) means a fiasco, *fetish* (choice C) means an odd obsession, and an *iconoclast* (choice D) is someone who attacks traditional beliefs.

47. The correct choice is B.
Enamored (choice A) means "in love [with]"; it is the only one of the choices that makes sense in the sentence. *Dissident* (choice A) means disagreeing, *laconic* (choice C) means terse, and *maudlin* (choice D) means overly sentimental.

48. The correct choice is A.
Only *wicked* (choice A) has the same meaning as *nefarious*.

49. The correct choice is C.
Only *calm* (choice C) has the same meaning as *placate*.

50. The correct choice is A.
A person who is *altruistic* is generous toward others, so choice A is the only answer that makes sense in the sentence. *Cantankerous* (choice B) means grumpy, *depraved* (choice C) means corrupt or evil, and *ethereal* (choice D) means airy or spiritual.

51. The correct choice is C.
Only *remove* (choice C) has the same meaning as *extricate*.

52. The correct choice is B.
Only *candor* (choice B) retains the meaning of the rest of the sentence. *Amity* (choice A) means friendliness, *flippancy* (choice C) means levity, and *repugnance* (choice D) is a strong dislike or distaste.

53. The correct choice is D.
Only *standardized* (choice D) has almost the same meaning as *homogeneous*.

54. The correct choice is B.
Only *careful* (choice B) has almost the same meaning as *meticulous*.

55. The correct choice is B.
Only *imprudence* (choice B) means the opposite of *sagacity*.

56. The correct choice is C:
Only *resemblance* (choice C) has almost the same meaning as *affinity*.

57. The correct choice is C.
Only *frugal* (choice C) retains the meaning of the sentence.

58. The correct choice is C.
This is an example of an implied subject, so the answer is *you*.

59. The correct choice is B.
Department (choice A) and *doors* (choice D) are nouns. *Front* (choice C) is an adjective.

60. The correct choice is B.
The focus of the sentence is on the mask. *Oxygen* (choice A) is an adjective. *Patient's* (choice C) is a possessive noun. *Mouth* (choice D) is a noun that is the object of the preposition *across*.

Verbal Skills Test 2

1. The correct choice is B.
The sentence is about the staff. Although choices A, C, and D are all nouns from the sentence, they are not what the sentence is about.

2. The correct choice is C.
This sentence has an implied subject, which is *you*. The other choices are nouns, but none is the focus of the sentence.

3. The correct choice is C.
The subject of this sentence is *nurse*. The three other choices are nouns, but none is the focus of the sentence.

4. The correct choice is A.
The word *his* early in the sentence is a clue that the doctor is male. This eliminates choice B. The sentence is about one doctor, not two or more, so that eliminates choice C. Choice D is the right gender but the sentence does not call for a pronoun in the objective case.

5. The correct choice is C.
This sentence requires the feminine possessive pronoun *her*. Choice A is not possessive. Choice B is plural and first person. Choice D is the wrong gender and not possessive.

6. The correct choice is D.
The first part of the sentence, with the word *tomorrow,* shows that the action will take place in the future. That eliminates choices A, B, and C.

7. The correct choice is A.
The first part of the sentence, with the word *yesterday,* indicates that the action took place in the past. That eliminates choices B, C, and D.

8. The correct choice is A.
The word *test* is an adjective modifying the noun *results. Immediately* (choice B) is an adverb. *Me* (choice C) is a pronoun, and *news* (choice D) is a noun.

9. The correct choice is A.
The word *parking* is an adjective modifying the noun *lot. Lot* (choice B) and *morning* (choice D) are nouns. *Up* (choice C) is an adverb telling *how* the parking lot fills.

$195.60

#128.48 due 12/18/2014
#128.48 due 1/15/15
"   "   2/12/15
"   "   3/12/15
"   "   4/9/15

paige
413-205-0906

(Shayley 10)
(Audree 7)
Addie Lynn &
sisters
P.O Box 162
Fountain Green, UT
84632

$$0.1 * x = \frac{5}{0.1}$$

$$x = \frac{5}{0.1}$$

$$\frac{5}{0.1}$$

$\dfrac{78}{15}$

$$\begin{array}{r} 3.13 \\ 15\overline{)78} \\ -65 \\ \hline 13 \end{array}$$

$$\begin{array}{r}.7\\4\overline{)30}\\ 28 \\ \hline 2\end{array}$$

$0.1\overline{)5.}$

$$\begin{array}{r} 250 \\ 18 \\ \hline 2000 \\ 2800 \end{array}$$

45.00

$$\begin{array}{r} 3 \\ 15 \\ \times\, 0 \\ \hline 0 \end{array}$$

$$\begin{array}{r} 2 \\ 15 \\ 4. \\ \hline 60 \end{array}$$

$\dfrac{4.5}{9}$

$\overline{405}$

$0.1\overline{)5}$

$$\begin{array}{r} 2 \\ 78 \\ 15 \\ 5 \\ \hline 75 \end{array}$$

$$\begin{array}{r} 65 \\ 5 \\ \hline 0 \end{array}$$

$\dfrac{5}{1} \times \dfrac{0.1}{1}$

$$\begin{array}{r} 1 \\ 15 \\ 15 \\ 30 \\ 35 \\ \hline 65 \end{array}$$

$10\overline{)50.}$ $5.$

$5.$

$5\overline{)0.1}$

$$\begin{array}{r}10\\\hline 0\end{array}$$

$0.1\overline{)5.0}$

$$\begin{array}{r} 250 \\ 82 \\ \hline 500 \\ 20000 \\ \hline 20500 \end{array}$$

$$\begin{array}{r} 15 \\ 4 \\ \hline 15 \\ 5 \\ \hline 75 \end{array}$$

$\$400 \quad 32\% \text{ off}$

$$\begin{array}{r} 9 \\ 100 \\ -32 \\ \hline 68 \end{array}$$

$$\begin{array}{r} 400 \\ 68 \\ \hline 2400 \\ 24000 \\ \hline 26.400 \end{array}$$

$\dfrac{78}{15}$

$$\begin{array}{r} 5.3 \\ 15\overline{)78} \\ -75 \\ \hline 3 \end{array}$$

5.3

$$\begin{array}{r} 15 \\ 15 \\ 30 \\ 15 \\ 45 \\ 5 \\ \hline 60 \end{array}$$

$\dfrac{60}{15}\;\dfrac{}{75}$

10. The correct choice is C.

The adjective *dozen* modifies the noun *victims*, and the adjective *emergency* modifies the noun *mode*. The words in choice A are both nouns. The words in choice B are both verbs. Choice D consists of the adverb *when* and the noun *mode*.

11. The correct choice is B.

The adverb *cautiously* modifies the verb *cut;* it tells *how* the surgeon cut. Choices A, C, and D are all adjectives.

12. The correct choice is C.

Terribly tells how the lounge reeked; *foolishly* how the interns ordered. The words in choice A are both adjectives. The words in choice B are both verbs. The words in choice D are both nouns.

13. The correct choice is A.

The adverb *easily* modifies the verb *obtain,* and the adjective *necessary* modifies the noun *prescriptions.* The words in choice B are both nouns. The words in choice C are both verbs. The words in choice D are both prepositions.

14. The correct choice is D.

The adjective *modified* modifies the noun *ambulance,* and the adverb *noisily* modifies the verb *roared.* Choice A includes a noun and verb. The words in choice B are both nouns. Choice C includes a noun and a verb.

15. The correct choice is A.

This is a fragment; it is missing a verb to be complete. It already has a noun and does not need an adverb and adjective.

16. The correct choice is B.

This is a fragment; it is missing a subject to be complete. It already has a verb and does not need an adverb or adjective.

17. The correct choice is B.

Adding a comma without a coordinating conjunction merely creates a comma splice. In choice A, the semicolon corrects the run-on. Choice C adds an appropriate conjunction. Choice D corrects the run-on by dividing it into two separate sentences.

18. The correct choice is C.

A colon is not the appropriate punctuation to correct the run-on sentence. Choice A correctly uses a comma with the conjunction *and.* Choice B corrects the run-on sentence with a semicolon. Choice D corrects the run-on sentence by dividing it into two separate sentences.

19. The correct choice is B.

The sentence calls for a conjunction that shows a contrast between Dr. Addison's current job and his habit of checking up on his former colleagues. The best conjunction choice is *yet.* None of the other choices makes sense in the context of the sentence.

20. The correct choice is C.

Choices A, B, and D do not make sense in the context of the sentence.

21. The correct choice is D.
Choice D is the only one that makes sense in the context of the sentence. Choices A, B, and C all contradict the sense of the sentence.

22. The correct choice is D.
Choices A, B, and C do not make sense in the context of the sentence.

23. The correct choice is B.
An independent clause, such as a sentence, can stand on its own. None of the other choices can do so.

24. The correct choice is C.
A dependent clause can never stand alone. Choice A is incorrect because any kind of clause includes a verb, and choices B and D are not characteristics of any kind of clause.

25. The correct choice is B.
Choice B is the only phrase that begins with a preposition.

26. The correct choice is D.
Under the nurse's desk is a prepositional phrase that begins with the preposition *under.*

27. The correct choice is D.
Surrounded is the only word in the list that is spelled correctly.

28. The correct choice is C.
Arithmetic is the correct spelling of the word.

29. The correct choice is D.
The word *mince* is a homophone for *mints;* the words are pronounced the same but spelled differently.

30. The correct choice is C.
In the word *handkerchief,* the letter *d* is not pronounced; it is said to be silent.

31. The correct choice is B.
Cemetery is the correct spelling of the word.

32. The correct choice is A.
Committed is the only word in the list that is spelled correctly. The others should be spelled *foreign, liaison,* and *possession.*

33. The correct choice is D.
The correct spelling is *rhythm.*

34. The correct choice is C.
An apostrophe is needed in the word *interns* to show possession.

35. The correct choice is C.
A comma is needed to set off the dependent clause *which opened two years ago.* The clause adds information but is not necessary to the sense of the sentence.

36. The correct choice is D.
A comma is needed at the end of the introductory adverbial clause *Because the entire staff was out with the flu.*

37. The correct choice is C.

Choices A, B, and D are plurals that do not require an apostrophe. Only *department's* requires an apostrophe to show possession.

38. The correct choice is C.

This is a run-on sentence. The two parts of the sentence need to be separated by a semicolon between *tonight* and *he*.

39. The correct choice is A.

Choices B, C, and D are plurals that do not require an apostrophe. Only *hospital's* requires an apostrophe to show possession.

40. The correct choice is B.

A colon is needed to introduce the list that follows the word *desk*.

41. The correct choice is D.

A quotation mark is needed at the end of the quoted material, which ends with the word *that*.

42. The correct choice is D.

This quoted sentence would be said with great urgency, so the proper end punctuation is an exclamation point. The sentence already has quotation marks, it is not a question, and there is no unnecessary information in it.

43. The correct choice is B.

Only a semicolon can be used to join two complete sentences without the addition of a conjunction.

44. The correct choice is C.

Choice A is the purpose of parentheses. Choice B is the purpose of a comma. Choice D is the purpose of a question mark.

45. The correct choice is C.

None of the other punctuation is required to indicate a speaker's actual words.

46. The correct choice is B.

A *eulogy* is a funeral speech given in praise of the deceased.

47. The correct choice is A.

Corpulent means obese or overweight.

48. The correct choice is A.

A synonym for *squalid* is *filthy*.

49. The correct choice is A.

A *mentor* is an older, more experienced person who provides help and advice to a younger person.

50. The correct choice is B.

Rules has nearly the same meaning as *protocol*.

51. The correct choice is C.

To *paraphrase* is to communicate the meaning of someone's words without quoting them exactly. None of the other choices makes sense in the sentence.

52. The correct choice is C.
A person who is *taciturn* is generally quiet and may not be very sociable. *Outgoing* (choice C) has the opposite meaning.

53. The correct choice is D.
Unwilling (choice D) has nearly the same meaning as *reluctant*.

54. The correct choice is B.
A *sedative* is a medication that calms a person's emotions.

55. The correct choice is A.
Apprehensive (choice A) means *worried that something bad may happen.*

56. The correct choice is A.
Authorize (choice A) has almost the same meaning as *sanction*.

57. The correct choice is B.
A person who has a calm demeanor may be described as serene or *placid*.

58. The correct choice is A.
Credulous has almost the same meaning as *naive*.

59. The correct choice is C.
An *infallible* person is someone who never makes a mistake.

60. The correct choice is A.
People who *collaborate* with each other work together as a team.

Reading Comprehension Test 1

PASSAGE 1

1. The correct choice is C.
Choice A is incorrect because acupuncture is used to treat more than just cramps. Choice B is incorrect because the passage does not say that acupuncture should replace medication. Choice D is incorrect because the study described in the passage was intended to find out if acupuncture was a valid alternative to traditional treatments, not to prove that acupuncture was a superior choice.

2. The correct choice is A.
Choice B is incorrect because there is nothing in the passage about comparing the costs of the different treatments. Choice C is incorrect because traditional treatment is said to be effective. Choice D is not mentioned in the passage.

3. The correct choice is B.
Choice A is incorrect because there are no references in the passage to other studies of acupuncture as a treatment for menstrual pain. Choice C is incorrect because the passage does not mention any testimonials from patients. Choice D is irrelevant to the question being asked.

4. The correct choice is C.
There is nothing in the passage to support choices A, B, or D.

5. The correct choice is D.

Choice A is wrong because the researchers concluded that acupuncture was a credible alternative treatment. Choice B is too broad a statement to be accurate. Choice C is never stated in the passage.

PASSAGE 2

6. The correct choice is C.

Choice A is incorrect because there is nothing in the passage about how to discipline young people. Choice B is mentioned but is not the focus of the passage. Choice D is too broad a statement to accurately describe the main idea of the passage.

7. The correct choice is D.

The passage states that sufficient brain development takes place by the early twenties. No other time period is mentioned.

8. The correct choice is B.

There is nothing in the passage to support choices A, C, or D.

9. The correct choice is A.

None of the procedures mentioned in choices B, C, or D is mentioned in the passage.

10. The correct choice is C.

Choice A is incorrect because lack of discipline was not the cause of the problem. Choice B is incorrect because surgery is not mentioned as a possible treatment. Choice D is incorrect because the developmental issues described in the passage are not necessarily brain abnormalities.

PASSAGE 3

11. The correct choice is C.

The main point of this passage is to show how exposure to toxins now can cause health problems later. The passage is not primarily about choice A, the prevalence of lead in the environment; choice B, what shin bones can reveal; or the items mentioned in choice D, which are included merely as similar examples.

12. The correct choice is A.

Choice B is wrong because the doctors are "increasingly concerned" about effects of lead, pesticides, and mercury, not about the process of normal aging; choice C is not supported by enough information; and choice D is the opposite of what the passage actually states.

13. The correct choice is D.

Choice A is wrong because there are several ways to detect lead, choice B is wrong because the passage shows that lead is still a problem, and choice C is proved wrong within the passage by the results from the tests on shin bones.

14. The correct choice is B.

Choice A is not supported by the quote, choice C is wrong because the doctor does not propose anything contradictory in his quote, and choice D is wrong because one person's opinion is not enough to prove anything about all doctors.

15. The correct choice is C.
Choice A is incorrect because there is no reason to conclude that the shin bone is the only place where lead accumulates, choice B is wrong because the bone's fragility is not a relevant factor, and choice D is wrong because the bone's proximity to the surface is also irrelevant.

PASSAGE 4

16. The correct choice is B.
Choice A is false based on the facts in the passage, choice C is a detail from the passage but not the main point, and choice D is an opinion and is not a relevant fact from the passage.

17. The correct choice is D.
Choices A, B, and C were all mentioned in the passage, but choice D was not mentioned.

18. The correct choice is C.
Choices A, B, and D were not mentioned in the passage as side effects.

19. The correct choice is A.
Only choice A was actually named as a purpose of sleep. Choice B may be true but is not mentioned in the passage; choice C is too broad a statement to be accurate; and as for choice D, although changes in brain chemistry are mentioned, they are not described as dramatic or occurring only during sleep.

20. The correct choice is D.
Nothing in the passage discusses the scientific acceptability of the German studies. Choice B is true but is not the conclusion that can be reached based on the passage, and choice C is the opposite of what the passage states.

PASSAGE 5

21. The correct choice is D.
Choice A is a very broad statement and is not the main point of the passage. Choice B is a supporting detail, and so is choice C.

22. The correct choice is C.
Although the ideas in choices A, B, and D are all mentioned in the passage, only choice C is indicated as the purpose of the survey done by the CDC.

23. The correct choice is B.
Choice A is a different meaning of the word *surfing*. Choices C and D are activities that do not define or reflect the concept of Internet surfing.

24. The correct choice is A.
Choices B, C, and D are all listed as possible risks, but choice A is not mentioned.

25. The correct choice is A.

Choice B is the amount of sleep teens need, choice C is the amount of sleep young children need, and choice D is a number not mentioned in the passage.

PASSAGE 6

26. The correct choice is C.

Choice A is wrong because other methods of punishing children are not discussed in the passage. Choice B is a supporting detail from the spanking debate and not the main idea of the passage. Choice D is wrong because there was no mention of a double-blind study.

27. The correct choice is A.

Choices B, C, and D are not the definition of the word *integral*.

28. The correct choice is B.

The summaries presented in choices A and D are both too sweeping to accurately reflect Gershoff's opinion about spanking, and choice C does not fit with Gershoff's opinion.

29. The correct choice is D.

Choices A and B are overly strong statements that are not supported by the passage, and choice C is not supported by anything in the passage.

30. The correct choice is B.

Choices A, C, and D do not accurately reflect the opinion of the American Academy of Pediatrics.

PASSAGE 7

31. The correct choice is C.

Choice A is not a logical conclusion from the details presented in the passage. Choice B is not correct because the passage does not prescribe "hard" exercise as a remedy for fatigue. Choice D is not correct because low-impact exercise helps with fatigue, not with the diseases mentioned.

32. The correct choice is C.

The group in choice A experienced no benefits, the group in choice B had more trouble with fatigue, and there was no such group such as the one mentioned in choice D.

33. The correct choice is B.

Choice A is wrong because athletes were not involved in the study, choice C is wrong because the scientists were observers, not participants, and choice D is wrong because those patients were part of a different study.

34. The correct choice is D.

Choices A and C are other meanings of the word *track*. Choice B has nothing to do with the word.

35. The correct choice is D.

Choices A and B are incorrect because there is nothing in the study to support the idea that exercise speeds healing or improves the effectiveness of medical treatments. Choice C may be true but it is not mentioned anywhere in the passage.

Reading Comprehension Test 2

PASSAGE 1

1. The correct choice is C.
The study showed no improvement in people who used aromatherapy, so choice C is the best answer. Choice A contradicts what is stated about lavender in the article, choice B is too strong an opinion, and choice D is not supported by the passage.

2. The correct choice is B.
The passage states that lemon and lavender are two of the most popular scents used in aromatherapy. Choice A is wrong because ease of finding the scents was not mentioned, choice C is wrong because the two scents are not described as helping with headaches, and choice D is never mentioned in the passage.

3. The correct choice is D.
It is reasonable to conclude that true believers in aromatherapy might tend to report positive results, even if their claims were not scientifically verifiable. Those claims would not necessarily be lies, so choice B is wrong; choice A is wrong because a person who believes in aromatherapy is not necessarily gullible; and choice C is wrong because there is no mention of anything that believers might gain if the study supported their belief.

4. The correct choice is A.
Scents such as lemon and lavender are perceived as safe and natural, so choice A is a logical conclusion. Nothing in the passage supports any of the other choices.

5. The correct choice is C.
The study described in the passage is not necessarily absolutely conclusive, so choice C is the only conclusion you can legitimately draw from the passage. The results of the study do not support any of the other choices.

PASSAGE 2

6. The correct choice is D.
Choice D expresses the main idea of the passage. Choices A, B, and C are supporting details.

7. The correct choice is B.
The first sentence describes the intense media coverage given to osteoporosis. Choice A is not a possible conclusion from that first sentence, and choices C and D are contradicted by the passage.

8. The correct choice is B.
Choices A, C, and D are all mentioned in the passage as factors considered in FRAX studies.

9. The correct choice is A.
Because smoking and alcohol are part of the FRAX calculations, it is reasonable to assume that they are considered to be possible factors in loss of bone mass. Choice B is wrong because cancer risk is not mentioned in the passage, choice C is wrong because it makes too broad an assumption, and nothing in the passage supports choice D.

10. The correct choice is C.
None of the other choices is mentioned in the passage.

PASSAGE 3

11. The correct choice is B.
Choices A, C, and D are all details that support the main idea of the passage.

12. The correct choice is A.
The quote from the CDC report supports the basic ideas presented in the passage. Choice B is wrong because the quote does not contradict any of those ideas, choice C is wrong because no statistics are cited, and nothing in the quote supports choice D.

13. The correct choice is D.
Choices A, B, and C are not based on any information in the passage.

14. The correct choice is C.
All of the other choices are specifically mentioned in the passage.

15. The correct choice is C.
Choices A, B, and C are all extreme conclusions that are not supported in the passage. Choice A is never stated. Choice B is wrong because the CDC merely recommends physical therapy; it does not insist that all elderly people be enrolled in physical therapy classes. Choice D is wrong because the quote says only that fear of falling *can* cause elderly people to stay home, not that all elderly people are staying home because of that fear.

PASSAGE 4

16. The correct choice is A.
Choice A covers the two main topics of the passage. Choice B is wrong because the passage is about far more than binging and purging, and choices C and D are wrong because both refer only to supporting details, not to the main idea of the passage.

17. The correct choice is D.
Drunkorexia refers to a combination of eating disorders and alcohol abuse. Choices A, B, and C are all incorrect because all three ignore the second factor (alcohol).

18. The correct choice is A.
Although eating disorders may also be linked to the conditions mentioned in choices B, C, and D, only the link in choice A is mentioned specifically in the passage.

19. The correct choice is B.

Treatment is the focus of the last half of the passage. None of the other choices is discussed.

20. The correct choice is A.

The point of the quote is to underline the link between eating disorders and substance abuse. The idea in choice B is introduced in another, earlier quote; choice C is wrong because the quote does not contradict the rest of the passage; and choice D is wrong because no new theory is mentioned.

PASSAGE 5

21. The correct choice is D.

Choice A and B are supporting details only. Choice C is wrong because it is an opinion that is not expressed in the passage.

22. The correct choice is A.

The other three choices are mentioned as ingredients that are monitored.

23. The correct choice is C.

Tap water and bottled water undergo much of the same kind of monitoring and regulation. Choice B is not true, and choices A and D are not supported by the passage.

24. The correct choice is B.

Because the bottled water industry is monitoring the levels of pharmaceuticals in water, it is reasonable to infer that there are concerns that someday those pharmaceuticals might be a problem. Choice A is wrong because there are no current standards for levels of pharmaceuticals in water. Choice C is wrong because nothing indicates that pharmaceuticals in water are extremely dangerous. Choice D is not supported by the passage.

25. The correct choice is C.

Choice C is the most reasonable conclusion that one can draw. Choices A, B, and D are not supported by the passage.

PASSAGE 6

26. The correct choice is B.

Choice A is wrong because the problem described is short-term memory loss, not long-term memory loss; choice C is wrong because the memory loss is not permanent; and choice D is wrong because lack of sleep is not the only factor suspected of causing memory loss.

27. The correct choice is C.

Although the other choices are mentioned, the Australian researchers placed most of the blame on hormonal shifts.

28. The correct choice is D.

The three categories listed in choices A, B, and C are all mentioned as being included in the study.

29. The correct choice is A.
The researchers "suspect," or *suppose,* that hormonal shifts are the cause of the problem. They do not *doubt* (choice C) this finding, nor are they sure enough to *conclude* (choice D) definitively that they have found the cause. *Decide* (choice B) does not fit the meaning of the sentence.

30. The correct choice is D.
Choice D best summarizes the conclusion of the passage. Choice A is wrong because the memory loss is not severe, choice B is wrong because the problem described is due to more than just lack of sleep, and choice C is wrong because forgetting phone numbers is merely one example of the problem.

PASSAGE 7

31. The correct choice is C.
Choice C best summarizes the ideas in the passage. Choice A is wrong because the passage does not recommend that people should move to sunnier climates. Choice B is wrong because it is contradicted by the passage. Choice D is wrong because men's problems with SAD are a supporting detail of the passage, not the main idea.

32. The correct choice is C.
Sunshine is the only meaning of the word that makes sense in the context of the passage.

33. The correct choice is A.
Lethargy means sluggishness. The meaning can be inferred from the connection with depression, social withdrawal, and chronic fatigue.

34. The correct choice is C.
Suicide (choice C) is the worst possible consequence mentioned in the passage. Depression (choice A), though painful, is not as dire as suicide. Choices B and D are not necessarily negative consequences.

35. The correct choice is A.
Choices B and D are possible treatments but not the primary one mentioned in the passage. Choice C is not mentioned in the passage at all.

Mathematics Test 1

1. The correct choice is A.
Both the spinning and yoga classes have seen participation go up over both years.

2. The correct choice is A.
Spinning saw an increase of 5 from 2006 to 2007.

3. The correct choice is C.
$(12 + 5 + 1 + 0 + 7) \div 5 = 5$

4. The correct choice is D.

5. The correct choice is B.

This is a proportion problem, so you can set up two equal fractions: 75 cents and 1 shirt on the left, and 1,500 cents and x on the right. Cross-multiply and you get $75x = 1,500$. Divide each side by 75 and you get $x = 20$.

6. The correct choice is D.

The fraction $\dfrac{60}{12}$ divides out to 5, which is the same as 500%.

7. The correct choice is C.

There are 100 centimeters in a meter, so there are 56×100, or 5,600 centimeters in 56 meters.

8. The correct choice is B.

If Jane has collected 132 stamps over 12 months, she has collected an average of $132 \div 12 = 11$ stamps per month.

9. The correct choice is A.

When you convert $2\dfrac{66}{84}$ into an improper fraction, you get $\dfrac{234}{84}$. Divide both numerator and denominator by 6 to get $\dfrac{39}{14}$.

10. The correct choice is A.

The question is asking for the circumference of the tire. Because the radius is 15, you can plug into the formula for circumference and get $C = 2 \times 15 \times \pi$, or 30π.

11. The correct choice is B.

The pair of shapes shows a triangle with another triangle inside of it and a side cut off. Choice B reflects the same changes, although it is rotated differently.

12. The correct choice is C.

Simplify to make it easier to translate: J is five more than twice F. Now you can see the mathematical equivalent for each word, $J = 5 + 2F$.

13. The correct choice is D.

14. The correct choice is C.

$33\dfrac{1}{3}\%$ is the same as $\dfrac{1}{3}$ of the pie chart. You know that a circle has 360 degrees total, so $\dfrac{1}{3}$ of 360 is 120 degrees.

15. The correct choice is C.

Remember, when you see a division sign and the bases are the same, you can just subtract the exponents.

16. The correct choice is C.

Because the only difference between the answer choices in this problem is the number of places behind the decimal, all you really need to do is count. There are three places behind the decimal in the original problem; therefore, there are three places behind the decimal in the result.

17. The correct choice is B.
0.6×70, or $6 \times 70 = 420$ and then you move the decimal one place to the left, giving you 42.

18. The correct choice is B.
You can use the Pythagorean theorem on this problem, but it is also a Pythagorean shortcut. A triangle with sides 30, 40, and 50 is similar to a triangle with sides 3, 4, and 5.

19. The correct choice is D.
Cherry pie has 29%, so you need to find other categories that add up to 29. Blueberry, peach, and key lime have 29% collectively, so choice D is the correct answer.

20. The correct choice is D.
You are looking for an answer choice (or two) that would give you greater than 42% collectively. Clearly choice B is greater than 42%, because it encompasses all the categories except apple and therefore totals 58%. Peach, key lime, and cherry add up to 50%, so choice C also works, making choice D the correct answer.

21. The correct choice is B.
Choices B and D are the only answers that are negative, so you can eliminate choices A and C. Because $\frac{1}{3}$ is a fraction between 0 and -1, it is not as far to the left as -3, and therefore not as small.

22. The correct choice is B.

23. The correct choice is B.
The formula for area of a circle is $A = \pi r^2$, so plugging the radius 4 into the formula gives $A = \pi 4^2$ or $A = 16\pi$.

24. The correct choice is B.
Remember, a stem-and-leaf plot displays the tens digit on the left and units on the right. All numbers represented must be listed, even if they are duplicates.

25. The correct choice is A.
Remember to take this in bite-sized pieces, with the easier stuff first. The line crosses the y-axis at -3, so you can eliminate choices B and D. A quick $\frac{rise}{run}$ or ballparking tells you that the slope is 2, so choice A must be the correct answer.

26. The correct choice is D.
Creating two equal fractions for your proportion, you could put 5 (berries) in the numerator and 4 (yogurt) in the denominator on the left, then 10 (yogurt) in the denominator on the right and x in the numerator. Cross-multiplying gives you $50 = 4x$, so $12.5 = x$.

27. The correct choice is C.

28. The correct choice is B.
18 is divisible by 2, 3, 6, and 9 other than itself and 1; 21 is divisible by 3 and 7; 25 is divisible by 5.

29. The correct answer is 36.

Translate: $45 = \dfrac{125}{100} \times x$. Solving further, you get $4{,}500 = 125x$, and you can divide both sides by 125 to get $36 = x$.

30. The correct choice is B.

$3 \div 5$ divides out to 0.6.

31. The correct choice is C.

This question is asking for area of a rectangle, so you just need to multiply the sides; $18 \times 12 = 216$.

32. The correct choice is B.

First, you need to convert 15:40 to a fraction and reduce it. $\dfrac{15}{40}$ becomes $\dfrac{3}{8}$, which is equal to 37.5%. This is a great one to have memorized so that you do not have to worry about the math on the actual test.

33. The correct choice is C.

34. The correct choice is D.

The wording on this one is just a little bit trickier than some others you have seen; first you have to determine that each child gets three cookies, because a package of six cookies is split between two children. If each child gets three cookies, that is the left side of our proportion: three cookies over one child. The right fraction is x over twelve children. Cross-multiply and you get $x = 36$.

35. The correct answer is 17.

Translate: $x = 2 \times 10 - 3$. Solve and you have 17.

36. The correct choice is A.

37. The correct choice is A.

Bowtie to find the difference; $28 - 9$ on top and 36 on bottom gives you $\dfrac{19}{36}$.

38. The correct choice is A.

There were three days with no rainfall, whereas no other amount occurred that many days, so 0 is the mode.

39. The correct choice is B.

The median of the ordered list $-8, -1, 3, 4$, and 12 is 3.

40. The correct choice is C.

Sven eats $\dfrac{3}{8}$ of the pizza, which has a total degree measure of 360 degrees. $\dfrac{3}{8} \times 360 = 135$.

41. The correct choice is D.

To convert Celsius to Fahrenheit, multiply by $\dfrac{9}{5}$ and then add 32. $60 \times \dfrac{9}{5} + 32 = 108 + 32$, so the correct answer is 140°F.

42. The correct choice is C.
The prime factors of 75 are 3, 5, and 5, giving you a sum of 13.

43. The correct choice is B.

44. The correct choice is A.
Dividing means subtracting exponents, so $\dfrac{y^7}{y^4}$ is the same as y^{7-4}, or y^3.

45. The correct choice is A.

46. The correct choice is C.
Using the Pythagorean theorem, $4^2 + 6^2 = c^2$. So $52 = c^2$, meaning that $\sqrt{52} = c$. The prime factors of 52 are 2, 2, and 13, so the 2s come outside of the root sign and $2\sqrt{13}$ is the result.

47. The correct choice is B.
The prime factors of 80 are 2, 2, 2, 2, and 5, so the two pairs of 2s can come outside of the square root sign and the 5 must stay in.

48. The correct choice is B.
The number 46 is not prime. However, 47 is prime, making it the smallest prime number in the answer choices.

49. The correct choice is D.
Be sure to set up a proportion: 2 walls and 90 minutes are on the left and 6 walls and x are on the right. Cross-multiplying gives $2x = 540$. Divide both sides by 2 and you have $x = 270$.

50. The correct choice is A.

Mathematics Test 2

1. The correct choice is D.
A stem-and-leaf plot displays the tens digit on the left and units on the right, displaying all numbers listed in the original presentation.

2. The correct choice is B.
Once you pare down the excess words, the problem is really asking what is 20% of 35, which is also $\dfrac{1}{5}$ of 35. $\dfrac{1}{5} \times 35 = 7$.

3. The correct choice is C.
First, you need to reduce. The fraction $\dfrac{60}{24}$ reduces to $2\dfrac{1}{2}$ or 2.5. Expressed as a percentage, $2.5 = 250\%$.

4. The correct choice is D.
This question is mostly a basic proportion, with 45 minutes over 1 day on the left and x over 7 days (remember to convert!) on the right. Cross-multiply and you get $315 = x$. However, the answer choices are expressed in hours *and* minutes, so you must divide 315 by 60 (the number of minutes in one hour) to get 5r15, or 5 hours, 15 minutes.

5. The correct choice is D.
Because 1 inch equals approximately 2.5 centimeters, multiply 48 by 2.5. Even if you only ballpark, 120 is the only answer that comes close.

6. The correct choice is C.
$(8 + -4 + 3 + 9 + 4) \div 5 = 4$

7. The correct choice is C.
First, you must convert the mixed number into an improper fraction. $2 \times 4 + 3 = 11$, so you get $\dfrac{11}{4}$ for our improper fraction. Second, dividing by a fraction means you need to flip it and multiply, so your problem is really $\dfrac{11}{4} \times \dfrac{8}{7}$. Multiply across and you get $\dfrac{88}{28}$, which reduces to $\dfrac{22}{7}$.

8. The correct choice is D.
The formula for the area of a circle is $A = \pi r^2$, so when you plug in a radius of 6 and get $A = \pi 6^2$, the area is 36π.

9. The correct choice is C.

10. The correct choice is A.
First, look at the easiest thing to tell at first glance; the line crosses the y-axis at 1, so you can eliminate choices B and D. The slope is $\dfrac{1}{3}$, which you distinguish from 3 by ballparking, because it is a very gradual slope, or you can determine it using $\dfrac{rise}{run}$.

11. The correct choice is B.
This problem uses a Pythagorean shortcut, but you can also use Pythagorean theorem if you forget the shortcuts. The sides of the rectangle are 5 and 12, so you can plug those in to the theorem and get $5^2 + 12^2 = c^2$. That brings you to $169 = c^2$ or $\sqrt{169} = c^2$, which solves as $13 = c$.

12. The correct choice is D.
You are looking for 20%, or $\dfrac{1}{5}$ of the pie chart, which has a degree measure of 360. $\dfrac{1}{5} \times 360$ is 72.

13. The correct answer is 92.
$(94 + 91 + 88 + 95) \div 4 = 92$; therefore, Polly's average on the four tests was 92.

14. The correct choice is C.
If a problem has exponents of the same base being multiplied, you *add* the exponents: $7^3 \times 7^5 = 7^8$.

15. The correct choice is A.
One way to do this problem is to reduce the answer choices until you find one that equals 15:8, which choice A does. Another way is to set the answer choices up as proportions with 15:8, and bowtie to compare them. The one that comes out with equal numbers on both sides is the equal ratio.

16. The correct choice is B.
$(3 + 14 + 10 + -7) \div 4 = 5$; therefore, the average of the list of numbers is 5.

17. The correct choice is D.
Because the question is asking for a prime number, you can immediately eliminate the even answer choices, A and D. The number 27 is not prime because it is divisible by 3, and 29 is prime.

18. The correct choice is D.
The answer choices with absolute value signs must be positive, so to find the largest value, pick the largest positive number, which is 7.2.

19. The correct choice is B.
The temperature between February and March only increased a slight amount—three degrees or so—compared with much larger increases between the other months.

20. The correct choice is B.
February and April both show an increase of more than ten degrees; they each increase by about 12 or 13.

21. The correct choice is B.

22. The correct choice is B.
To convert Fahrenheit to Celsius, subtract 32 and then multiply by $\frac{5}{9}$. $(90 - 32) \times \frac{5}{9} = 32\frac{2}{9}$, or approximately 32.

23. The correct choice is B.
Translate: "One dollar more than half its normal price" when the normal price is 15 translates into $\frac{1}{2} \times 15 + 1$, which is the same as choice B.

24. The correct choice is A.

25. The correct choice is C.
You are dividing by a decimal, but remember that you can ignore all decimals until the math is complete. $34 \div 2 = 17$, and because you are dividing, you subtract the number of digits behind the decimal in the divisor from the number of digits in the dividend. $1 - 1 = 0$, so you do not need to move the decimal point, and it stays 17.

26. The correct choice is C.

27. The correct choice is A.
This problem can be done by comparing individual fractions, but it is probably more time consuming than the alternate, which is converting the fractions into decimals so that they are easier to order. $\frac{1}{8} = 0.125$, $\frac{2}{5} = 0.4$, $\frac{1}{2} = 0.5$, and $\frac{3}{4} = 0.75$, so that is the order they should be in from left to right.

28. The correct choice is B.
The prime factors of 28 are 2, 2, and 7, so their sum is 11.

29. The correct choice is B.
Ignoring the decimals, 38×235 is 8,930, and there are four digits behind the decimal in 0.38 and 2.35, so you move the decimal four places to the left to get 0.8930 or just 0.893.

30. The correct answer is 36.
Translate: $x = 0.6 \times 60$. Multiplying it out gives you $x = 36$.

31. The correct choice is C.
Set up a basic proportion with 45 (cents) over 2 (holes) on the left and x over 10 (holes) on the right. Then you can cross-multiply to get $45 \times 10 = 2x$ and solve to get $225 = x$. Of course, you then need to express that in dollars to fit the answer choices, and 225 cents = \$2.25.

32. The correct choice is C.
The problem asks for area of a triangle, so you need to plug the numbers you are given into the formula for area of a triangle, $A = \dfrac{1}{2}bh$, giving you $A = \dfrac{1}{2} \times 10 \times 9$, which solves to $A = 45$ in^2.

33. The correct choice is A.
The first pair of shape clusters shows the same set of shapes, but reorganized. Choice A is the only cluster that completes the second pair in the same way; the shapes aren't rearranged exactly as the first pair were, but all of the other answer choices contain shapes that aren't in the first cluster of the second pair.

34. The correct choice is B.
$\dfrac{7}{8}$ divides out as 0.875, so choice B is the correct answer. This is a great one to memorize if you have not already!

35. The correct choice is D.

36. The correct choice is C.
The number of donors on Tuesday was about 25 and from Tuesday to Wednesday, that number increased by about 25. That is a 100 percent increase from Tuesday to Wednesday.

37. The correct choice is C.
The decrease from Wednesday to Thursday is the only decrease over 10, which you can tell by estimating using the gridlines on the chart.

38. The correct choice is A.

39. The correct choice is D.
$(23 + 8 + 2 + 7) \div 4 = 10$

40. The correct choice is D.
$\dfrac{7}{35}$ divides out to 0.2.

41. The correct choice is B.
This is a basic proportion problem; set up 5 over 2 on one side and 30 over x on the other side. Cross-multiply and you get $5x = 60$, which solves to $x = 12$.

42. The correct choice is D.

43. The correct choice is B.
The prime factors of 56 are 2, 2, 2, and 7. One pair of twos can come outside the radical, and the other 2 and the 7 must stay in.

44. The correct choice is D.
This problem is basic translation, but be careful about the meaning of "three years younger"; it can be tricky to tell when you need to subtract.

45. The correct choice is B.
Let's translate: "5 is what percent of 40" becomes $5 = \dfrac{x}{100} \times 40$, or $5 = \dfrac{40x}{100}$.

Multiply both sides by 100 and you get $500 = 40x$; divide each side by 40 and you get $12.5 = x$. Therefore, 5 is 12.5 percent of 40.

46. The correct choice is A.

47. The correct choice is D.
Because the problem is looking for area of a rectangle, you just need to multiply the length and the width. $90 \times 85 = 7{,}650$.

48. The correct choice is D.
First, convert the integer and mixed number into improper fractions. 3 becomes $\dfrac{3}{1}$ and $1\dfrac{5}{6}$ becomes $\dfrac{11}{6}$. You can bowtie $\dfrac{3}{1} - \dfrac{11}{6}$ to equal $\dfrac{18-11}{6}$, which becomes $\dfrac{7}{6}$.

49. The correct choice is C.
Remember to factor the 2 out of both terms; there is an answer choice that is otherwise correct and it does not have the 2. Otherwise, the greatest number of x's that you can factor out is 4 and the greatest number of y's you can factor out is 3; the part inside the parentheses remains the same in all answer choices, so you do not even need to worry about the rest.

50. The correct choice is A.
Translate: "Bob is 5,000 less than the sum of Al and Carl" (yes, the problem is actually talking about their salaries, but we are simplifying the language) translates to $B = -5{,}000 + A + C$, which can be rearranged to fit choice A.

Science Test 1

1. The correct choice is A.
Isotopes have the same number of protons and are the same element. What makes them different is the number of neutrons present, which makes the mass number vary as well.

2. The correct choice is A.
"Amphi" means both (amphitheater, amphibian). An amphoteric substance can act as either an acid or base.

3. The correct choice is C.

In a chemical reaction a compound may be broken down and transformed into other compounds. Elements, however, are not broken down chemically during a reaction.

4. The correct choice is D.

A hydronium ion concentration of 1×10^{-7} M in a solution translates into the solution having a pH of 7. This pH value indicates a neutral solution that is neither acidic nor basic.

5. The correct choice is C.

After 24 days, the sample has undergone three half-lives. During the three half-lives we see that the amounts change as follows: 1 whole $\rightarrow$ ½ $\rightarrow$ ¼ $\rightarrow$ ⅛, where an arrow represents 8 days (one half-life).

6. The correct choice is D.

Carbon-12 is not an emanation of a nuclear decay. Radioactive substances that undergo a natural transmutation give off alpha particles, beta particles, and gamma rays.

7. The correct choice is D.

A strong acid has a very low pH value and more hydronium ions present in solution.

8. The correct choice is A.

The symbol for potassium is K (for calcium, Ca; for carbon, C; and for phosphorus, P).

9. The correct choice is D.

Exothermic reactions release heat, whereas endothermic reactions absorb heat.

10. The correct choice is B.

Boyle's Law demonstrates the inversely proportional relationship between pressure and volume. This should not be confused with Charles' Law, which relates temperature to volume.

11. The correct choice is C.

An ionic bond is formed between a metal and a nonmetal. The metal (Mg) loses electrons to the nonmetal (Br).

12. The correct choice is C.

Chlorophyll absorbs red and blue light best; 665 nm corresponds to red light, whereas 430 nm corresponds to blue light.

13. The correct choice is A.

The xylem of the plant carries materials from the roots, upward throughout the plant.

14. The correct choice is D.

When placed in distilled water, a cell has a higher concentration of solutes inside and a very low concentration of solutes outside. In an effort to dilute the concentration of solutes inside the cell, water flows into the cell, causing it to swell and possibly burst.

15. The correct choice is B.
Cytokinesis literally means "cytoplasm movement." This occurs during telophase and is the final phase of cell replication.

16. The correct choice is A.
Carnivores are meat eaters, whereas herbivores are plant eaters. Consumers are organisms that eat others, and decomposers help decay materials so that they can be recycled in the environment.

17. The correct choice is B.
During metaphase, the chromosomes line up near the equator of the cell in preparation for the separation of the chromosomes and the pinching of the cytoplasm.

18. The correct choice is A.
The term *lysis* means "to split." The enzymes in lysosomes break down substrates into desired products.

19. The correct choice is A.
The lock-and-key model describes how the substrate must fit into the active site of an enzyme for the reaction to take place.

20. The correct choice is D.
Organisms that contain chlorophyll are most likely green.

21. The correct choice is B.
Proteins, lipids, nucleic acids, and carbohydrates are the four major organic compounds that are important to living things. Synthetic polymers, although they can be placed into living things, are not formed by the body naturally.

22. The correct choice is A.
Glucose is a simple sugar and is what carbohydrates and starches need to be turned into so that they can be used by cells.

23. The correct choice is D.
The wavelike movements of muscles in the digestive system is called peristalsis. This pushes food through the digestive tract.

24. The correct choice is C.
Atherosclerosis is the hardening of the arteries. As cholesterol builds up, the opening in the artery closes, leading to a heart attack.

25. The correct choice is B.
The esophagus connects the mouth to the stomach. The epiglottis covers the glottis so that food does not enter the windpipe or lungs. The anus allows the release of fecal matter from the body.

26. The correct choice is A.
The three types of muscles are smooth, skeletal, and cardiac. The nerves do not need muscles to function.

27. The correct choice is A.
The heart is made of muscle. This type of muscle is called cardiac muscle.

28. The correct choice is C.
Vitamin D helps with the absorption of calcium so that teeth and bones can grow and develop properly.

29. The correct choice is B.
Synapses are the spaces between neurons. This space serves to allow neurotransmitters to move between the neurons.

30. The correct choice is B.
The villi (microvilli) in the small intestine act the same way roots do, to increase the surface area so that more substances can be absorbed into the body.

31. The correct choice is C.
Gases diffuse through membranes and into the blood. This happens at the capillaries located at the alveoli.

32. The correct choice is A.
The average person in good health has a pulse of about 72 beats per minute and a blood pressure of 120 over 80 mm Hg.

33. The correct choice is A.
Optic refers to the eye, where the retina is located. Olfactory refers to the nose, and auditory refers to the ear.

34. The correct choice is B.
Smooth muscle is the type of muscle found in the digestive system.

35. The correct choice is A.
The mandible is the jaw bone. The ribs are located in the chest, whereas the radius and femur are located in the arm and leg, respectively.

36. The correct choice is C.
The term *renal* refers to the kidney. The term *pulmonary* refers to the lungs.

37. The correct choice is A.
Although many anatomical structures contain valves, the bicuspid valve is located in the human heart.

38. The correct choice is D.
Accessory organs aid other organs. In this case, the liver, pancreas, and gallbladder all aid the organs of the digestive system by secreting digestive juices into the digestive tract. The stomach is part of the digestive tract and does not fall under the category of accessory organ.

39. The correct choice is C.
Bile is produced in the liver and is stored in the gallbladder. The function of bile is to emulsify fats, allowing them to be easily absorbed and digested by the small intestine.

40. The correct choice is A.
When a solute is added to a solvent, the boiling point increases and the freezing point decreases.

41. The correct choice is B.
The equation $P = IV$, power equals current times voltage, is the equation to use. Dividing the power by voltage gives $I = P/V$, and 60 watts/110 volts is 0.55 amperes.

42. The correct choice is A.
Transverse waves do not have areas of compression and expansion as they move perpendicular to the direction of the wave.

43. The correct choice is B.
According to the equation, $v = f\lambda$, the frequency is equal to the velocity of the wave divided by the wavelength. Dividing 20 m/s by 4 m gives $5\,s^{-1}$.

44. The correct choice is C.
Because of its smooth surface, the angle of incidence is expected to be equal to the angle of reflection.

45. The correct choice is C.
Dispersion is the breaking up of white light into the colors of the rainbow.

46. The correct choice is D.
Refraction is the bending of light that takes place as light travels from one medium into another. It occurs because of the change in speed of the light.

47. The correct choice is D.
The formation of an ion depends on the loss or gain of electrons. If the ion is negative, then the ion must have gained a negatively charged electron.

48. The correct choice is A.
The correct unit for current is amperes.

49. The correct choice is B.
The symbol shown is the symbol for ohms, the unit for resistance.

50. The correct choice is D.
Rearranging the equation, we find that the current is equal to the voltage divided by the resistance, $I = V/R$.

51. The correct choice is A.
Lights connected in parallel have an advantage over those connected in series in that, should one light bulb break or die out, the others will remain lit.

52. The correct choice is B.
The voltage, V, is equal to IR, current times resistance.

53. The correct choice is D.
Electrical potential is measured in volts. The other three choices, ohms, watts, and amperes are resistance, power, and current, respectively.

54. The correct choice is A.
Power can be found by multiplying V by I. This gives 220 watts of power.

55. The correct choice is D.
According to the equation $P = IV$, the current is P/V. Dividing 1,525 watts by 110 volts gives 13.9 amperes.

56. The correct choice is A.
Only choice A demonstrates the correct units for impulse, N·s. In addition, the impulse can be calculated by multiplying the force by the change in time, $p = F\Delta t$.

57. The correct choice is D.
The 10-kg object had a change in its velocity by $10\,\text{m/s}$. Using the equation $p = m\Delta v$, we find that the correct answer is $100\,\text{kg·m/s}$.

58. The correct choice is D.
The plane traveled a total distance of 1,000 miles, but because the plane returned to its original point of origin, its displacement is 0 miles.

59. The correct choice is C.
The reaction $2NaI + Cl_2 \rightarrow 2NaCl + I_2$ shows a single replacement as the chlorine replaces just one element, the iodine.

60. The correct choice is C.
When attached to the electromagnet, the potential energy (PE) of the car is $367.5\,\text{kJ}$ because PE = mgh, and PE = $(1,500\,\text{kg})(9.8\,\text{m/s}^2)(25\,\text{m})$. As the car falls, all $367.5\,\text{kJ}$ of PE are converted to kinetic energy. On hitting the ground and making a sound, the car will no longer possess any PE.

Science Test 2

1. The correct choice is D.
The valence electrons are the outermost electrons in an atom. These electrons are of importance because they are the electrons that are lost, gained, or shared in a reaction.

2. The correct choice is B.
Litmus, red or blue, is blue in a base and red in an acid. Phenolphthalein is colorless in acid and pink in base.

3. The correct choice is D.
The alcohol functional group is the group that has an –OH group bonded to the carbon chain. The other choices show an ether, an alkyne, and an aldehyde, respectively.

4. The correct choice is D.
Values for pH just above 7 are basic. Given that the pH of this blood is just above 7, it indicates that the blood sample is a weak base.

5. The correct choice is A.
The ability to evaporate is a liquid's volatility. A more volatile liquid evaporates faster.

6. The correct choice is A.
Nonpolar compounds have no overall polarity. Diatomic molecules, such as F_2, have two of the same element chemically bonded. Because the elements have the same electronegativity, they share the electrons equally and form a nonpolar covalent bond.

7. The correct choice is C.

Sublimation is a change from solid phase to gas phase with no liquid phase in between. Other substances that can sublime are dry ice (solid carbon dioxide) and mothballs (naphthalene).

8. The correct choice is B.

The upper right portion of the periodic table includes the nonmetals. These include the noble gases, halogens, and the elements S, P, O, N, and C.

9. The correct choice is B.

Allotropes are different forms of the same element. Diamonds and graphite are made from carbon. Other examples of allotropes are ozone and oxygen gas, which are allotropes of oxygen.

10. The correct choice is B.

Balancing equations is quite tricky and requires lots of practice to master. On examination of the first substance, we see that methane gas has one carbon atom. There is also one carbon atom on the right side of the equation. There is no need to balance this. There are four hydrogen atoms on the left side. To balance this, we change the coefficients so that there are four hydrogen atoms on the right. This is done by placing a 2 in front of the water:

$$\_CH_4 + \_O_2 \rightarrow \_CO_2 + 2H_2O$$

Inspection of the oxygen atoms shows just two atoms of oxygen on the left but a total of four oxygen atoms on the right (two from the water and two from the carbon dioxide). We change the coefficient of the oxygen gas to a 2 so that there are four oxygen atoms on the left. Now the equation is balanced:

$$1CH_4 + 2O_2 \rightarrow 1CO_2 + 2H_2O$$

11. The correct choice is A.

Water has a density of $1\,g/mL$. To float, the object must have a density that is less than that of water. The object labeled W floats and objects X, Y, and Z sink.

12. The correct choice is B.

For the substance to decay from 40 grams to 10 grams it must undergo two half-lives ($40 \rightarrow 20 \rightarrow 10$). If it takes 16 days for two half-lives to occur, it takes just 8 days for one half-life to occur.

13. The correct choice is D.

To become a female, each parent must give an X chromosome so that there are two X chromosomes present. The mother of the human fetus always gives an X chromosome, whereas the father can provide either an X or a Y. Because the variation lies with the father, the father's sperm determines the sex of the fetus.

14. The correct choice is A.

The sun provides plants with the energy to grow. It is the producers who serve as the basis for the food that other organisms consume.

15. The correct choice is C.
Both lipids and carbohydrates contain carbon, oxygen, and hydrogen. Although both proteins and nucleic acids contain nitrogen, only the nucleic acid has a phosphate group.

16. The correct choice is A.
Cellular respiration includes the other three processes; glucose is broken down into other substances in a number of different processes. The processes have one goal, to produce the ATP which is needed by our cells.

17. The correct choice is D.
The chlorophyll in plants absorbs red and blue light best.

18. The correct choice is C.
The scientific name of an organism includes its genus and species.

19. The correct choice is C.
Insects are classified as herbivores because they eat plants. This is not to be confused with producers, which are the green plants.

20. The correct choice is B.
For the plant to be short, it must have alleles that are tt. For the plant to be tall, it must have alleles Tt or TT. Crossing Tt with tt gives the following: Tt, Tt, tt, and tt. This cross demonstrates that 50 percent of the plants are short.

21. The correct choice is C.
Photosynthesis creates glucose and oxygen gas from carbon dioxide water and light energy. Respiration takes oxygen gas and glucose to make energy, carbon dioxide, and water.

22. The correct choice is B.
Flowers have the organs that are responsible for sexual reproduction. The male reproductive organs are called stamens and the female reproductive organs are called pistils.

23. The correct choice is B.
Monosaccharides, such as glucose, can join to form long molecules called starches. Amino acids would form proteins, and nucleic acids would form DNA and RNA.

24. The correct choice is D.
Catalysts are not consumed or altered during a chemical reaction. Catalysts lower the activation energy of a reaction and then proceed to carry out this process again and again, without being destroyed.

25. The correct choice is D.
The rectum serves stores fecal matter before it is eliminated from the body. The mouth, small intestine, and stomach all have gastric juices containing enzymes to digest foods.

26. The correct choice is A.
The septum is the part of the heart that separates the left and right sides.

27. The correct choice is C.

Tears, urine, and mucus are all primary lines of defense, because they work to prevent infection. Inflammation is an example of a second line of defense, because it works once the body has been infected.

28. The correct choice is D.

The epiglottis covers the larynx so that food does not enter; this ensures that the food goes down the esophagus.

29. The correct choice is B.

The liver works to clean and detoxify the blood. The liver also produces bile, which is stored in the gallbladder.

30. The correct choice is B.

Estrogen is a hormone produced by females. It is produced in the ovaries and not in the adrenal medulla.

31. The correct choice is D.

The central nervous system is composed of the brain and spinal cord. This is easy to remember because they lie down the center of the body.

32. The correct choice is A.

Ligaments hold bone to bone. Tendons hold muscle to bone.

33. The correct choice is D.

Choices A, B, and C are parts of the female reproductive system. The epididymis is part of the male reproductive system and lies on the testicles.

34. The correct choice is A.

The iris and retina are just a few of the many parts of the eye.

35. The correct choice is A.

Posterior refers to being behind. The kidneys are behind the small intestine.

36. The correct choice is B.

Enzymes can be identified by the ending -*ase*. Proteases are enzymes that digest proteins.

37. The correct choice is C.

Antibodies, killer T cells, and phagocytes all work to destroy foreign invaders in human bodies. Viruses are an example of these invaders.

38. The correct choice is D.

The diaphragm is the muscle that moves to create a void space in the chest. This allows air to rush through the respiratory system and fill the void space created.

39. The correct choice is D.

White blood cells are produced in the bone marrow and not by the skin.

40. The correct choice is A.

Although all four choices are associated with the nerve cell, the synapse is not an actual part of the nerve cell. Instead, the synapse serves as a gap between nerve cells in which neurotransmitters move from one nerve cell to another.

41. The correct choice is C.
The other name for the digestive system is the alimentary canal. One mnemonic device to remember is that the word *aliment* is French for *food.*

42. The correct choice is C.
A vector quantity has both a magnitude and a direction. A scalar quantity has only a magnitude.

43. The correct choice is A.
Only choice A has both a direction and magnitude, making it a vector.

44. The correct choice is D.
The velocity is the change in distance over time. This object went 100 m in 10 s, making the velocity 10 m/s.

45. The correct choice is A.
Velocity = distance/time. Rearranging the equation, distance is equal to time multiplied by velocity. This gives (15m/s)(5s) = 75 m.

46. The correct choice is B.
An object that has a constant velocity does not experience any acceleration because there is no change in the velocity, a component needed to calculate acceleration.

47. The correct choice is D.
Acceleration is defined as the change in velocity over time, $a = \Delta v / \Delta t$.

48. The correct choice is B.
Momentum, p, is equal to mass times velocity. Choice B has least momentum, 20 kg·m/s.

49. The correct choice is B.
The equation for momentum reflects mass multiplied by velocity.

50. The correct choice is C.
Because the equation for momentum multiplies mass (kg) and velocity (m/s), the units are kg·m/s.

51. The correct choice is D.
The newton is the unit of measure for force, which is calculated by the formula $F = ma$. Multiplying mass (kg) by acceleration (m/s^2) gives kg·m/s^2.

52. The correct choice is A.
Newton's first law addresses inertia and states that an object at rest will stay at rest and that an object in motion will stay in motion. This changes if the object is acted on by a force.

53. The correct choice is B.
Acceleration of an object requires a force. This can be calculated using the equation $F = ma,$ as described by Newton's second law.

54. The correct choice is C.
Newton's third law states that when an object applies a force to a second object, that second object applies an opposite and equal force to the first object.

55. The correct choice is C.

For the object to come to rest, a force must act on it. One possible force is the friction that exists between the object and the table.

56. The correct choice is C.

Work, W, is equal to force times distance, Fd. This gives, using the correct units, 15 N·m.

57. The correct choice is B.

$W = Fd$ or $F = W/d$. The work, 100 N·m, divided by 20 meters, gives a force of 5 N.

58. The correct choice is A.

Conservation of energy tells us that energy can neither be created nor destroyed. The total energy of a system, however, can be converted from one form to another.

59. The correct choice is D.

Energy is measured in joules. Height is a distance, d, and is measured in meters.

60. The correct choice is A.

The term *olfactory* refers to the nose and nasal cavity.